CITIES IN TRANSITION

Also by Michael Middleton

Man Made the Town

MICHAEL MIDDLETON

CITIES _in_ TRANSITION

The Regeneration of Britain's Inner Cities

Michael Joseph
LONDON

MICHAEL JOSEPH LTD

Published by the Penguin Group
27 Wrights Lane, London W8 5TZ, England
Viking Penguin Inc., 375 Hudson Street, New York, New York 10014, USA
Penguin Books Australia Ltd, Ringwood, Victoria, Australia
Penguin Books Canada Ltd, 2801 John Street, Markham, Ontario, Canada L3R 1B4
Penguin Books (NZ) Ltd, 182–190 Wairau Road, Auckland 10, New Zealand

Penguin Books Ltd, Registered Offices: Harmondsworth, Middlesex, England

First published in Great Britain 1991

Copyright © Michael Middleton 1991
Maps by Peter McClure

Printed in England by Clays Ltd, St Ives plc
Filmset in 11 on 12½ Monophoto Photina

A CIP catalogue record for this book is available from the British Library

ISBN 0 7181 3242 4

CONTENTS

LIST OF ILLUSTRATIONS

Photographs other than those attributed above are the author's

ACKNOWLEDGEMENTS

AN ENORMOUS literature attaches to the subject of this book. Over the past twenty years surveys, studies and reports without number, for the most part official or academic but stemming also from the private sector, the voluntary organisations and individual writers, have examined in detail the many problems associated with urban decline and have set out varying strategies for urban regeneration, especially for specific areas. There would be little point in a book of this nature, even were it possible, to seek to list them all here. I have nonetheless to express my indebtedness to their begetters for much of the information in the following pages; sources of particular quotations and figures are given in Appendix B. As will be apparent I have also plundered the daily press for headlines and comment. It would have been nice to have junked a lot of the figures and statistics – for they make for boring reading – but without their stiffening too many statements would have remained too generalised. I can only advise those for whom such things are an instant switch-off to skip them and press on regardless. Three small points. If some of the figures seem less than totally up to date, it may be that they are simply the latest available; those stemming from the 1981 census, for example, can only be updated by this year's 1991 census. Others will undoubtedly have been superseded by the time the book is through the printing presses; the broad trends they mirror are unlikely, however, to be affected. Area measurements are mostly approximate.

I have received help from many quarters. The Department of the Environment and the Welsh Office have furnished me with useful material. The Scottish and Welsh Development Agencies have given generous assistance. The Housing Corporation, Scottish Homes and the Countryside Commission provided me with information.

1

All the Urban Development Corporations responded readily to my various demands. A number of County, Borough and District Councils, and in Scotland Strathclyde Regional Council, provided me with invaluable detail. From the private sector, Business in the Community, the Civic Trust and the Urban and Economic Development Group (URBED) were among those who furnished me with helpful material.

Among those who personally gave of their time, or in other ways offered me access to their experience, were:

Martin Bradshaw, Director of the Civic Trust; Director of Planning, West Yorkshire Metropolitan Council, 1974–86.
Honor Chapman, of Jones Lang Wootton, and Board Member, Cardiff Bay Development Corporation.
Jim Cocker, of Birmingham City Council Development Department/ Birmingham Heartlands.
Sir Andrew Derbyshire, Senior Partner RMJM, Board Member, London Docklands Development Corporation, 1984–1988.
Michael Ellison, Chief Executive, Calderdale Metropolitan Borough.
Martin Eagland, Chief Executive, Leeds Development Corporation.
Bill Hay, Chief Executive, The Newcastle Initiative.
John Fox, founder of Welfare State International.
Bernard Hunt and John Thompson, of Hunt Thompson Associates.
J. R. Lewis, Assistant Planning Officer, Mid Glamorgan County Council
John Lockwood, Director, 'Calderdale Inheritance' programme.
Ian Page, Director of Marketing and External Affairs, Black Country Development Corporation.
Richard Penn, Chief Executive, Knowsley Metropolitan Borough, 1981–89, now of Bradford Metropolitan Borough.
John Pickup, Director of Planning, Cardiff Bay Development Corporation.
James Rae, Director of Planning, City of Glasgow.
Dr John Ritchie, Chief Executive, Merseyside Development Corporation.
Barry Shaw, Director of Urban Design, London Docklands Development Corporation.
The Rt Revd David Sheppard, Bishop of Liverpool.
John Thacker, Chairman, Shepheard Epstein Hunter.
Neville Whittaker, Director, North East Civic Trust.
Allen Williams, lately Regional Director Valleys, Welsh Development Agency.

To all of these I am deeply grateful. I spoke, too, to many others, some of whom did not wish to be named – which does not diminish my indebtedness to them.

I am grateful to those listed in the table of illustrations for the use of photographs, and to Glasgow City Council for help with map material.

Finally my thanks are due to Andrew Hewson who first suggested the book;' to Lesley Arden who transferred it to her word processor so impeccably; to Sir James Swaffield for his many helpful comments on reading the manuscrpt; and to Messrs Michael Joseph who have seen it through the editorial and production process with marked patience and good humour.

These acknowledgements should perhaps end with a declaration of interest by the author. I was Director of the Civic Trust in London from 1969 to 1987; and I am a member of the Cardiff Bay Development Corporation's Design and Review Panel.

1

INTRODUCTION

One thing hastens into being, another hastens out of it. Even while a thing is in the act of coming into existence, some part of it has already ceased to be. Flux and change are forever renewing the fabric of the universe, just as the ceaseless sweep of time is forever renewing the face of eternity.

Marcus Aurelius, *Meditations*, 6:15

ALL CITIES are in a state of transition, of becoming – of becoming bigger, smaller, better, worse, or maybe just *different*. The process of change can be so slow as to be hardly apparent from decade to decade. It can happen so violently that to those involved it seems almost cataclysmic. Many British cities have been subjected, since World War II, to successive waves of change – to large-scale slum clearance, to massive highway construction, to the comprehensive redevelopment of their central areas. Over the past quarter-century extensive areas of urban Britain have fallen into decline and decay. A complex of interrelated problems associated with the 'inner city' has forced itself upon the public consciousness and for fifteen years, more particularly during the past decade, we have been struggling to find ways of dealing with it. Urban regeneration has become a national priority. It is the subject of this book.

That we face problems should not astonish us. Much of the world is being shaken by changes – political, industrial, economic, social – perhaps as widespread and profound as ever before compressed into a like period. It would be naive to believe that Britain could somehow have escaped the shock waves. Small surprise that we are being forced totally to restructure long-established frameworks. Small surprise that our towns and cities, reflecting as always the society they serve, now face change on a scale unprecedented since the second half of the last century.

To a large extent it is a problem of our own making. For generations we have failed to plough back into our towns and cities the basic resources needed to keep them in good working

4

order. A very large part of our building stock is unfit. Drainage and water-supply systems are almost everywhere in need of fundamental repair and improvement. Road and rail transportation systems creak under the strain, and from time to time collapse. Derelict land and waste lots fester, often for a generation and more. The public realm looks increasingly seedy and uncared for, with graffiti, litter and vandalism everywhere apparent. We have yet fully to grasp that the maintenance, renewal and improvement of our towns and cities presents a challenge no less demanding than that which faced the earlier city *builders*. 'The problems we face now,' one city planning officer said to me, 'are simply a measure of the extent to which we were guilty of bad housekeeping in times past. We allowed things to build up. Other cities did the same. And because, finally, we all had to do something dramatic, they had to invent a new word for it: regeneration.'

To this long standing reluctance to spend on keeping our corporate house in order, industrial collapse and resultant unemployment have added new urgencies. Three things dominate the 'inner city'. They are poverty, lack of job opportunities, and a crumbling environment. There are others – like health, crime, race relations – but they are attendant problems. *All* these factors interact. Only holistic strategies and programmes which address them all can lead to long-term, self-sustaining regeneration.

To set out the nature of the problem is one thing. It has been surveyed and analysed in study after study. To establish with any precision the effects of the steps we are taking to meet it is altogether another matter. It is like trying to photograph a moving subject. A fraction of a second later the image has changed. Half a minute later the background has changed. Official programmes come to the boil, and mysteriously cool, the original hype left hanging in the air like the smile of the Cheshire Cat. Elections come and go, Ministers come and go, fashions come and go, all producing sometimes quite startling policy reversals at national and local level. Big development companies go to the altar – for the biggest of today's projects tend to be beyond the capacity of a single concern – but as quickly file for divorce. Projects come to Public Inquiry, perhaps after years of work, are returned to the drawing board, swap architects, swap backers, run into economic recession and are ditched. For the very context in which measures have to be drawn up is all the time itself in flux. Inflation rates go up and down, mortgage rates go up and down, employment figures go up and down. Forecasts and projections fluctuate wildly. By those with an axe to grind statistics are shuffled as confusingly as the lady in the three-card trick. As this book goes into production a number of the points made in the final chapter, in relation to the role and workings of local government, are about to be given an airing, it is reported, in a forthcoming Government Consultation document. By the time it is in print the wheel will have turned again, some of it will be sadly out of date, new thrusts – and failures – will have developed. We are looking at a continuing process without beginning or end.

Scarce a day passes but that some aspect of all this is given momentary prominence by press or television. Conferences debate the subject it seems almost weekly. By 1990 there was even an inner cities magazine. At least a glancing reference to 'the inner city' is almost *de rigueur* in the speeches of any politician worth his salt. Mrs Thatcher lent it her imprimatur in her famous aside after the 1987 election. The Prince of Wales has tirelessly lent his weight to the encouragement of the troops in the field. And yet . . . somehow the overall picture remains fuzzy, blurred, confused.

Every claim is met by its counterclaim, every positive by a negative. The headlines seem irreconcilable. '£3 bn scheme to train workers for twenty-first century' – but a month or two later 'Labour leak exposes plan to cut £300 m from training funds'. '£1 bn Underground extension to serve Docklands' we read – but in the same month: 'Docklands scheme an "irredeemable failure"'. '£500 m boost for the cities' – good news, surely; yet, within weeks, 'UK cities are poor relations' (findings of an EEC study) and, within a month or two, 'Poll tax curbs force councils to implement sweeping cuts'. On the one hand 'Britons enjoy unprecedented affluence and materialism'; 'Standards of living accelerate' and 'British quality of life among the best in the world'; yet on the other, 'Poverty rose faster in Britain than any other EC state'[1]; 'Business failure rate soars by 83%'; '974 hospital beds closed in London' and 'Unhoused families rise by 30%'. Clearly it is the best of times, the worst of times.*

The headlines, of course, are but froth on the surface of a torrent of activity which in fact runs deep and wide. Glossy publications from HMSO detail the thrust of the government's 'Action for Cities' programme. Newspaper supplements, magazine articles, radio and television interviews, advertisements and promotional videos, spell out the aspirations and achievements of the Urban Development Corporations, the government's lead

---

* To minimise bias these few rather random headlines have been culled almost entirely from one newspaper, *The Times*, over eighteen months or so.

agencies in regeneration, and other areas of the country. Competitions and awards highlight special endeavour. Important initiatives stem from the business world, the Church, the voluntary organisations. There are pictures of garden festivals, waterside housing, new roads being constructed, new science parks, convention centres, shopping centres, stadia. And there are the people . . .

Here is Chris Patten, sitting improbably all by himself at a desk set in the middle of six derelict acres in Liverpool; a national VAT centre is to be constructed on the site.

Here is Paul Reichmann in his little *keepah* skullcap, bending over a model of Canary Wharf: the retiring man who came with his brothers from Canada (where their company Olympia & York is said to be worth £15 billion) to rescue the biggest development of its kind in Europe, and to change the whole nature of development in Britain.

At the other end of the spectrum: a Nottinghamshire miner, Roger Brunt, and his wife. Together they have created a 2.5 acre/ 1 ha wildlife mini-park on what was a rubbish dump behind their home in Newark. It was paid for by overtime put in at the pit, and then by a *Times*/PM award of £5,000.

Here a broadly smiling figure, lightly bearded, dark suited, showing a couple of inches of white cuff, looks out from the page.[2] He is standing in a flag-decked St George's Square in Glasgow, and it was he, Michael Kelly, who coined in the mid eighties, as Lord Provost, the slogan 'Glasgow's Miles Better'. A small thing? There are those who think it marked the turning point in renewal of confidence in the city.

Another kind of confidence-building: Joe Souza, coach to the cast of the Lloyd Webber roller-skating musical *Starlight Express*, has taken a gang of rowdy, truant-playing, street tearaways from an Islington estate and turned them, over nine weeks, into a disciplined (roller-skating) part of a specially written community play commissioned by All Change Arts.[3] 'When I first saw them,' Souza is quoted as saying, 'I thought, what on earth am I letting myself in for? I was used to teaching professionals, not a bunch of stroppy teenagers.' But it worked. 'They not only learnt how to roller-skate properly but they learnt how to fit in with the diverse group of people in the play.' 'One of the things I learnt from what Joe taught us,' says 15-year-old Wayne Hastie, who now wants to become an actor, 'was respect for other people and self control.'

Who is this proclaiming the virtues of the free market and provincial regeneration? No report from the North East can do without a picture of John Hall, the miner's son from North Seaton, and now Sir John, arms outstretched in triumph against the background of his £200 million Gateshead MetroCentre, created on what was derelict land and one of the largest covered shopping complexes in Europe. 'The whole,' he says of the regeneration process, 'can only have life and vigour if the parts are alive and vigorous.'

Alive and vigorous? In South Wales they tell of a little old lady in the Cynon Valley, who rang officialdom one day to say the centre of her village was a mess and what about it? – who extracted £20,000 each from the Council and the Welsh Development Agency to put things right.

So many threads, at so many levels: corporate and costly, personal and parochial. The eighties produced some runaway successes – but also sad failures. So many business start-ups – but the closures and lay-offs continue. So many houses – but so many that no one wants to live in. So many people labouring so hard – so many others feeling that they are being trampled upon. Here is a public demo against the construction of a new road to London Docks. Here is the Royal Society for the Protection of Birds opposing the passage through Parliament of the barrage proposals for Cardiff Bay. Here is the city of Bristol resisting to the last the imposition of a Development Corporation upon its territory. A confused picture, in which the parts never seem quite to make up a whole.

The following pages attempt an overview of all this, a broad progress report that will give a whiff of how things have actually been shaping during the 1980s. It is inevitably patchy and incomplete. There is no way that justice could be done, nationwide, to so many agencies, so many projects, so many people. An entire book could hardly record the full story of any single one of the areas I visited. I hope that most of the *types* of contribution being made to physical regeneration find a place somewhere or other in these pages. The reader should not assume, however, that these examples are unique; comparable programmes are likely to be found in many other parts of the country. I am very conscious, indeed, of the volume of effort represented by all the towns and cities, organisations and individuals who do *not* figure here, and can only express my admiration for them collectively. Only a tiny number slide into the 'photo-opportunity' pictures staged for the great and the good. Most are unknown outside a very limited circle. Too often they are presented as a faceless 'They'. Thus Anne Robinson, in the *Daily Mirror*, lambastes those battling to bring new life to Liverpool: '. . . one sharp-suited out-of-town expert after another has been allowed to tell Liverpool what's good for it.

But none of them in their bossy sermons, their finger-wagging lectures, their absurd solutions has been able to rob Liverpool of its ... spirit and its humour.'[4]

Can she have met any of 'them'? The most heartwarming thing for me, in my forays about the country researching for this book, was to meet so many committed people – in the public service, in business, in the voluntary associations – labouring so hard, in the face often of quite inadequate resources and all sorts of political and procedural frustrations, to turn round the fortunes of the communities in which they work, and thereby those of the nation.

I hope that something of this comes through in the pages which follow. The book looks first at the nature of the problem – familiar up to a point, but it has to be said again if sense is to be made of the action programmes we have adopted. There follows a glance at the mechanisms at present in place by which these programmes are effected – for the most part but dimly understood, I suspect, by those not actively engaged in such matters. The middle – and main – section surveys, albeit with many gaps, something of what has actually been happening on the ground, mostly in the big conurbations* but certainly not solely in the 'inner city' in the literal sense of the words. In this round-up are to be found beacons of hope, mistakes, experiments, grim reminders of how much yet remains to be done. One or two general themes – housing and derelict land for example – are then considered in their own right, for they embody values and approaches which transcend site-specific boundaries. Last of all, a final chapter seeks to identify some possible pointers for the future. How can we avoid the creation of similar problems in the years to come? Have we any real idea of the kind of towns and cities we should be aiming to create? It does not pretend to definitive solutions. They do not exist. But as we move towards the next century our present preoccupations with urban regeneration must surely come to be recognised as part of the wider challenge of how to handle the management of change generally.

If this book concerns itself primarily with the physical environment, it is because of my belief that, in the last analysis, with education, environmental quality is the key to everything else. Business and industry will not invest in a shot-up area which gives the impression that it sees no future for itself. We have to create whole quarters, whole towns, whole cities, which are desirable, exciting, enriching: where people actually *want to be*. The

* The term was coined by Geddes in his *Cities in Evolution*, 1913.

stakes are now very high. We are in direct competition with cities and life-styles worldwide. It will not do to plead that we cannot *afford* to do things properly. We cannot afford *not* to. Our very future depends upon it.

Change of this nature, on this scale, will not happen of itself. No magical inevitability attaches to it. It implies a conscious choice of priorities nationally, a consensus attitude of mind which permeates all else that we do, vote for, invest in, do without. It is possibly the biggest peace-time challenge Britain has had to face in this century. Its full acceptance will alone enable us to enter the next as a buoyant, confident society of civilised values.

PART ONE

PROBLEMS AND POLICIES

If way to the Better there be, it exacts a full look at the Worst.

Thomas Hardy, *In Tenebris*, II

The purpose of government . . . is the happiness of the common man.

Lord Beveridge, *Social Insurance*

2

INNER CITY – AND BEYOND

THREE SNAPSHOTS
Here in the High Road the bright plastic of the betting shop fascias flash like beacons. Wire mesh covers most of the other windows – the video hire places, the washateria, the caff, the tiny 'supermarket' – unpainted most of them for a generation. Others are boarded up, flyposted, their upper windows rimmed with jagged glass. The Town Hall once bore a florid air of confidence; it is drab now, its clock stopped twenty years ago, it has given up the struggle. Weeds push through the pavements, even sprout from the shopfronts. A sheet of torn polythene, caught in some overhead wire, flaps and claps in the wind. Paper swirls about one's feet, lifting from time to time to swoop amidst the traffic. A couple of empty beer cans in the gutter make a *gamelan* jangle as they skitter this way and that with each successive gust. In the alleys and side roads collapsing buildings are shored up by great baulks of timber. A mongrel scavenges one of the waste sites, among the stained mattresses, the rusting oil drums, the sodden heaps of – what? Aerosol tags, venom and obscenities are scribbled over every surface with relentless, mind-blowing monotony.

The High Road is quite animated, in its way. There is a group waiting for the pub to open. One of them, short of breath, sits on a low wall, wheezing. A middle-aged Pakistani steers an unwavering course with measured tread, his wife an acceptable yard and a half behind him. Two black tearaways on skateboards zig-zag the pavement at speed, conscious of their prowess. Other young drift through an 'amusement arcade' of one-armed bandits, in a state almost of hypnosis. Three girls, chattering, click-clack on high

13

heels towards adventure. A very old lady, with matchstick legs, pushes an almost empty basket on wheels slowly, slowly, to the supermarket. From a pile of cardboard under an arch, if you look carefully, four legs protrude.

This is the face of the inner city.

Turn the page. The image changes. On the maps this area straddles the green belt. The high-rise towers, stained now, their ground-floor windows and garages breeze-blocked up, look as though they were off-loaded wherever a cheap site offered. This was good farmland once, and indeed, from the upper floors of the flats, in the distance you can still see the corn ripen through the summer. But at ground level it is a featureless panorama of puddled tarmac and cracked concrete, of chain-link fencing and corrugated iron and barbed wire. There is no High Street here. Roads traverse the area but there is little traffic. The one-time clutch of small neighbourhood shops has been empty now for quite a while – one or two put to the torch, the rest with their protective boarding long since smashed open, aerosolled; dark caves for glue-sniffers and crack-pushers. This is a no-go area for postmen and milkmen; police do not go singly. There is an eerie absence of movement, an almost complete silence. Some boys lean aimlessly, warily, in a doorway. Behind steel-protected doors in the four-storey walk-ups are single-parent families, squatters, runaway kids from home, the elderly and infirm. Occasionally a figure scuttles to the bashed-up bus stop to make the journey into town – to collect benefit, to shop for a couple of days, to look in at the Job Centre. There is not much else to look forward to. Tomorrow will be as today, next week the same as this, and next year probably the same as this year.

One of the faces of deprivation.

Turn the page again. Another image. Rotting sites that once hummed and crashed with heavy engineering and the lighter industry that went with it, unrolling, seemingly endlessly, across the landscape. Rusting sheds, with gaping rents in their corrugated-iron roofs, the detritus of the past scattered across the blackened, soured and festering wasteland. Silent derricks, silent chimney stacks, bits of concrete road that were once filled with thousands of men cycling and marching to work, which now lead nowhere. Here, screaming gulls tumble over a waste tip. Here is a vast buff-coloured area, the size of a small town, flattened, not yet weed-grown, where the dust lifts in the wind, its billboard plea for fresh investment as yet unanswered. Here, in limbo now, two streets of Victorian workmen's cottages; and here a little estate of red brick semi-ds, band-box new – but why at this particular spot?

Half a mile away, apparently at random, a patch of wasteland has been carefully municipalised into grass and crescent rosebeds – but why here, where there is little to look at from the single park bench except the passing traffic? For this sub-region of despair is threaded through by motorways and trunk roads, carrying each its thrumming stream of cars and heavy freight lorries, speeding through, but never stopping. Life itself by-passes this whole area. Get off the highway and you might see a flight of pigeons being released, or a couple of whippets being walked to the old dockside, or some washing being put on the line, but little more. Faces, if you see them, are not elderly; they are just the faces of a discarded generation. This gaunt land lacks jobs. It lacks focal points where the sense of community can flourish. It has lost its *raison d'être*, its sense of organised purpose, and knows not where its future lies.

Another of the faces of decline.

The conditions of urban decline have been set out *ad nauseam*. First – concentrated poverty, arising primarily from an absence of job opportunities; to which, in many cities, additional desperation is lent by concentrations of immigrant workers and ethnic minorities who find it even more difficult to obtain long-term employment. Second – declining services. There are fewer buses, schools and clinics close down or are amalgamated with others at a distance from the community, potholes scar the roads and pavements, dustbins are emptied less frequently, parks and open spaces go to seed. Housing decays because owners can no longer afford to undertake needed repairs and the level of rents received means that it is simply not worth the landlord's while. Upper floors fall empty. Shops, cafés go down-market and finally out of business. All this discourages fresh investment in the area and disappearing jobs are not renewed. Third – increased crime rates. Those who remain, from boredom, bitterness and frustration, occasionally from real need, take increasingly to vandalism, muggings – and at intervals, maybe, to riot, arson and looting. Fourth – there is an outward migration of population: of the younger and more skilled in search of jobs elsewhere; of those who can afford it to accommodation in more desirable areas; of traders and small businesses because their turnover is no longer sufficient to cover inner-city rents and rates, or because repeated theft and vandalism of their premises has finally knocked the stuffing out of them.* Fifth – this outward migration, leaving

---

* Insurance premiums are five times higher in the big cities (e.g. London, Liverpool, Manchester, parts of Glasgow) than elsewhere.

larger and larger areas of property empty, results in plummeting revenues from local taxes at the very time the public authorities face the need for increased social work, policing, health care and housing repair. All interlocked, these things lead to a descending spiral of decline – which may continue over decades, perhaps even generations, and is not to be reversed overnight.

These are the ills of the 'inner city'. The term slid into general use, this side of the Atlantic, in the early 1970s – replacing the earlier 'twilight areas'. By now it is a cliché and we all know its connotations. Or do we? It can prove more slippery than at first imagined. To start with, where *is* the 'inner city'? It may indeed mean the historical heart of a city, where are concentrated its administrative functions, its central business district, its shopping, cultural and leisure attractions – an area with a high and affluent daytime population, but, at the same time, embracing low-income resident ghettos of deprivation. More commonly it is likely to be, not so much 'inner', as the area sandwiched between this inner core and the outer suburbs – in London, for example, Tower Hamlets or Brixton. Here we are likely to find square miles of Victorian housing, much of it so run-down as to be uninhabitable but nonetheless filled with close-knit Asian families at exorbitant rentals, single parents with their children, squatters, young people from afar in search of work. Even more confusingly, the problems we associate with the 'inner city' may turn out rather to be found in the 'outer' city – the outer, peripheral estates so recklessly thrown up, with the best of intentions, in the 1950s and 1960s. The well-meant but brutally thoughtless slum-clearance programmes of Glasgow and Liverpool, to name but two examples, which hoovered up communities and dumped them in high-rise, 'overspill' flats on the perimeter of the city or beyond, simply created a series of new social time-bombs for the disposal squads of today. The urban fringe may well present bigger problems than the 'inner city' itself. But there is yet a further dimension. 'Inner-city' symptoms are not confined to the great conurbations. They can be found in the mining valleys of South Wales, in parts of county towns, in seaside resorts and in rural areas. Their effects upon the individual there are no less devastating than in the great conurbations. Cumulatively, the wellbeing of such areas is of no less significance to the nation than that of the more obvious concentrations in the big cities, which are only, by reason of their scale, less easily overlooked and tend to overlay, in the public mind, the comparable problems of smaller places.

Though the outward signs of decline have so much in common

everywhere, how different are all these towns and cities – in their traditions, their appearance, their fierce local loyalties. For a start, the density of built-up areas can differ widely. Bristol, covering 42.3 square miles/109.5 sq. km., has a population of 393,800; Liverpool, covering a very similar 43.6 square miles/113 sq. km., has 491,500; while Bradford, with a comparable population of 463,500, covers 143 square miles/370 sq. km. The speed and nature of change ranges over a wide spectrum. Some areas, for this reason or that, are haemorrhaging fast and need first aid to staunch the flow. Some have existed for an appreciable time on an unchanging plateau of deprivation. Some are blighted by uncertainties attaching to the *threat* of change – large-scale new development, projected new transport systems and the like. In others again traditional activities are being diminished and the existing communities dispossessed by the strength of market-led office development and associated gentrification.

There are no rules of thumb. To get to grips with the realities of urban decline and deprivation we have to abandon broad brushstroke classification and begin to concern ourselves with area and *neighbourhood* characteristics. We need to disaggregate overall statistics, and use a smaller mesh. There can be wide local variations in, for example, the figures for population change or unemployment. Between 1971 and 1981, in Liverpool as a whole, the number of residents in work declined by 26.1 per cent; in the inner city the figure was 34.3 per cent (or more than double that in the 'outer' city); in Toxteth it was 38.6 per cent. Strathclyde in 1988 had an overall level of unemployment of 18 per cent, but in a good many areas this rose to 30 per cent, and in the worst to 60 per cent. During the early 1980s black and other ethnic groups sometimes found themselves three-quarters unemployed, or even more, in cities where the overall rate was not far from the national average.* And just as there are pockets of decay and deprivation in prosperous boroughs and districts, so in others, side by side with poverty and squalor, are to be found charming little squares and cul-de-sacs from the eighteenth century, handsome rectories and public buildings, the vigorous life of street markets.

What then are the indicators by which we can measure deprivation? The government use eight: unemployment, overcrowding,

* Unemployment figures are constantly disputed because of repeated changes of definition and in entitlement. The government admits to five 'significant' changes between 1979 and 1991; others put the number at about thirty. Professor Bernard Benjamin, for the Economic and Social Research Council, has called it 'the classic example' of the government's confusing use of statistics.

single person households, households lacking or sharing basic amenities, lone pensioners, an immigrant Commonwealth head of household, population change between censuses, and mortality rates. These are boiled up and put in the blender to produce what are known as 'Z' scores (which are used to help determine the amount of government grant aid to be made available to different areas). However, academics and others have found these headings alone too crude a measurement, and at different times have thrown additional factors into the calculation.* Such additional indicators have included educational attainment (significant in the search for jobs), homelessness, numbers of empty properties, car ownership (an important factor in areas where public transport is minimal), the degree of assisted housing, residential prices and rental levels, numbers of owner-occupiers, retail turnover, business starts and closures, numbers of planning applications (as an indication of the state of the local economy). All statistics can be massaged to make particular points, and some of these factors are clearly difficult or impossible to quantify with accuracy. Sometimes quantification alone, without further information, is anyway not in itself helpful. Does the preponderance of pensioners in the age-groups profile arise because the young and able-bodied have fled the area, or because the elderly, for one reason or another, have flocked to it as a place in which to retire? Inner-city crime statistics can be horrific – but then, upon examination, rural statistics no less so. Behind each seemingly clear-cut picture lie many ambiguities. Nonetheless, in the absence of some at least of the more 'robust' of these additional factors, official rankings do not always accord with the uncluttered evidence of one's own eyes. Contrasts can be very simple. Consider some of the more obvious facilities available in Bracknell New Town, Berkshire, and Easterhouse, one of Glasgow's outer estates. Both have populations around the 50,000 mark. Bracknell, with 660,000 sq. ft./61,300 sq. m., has six times the shopping floorspace in the town centre that Easterhouse has. Bracknell has 23 post offices; Easterhouse 5; 15 banks as opposed to 1; 8 libraries as opposed to 2.[3]

For those actually living in the 'inner city' these things are more immediate than the finicking distinctions of analysts. Their problems are unambiguous. They revolve around poverty, housing and jobs. Let us look a little more closely at these things.

*

* D. Eversley and I. Begg, for example, for the Economic and Social Research Council, have collected data at ward level of over 70 indicators.[2]

Staining all other deprivation statistics – although, curiously, not included amongst them – are the hard facts of poverty. To seek to reduce poverty to a minimum, if not totally to eliminate it, is a fundamental mark of a civilised society. But what *is* poverty? Can one speak of absolute poverty, or only of relative poverty? Merely to pose the question leads one speedily into social, economic and philosophical quicksands.

Absolute poverty, as it exists in the Third World, a tenuous clinging to existence, is all but unknown in Britain today. The grinding hardships which brought the Jarrow Marchers to London in the 1930s – threadbare, hungry, cold – have faded into history now, eliminated for all but a tiny handful by the safety nets of the Welfare State. Gone now the once common-enough sight of grimy toes sticking through gaping shoes of working-class children. Gone now the privy in the back yard. Fifty years ago the working day, for those in jobs, was long, and a week's holiday a year the norm. Today nearly all manual workers are entitled to four weeks holiday a year (a fifth to five weeks or more) and 60 per cent take at least one long holiday away from home. As national prosperity has risen, so have real disposable incomes per head – at least for those in employment. On average, each household was one-third better off in 1990 than in 1980. Most of the present generation are enjoying an affluence undreamed of by their parents and grandparents. But for the others? In May 1989 Mr John Moore, the then Secretary of State for Social Security, claimed that affluence now spreads right across the board. Indeed, he seemed almost to deny the very existence of poverty. 'Not only,' he was quoted as saying, 'are those with lower incomes not getting poorer, they are substantially better off than they have ever been before.' The *Times* headline ran: '"Poor" Britons have never had it so good, says Moore'. Department of Social Security figures indeed show a rise (in 1988 terms) of £15.38 a week in unemployment benefit since 1948; of £16.38 in income support for a single person; of £23.78 in retirement pensions. Half the poorest fifth of the population, Moore told his audience, have a car, a telephone, central heating. Nearly all have a television set. 'It is hard to believe,' he said, 'that poverty stalks the land when even the poorest fifth of families with children spend nearly a tenth of their income on alcohol and tobacco.'

But statistics can be assembled in many different ways. Measured against average earnings, unemployment benefit *fell* over the same period from 1948 by 2.8 per cent; income support by 1.2 per cent; and retirement benefits alone show an increase – of 1.3 per cent. A London School of Economics analyst, Malcolm Wicks, estimates that, between 1979 and 1986, the top fifth of households enjoyed a 26 per cent increase in their living standards; the lowest fifth a drop of 6 per cent.[4] In May 1991 the House of Commons (all party) Select Committee on Social Security offered two alternative readings of the 1988 figures. Using median figures (i.e. the mid point of the data) as the basis, the population as a whole enjoyed a 33.5 per cent rise in income between 1979 and 1988; the poorest groups 2 per cent. Using *mean* figures, the latter groups showed a real fall in income of 6.2 per cent.[5]

Other analysts, using other periods, have produced other figures to show how we distribute our increased prosperity. However, comparative figures of this kind bring us no closer to a definition of poverty. The European Community's yardstick covers anyone receiving less than half the average income in a given society. Nigel Lawson, when Chancellor of the Exchequer, endorsed this approach. After his 1988 Budget he said: 'Half average earnings [then running at around £240 a week] – that's poor.' On this basis poverty in Britain doubled from nearly 5 million people in 1979 to 10.5 million in 1987 – a faster rate than in any other Community country. The official rule in this country has it that poverty begins at or below 140 per cent of the level at which government income-support measures begin to operate (currently £51.45 per week for an adult couple). This puts about 15 million people, or nearly one third of the population, at poverty level – a proposition that John Moore refused to accept. 'It is utterly absurd to speak as if one in three people in Britain today is in dire need. These claims are false and they are dangerous.' Inequality or an absolute of destitution – which provides the more realistic basis for the alleviation of hardship? And how should destitution be defined in the late twentieth century? A recent General Household Survey gave one million, or 14.5 per cent, of British homes in 1986 as having a gross income of less than £65 a week (with 472,000 households below £45). Such conditions are concentrated in the inner cities. One in five in Southwark earns less than £50 a week.[6]

All such statistics and propositions do little more than provide pointers. Every individual's circumstances are affected by a web of give-and-take elements: housing benefits, disability payments, children's allowances, national and local taxes, special allowances and dispensations.* Over and above the small type, however, is

* Social Fund payments to the poorest to meet their basic needs are now discretionary. In a recent case applicants were refused because it was thought that the local office had run out of money; in a subsequent High Court case the procedure was found defective.

the cardinal truth embodied in a brief sentence in the 1985 report of the Archbishop of Canterbury's Commission on Urban Priority Areas, *Faith in the City*[7]: 'Poverty is not only about shortage of money ... It is about rights and relationships, about how people are treated and how they regard themselves; about powerlessness, exclusion and loss of dignity. Yet the lack of an adequate income is at its heart.'

The dripping walls of the system-built 1960s flats are real. The stench of urine on the staircases (the lifts have been out of order for months) is real. The three attacks upon old people in the dark approaches over the past two months are real. Poverty is not being able to move elsewhere; being dependent on one's points in the Council's housing list, with maybe a five-, ten-, fifteen-year wait before being offered acceptable alternative accommodation.

Joblessness? 'Get on your bike!' says the Cabinet Minister. But when whole sub-regions offer many fewer job opportunities than there are those seeking them, the search for work must extend to more distant parts of the country. How then, even with a job, is the council tenant without capital to move and rehouse his family?* Poverty is being frozen out of opportunity. Poverty is being brought up with Mum and Dad in a 'hostel' bedroom not much bigger than a broom cupboard. It is the aimlessness of unchanging days and weeks and years without work. It is finding employment doors closed against one because of the colour of one's skin, or because one lacks the skills for the new kinds of job which are coming into existence. It is having to spend 80p return every time you have to go to town to shop, because the little local stores have been put to the torch and the traders have gone away.

Absolute poverty still exists. There are the vagrants and drop-outs, the paperbag communities, the young who have run away from home and gravitated to the pavements of the big city. But for the nation as a whole poverty no longer centres upon actual homelessness, actual hunger, disease and sanitation. Poverty today is being locked into an existence from which there is no escape. It is the removal of choice, the denial of *access* to another way of life, powerlessness over one's future. It is the source of the family tensions and breakdowns to which hopelessness leads; the despair which settles over inner cities and outer estates like a miasma.

*

* Local authorities are under no obligation to house those who have rendered themselves homeless – for example by moving to another part of the country in search of work. Single people – other than the elderly and the handicapped – anyway have no statutory *right* to housing.

21

Decent housing is central to the self-respect and wellbeing of the individual. By extension it is central to the self-respect and wellbeing of the nation. It is a key factor in the problems of the inner city and the outer estates.

> If the base for so much of our lives is insecure, damp, cold or overcrowded, then the attainment of almost all goals is made more difficult. Personal problems – of old age, of infirmity, of poverty, of unemployment, of educational achievement and so on – are magnified . . .
>
> The negative aspects of our lives – ill health, vandalism and crime, racial prejudice, loneliness, mental illness, family break-up – are multiplied and exaggerated by housing shortages and bad housing conditions. The cost of curing these social ills is correspondingly increased although it never appears in any housing accounts.

Inquiry into British Housing report, 1985[8]

This Inquiry, chaired by the Duke of Edinburgh, was initiated to coincide with the centenary of the monumental 1885 report of the Royal Commission on the Housing of the Working Classes. To read now any of the great nineteenth-century reports on housing is like looking through the wrong end of the telescope, so unbelievable and remote seem the horrors they document: 2,400 people sleeping in 853 beds[9]; courts of up to twenty houses, boasting a single privy between them; a life expectancy of seventeen years for the labouring classes in Manchester. In the 1880s, in parts of the Boundary Street area in the East End of London, the death rate was still four times that of London as a whole (one child in four died in its first year). Anonymous ghosts, arising from pages in national archives. Today's problems are as distant from these as they in their turn were from the disease and hunger of mediaeval times.

Today a population of some 55 million lives in around 21 million households. The figures reflect the steady improvement in space and occupancy standards since the beginning of the century. The population has more than doubled, but whereas in 1911 the average household consisted of over four people, in 1987 it was 2.52. Another, and no less significant change has taken place over the same period. In 1913 90 per cent of all housing in Britain was rented; only one tenth was owner occupied. By the middle 1980s, through increased affluence and energetic government policy, some 65 per cent was owner occupied. However, these cheerful statistics do not tell the whole story. Estimates of the state of the nation's housing stock vary, some putting the number which are unfit, lack a basic amenity, or need substantial repair, as high as one quarter of the total – or around 5 million homes. A middle-of-the-road figure comes from the Association of District Councils' 1989 report *A Time to Take Stock*. Completed from government surveys[10], this suggests that nearly 3 million houses in England and Wales require urgent modernisation, at a cost of £36 billion. The government itself reckons that 4 million local authority houses need repairs costing (a surely modest?) £4.3 billion. However the arithmetic is computed, the scale of the problem remains daunting, and the National Audit Office has estimated the maintenance backlog to be growing by about £1 billion a year.

Nor has homelessness been abolished. Suggested figures for those with no home of their own have varied between one third of a million in England and Wales (Department of the Environment, 1981) and the 1.2 million reckoned to be on English local authority housing lists (an unreliable guide). The word itself is used in different ways. The number of 'statutory homeless' (i.e. those for whom local councils *have* to find accommodation) was put by the government in March 1990 at 125,000; some 41,000 families are being put up temporarily, with about 12,000 in bed-and-breakfast 'hotels'. Many of these are notoriously cramped, dirty, dangerous (fire risk) and quite unfit places in which to bring up children.* In the big cities it is impossible to be unaware of the growing number of those sleeping rough in cardboard-and-paperbag communities. There are currently thought to be some 5,000 of them, with the problem most acute in the sixteen- to eighteen-year-old group. Precise figures for these various categories are clearly impossible to establish. What is clear is that an unacceptable number of people are living in unacceptable conditions. Nor is their number growing less. DoE figures for homelessness issued in March 1990 showed a 10 per cent increase over the previous year. The (Conservative controlled) London Boroughs Association, a few months before, had put the comparable increase in London at 30 per cent, and blamed this on the government's restrictions on council-house building. One thousand people are said to seek help from local councils each working day on homelessness-related problems.

* It is also an absurdly profligate way of dealing with the problem. The example was quoted in 1989 of a homeless family being lodged in an £800-a-week seaside hotel, paid for by the Council which had evicted them for not having paid £250 in rent arrears. At the time of the report the hotel bill had amounted to £6,785, while the family's home remained empty. In December 1990 Shelter estimated that councils were spending twice as much on temporary accommodation for families as it would cost to build them new homes.[11]

Homelessness and the state of the housing stock are indeed fundamental indicators for the inner city. One guide to what is being done about the latter is offered by the rates of slum clearance and of new house building. Again the figures make depressing reading. In the mid eighties slum clearance amounted to no more than 20,000 properties a year for the whole of Britain – a rate which, it has been pointed out, assumes a natural – or perhaps *un*natural – life for all property of a thousand years.* During the five years from 1979/80 to 1984/85 public expenditure on housing declined by 54.6 per cent. In 1988 24,800 public sector houses were completed, compared with 140,000 in 1977. Housing association completions were down from 16,300 in 1979 to 9,200 in 1989. Investment in new house building, in fact, is now lower in this country than in any comparable nation, both as a percentage of the gross national product *and* in relation to the number of houses built per thousand of the population. Little to look forward to here for those locked into grossly inadequate homes.

Hidden within the overall statistics are more specific areas of hardship. It is not only the *number* of homes which is important – Merseyside planning officers, for example, reported, not withstanding demolitions, a doubling of vacancy rates between 1971 and 1981, with 60,000 council dwellings hard to let [12] – but rather availability of the type of accommodation which is needed and fit to live in, in the places where it is needed. The shift towards private ownership is obviously healthy (though in every area there are those who, perhaps as a result of job lay-offs, or rising inflation and interest rates, cannot keep up with their mortgage payments and find their house, on which they had pinned so much, repossessed).† There remains, however, a substantial proportion of the population for whom access to ownership is closed: the young (including students), the elderly, the essentially mobile, the unemployed, immigrants, the most deprived and vulnerable. They simply do not have the money.[13] For these there is an absolute need for rented accommodation, and it is a need which is particularly urgent in the big cities.

Historically, it was this need which the immense public-housing programmes of the local authorities set out to meet. Public housing on this scale – at the end of the 1970s councils were accommodating some 18 million people – was unique to this country in the western world. It was a role made necessary by the progressive

* Twenty million houses, divided by 20,000 demolitions a year.
† Repossessions reached a record high by the autumn of 1990.

decline of the private sector in this part of the market, an area rendered unprofitable by rent controls, security of tenure for the tenant (which reduced the asset value of the property) and the increasing costs of maintenance and management. Now that local authority building has all but ceased – Exchequer subsidy towards public housing was £2,029 million in 1980/81, fell to £656 million by 1984/85, and now goes to only about fifty councils (out of 319) – the burden has fallen upon the housing associations. Admirable though their efforts are – and they have expanded greatly over the last decade or so and are now responsible for over 600,000 homes – it is questionable whether they can meet the full demand for rented accommodation at reasonable levels. To the extent of the shortfall, hardship will continue.

And what of the state of the accommodation that *is* available? Much local authority housing has been excellent. Many earlier estates (for example by the London County Council) have considerable charm today and have been designated as conservation areas. After World War II central government, through its Housing Manuals, set space and design standards, and the best public housing was certainly better designed than its equivalent in the private sector. The very scale of the operation, however, encouraged a rule-of-thumb approach. Much from the inter-war years, and from the 1950s and 1960s, was monotonous in style, mechanistically repetitious in layout, and altogether lacking in character and delight. With the drive to system-built high-rise flats and towers – encouraged by government subsidy which increased in jumps with every so many extra floors – these weaknesses were compounded.

With hindsight the shortcomings of the high-rise estates are all too glaringly obvious. The anonymity of the buildings themselves, and the abject failure in many cases to create even a minimally decent setting at ground level, combined to depress the spirits of those decanted into them. But design weaknesses at a deeper level made possible, or exacerbated, the siege mentality now to be encountered in so many such estates. 'Walkways in the sky', common entrances, hidden corners which are not overlooked, communal spaces which belong to no one, poor lighting, these are among the things which encourage violence and vandalism. In America Oscar Newman analysed the factors making for 'defensible space' in the early 1970s. In this country Dr Alice Coleman has broadened these to embrace a wider range of elements encountered in the 'sink' estate (including litter, graffiti, damage and the prevalence of faeces in public areas).[14] The 1980s team she headed from the Land Use Research Unit at King's College, London, studied over 4,000 *blocks* of flats in all parts of Britain as well as overseas, but concentrating on two 'inner city' London Boroughs where *every* such block was surveyed. Among the factors the team identified as important were: the size and height of the blocks, the number of dwellings in each block and the number served by each entrance, the positioning of that entrance, corridors and upper walkways, the spatial organisation of flats within the block (one floor, two floors) and of the spaces around the block (walls and fences, play areas, communal areas, opportunities for and hindrances to surveillance, etc.). Modifications to these are now becoming the commonplace of refurbishing such estates; but radical redesign, though increasing, remains the exception rather than the rule.

The sheer volume of public housing has led to problems of maintenance. Alice Coleman's survey was concerned with externals; interiors open up a further range of problems. Deck-access housing in Manchester was reported in the middle eighties as leaking, without heating, stinking from back flows of sewage, infested by cockroaches, and badly vandalised. Large areas of pre-World War I housing, by modern standards, are unfit to live in. The sums now required to renew or rehabilitate all this crumbling property totally outstrip the resources available to the local authorities concerned. Sometimes, it would seem, the will too is lacking.

> The house next door was owned by the local authority [a London Borough] but inhabited by young squatters, who seemed acceptable and who looked after the property. But the council evicted them and wrecked the house, smashing internal fittings and boarding up doors and windows to make it uninhabitable. The council then abandoned the property, letting the garden become overgrown and infested, allowing water pipes to burst.
>
> Letter, *Sunday Times*, 28 May 1989

Public attention concentrates on public housing – properly, for public authorities should maintain exemplary standards – but it has to be said that disrepair is more widespread in the private sector than the public. Although up to £14 billion is spent annually on privately owned housing alone,[15] disrepair is reckoned to be on the increase. There seems to be little doubt that the total needed properly to remedy defects in the *total* housing stock is of the order of £35 billion or more. And that excludes slum clearance and new construction.

*

Jobs. What brought the 'inner city' into prominence was, of course, the calamitous collapse of Britain's traditional industrial base and the trauma of the unprecedented unemployment which ensued. (For thirty years full employment had been a specific objective of economic policy and from 1945–74 unemployment had averaged less than two per cent.) The story scarcely requires retelling at length for its climax was reached within the past decade and its effects are with us still. What is sometimes forgotten is just how far back the roots of our present situation go. At the very zenith of Empire, when Britain's industrial and economic power was dominant throughout the world, when the volume of our exports was unprecedented, when Establishment affluence was at its most ostentatious, and a new century promised unbeliev-able developments in every direction, our worldwide commitments were already overstretching our economy. In 1903 Joseph Chamberlain, as Colonial Secretary, was referring to Britain as 'the weary Titan, staggering under the weight of its own orb'. The conditions for decline already existed – under the surface. The picture was blurred by two world wars, with the prodigious demands they made upon industry. And if, in between, standards of living fell savagely in the 'Great Depression', that after all, we told ourselves, was something which affected the whole wide world and not just Britain.

By the second half of the 1940s, however, the dissolution of Empire, the wartime sale of our overseas assets, the overwhelming productivity of the United States, and the first signs of intense industrial competition from newly developing nations, meant that the harsh realities could no longer be overlooked. Three genera-tions had failed adequately to modernise, repair, reinvest – in the railway system, the mills and foundries of the industrial North, the ports, housing, the Victorian drainage systems of the cities, and much, much else. New technologies were developing, new needs emerging. Inexorably, it seemed, the great industries wound down. Britain's share in total world exports was 25.5 per cent in 1950; in 1979 it was 9.7 per cent. At the turn of the century we built half the world's ships; at the end of the eighties the figure was 0.77 per cent. The chimney stacks and mill complexes of Lancashire and Yorkshire fell smokeless, silent and still. The furnace glow of great steelworks no longer warmed the night skies. Beeching's surgery excised long miles of track from the railway system. The first of the docks closed ... It turned into a rout. Coal production, which had peaked at 287 million tons just before the 1914 war, then employed over one million men. By 1960 the workforce was down to 634,000; today it is around 80,000 and still shrinking. In South Wales, output shrank from

270,000 tons in 1920 to 110,000 in 1945 and to 3,000 or less today. Now the heaps of coke and anthracite in Cardiff Docks are likely to be *inward* bound from abroad.

Coal, steel, textiles ... the knock-on effects of decline became pervasive. Car manufacturers disappeared, or fell to foreign companies, leaving only, sometimes, their marque behind as a memory of a once flourishing firm.* As the main industries declined so, inevitably, did the secondary, support firms who supplied components. So, too, the ports. The tonnage entering Liverpool docks in 1922 was 31.6 million; by the early 1980s it had dwindled to less than 10 million. Shipbuilding and ship repair shrank in sympathy. As late as 1978 British Shipyards had twenty-eight yards and 86,700 employees. Ten years later it was four yards and 6,000 employees. In 1988, with the disposal of the Govan yard on the Clyde and the closures on Tyneside, the multi-billion-pound effort to maintain a British shipbuilding industry had all but come to an end. The then Head of the Civil Service, Sir William Armstrong, described its function in 1973 as 'the orderly management of decline'; scarcely a rallying cry.[16] By the end of the decade decline seemed out of control. Between 1978 and 1983 alone manufacturing industry contracted by 10 per cent and the latter year saw our first trading deficit in manufactured goods since the Industrial Revolution.

All this is depressingly familiar, but it has to be stated again if the problems of the inner city are under scrutiny. The effects upon the cities were catastrophic. Liverpool lost one third of its population in ten years; inner Glasgow 37 per cent. In all parts of the country – even in parts of the relatively prosperous South East – the bitter picture was repeated. A report for the European Commission in 1988 placed five UK cities amongst the seven in Western Europe suffering most severely from decline. (Only one British region, the South East, rose above the EEC *average* in prosperity.)

Of course the full picture is a lot more complicated. As a result of the great shake-out, industry is much 'leaner and fitter'. We have replaced our lost overseas investments with new ones. A new generation of industries, from electronics and high technology to tourism, are flourishing. Trade routes have changed; if the tonnage passing through Liverpool and London has plummeted, in Dover and Harwich it has risen and the Channel Tunnel will change things again. Nor are all the problems of our own making. New technologies will displace older until the end of time. The strengths

---

* Austin's was finally phased out from 1989, after eighty-four years.

and weaknesses of other economies, some at the other side of the world, can, sometimes it seems unfairly, affect our own. The competition posed by newly emergent countries, the discovery elsewhere of new natural resources – such things have to be accepted as natural hazards. Febrile and volatile international exchange rates, exacerbated by 'hot money' speculation, can fundamentally affect the flow of exports and imports, and thereby whole industries.

Nor, by the same token, are all these problems confined to Britain. In the United States the dispersal of business, and the outward pull of suburb and countryside for the more affluent, have turned many city centres into crime-ridden wastelands. In Europe, decline marks a swathe of nineteenth- and twentieth-century industrial centres stretching from Turin, through the Saar, the Ruhr and southern Belgium, across parts of Scandinavia and the North of England to Glasgow and Belfast in Scotland and Ireland. It includes textile towns like Norrköping in Sweden to Roubaix-Tourcoing in northern France; steel and mining towns like Limbourg in the Netherlands to Dortmund in the Ruhr. (Dortmund's coal and steel workers, for example, will have dropped, it is thought, by three quarters between 1960 and 1990, from 80,000 to fewer than 20,000 – and maybe to 16,000.) Around a hundred shipyards in Europe changed hands during the eighties. All this is the outward evidence of a fundamental restructuring of world industry – the completion of a cycle which started the frantic urbanisation of these places in the first place.

Change is never a comfortable process. But though it be cold comfort to those who have lost their livelihood, the regional, continental and global thrust towards rationalised production and distribution will continue – and continue to bring increasing benefits to the consumer on a scale inconceivable a mere generation ago. The clock is not to be put back. Throughout history cities have waxed and waned. Who knows – in a hundred years, with another shake of the kaleidoscope, the new industrial areas of Japan and South Korea, Taiwan and Brazil, may be in decline. What is certain is that, if the hard-hit cities of the West are to be great again in the future, it will not happen by divine providence. Self-help alone will bring about their regeneration. Some of the means we have adopted to this end are outlined in the following pages.

3

POLICIES AND PROGRAMMES

NATIONAL POLICIES, notwithstanding party-political claims, are seldom created *ab initio*. They emerge from, are built upon, or react against, a great weight of previous practice, often stretching back over generations. Like English case law they are linked in a continuously evolving process.

To chart the development of official intervention in urban problems is to chart the slow appreciation of their complexity. It began, in the wake of the great cholera outbreaks of the mid nineteenth century, with the steps taken to deal with public sanitation. Liverpool, to its credit, was the first city in the country to appoint a Medical Officer for Health.* Nonetheless, there was furious public opposition when, in 1853, the Corporation, having spent nearly £63,000 on Improvement (meaning, largely, improved hygiene) the previous year, attempted to levy an Improvement rate for the year ahead. The outcry prompted the *Liverpool Mercury* to remonstrate:

> We have been too long idly hoping that improvements would drop from the clouds without any effort on our part – too long looking up to the corporate purse in order to save our own.[1]

It is a cry still heard in our own day, and, at a number of levels, colours the debate on how best to regenerate our cities.

Once the national sanitary battle had been won – and the dramatic improvement in public health which resulted perforce

---

* He it was who advised the Sanitary Commission sent out to investigate the Crimea scandals exposed by Florence Nightingale.

clinched that argument – attention turned increasingly to housing. Indeed, for half a century and more, health and housing were seen as two sides of the same coin, and were dealt with, in so far as they were, by the same government department. The first model estates were built by philanthropic charities and industrialists, but 1851 legislation empowered local authorities to build lodging houses for the labouring classes, and seventeen years later they were given powers to deal with slum clearance and to build on the cleared land. Some of the bigger cities – notably Liverpool and, north of the Border, Glasgow – sought to use these powers, but not, it must be admitted, very effectively. Gradually, however, between 1880 and 1980, and especially during the second half of that period, the provision of low-rental housing coupled with slum clearance came to be seen as a major public responsibility – to the point where, in the 1970s, some 18 million people were being housed by local councils. This particular sense of responsibility has powerfully coloured left-wing politics to the present day (though the passion for demolition has nearly always outstripped the provision of new homes).

The growing concern with housing led inevitably to consideration of other environmental factors – roads, the siting of industry, leisure provision; indeed, eventually, to the design of whole towns and cities, and the balance between town and country. The potential for official intervention in these matters was extended, rather uncertainly, by the 1909 Housing and Town Planning Act. If, in fact, little planning was done in the first half of the century, that was largely because workable mechanisms had not been put in place. It has to be remembered that local government, as we know it today, only gradually replaced the earlier ramshackle network of small-scale vestries and boards for this and that, none of which were in a position to pursue strategic programmes, or to match the thrust of free enterprise chasing profits by the easiest routes. Not until the Local Government Act of 1888 did elective County and County Borough Councils come into existence; and six years later the Urban and Rural Districts and Parish Councils were set up. Although numerous towns and cities built themselves astounding Town Halls the public purse was, by today's standards, minimal; to create the administrative machinery required for dealing with environmental abuse on any scale was beyond the political will of the times.

The decisive moment was reached only at the end of World War II, in a consensus euphoria that the rational planning of available resources would enable us, once and for all, to get our cities right;

to clear the slums which the Luftwaffe had missed and ensure decent living standards for all sectors of the community. We would hack out the tangled undergrowth, the diseased and dead wood, let in sun and air, plant new towers and clusters to articulate the formless mass of the metropolitan jungles. A hierarchy of traffic routes would provide easy communication between cities, neighbourhoods, individuals. Work, home and recreation would be kept apart. All the old confusions would be sorted out.

The objectives were lucidly stated by Lewis Silkin, Minister of Town and Country Planning (such a Ministry itself being a new concept from the mid-war years), in the debate on the Second Reading of the 1947 Bill which gave Britain its planning system. They were

> to secure a proper balance between competing demands for land, so that all the land of the country is used in the best interests of the whole people . . .
>
> . . . these conflicting demands for land must be dove-tailed to-gether. If each is considered in isolation, the common interest is bound to suffer. Housing must be so located in relation to industry that workers are not compelled to make long, tiring and expensive journeys to and from work. Nor must our already large towns be permitted to sprawl, and expand, so as to eat up the adjacent rural areas and make access to the countryside and to the amenities of the town more difficult. Green belts must be left around towns, and the most fertile land kept for food production. The continued drift from the countryside must be ar-rested . . .
>
> . . . between the wars industry tended to concentrate in the South of England, with the result that the towns in the South, especially London, grew too large for health, efficiency and safety, while some of the older industrial areas suffered chronic unemployment.

Surveying the havoc wrought upon so much of Britain over the following thirty years, it is easy to dismiss the aspirations of those days. But who is to say that they were wrong? In today's market-led economy it is salutary to ponder the irreversible damage done to the face of Britain by uncontrolled capitalism over the previous century, the blatant shortcomings of which made the Town and Country Planning Acts inevitable. For the failures of our post-war policies and programmes we have to look, not at the aspirations which underlay them, but at the political, economic and social factors which affected their execution.

*

It was a time of big visions. Shortages of every kind inhibited major developments for a decade or so after the war, but the New Towns programme was successfully initiated, and all the demographic and industrial projections pointed to steady expansion. Taking their cue from Abercrombie's work on London during the war, cities in all parts of the kingdom hurled themselves into massive replanning on a scale never before conceived of in Britain. London, Coventry, Plymouth, Glasgow, Liverpool, Newcastle, Birmingham, Sheffield and the rest, committed themselves with ardent enthusiasm to a future which would, no one doubted, transform the quality of life in their inner cities and far beyond.

It was not to be. It has become the conventional wisdom to rubbish 'the planners' – a convenient term in the public mind for architects, local authorities, property companies, traffic engineers, politicians and civil servants, as well as the real thing. In fact, in those post-war years, Britain's cities drew upon professional talents of a high order, many of their architects and planners drawn from the idealistic training ground of the London County Council Architect's Department. Colin Buchanan, then a civil servant and now Sir Colin, in his seminal *Traffic in Towns* provided the rationale for new traffic systems. The professionals' political masters were mostly no less dedicated to the same social-engineering ideals, and some, like T. Dan Smith in Newcastle-upon-Tyne, brought exceptional vision and entrepreneurial flair to the task.

So what went wrong? Seen in retrospect it was all absurdly overconfident. The projections on which everyone was working until the early seventies proved to have been grossly overestimated. The post-war 'baby boom' petered out. Loss of Empire began to affect overseas markets; complacency and bizarre manning agreements industrial productivity. Costs escalated. Councils faltered and then lost their political will. Half-completed road systems were never finished (leading to bottle-necked stop-go confusion). The raised walkways intended to link buildings and areas – separating the pedestrian from the traffic – were never connected up (so never used). The lawns and the Letraset trees, the shops and the playgrounds, shown on the drawings, failed to materialise around the new estates. It all became too much to handle. Maintenance was skimped scandalously (so that the new flats into which people were at first so delighted to move degenerated into new vertical slums). Opinion turned violently – and rightly – against the needless destruction of familiar areas and well-loved landmarks (so often left barren and unbuilt upon after the clearances). Above all, at no point were the people concerned asked what they themselves wanted, as the advancing juggernaut of Progress broke up their long-established communities and scattered them in new estates far from the surroundings they knew.

We contrived to fall between all possible stools. The initial visions of the 1950s were never seen through to completion – but clearance obliterated much of character from the past and changed the face of our towns and cities irrevocably. We moved people in great numbers from intolerable conditions into accommodation which we needlessly allowed to become intolerable. What had started as a brave crusade into new territory ground to a halt in the mid seventies, in part because the nation was reeling under the effects of the oil crisis, galloping inflation and escalating industrial decline, but no less because the original vision had faded beyond recall. Thereafter our approach to urban planning would never be quite the same again.

By 1974, as we know from Barbara Castle's diaries, the inner city had made its way – as a distinct complex of problems – to the Cabinet table. Unease had been building up for some years. It was becoming all too clear that, whatever else they had achieved, the policy objectives of the 1947 Act had not led to an improved quality of life in the cities. Ghettos of deprivation had already become a matter of acute concern in the United States; the end of the sixties saw a flurry of legislation in Britain aimed at ameliorating some of the same difficulties. They were seen solely as social problems, and were tackled by the Home Office and the Department, of Education. These excursions into the 'twilight' areas have been likened to a form of 'action-research' and need not detain us here. Notwithstanding the creation in 1971 of the Department of the Environment – at first embracing the Departments of Housing and Local Government, Transport, and Works* – the government machine was not yet ready to think in terms of more integrated initiatives, as Peter Walker, first to head the new department, discovered. (He attempted, for example, to get something moving in London's decaying docklands.) By 1974, however, there was a clear need to bring urban problems into clearer focus. OPEC had quadrupled the price of oil and the economy seemed to be in free fall. Earlier assumptions on population growth were blown away like chaff in the wind (predictions for the end of the century were dropped from 66.4 million to 52.2 million). Local government was in the throes of total restructuring (83 County Boroughs, 259

---

* Transport was subsequently hived off again, a step regretted by many.

Borough Councils, 522 Urban District Councils and 488 Rural District Councils were being replaced by 36 Metropolitan Districts, 290 Districts in England and 37 Districts in Wales; in Scotland the Counties disappeared altogether to be replaced by much larger Regions – the Greater London Council and enlarged London Boroughs had been created ten years before). The new Labour government realised that the alleviation of poverty and deprivation had to be set within a more structured framework – but to do so effectively much more information was needed. Three prototype areas were chosen for study – Liverpool, Birmingham and the London Borough of Lambeth – these 'Inner Area Studies' being probably the first of their kind in Western Europe. In Scotland and Wales two new-type Development Agencies were created to initiate regeneration schemes. A Cabinet Committee was set up to undertake a major ministerial review of the whole subject, and out of all this a new policy framework was set forth in the White Paper of June 1977.

The essential new element in the White Paper was the inclusion for the first time of the economic factor. Dispersal was dropped; every effort was to be made to restore business and industry's confidence in the inner city; the Urban Programme was moved from the Home Office to the Department of the Environment and funding for it was raised from about £30 million in 1977/78 to nearly £100 million the following year. Resources were to be concentrated on the worst areas. 'Inner City Partnerships' (in the first instance between the government and local authorities, though it was hoped to bring in the private sector and voluntary organisations wherever possible) were set up in Liverpool, Manchester and Salford, Birmingham, Newcastle and Gateshead, and the London Boroughs of Hackney, Islington and Lambeth; a larger number of 'Programme Authorities' was designated, to prepare special Inner Area Programmes, and a number of 'Designated Districts'. All of these became eligible, in some measure, for assistance under the enlarged Urban Programme. The White Paper in particular saw at last the need to interweave the whole range of main policies and programmes, and to 'bend' them towards increased aid for the inner cities. The Inner Urban Areas Act, the following year, gave effect to the policies it set out. This, then, was the general framework inherited by the incoming Conservative government in 1979. White Paper and Act – amended, pulled around, filled out – for some years continued to form the broad basis for government action in the Thatcher decade, and indeed have never been wholly supplanted.

The general objectives of the new administration need no

35

elaboration. It has sought to reduce the degree of government intervention in public life, and the degree of public dependency upon government. It has sought to replace all forms of planning by the dynamic of the market economy, and to restrict the governmental role to one of regulation. With Adam Smith – perhaps the originator of the 'trickle-down' theory – it has linked the improvement of living standards across the board to an expanding economy, in the absence of which the poor can only become poorer. To these ends it set out to galvanise the supply side of the economy, to undermine entrenched corporatist assumptions wherever they might be found, and to reshape the Welfare State in the light of escalating demands upon it. It is within this framework of ideas that over twenty specific legislative actions taken in relation to urban regeneration and the inner city have to be seen.

First, throughout the 1980s, the government set out to woo the private sector and induce it, by one means or another, to take a much bigger share of the responsibility for urban renewal. Secondly, by the same token, through no fewer than fifty legislative enactments, it has sought steadily to clip the wings of local government, reduce its responsibilities and tightly to control its expenditure.* The introduction of the Block Grant system made possible a progressive reduction of grant to high-spending councils; restructuring of the Rate Support grant has cost councils generally some £22 billion since 1978. Housing responsibilities have increasingly been whittled down and virtually no house building is now being undertaken by local councils. Competitive tendering for Council services was introduced. In 1986 the Metropolitan Counties (Greater Manchester, Merseyside, Tyne and Wear, West Midlands, South Yorkshire and West Yorkshire, together with the Greater London Council), seen by an earlier Conservative government as strategically essential little more than a decade before, were given the chop. And as the eighties ended the introduction of the community charge, and the capping that came with it, created new confusions. Many of these moves were directed towards a more precise targeting of inner-city funding (though some would say more arbitrary), one aspect of which, a curious contradiction of the government's declared aims, has been the marked increase in centralised decision-making by Whitehall.

* Local authorities derive their main revenue in part from local taxes/community charge/or equivalent; in part from government grant for specified purposes. Substantial capital expenditure is usually met by (interest bearing) loans sanctioned by government. All three sources, since 'capping' was introduced, are thus subject to tight government control – as is funding from the European Community.

Against this background, a wide range of new initiatives was taken which distinctively coloured the Thatcher decade. These might all have been put in hand anyway – certainly some were already in the pipeline – but they were lent additional urgency by the events of 1981 and 1982.

The riots should not have been the surprise they were. Bloody confrontations are by no means unknown in our history – even our not-so-distant history. America's race riots filled our newspapers and television screens in 1968. Here, unrest was evident to those with half an ear to the ground. In 1976 Sir Reg Goodwin, Leader of the then Greater London Council, was suggesting that 'the possibility [of] . . . civil disorder on a scale we have not previously encountered in this country is now real enough to justify urgent intervention'.[2] To what extent are such prognostications self-fulfilling? The reality of this one was confirmed in 1980/81, when large numbers in Notting Dale, Brixton and Southall in London, in the St Paul's district of Bristol, Moss Side in Manchester, and, finally, Toxteth in Liverpool, took to the streets. Of these ugly events Brixton was the most serious, to be followed, in 1985, by the worst of all, on Broadwater Farm Estate in Tottenham (completed a mere twelve years earlier), in the course of which a policeman was murdered and firearms were used for the first time in such a situation in Britain. Nonetheless it was Toxteth in particular which shook the nation. The *Guardian* called it 'the most frightening civil disorder ever seen in England'. Thereafter the inner city was on the national agenda as never before.

In an unprecedented move for a Cabinet Minister, Michael Heseltine, the Environment Secretary, took himself to Merseyside for three uninterrupted weeks. He subsequently described the period as 'a seminal experience' ('one of those priceless formative experiences from which every politician takes strength'). As chairman of the already existing Inner City Partnership for Liverpool he had good knowledge of the area's escalating difficulties. Now, however, he was freshly appalled by the conditions to be found there. All his previous thinking was confirmed and reinforced. 'We had,' he says, 'to create a wider economic base for the regeneration process. The essence of the task was to inject *quality* into the environment to make it desirable in the marketplace. Improve the environment, clear out the negative values [meaning dereliction, the absence of roads and services and essential infrastructure] – then private enterprise will come in.' He was impatient of the impotence of 'the dependent society'. 'There simply was not the capacity to reverse

37

the process of decline. Greater economic independence was vital if resources were to be brought to bear upon the problem.'[3]

The thrust to harness new resources was to be effected, overall, through an expanded and more precisely targeted Urban Programme. However, it was through the creation of a quite new range of agencies and mechanisms – Urban Development Corporations, Task Forces, City Action Teams, Garden Festivals, Enterprise Zones (with Simplified Planning Zones in the wake of these) and private-sector bodies to take over council housing estates – that the assault upon the worst-hit areas was to be mounted. All these are to be found on Merseyside; several arose directly from Heseltine's three weeks there and were 'test-bedded' there.

The existing Partnership mechanism in Liverpool seemed to Heseltine little more than a jousting ring for acrimonious bickering between City and County – much as, over ten years, London's local authorities and the GLC had found themselves unable jointly to initiate action on the scale necessary to breathe economic life back into the docklands. The chosen instrument to replace it was already in the pipeline. The Local Government Planning and Land Act 1980 empowered the government to create 'Urban Development Corporations', to do for the regeneration of existing cities something of what the New Towns Corporations had been doing on 'green-field' sites for more than thirty years. The first two such Corporations came into existence in 1981, for Merseyside and London's Docklands. They were single-purpose authorities, with power to acquire and assemble land, to redevelop it, and exercise planning control over its development by others – but having no responsibilities for education, policing, public health and the many other matters with which the ordinary local authority is concerned. Like the New Towns Corporations they were appointed and financed by the government. Local authority reactions were predictable. The Corporations, as unelected bodies, were an infringement of democracy, designed to impose the government's will upon a defenceless public, part of an overall strategy to reduce the competence of local government. As we shall see, these resentments have not disappeared. Heseltine deals with them breezily. 'The charge of undemocratic,' he says, 'stands not a whit. We put Labour councillors on the Corporation Boards and they were happy as sandboys – and could then go back to their Councils and say they had fought things every inch of the way. Anyway the Corporations were not innovative. The mechanism had been applauded in the New Towns, which are seen internationally as one of the great triumphs of planning in Britain.'

There are now ten UDCs in England, and one in Wales – a second generation, after the first two, having been created in 1987 for Teesside, Tyne and Wear, the Black Country and Trafford Park, with Cardiff Bay in Wales; and a third generation, a year later, for Leeds, Sheffield, Central Manchester and, after a struggle by the City which went to the House of Lords, Bristol. The first generation have a projected life span of about fifteen years; the second of seven to ten years; the third – the short, sharp shock treatment – of five to seven years. The areas covered by the Corporations vary greatly in size, from Teesside's 11,260 acres/4,560 ha to Bristol's 890 acres/360 ha. So, too, does the nature of their problems. Some have had to face daunting tasks of land reclamation; others cover the very heart of a bustling city. Some have had few local residents to consider; others have had to be intimately concerned with local communities. All have as their primary objective the bringing about of industrial or commercial regeneration. As the number of corporations has increased, so, of course, has the government's funding. Overall, in 1989/90, the English UDCs received more than £250 million, the total investment since 1981 being of the order of £800 million. This is meant to achieve a public/private sector gearing of 1:4. As we shall see the reality has so far been very different, the ratio in London's Docklands being a staggering 1:12, in Merseyside a worse than reversal of the official target at 4.3:1. The nature and work of the Corporations will emerge in greater detail in later pages; suffice it here to register them as the government's main instrument of policy for dealing with the inner city in the 1980s.

More experimental has been the introduction of Garden Festivals, Enterprise Zones and Freeports. The notion of the national and international Garden Festival, used for some time in West Germany as a means of reclaiming derelict land to a social end, was introduced into this country at Michael Heseltine's suggestion, the first such being organised by the Merseyside Development Corporation on the site of an immense refuse tip south of the city centre. Since then others have been mounted at two-yearly intervals in Stoke-on-Trent, Glasgow and Gateshead, with Ebbw Vale due in 1992.

The Enterprise Zone seeks to encourage industry to locate within a certain designated area – the essential infrastructure having been created by the local authority or development agency – through the incentives of freedom from local taxes for ten years, and minimal planning restrictions. There were, in 1990, seventeen in England; four in Scotland; and three in Wales (with two more in Northern Ireland). No more, however, are now to be created.

The Freeport concept has a long history in other parts of the world – Hamburg, Taiwan and Mexico City are three current examples from a total of maybe 400 or so. In essence the Freeport is treated as though it were foreign territory: no tariffs or duties are levied on goods coming in or going out. Reduced taxation and regulations within it facilitate processing and manufacture – and thereby employment. Hamburg's Freeport, for example, generates some 20,000 jobs directly within the area itself, and maybe 40,000 more through support firms operating outside. To date, Liverpool's is probably the most successful of those set up in Britain.

Over the greater part of the country, which remains unaffected by Development Corporations, Garden Festivals or Enterprise Zones, the regeneration process is carried out through a complex web of grants and loans and EEC funding, administered through a range of government departments and agencies. Regional-aid policies developed over more than forty years overlap and blur into current inner-city policies. Confusion is compounded by the frequency with which the names of grants, and the rules governing them, are changed. At the centre remains the Urban Programme, targeted now upon fifty-seven designated towns and cities – the 'Programme Authorities'. The Urban Programme is by way of being a holdall for assistance in a number of fields, stemming from various government departments. In 1988/89 some 64 per cent of its resources came from the Department of the Environment, 16 per cent from Education and Science, 16 per cent from Health, and 4 per cent from Transport. The most noticeable trend over the eighties has been a reduction in expenditure on social programmes and a corresponding rise in expenditure on those with economic objectives. Up to 10,000 projects a year are assisted in this way.

There are grants and loans, previously available under two different headings but now consolidated as City Grant, to be had from the Department of the Environment. City Grant's essential purpose is to support capital projects which will strengthen and revive the local economy, improve the environment and encourage private investment by fitting land for development (i.e. removing the 'negative value') and assisting work which could not otherwise go ahead. In recent years the emphasis has shifted from local-authority schemes to private-sector projects, the largest to date being a £17 million grant towards the redevelopment of Hull's Victoria Dock. City Grant, with the two grant programmes it replaced, had put out, by 1989, some £1.2 billion, including about £300 million under the previous system. Benefits include the reclamation of 1,700 acres/688 ha and an estimated 42,000 new jobs.

Housing needs separate consideration, and here very fundamental changes have taken place. In the 'sale of the century' (there were quite a few of these during the 1980s) local authorities were pushed by the government into disposing of a great part of the estates they held – in some cases all. The 'right to buy' had been included in a draft Housing Bill of the outgoing Labour administration in 1979. It chimed in admirably with the privatisation ethic of the Thatcher government, and, aided by discounts on purchase prices and the longstanding provisions for mortgage relief, the result has been, as we have seen, an increase in home ownership from 10 per cent in 1913 to some 65 per cent today.* At the same time Councils have been restrained financially from new housebuilding by the drastic reduction in, or in many cases total removal of, Government Housing Subsidy, coupled with tight control over capital spending generally (including the use – even for housing purposes – of the proceeds of housing sales). The onus for providing further homes for sale has fallen squarely upon the private sector, and for homes at lower rental levels upon the Housing Association movement.

Early housing associations – local co-operatives and charitable trusts – began to appear a century ago. By World War I there were about sixty. Only after World War II, however, was their potential taken seriously by successive governments. A new agency, the Housing Corporation, was brought into being in 1964 specifically to administer 'cost-rent' schemes and to encourage 'co-ownership societies'. Loan capital was made available from a £100 million fund. Over the next quarter-century this has grown, notwithstanding intermittent cutbacks occasioned by the state of the economy, a hundredfold, and today housing associations in all parts of the country are struggling, in harness with local authorities, to meet the need for rented accommodation. For the tenants of existing council estates the government has offered three choices: to continue under local authority management, to opt for management by a private enterprise company, or by an existing housing association or new co-operative of their own for the purpose).

An early marker in demonstrating how greatly a 'sink' estate could be transformed, with the active participation of its tenants, from unlettable to highly desirable, was Lea View House, in Hackney (1980–83). 'Compared to what we had,' said one tenant,

---

* It is interesting to note that in prosperous Germany, for example, the figures are more or less exactly reversed, with 60 per cent of Germans happy to live in rented accommodation.

41

'this is paradise.'[4] Another was set up as a result of Heseltine's dramatic three-week visit to Merseyside in 1981. Arising directly from his spur-of-the-moment invitation to some of the great and good among business leaders to join him there, joint arrangements were put in hand for a new body, in which the main input came from the private sector, to assume responsibility for a single-tenure housing estate in Knowsley and gradually transform it, through a mixture of improvement and new building, into a more acceptable, mixed-tenure area. Comparable projects have since become widespread in many parts of the country – some, inevitably, more successful than others. In 1985 the Department of the Environment set up, within the department, the Estate Action programme. Based largely on the experience gained by the earlier Priority Estates Project dating from 1979, Estate Action seeks to build upon the lessons learnt from transformations already effected, and to promulgate the principles by which run-down estates can be improved and managed in conjunction with the tenants themselves. It can assist local authorities in this direction by means of targeted loan sanctions which supplement the normal allocations from government. Such assistance rose from £50 million in 1986/87 to £190 million in 1989/90. In relation to the scale of the problem, however, a budget of this nature tends to produce minor improvements rather than thoroughgoing restructuring. Funding is of the essence. Towards the end of the decade an ill-starred initiative from Whitehall proposed the creation of a series of Housing Action Trusts, which, under DoE auspices, would take over estates from local authorities, improve them with public and private resources, and manage them. Properties would then pass to new owners under the Tenants' Choice scheme. Pilot schemes were mooted for Lambeth, Southwark, Leeds and Sunderland; the level of government assistance proposed for the programme was £125 million spread over three years. However, HATs foundered, first because the proposed funding quickly proved totally inadequate; secondly because – to governmental surprise – tenants made it clear that they did not want them.*

From a different part of the DoE comes another source of funding – in 1988/89 totalling over £77 million – to assist the clearance and restoration of derelict land, a subject touched upon in greater detail in Chapter 13. During the 1980s Derelict Land Grant has been bent increasingly towards the reclamation of

---

* There are indications that Michael Heseltine, back at the DoE, may try to breathe new life into the idea. See page 236.

urban sites and has played a major part in many of the schemes cited in the following pages. The same year of 1988/89 saw 830 acres (336 ha) cleared in the fifty-seven designated areas.

We are still, however, scratching the surface of the full range of official support programmes directed towards the inner city. Other departments have their own mechanisms. Emphasis has rightly been given to training programmes, with the Youth Training Scheme of the Manpower Services Commission, whose results ranged from superlative to negligible, giving way to schemes shaped more precisely with local industry and geared to the specific skills they require. Promotional and investment agencies have been encouraged in many parts of the country. Road building has opened up new sites for industrial and commercial use. Innovative crime-prevention schemes have been introduced. But in addition to all the main departmental inputs, those of a whole number of government quangos have to be considered. There are the Scottish and Welsh Development Agencies; the Housing Corporation, already noted, with its equivalents in Scotland and Wales; the Development Commission, which spends about £14 million a year on workshops built and managed by English Estates; English Heritage, for the restoration of historic buildings and areas; the Tourist Boards for projects assisting tourism; the Countryside Commission for improvements in the urban fringe. From the European Community come substantial – though now for the UK declining – grants and loans. These have underpinned many of the projects described in this book.* Small wonder that to the uninitiated all this suggests a hall of mirrors, criss-crossed with tripwires, the positioning of which is all the time being changed. The National Audit Office, the governmental watchdog body, commented in September 1989: 'Government support programmes are seen as a patchwork quilt of complexity and idiosyncrasy. They baffle local authorities and business alike. The rules of the game encourage compartmentalised policy approaches rather than a coherent strategy ... [so that] – key organisational structures have fallen into disrepair.'[5]

It is certainly not easy to judge how much coordination exists within the official machine. One – limited – mechanism to this end stemmed, like so much else, from Heseltine's sojourn on Merseyside. In the wake of Toxteth he set up the Merseyside 'Task Force'. This brought together the Regional Directors of the Departments of Environment, of Employment, and of Trade and Industry,

* For a note on the main European Funds, See pages 287–290.

under a young Under Secretary from London, Eric Sorensen. It applied itself not just to Liverpool but to the much wider Merseyside Special Development Area. The previously existing Inner City Partnership – disregarded by Heseltine – withered away and the Task Force became the channel through which government funding was steered. From it, with Sorensen's eventual arrival back in London to head the DoE's Inner Cities Directorate, developed a much wider network of 'Task Forces' and 'City Action Teams' within a number of the fifty-seven Urban Programme Authorities. There are currently eight CATs (one has a slightly different title), composed of senior civil servants from the regional offices, whose job is specifically to coordinate government action at the local level. The sixteen Task Forces exercise something of the same function for more limited areas, but, in conjunction with local authorities and local organisations, can pump-prime modest local initiatives. The Task Forces are short-term; their locations change from year to year as and when it is considered that they have served their purpose (or, as some would have it, when there is thought to be a danger of their staffs 'going native').*

Nationally, the rationale by which resources are distributed remains obscure. Rivalry, and sometimes infighting, exists between the government departments concerned: Environment, Trade and Industry, Employment, Transport, Education, Health, Social Security, the Home Office. The Urban Development Corporations report to Environment; until summer 1989 the Task Forces reported to Trade and Industry, and an Inner Cities back-up team was to be found in Downing Street. Ministers come and go as the pack is shuffled and redealt (there have been six Secretaries of State at Environment alone in nine years; add in the other departments and all the Ministers and junior Ministers involved) and with each change there tends to be a change of emphasis.

Following Mrs Thatcher's post-election *ad lib* of 1987 great efforts have been made to give government programmes a semblance of greater coherence. In the spring of 1988 the Prime Minister, flanked by no fewer than six senior Ministers, launched a new £3 billion drive under the promotional tag: 'Action for Cities'. A glossy brochure brought together for the first time the essential elements of the government's various programmes, and Ministers stumped the country to meet the private sector over a series of 'working breakfasts'. (It was characteristic, if newspaper reports are to be believed, that in some cases local authority representatives

* Merseyside's remains a little different.

44

were not invited.) Critics were quick, not unfairly, to point out that 'Action for Cities' contained little that was new, and only 'old money masquerading as new'. The government, not unfairly, responded that the initiative represented a move to better coordination of official action and would thus squeeze more from the money being spent. It may be thought that even *recognition* of the need for greater coordination marked a significant step forward.

So – can we be said at last to have got a grip on these deep-seated problems which have dogged us ever since the Industrial Revolution? Let us briefly recap.

Over a century and a half, public concern with the urban environment has developed from matters of public hygiene to encompass housing conditions, then the planning of towns, a whole range of social problems, and now the economic base upon which all else has to be built. We have seen an initial reluctance to admit society's moral responsibility in such matters change to the point where an elaborate structure of official machinery has been built up to deal with them, with important additions and modifications made to this machinery during the 1980s. This sketch has, however, almost totally omitted the part played by the unofficial world – the private sector and the many independent agencies and associations with social and environmental concerns. One of the marked features of the 1980s was the development of fruitful new working relationships between the most diverse organisations, in many cases directly encouraged and assisted by government.

More fully to harness the resources of the private sector to the regeneration process was of course, from the outset, a major objective of the Thatcher administration. Helped along by the sort of inducements already noted, private enterprise has moved more confidently into often complex partnerships with local authorities, government agencies and voluntary associations – not only in housing but in the creation of shopping centres, office accommodation, marinas, hotels and much else. For particular projects powerful consortia have been formed. In Birmingham, for example, a group of construction companies has set up, with the City Council, what is in effect a private-sector development corporation. Elsewhere a comparable consortium, under the banner of the 'Phoenix Initiative', is seeking opportunities to undertake renewal projects on a sizeable scale. Where the pickings have looked rich enough – and before the catastrophic downturn in the market at the end of the eighties – developers have fallen over themselves to get in on the act, and the scale of their investment has been

45

enormous. It would be unfair, however, to dwell only upon these. There has been acceptance in other cases of a definite risk element, and, overall, an increasing thrust towards wider corporate initiatives aimed at urban renewal.

As a direct result of the study tour of Merseyside which Heseltine laid on for top industrialists and businessmen in 1981, a 'Financial Institutions Group' was formed (its members seconded by their companies). From this sprang, for government, the notion of the Urban Development Grant (now City Grant) as described above, and, for the private sector itself, a new organisation, 'Business in the Community', 'to act as a focus and catalyst for the greater involvement of business in local economic development and regeneration . . .' This was new territory and BIC did not find it easy to engage effectively with the many other organisations already in the field. However, support for it has grown steadily – nearly two thirds of *The Times'* 'Top 100' companies are among its more than 330 members – and the Prince of Wales has been active on its behalf. With growing confidence BIC is now branching out in a number of directions – it has for example set up a number of area-based 'Business Action Teams' and half a dozen 'Neighbourhood Partnerships' – but its most solid achievement to date is to have encouraged into existence a network of nearly 300 Enterprise Agencies, in all parts of the UK, with an annual budget between them of around £30 million. In the late eighties the CBI set up its own study group and task force to broadly similar ends, establishing its flagship in Newcastle as 'The Newcastle Initiative'.

No less valuable are the promotional agencies – regional or city based – formed by local business leaders (often in conjunction with the public authorities) to bang the drum for their particular area and stimulate inward investment by the private sector. In yet another direction, as the foreseen skills shortage of the 1990s looms ever closer, companies have shown themselves responsive to the need for improved training (the CBI claims annual employer spending on training of more than £18 billion). In a 1988 initiative, the 'Inner City Compacts' scheme, over fifty education authorities agree their standards with companies in return for promises from the latter of jobs for their pupils meeting those standards. 'Compacts' will now come under the control of newly formed Training and Enterprise Councils, the role of which will be expanded as the government's Youth Training Scheme is run down – forty were under way within nine months of the launch of the new scheme.

The private-enterprise picture shades into the even more

private-enterprise world of many voluntary and non-profitmaking organisations – supported, most of them, in differing degrees by government, business and industry, and charitable trusts – as well, of course, as their own memberships. The whole concept of the 'voluntary', unofficial body, working *pro bono publico*, is stronger in Northern Europe than the Mediterranean countries (in France the Code Napoléon has little place for such things), but it is strongest of all in Britain and North America. Perhaps it is their very proliferation, and the fact that their roots go back a century and more, which cause them so often to be taken for granted. In the environmental field they have blazed the trail and created the first exemplars in model housing, the development of planning concepts, and community consultation and participation. There are societies and associations for the alleviation of poverty and destitution, for the young, for ethnic minorities; which clear waste ground, find new uses for decaying buildings, create managed workspace, playgrounds, urban farms, and cultural facilities; which sponsor their own positive proposals for public discussion ... an extraordinary spectrum of bodies chipping away, here and there hacking away, at facets of a problem at once national and local.

A particular strength of the voluntary movement has been its ability to work in a completely independent 'enabling' capacity – by placing its expertise at the disposal of a community, to explain potentials intelligibly, to show alternative ways forward, to open doors, advise on sources of funding, to assist with technical problems and, knowing the ropes, to act disinterestedly as go-between in the community's dealings with officialdom. In other words, to make things happen. It is an activity better summed up in the French words *'animation'* and *'animateur'* than our more passive equivalents. At the national level there are several bodies acting as catalysts in this way, among them the Civic Trust, currently active in two score towns and cities; the Urban and Economic Development Group (URBED); and, at first on city fringes, but increasingly in inner areas the Groundwork Trusts, originally set up by the Countryside Commission and the Department of Environment. Mention must be made too, among the Church of England's follow-up moves to *Faith in the City*, of the Church's Urban fund, which raised £11 million in its first year. Working in harness with local councils and government departments, these and others bring together into new partnerships organisations both official and unofficial, provide them with a vision and a strategy, often providing access to funds which would not otherwise be available, and advising the ordinary citizen on what they can do personally.

By any standards the Thatcher decade was one of the most remarkable of recent political history, and not only for the length and style of her rule. The shake-out of 1981/82, until then perhaps the worst recession in this century, made possible some dramatic industrial turnrounds; British Steel, as one example, is now cited as one of the most successful steel producers in the world. Annual growth, which had dropped to about 1 per cent between the early seventies and the early eighties, returned to a 3 per cent burst in the second half of the eighties, outstripping for a time that of all our European partners. Unemployment, from its horrifying peak in 1981, was more or less halved. Inflation, for a while, dropped to a point that was almost acceptable. By 1988 Nigel Lawson was able to claim that announced and executed privatisations had accounted for nearly two thirds of the state commercial sector. Government spending, as a percentage of the GDP (29 per cent in 1932 but 50 per cent by the mid seventies) today has been brought down to about 39 per cent. Above all, attitudes and perceptions were changed profoundly – to the point where it is possible to see Labour Party policies as having been as greatly affected by the Conservative eighties as were Conservative policies by the Labour years after World War II.

But the problems of half a century and more do not disappear in a decade. In 1987 the foreign press were lauding the British 'economic miracle'; the once 'sick man of Europe' wrote *Handelblatt* in March 1988, 'has become the most dynamic economic nation in Europe' – but within three years inflation was once more rising stubbornly, to a level of all but 11 per cent; unemployment, after its steady fall, was once more galloping upwards at an alarming rate; the economy was once more deeply into recession. If productivity was up, production output was down; the number employed in the manufacturing industries fell below the five-million mark for the first time on record; in the last quarter of 1990 fifty companies a day were going out of business, and by 1991 it was 900 a week. As Britain entered the decade, likely to be so crucial to the western world in so many ways, all the old stop-go spectres loomed afresh – affecting, inevitably, amid much else, our efforts to renew the cities.

In the euphoria of the eighties boom, there was a feeling that 'if we can't do it now, it can never be done'. But the impact upon renewal programmes of the 1989/90 collapse of the construction/

property development market was tellingly symbolised by the standstill in the enormous Royal Docks area of London's Docklands, from which the various developers had withdrawn, taking their exciting plans with them. The construction of needed roads, bridges and transit systems was in many cases put on hold. Homelessness was on the increase, older housing as we have seen, still needed billions spent on it, new housing was at a twenty-five-year low (more houses were built in the late forties than the late eighties), home repossessions soared to nearly 44,000 in 1990 and 'Builders fear 25% bankruptcies' was the headline. One fifth of critical sewers were in danger of collapse in some parts of the country. Hospital wards were closed for lack of funds, schools for lack of teachers. The filth and squalor of the streets remained a matter of national embarrassment.

Confusing signals then. Government commitment to the inner city, and to urban regeneration generally, appeared – at first glance – firm. By 1990 the 'Action for Cities' programme was being costed at £4 billion. However, when the total is broken down, some interesting aspects of resource allocation emerge. For example, the Development Corporations have come increasingly to dominate Urban Programme funding. Many areas of decay and deprivation lie far beyond the boundaries of the UDCs but support for these is declining as an ever-increasing share, currently a third or so of the total, goes to the Corporations. Break down the £800 million allocated to the Corporations and you find over £500 million of it going to the richest – London Docklands. In November 1989 the government announced a 37 per cent increase in expenditure on regeneration over the next two years; of the additional £420 million involved, no less than £359 million was earmarked for the LDDC. By 1989 some £1.2 billion had been committed in City Grant and the two predecessor schemes it superseded. However, the *total* of £34 million allocated for 1988/89 was only £6 million more than went to one *single* UDC that year (Tyne and Wear). Between 1983 and 1990 Urban Programme Grant fell by 28 per cent in real terms, and was expected to fall by another 14 per cent by 1991/92. Of the fifty-seven eligible Programme Authorities, twenty-eight received nothing in 1988/89; of the thirteen eligible London Boroughs, nine got nothing. Or consider, in another direction, the position of the Housing Corporation – the principal banker for the housing associations. The Corporation's budget is scheduled to rise to a record £1.3 billion from 1990, but – apart from cutbacks forced upon it in the meantime by cash-flow problems – that does not compare with the £2 billion a year Housing Subsidy which went to local authorities at the beginning of the eighties.*

This now-you-see-it-now-you-don't principle blurs efforts to gauge the results of government spending at the receiving end. For Whitehall the eighties represented a more deliberate targeting of resources; for local authorities they represented shrinking means and independence. The loss, for example, between 1979 and 1989, of £22 billion resulting from the re-ordering of Rate Support Grant enormously outweighed the funds made available through the Urban Programme. The progressive diminution – some have called it marginalisation – of the local authority role during the eighties represented a profound shift of traditional responsibilities in the public domain. The Thatcher administration's intrinsic mistrust of local government, and frustration with its policy weaknesses, was mirrored in the weary unease with which councils viewed each new government demand and every smart new underfunded initiative. Abolition of the Metropolitan County Councils left the conurbations without strategic management, the very need for which had brought the Counties into being in the first place. (London is now the only capital city in the western world that has no single authority to guide, for example, its planning and transport.) Urban regeneration is essentially a strategic problem and the considerable areas previously supported by the Metropolitan Counties can find little to comfort them in the geographically much more limited work of the UDCs. Small wonder, as they have found themselves increasingly hedged in, that local authorities have become uncertain as to the future role the government sees for them. 'There are important sources of friction,' said the Audit Commission in the report already noted. From another direction the CBI, in a report published at the end of 1988, stated: 'One of the clearest messages to emerge is that the efforts to turn around Britain's cities will be shackled so long as the present uneasy relations between central and local government exist.'

Conflicting signals, then; confusions and contradictions. On the one hand a new confidence, a new buoyancy; on the other, new frustrations and old, old problems still to be solved. Something of what these things mean at local level will become clear in the following chapters.

* And where does the money go? The DoE was admonished by the National Audit Office in September 1989 for its failure to ensure that its £4 billion p.a. was going to the areas of greatest need.

A numer of the agencies, measures and mechanisms mentioned in this chapter are described more fully in Appendix A.

PART TWO

PLACES

Change is not made without inconvenience, even from worse to better.

Richard Hooker (1554?–1600), quoted by Dr Johnson in his
Preface to the *Dictionary*

When we build, let us think that we build for ever.

Ruskin, *The Seven Lamps of Architecture*

4

LONDON'S DOCKLANDS

The warehouses are roofless and empty; the walls are crumbling
down; the windows are windows no more; the doors are falling
back into the streets; the chimneys are blackened, but they yield
no smoke. Thirty or forty years ago . . . it was a thriving place;
but now it is a desolate island indeed. The houses have no
owners; they are broken open, and entered upon by those who
have the courage; and there they live and there they die.

LONDON'S DOCKLANDS. Not the Isle of Dogs in the twentieth
century but Southwark in the 1830s, as Dickens saw it in *Oliver
Twist.*

The East End, cut off by the residentless Square Mile of the City,
has always been remote from the Boroughs lying to the west –
another world, a city within a city. Its fortunes turned upon the
river. First the little creeks and estuaries of London's lost streams;
by the end of the nineteenth century 118 sufferance wharves; then
the 33 miles of dock quay controlled by the Port of London
Authority. With the port came all the activities ancillary to
waterborne trade, and manufacturing, and waves of immigrants –
notably, in the mid nineteenth century, the Irish and, forty years
later, Jews from Eastern Europe. In the teeming, stinking warrens
of Stepney, Poplar, Limehouse, Wapping, Southwark, Bermondsey,
Rotherhithe and Deptford, disease, drunkenness and prostitution
were ubiquitously rife. This was the greatest port in the world,
but, save for those who lived and worked there, and the
philanthropists and social workers who ventured into it, for most
it remained hearsay territory.

Living conditions looked up, got worse, looked up, got worse.
Marked improvements in housing were effected by the London
County Council and the local authorities. But times were hard in
the 1930s, dock labour remained casual until after World War II,*

* For forty years until guaranteed employment was abolished in the eighties.

53

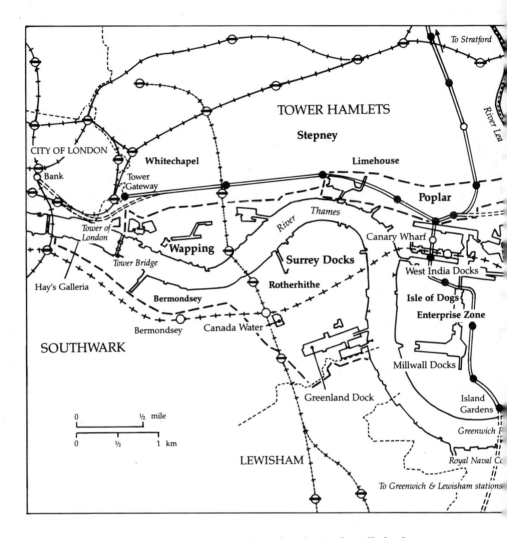

and during that war mass bombing by the Luftwaffe laid waste to vast areas. Willowherb took over, casting autumn clouds of drifting seeds across the wastelands.

London was for many years the biggest city in the world. It was the financial centre of the world. It was the largest manufacturing city in Britain. And it became these things because it was the biggest port. Until the 1950s a river trip from Westminster to Greenwich gave a breath-taking picture of what it was to be a great maritime power. Thames barges with their brown sails, tugs trailing their lighters, ships great and small from every quarter of the globe, and, piled in depth in one dock after another, the masts and funnels of hundreds more.

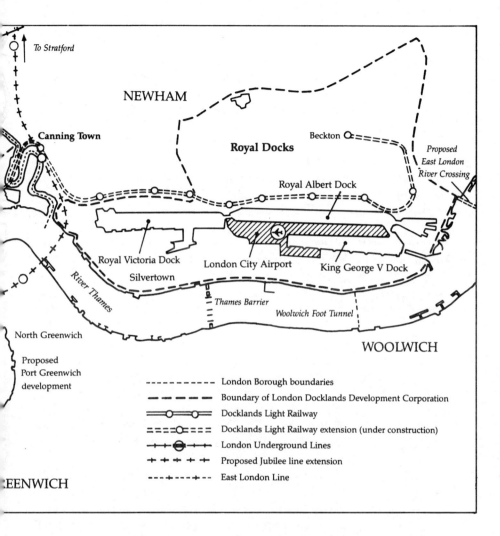

To Stratford

NEWHAM

Canning Town

Beckton

Royal Docks

Proposed
East London
River Crossing

Royal Albert Dock

Royal Victoria Dock
Silvertown

London City Airport

King George V Dock

River Thames

Thames Barrier

Woolwich Foot Tunnel

North Greenwich

WOOLWICH

Proposed
Port Greenwich
development

GREENWICH

- - - - - - - - - - London Borough boundaries

— — — — — Boundary of London Docklands Development Corporation

═══○═══○═ Docklands Light Railway

═══○═══ Docklands Light Railway extension (under construction)

+━●━+ London Underground Lines

+ + + + + Proposed Jubilee line extension

- - + - - + - - East London Line

Nonetheless, insidiously, from the early days of the century, problems multiplied. By the sixties decline was apparent and irreversible. Greater London itself lost 1.5 million people between its 1939 peak and 1977. Between 1961 and 1977 half a million manufacturing jobs had gone. Containerisation came, the coastal coal trade ceased, air transport mushroomed. One by one the great docks closed – East India Dock, London Dock, St Katharine's, and in 1970 Surrey Docks. Some 10,000 docks-related jobs went between 1966 and 1976, and another 8,000 in the five years after that.

All this is familiar, but needs briefly to be restated if the psychology and fierce local loyalties of Docklands are to be understood.

For generations the East End, the city within a city, was more or less left to its own devices, its hardships, and the only way of life it knew. (In 1970 the Isle of Dogs communities declared symbolic UDI in protest against successive governments' neglect and broken promises.) Small surprise that, now that way of life has gone for ever, the East End has not found it easy to adjust to quite other possibilities; that it views with suspicion the interventions of strangers from elsewhere – parasites, as it sees them, bent on extracting profits from the area that never came its own way. In the words of one elderly resident: 'When they could have helped us, they didn't want to know. Now they think they can make money here, they still don't want to know.'

When Peter Walker came to the new Department of the Environment in 1971 he commissioned, with the GLC, a study of the whole Docklands area from R. Travers Morgan and Partners. When, two years later, their report was published – it contained a range of alternative strategies and scenarios for debate – it was howled down by the Greater London Council and the Boroughs (and for good measure, the Unions). Local needs, they said, had been disregarded; there had been no proper consultation; and they objected strongly to the suggestion that a special agency might be created to tackle, or at least coordinate, what had to be done. Nonetheless it was clear that *something* had to be done, and a Docklands Joint Committee was set up, with representatives from the GLC and five riparian Boroughs, plus a number of coopted members. Work began on a new strategy.

Over the rest of the seventies ideas, proposals, projects came and went, were carried out or ditched. American proposals for a vast trade mart in Surrey Docks were approved, but evaporated. The GLC flew some ideas kites for possible developments. Around 800 homes were built and 1,500 more started; factory space was created; arrangements were made to relocate Billingsgate Fish Market. Yet, a fundamental dynamic was lacking. The Joint Committee had no powers to acquire land, nor had it resources on anything like the scale necessary. (It is interesting to note now, in the light of subsequent events, that the Joint Committee's strategy called for a public expenditure commitment of £1,140 million, with only maybe £900 million from the private sector.) With the change of government in 1979, official attitudes changed. Michael Heseltine came to the Department of the Environment. It seemed to him clear that without new machinery Merseyside and London's Docklands would continue to stagnate. 'I flew over the East End in

1973,' he says, 'when I was a junior Minister in the DTI, on the way to Maplin. It was exactly the same in 1979. The local authorities had done nothing. *Nothing.* Everyone was involved. No one was in charge. No structure existed where decisions could be taken instead of referred somewhere else for yet more consultation.' [1] Legislation was put in place for the creation of new-type urban development authorities, on the lines of the New Towns. Intensive petitioning against the proposed Docklands body ('a major blow to the future of the area,' said the leader of the Tower Hamlets Council) led to its reference to a Select Committee of the House of Lords, which nonetheless accepted the need for such an agency. The Merseyside Development Corporation and the London Docklands Development Corporation came into existence on 25 March 1981 and 2 July 1981 respectively. In the same year the 'Royals', the Royal Victoria and Royal Albert Docks, each a mile long, closed, as had West India and Milwall the previous year. One alone was still active. The trading centre of Empire and Commonwealth had fallen silent, save for the lap of the tide on the mud and the greened piles.

Nine years and four months later the tallest building in Europe* was 'topped out' on Canary Wharf in the Isle of Dogs, centrepiece of the biggest commercial development on this side of the Atlantic. The LDDC is the flagship of the government's urban development fleet; the explosion of activity in the Isle of Dogs at once the justification and the triumph of the Thatcherite ethic of releasing the free play of market forces. By 1988 an expenditure of £440 million of public money had levered ten times that sum – £4,400 million – of private investment (a looking-glass reversal of the Joint Committee's proposals of ten years earlier). Before the recession the Corporation saw private investment as likely to total no less than £15.7 billion by 1993. By 1990 some 17.5 million sq. ft./1.6 sq. m. of commercial development had been completed, with Canary Wharf alone promising over 12 million sq. ft./over 1.1 million sq. m. on completion. Around 13,000 homes had been built, with nearly 20,000 hoped for by 1993, and the population had risen by 56 per cent since 1981. A new light railway was in operation; a new airport was functioning. Some 28,000 new jobs had been created, with tens of thousands more expected in each year to come, to an anticipated 200,000 at the end of the century. [2]

All this, and it is still only the beginning, represents a colossal

* Until exceeded by a tower in Frankfurt.

achievement. London's centre of gravity has been shifted eastwards irrevocably. If proof were needed it is to be found in the total redesign of the London Underground map in 1990. Never again will the East End and the South Bank boroughs be cut off from the rest of the metropolis as in the past. Yet, throughout the eighties, savage criticism came from many quarters.

To many architects much of the area seemed a disaster zone.

> The central area of Docklands, the enterprise zone in the Isle of Dogs where no planning rules obtain, contains some of the very worst new buildings in Europe (with occasional exceptions, such as Cascades).* In their vulgarity and their insensitivity to place and to each other, the buildings of the enterprise zone epitomise Thatcher's Britain in all its philistinism and selfishness.

Thus Peter Davey, in the *Architectural Review* for April 1989.

Planners have been no less scathing (more especially in relation to the Isle of Dogs) – about the failure properly to link land use and a transport infrastructure; about the absence of any spatial structuring or urban-design framework aimed at producing, not just development, but areas of sufficient character to remain attractive into the next century. Walter Bor, a past President of the Royal Town Planning Institute, has called Canary Wharf an 'appalling mistake'.[3] Chris Shepley, as President of the RTPI, in 1989 spoke of 'irredeemable failure'.[4]

Political, local authority and community antagonisms have boiled over at intervals and have not disappeared. Southwark Borough Council has remained the most aggrieved of the three authorities concerned, and withheld cooperation with the Corporation for years. There have been numerous clashes of opinion with community groups, most notably over proposals for Limehouse Basin, new roads, and the airport. The National Audit Office and the House of Commons Employment Committee have at various times criticised the Corporation for lack of financial controls, limited provision of affordable housing, and lack of public consultation and involvement. In April 1988 the Labour Environment spokesman, Allan Roberts, went so far as to say: 'I would rather the Docklands were still derelict than what has happened.'

Clearly there must be lessons to be learnt, in a whole number of different directions, from the experience gained in this remarkable experiment.

*

* A distinctive apartment building at Hope Sufferance Wharf.

The designated area covered by the LDDC amounts to some eight square miles, or over 5,000 acres/2,050 ha, of which 450 acres/ 180 ha are water – the largest regeneration enterprise of its kind, it is reckoned, in Europe. It overlaps three London Boroughs – Tower Hamlets (which covers about one third of the LDDC area), Newham and, on the other side of the river, Southwark. Each of these, of course, stretches widely outside the LDDC area. The Corporation is unable to make statutory plans, but, within its boundary, it acts as Development Control Authority and decides (in consultation with the Boroughs) all planning applications (save in the Enterprise Zone created in the Isle of Dogs where planning restrictions are virtually non-existent). All other responsibilities – housing, roads, education, health, the social services and so on – remain with the Boroughs. In pursuit of its fundamental *raison d'être*, regeneration, the Corporation can acquire, assemble, own and sell land. (At its inception it received some 650 acres/260 ha from the Port of London Authority and the local authorities under a number of vesting orders.) Its main sources of income derive, first, from direct government grant (in 1989/90 it was over £245 million); secondly, from the disposal of land and property after its restoration and the provision of essential infrastructure, and services (between 1984 and 1989 this amounted to £253 million).

From the outset the government has seen the UDCs as small, quick-moving, entrepreneurial units, working to the maximum extent possible with the private sector and a minimum of in-house bureaucracy. They have thus depended for the most part upon outside consultancies rather than 'in-house' staff. The Corporation Boards (answerable to the Department of the Environment, which appoints them) consist of up to thirteen members. The Boroughs are entitled to put forward names for consideration as Board members, but to date, in London, only Tower Hamlets has elected to do so. The Board is advised by three committees – the Executive, Planning and Audit Committees. Under the Chief Executive there were, until January 1991, central divisions for Development, Employment, Community Services, Marketing, and Finance and Administration. Geographically, the 8 square miles are divided into four sub-areas – Surrey Docks, Wapping and Limehouse, the Isle of Dogs, and the Royal Docks and Beckton; multi-disciplinary teams were based in these sub-areas but are now to be merged into four newly created central divisions. In all, by 1990, some 400 people were working for the Corporation; of these, however, maybe 150 or fewer were whole-time in-house staff, the remainder working for outside companies and consultancies. These figures are generous compared with other Development Corporations but tiny compared with local authorities generally.

So frantic has been the pace at which events have moved since 1981, it is not easy to paint a coherent picture of the totality. The corporation's problem at the outset was one of credibility (did it mean business?); of overcoming the legacy of stagnation and inertia resulting from long decline (*how* actually to make things happen?); of changing people's perceptions (*why* should anyone move to such a forsaken area which lacked, amongst much else, adequate communications and access?). The Board, under its first chairman Nigel Broackes, took several quick decisions. It set itself against any further filling in of water space (as had been recommended in some of the 1973 proposals, and as had been carried out, for example, in Surrey Docks where only Greenland Dock remained. The water clearly represented a tremendous asset, environmentally and for sporting activities. To attract developers it designated the greater part of the Isle of Dogs – nearly one third of which it owned – as an Enterprise Zone, thereby freeing it to all intents and purposes of planning restrictions and its tenants, for ten years, of various fiscal liabilities. It began negotiations to acquire land, preparatory to fitting it for development. It sought, and obtained, government support for a new light railway, running from Tower Hill to Stratford. This would be developed by the LDDC and the GLC, and operated by London Underground. (It had been a body blow when London Transport, in 1980, scrapped plans for an extension into Docklands of the Jubilee Line.)

Here something has to be said about the Corporation's first Chief Executive, Reg Ward, for he above all shaped the Corporation's approach to the challenge of the early years. Ward's background had been civil service (he once worked for HM Inspector of Taxes) and local government (a New Town, and as Chief Executive in Coatbridge and in Hammersmith). His management style has been described as 'mercurial, visionary and sometimes maverick'. Notwithstanding – or because of – his own background experience, he has expressed scepticism of local government's ability to generate economic activity, and of planning controls generally. His instinctive opportunism, his mistrust of formal controls and guidelines, found full support at Board level. Heseltine, as was to be expected, was sympathetic and helpful. Wherever possible LDDC was given the wink to cut administrative corners in what was seen by all as a fight against time. Those who had dealings with the Corporation in its earlier years recall manic flurries of activity, conducted almost on a day-to-day, *ad hoc* basis, alternating with constantly changing addresses (as staff were moved to newly renovated buildings, and then maybe back again) and periods of total silence (as some new project was chased or new crisis dealt with). With hindsight, critics of the first waves of development are not few – but could it have been otherwise? How else could the whole process of development have been got moving quickly, the act of faith given validity? The question is central to the achievement of design standards in renewal programmes everywhere.

Edward Hollamby – ex LCC and Lambeth Borough, for the first years LDDC's chief architect-planner (though not a chief officer) – sought to establish for the Isle of Dogs some sort of physical vision. He commissioned from Gordon Cullen, the grand old man of 'townscape', a handsome *Guide to Design and Development Opportunities*. Unfortunately this romantic view of what might be was not grounded in any Corporation strategy or system of controls. It is not unfair to categorise this first phase in Docklands as an acceptance of anything by anybody prepared to invest there. Actual developments were small scale – big sheds for industrial purposes and rather suburban private-sector housing – 'Widow Twankey' housing in the words of Sir Andrew Derbyshire, for five years Chairman of the LDDC's Planning Committee. Attracted by the fiscal reliefs of the Enterprise Zone some 'names' began to trickle in from Fleet Street and television. Little of this, however, did much for the environment and it is ironic that what was probably the best of these 'first-generation' buildings, Nicholas Grimshaw's Heron Quays, is a few years later under threat of demolition to make way for the megastructures popping up around Canary Wharf.

Canary Wharf was the 'Big Bang' which announced the take-off of business confidence in Docklands and ushered in LDDC's second phase. At a stroke the Isle of Dogs moved into the international league. In October 1985 G. Ware Travelstead, with First Boston/ Credit Suisse, announced proposals for 71 acres/29 ha in this northern part of the Isle of Dogs. Nearly 12 million sq. ft./more than 1 million sq. m. of office space would be created on 24 acres/ 9.6 ha of the site, at a cost of £1.5 billion. Public attention centred upon the scheme's three fifty-storey towers – to be the highest in Europe – but one and all were stunned by a scale of development hitherto unknown in Britain. Vociferous opposition was noised in many quarters. The views from Greenwich hill would be ruined. The Docklands Forum, an umbrella group for residents in the area, denounced the whole concept as inimical to the interests of the community. The GLC, its own days numbered but an original co-sponsor of the Docklands Light Railway, geared itself to sue the LDDC for its (and the Secretary of State's) proposal to hand the railway over to the developers. There was everywhere unease about Lower Manhattan densities being funnelled on to this one site when square miles of decay stretched around on both sides of the river. Nearly everyone objected to a scheme of this size escaping, by reason of its siting in the Enterprise Zone, the public scrutiny and debate of a Public Inquiry. It had never been part of the Enterprise Zone concept to provide an escape hatch for anything making so profound an impact on so large an area around as this. LDDC and government were roundly attacked. But LDDC were bound by the rules of the game – not to mention the promise of 40,000 new jobs; and the Secretary of State refused to bend the rules and 'call in' the proposals.

However, as seems ever to be the case in projects of this size, the scenario was to undergo rewriting. Was it because LDDC, defensively, began to insist on certain conditions – the use of high-quality materials, firm completion dates, the appointment of a joint corporation/developer design-review board, wide consultation, and so on? For one reason or another, the developers experienced difficulties. The project languished, neither alive nor dead, for nearly two years, until in mid 1987 it was taken over – rescued might be the better word – by the privately owned Canadian company of Olympia & York, already known for their New York World Financial Center and Toronto's First Canadian Place. Their scheme proved to be less bombastically grandiose (though retaining the essential nature of the earlier) and rather more realistic. But not much smaller. It will produce a vast 10 million sq. ft./930,000 sq. m. of office space, 750,000 sq. ft./ 69,700 sq. m. of retail and leisure space, (150 shops and restaurants rising to 250) an extensive riverside promenade, and substantial contributions to the transport infrastructure. Costs are estimated at £3–4 billion. Work on site began in spring 1988; by 1989 waterborne batch plants on floating pontoons were churning out the enormous quantities of cement required for the foundations.

The starting gun had been sounded and the scramble for docklands land was on. Olympia & York were said to have paid about £80 million for their site; a year later, with no work yet undertaken, it was estimated to be worth around £280 million. Sites which could not have been given away three or four years earlier began to fetch £4 million an acre. Luxury 'yuppie' housing shot up wherever a glimpse of water offered – sometimes in converted warehouses, more frequently in new schemes of a 'post-modern' with-it-ness. ('Yuppie', incidentally, to indigenous Docklanders, means merely a rich interloper from elsewhere.) Such was the rush to this hitherto unknown land that the number of estate agents there went up from one or two to forty or more, and many of these new homes were sold 'off the drawing board', often as an investment in the hope that values would continue to escalate vertiginously.

In all directions activity was on the boil, tower cranes herded like giraffes. The Light Railway opened, a cheap and cheerful switchback, after problems with its computerised automation (which have never disappeared). Totally inadequate for the pressures now lying ahead, it nonetheless opened up the Isle of Dogs effectively for the first time. No less dashingly, after inevitable objections on the score of noise, the City Airport opened to the east, between the Royals, with two lines flying small STOL (short take-off and landing) planes to the Continent. This in turn was serviced by a new river bus plying regularly from Westminster. The vast London Arena opened in 1989 for pop concerts and mass happenings, and later in the year, in Wapping, the converted (Grade I listed) Tobacco Dock as a specialist shopping centre. In Southwark things were afoot from Southwark Bridge to Surrey Docks. Few of the big new buildings offer any distinction but here and there the spaces between them have been exploited. St Mary Overy Dock – an inlet just beyond the LDDC's boundary – has been retained by the Borough, and houses now the *Kathleen & May*, originally the *Lizzie May* of Bridport. In the middle of 'London Bridge City', a few hundred yards to the east, eventually to produce a million sq. ft./nearly 93,000 sq. m. of mixed development, Hay's Wharf has, conversely, been filled in and the space between the buildings glazed over to form the Hay's Galleria – well and sturdily detailed. In Surrey Docks the big shopping complex of Surrey Quays Centre has unfolded in phases, with the Scandic Crown Nelson hotel near by, and Greenland Dock has emerged as perhaps the best-designed LDDC scheme to date. Modest but increasing provision was being made for open space (for example an ecological park in Surrey Docks, Russia Dock Woodland and new landscape at Canada Water); for the arts; for water sports; for training. This was the general nature of what may be called the second phase of the LDDC's brief existence.

Almost imperceptibly, in the second half of the eighties, changes of emphasis could be detected in the Corporation's attitudes and programmes. Its second Chairman, Sir Christopher Benson – Chairman also of MEPC, the country's second largest property company – did much to defuse clashes of interest. It was in character that, during his reign, he sought to bring community interests more purposefully to the fore in the Corporation's planning and programmes. 'It is vital,' he wrote in the 1987/88 report, 'that the Corporation plays a major role in helping the old Docklands communities to feel part of the new developments that have sprung up during the past few years, and this is where we are now directing much of our energies.' Bolstered by its new economic strength, the Corporation knew, moreover, that it was now in a position to take a tougher line with developers than at the outset. The whole question of quality began to be addressed more seriously. Reg Ward's successor, Michael Honey, had previously been Chief Executive of Richmond-on-Thames – but, also, he was an architect. In one of his first statements he said that he saw his main role 'as that of building bridges and creating partnerships with the local authorities and the local communities'. But he also said, 'We expect standards of excellence in Docklands' – and within a month or two had appointed a Head of Urban Design, Barry Shaw, previously Area Director in Surrey Docks (and before that doing a similar job for Southwark Council). As an earnest to the outside world that design was now going to be taken seriously, taking a leaf out of Cardiff Bay Development Corporation's book,* a design-review panel of eminent architects and others was appointed; design staff were augmented.

There was a feeling that a less frenetic pace of development should now be the order of the day. Support for this was forthcoming in January 1989 when David Trippier, the then Minister for Inner City Coordination, urged a more gradual approach in future – partly on grounds of overheating in the construction industry, partly on qualitative grounds. Who could have imagined *that* three or four years earlier? Perhaps he had done no more than sniff the wind, for interest and mortgage rates rose with inflation throughout the year, the property market sagged, new houses refused to sell, the smiles on the faces of the housebuilders and developers began to look like fixed grins. Worse was to come. By summer 1989 half-finished projects, like the Cumberland Mills development, were being sealed up; Free Trade Wharf in Wapping was stopped; other projected schemes were shelved. In August Kentish Homes (previously responsible for the Cascades apartments

* See p. 135.

near Canary Wharf) collapsed; their ambitious project for the old Bryant and May factory at Bow, scene of the famous match girls' strike in the 1880s, went into receivership with only half the 638 flats built. Upriver, near Tower Bridge, the headlines read: 'Conran's Docklands vision becomes a nightmare at Butler's Wharf'. By the start of 1990 empty homes were being offered at 'half price' ('you pay half now, half in three years time') – to be followed by similar incentives for commercial premises. Most significant of all, Godfrey Bradman pulled Rosehaugh out of the Royal Docks where, with Stuart Lipton of Stanhope Properties, the two companies had been working on ambitious and imaginative plans for the biggest single site in Docklands. Given three months by LDDC to decide his own course of action, Lipton followed suit in the summer. The airport was losing money. The river-bus service had to be rescued. Tobacco Dock failed to attract custom. There was doubt about the future of the London Arena. Heads were shaken, all the old doubts renewed.

Through all this the rise and rise of Canary Wharf continued unabated. Cesar Pelli's fifty-storey tower was going up at the rate of one floor every three days, to reach its full 800 ft./244 m. in November 1990. The management of the construction process itself, with waterborne offices and batch plants, the need for temporary roads over the watercourses to provide access, the creation of all the infrastructure and surroundings at the same time as the buildings, called for considerable ingenuity. The first phase, offering 4.5 million sq. ft./418,000 sq. m. of floor space, was due for completion in the summer of 1991. By the end of the nineties, when all thirty buildings are on the site, this will have been augmented by a further 6 million sq. ft./590,000 sq. m. Rumour had it that, notwithstanding Olympia & York's powerful inducements and legendary powers of persuasion, by autumn 1990 only half of the first phase had been let. For the Reichmanns, presiding over Olympia & York, it may be surmised, this did not call for the panic button. They are long-term players and for them the question hanging over Canary Wharf is assumed to be not *if* but *when*. Mid 1991 saw the later phases of Canary Wharf put on hold indefinitely, but the sheer critical mass achieved on Canary Wharf cannot help, in their philosophy, but bring success sooner or later.

For the Docklands Corporation itself the recession was a serious blow. In 1989/90 land sales fell from £115 million to £24 million and for the first time the Corporation made a financial loss with a deficit of £4.25 million. Marketing ceased totally. What had been foreseen as the third main phase of its existence, the development of the Royal Docks, collapsed; the plans drawn up by Richard Rogers, Terry Farrell, Francis Tibbalds and others must be assumed to be dead. ('In my experience,' says Barry Shaw, 'a scheme has a shelf-life of about a year. After that *something* has fundamentally changed and you're lucky if you can retrieve anything.') With the Royals at a standstill, the LDDC's third phase has come to be centred upon the provision of essential transport infrastructure: in the first instance to deal with the massive requirements that will be generated when Canary Wharf comes into effective use; secondly, by further eastwards penetration, to open up the Royals and the airport to encourage development there; thirdly to link the areas south of the river to the Isle of Dogs and the City. There are half a dozen or so elements in this: the extension of the Light Railway westwards into the City, to link into the Underground system by mid 1991; its extension eastwards to Beckton; this ties in with the enlargement of the airport for use by larger planes and the creation of a new river crossing to the east of the Isle of Dogs; the extension of the Light Railway southwards to Greenwich and beyond; renewed proposals for extending the Underground Jubilee Line eastwards (as originally intended); and, among various roadworks, the building of the 'Limehouse Link' to join The Highway (from the Tower of London) to the Isle of Dogs.

All these have been the subject of much behind-the-scenes haggling and front-of-curtain wringing of hands, of private enterprise brinkmanship and governmental dithering – the latter reflecting of course the total absence of any transport strategy for London as a whole.* The end of the eighties saw cancellation of the high-speed Channel Tunnel link as an early priority and uncertainty as to the service's London terminus. A clutch of road proposals fell by the wayside. No fewer than three new Underground lines were under discussion – a BR cross-London link (at its fullest from Heathrow to Stanstead and Southend, but in the short term to Paddington and maybe Stratford); a south–west north–east line from Chelsea to Hackney; and the extension of the Jubilee Line already mentioned. All these were at different times the subject of on-off pronouncements by the government.

By early 1991 the situation was as follows. Outline approval had been given in principle to the Heathrow to Paddington section

---

* The London Planning Advisory Committee, set up by the Boroughs after the abolition of the GLC, has estimated at £8 billion the expenditure necessary on essential transport schemes for the Capital during the 1990s.

of the cross-London link, the Jubilee Line extension, and the southwards extension of the Docklands Light Railway. Particular controversy attached to the route to be chosen for the Jubilee Line. The Boroughs south of the river are notoriously ill-served by public transport and this has hindered their development. They were therefore incensed when they learnt that the Jubilee Line had been 'hijacked' by Olympia & York (who were initially reported as putting £400 million into its construction – a figure which shrank in later reports), so that it would turn northwards to Canary Wharf rather than continue south of the river. Another strand was added by the call for it to service the £300 million development – 'Port Greenwich' – proposed by British Gas on a 240 acre/97 ha site on the Greenwich peninsula. When the Department of the Environment announced the likely elimination of the stations at Bermondsey and Southwark, on the grounds that they would be marginal and uneconomic, feelings ran high. For the first time, it is said, since Transport was hived off from Environment, the DoE intervened in such an issue to put a contrary view. Working through the local Task Force, the case was made that the social and regeneration benefits accruing from the two stations would quite outweigh the DTp's more narrow cost-benefit arguments – and the £30 million gap they represented. In the event, stations at Southwark, Bermondsey and north Greenwich were confirmed by a House of Commons select committee in the spring of 1991.

Nor did things go smoothly elsewhere. The Limehouse Link, running underground for a mile or so in a four-lane tunnel, has been called, at around £170 million, 'the most expensive road in the world'. However, its construction has involved noise, disruption and the demolition of 113 council houses (the only such case in the Docklands development area in ten years). Although the LDDC, in conjunction with Tower Hamlets, will rehouse those affected – as well as offering a £35 million package of community sweeteners – tenants, predictably, marched on to the site and for a while stopped the bulldozers. Equally predictably the plea to be allowed to use bigger planes from the airport met with vociferous local opposition. The fifty-eight groups making up the Newham Docklands Forum promised mass demonstrations and to fight it at every stage. The use of bigger planes in turn depended upon the design of the proposed new bridge, the East London River Crossing, between Thamesmead and the Royals. This became the subject of a battle between the Department of Transport, proposing a very orthodox bridge, and almost everyone else who backed an infinitely more elegant bravura design by the Spanish architect Santiago

Calatrava – commissioned, interestingly, by Stanhope Properties who were still committed to the idea of some sort of development on the north side but were refusing to move until the bridge issue was resolved. All these matters, costing between them, several billions of pounds, were LDDC's principal preoccupation at the beginning of the nineties.

They were not, however, the only preoccupation. Reference has already been made to the political difficulties existing between the LDDC and the local authorities, and to the Corporation's growing realisation of its obligations to the local communities of Docklands.

In autumn 1989 Southwark Borough Council published a report on the first eight years of the LDDC as they affected, in the Council's view, the riparian belt from London Bridge to Surrey Docks. It was titled *Broken Promises.* It recorded how, after the Port of London Authority closed Surrey Docks in 1970, the Council acquired the land for housing and industry, cleared it, filled in and consolidated the water areas, and had the infrastructure of roads, sewers and river walls well in hand. Some industrial units and 300 homes were built. Parks and playing fields were laid out. Work stopped with the Local Government Planning and Land Act of 1980, and the land was acquired compulsorily the following year by LDDC. 'This of course,' in the words of the report, 'gave the UDC a head start.' At Cherry Gardens land acquired by the Council for housing, but not built upon because of government spending restrictions, was 'vested' by the LDDC at a lower price than had been paid for it. After a local campaign against the 'luxury' houses for sale proposed by the LDDC, the Corporation released the land and the Council had to borrow £4.8 million to buy it back for the scheme it had always intended there. Water under the bridge now, but not forgotten.

The promises? 'The LDDC promised to respect the local authority's plans. It promised to involve the local people. It promised to build houses for rent and to create local employment. It promised to create a new environment for the people of South and East London to enjoy. Eight years on the LDDC is hailed by some as a success. Local people don't see it that way.'

The LDDC had refused to accept the policies embodied in the Council's draft Local Plan and the Secretary of State directed the Council not to adopt it. Unemployment in Southwark had risen from 11.3 per cent in 1981 to 17.1 per cent in 1988; in Bermondsey it had doubled to over 6,000 since 1984. The average annual household income in Southwark is barely half the national average; 18 per cent of all households have an income of less than £50 a week. One in three dwellings is unfit, lacking basic amenities, or in need of major repair; over 4,000 households lack or share basic amenities like a bath or toilet. Even excluding the young and single (who do not figure in the statistics), homelessness more than doubled between 1981 and 1986.

The Council points to such things as the Corporation's offer of £1.2 million to induce a firm employing 400 to move out; to its failure to negotiate agreements with incoming employers to employ local labour; to the net gain of less than 10 per cent in rented accommodation and 6 per cent shared-equity mixed tenure, compared with its declared aims of 25 per cent and 25 per cent; to its failure to produce the up-to-100-per-cent funding promised for improvements to existing estates. 'No one disputes,' the report concludes, 'that [the local] community is experiencing change. New developments have enabled many new people, mostly young, mobile, with sufficient resources, to move into the area. Their needs and demands are different from those of the population at large – but the needs of the original community are still as great and increasing . . . Time and space in Surrey Docks are running out.'

Such concerns, as we shall see, have not been confined to London; they have arisen in some degree in several of the cities where UDCs have been set up. The later Corporations, however, have been very conscious of the problems encountered by their predecessors – the ice-breakers, as it were, in previously uncharted waters – and have tried to profit from their experience. As has been indicated, the LDDC itself has latterly worked hard to overcome some of the difficulties arising from its first years – to strengthen relations with the local authorities, and to develop its support for the local communities. In 1987 the Corporation signed a 'Compact' with the Borough of Newham; the following year it signed an 'Accord' with Tower Hamlets. These are intended to address some of the shortcomings in previous relationships – most specifically on the provision of land for low-cost, low-rent housing; in the training and use of the local workforce; and in assistance for the communities.

In 1988 a new Director of Community Services was appointed, who now has about sixty staff working with her. Training, resource and technology centres have been created to help local people acquire new skills, from the building trades to computer technology. In 1988/89 the Docklands Enterprise Centre was established in Southwark, at a cost of £1.2 million, to provide workshop units, training and advice for young people setting up their own businesses. Some £10 million was put into the construction of the Tower Hamlets Post 16 College. 'Brainpower' was launched, a pilot scheme to enable Docklands residents to enter advanced or further education irrespective of previous formal qualifications. And nearly £2 million funding went to assist primary and secondary schools in the area. For local organisations the Corporation has a fund of £1 million or so a year, distributed by the organisations themselves through a committee ('They're very logical. They turn down things we would have approved'). Specific projects have attracted additional funding; for example £1 million start-up money went to help fund the Docklands Sailing Centre. Overall, real efforts are made to keep local people and their representatives in touch with what is happening. 'On the ground,' one LDDC man told me, 'we have to consult at least as widely – probably more – than the local authorities, but it's within a different framework.' 'In the Surreys,' says Barry Shaw, Head of Urban Design, 'we mended fences with the community.' In the Royals, until recession brought everything to a halt, the developers laid on coach tours for local people to explain their proposals; land was offered for social housing; the Compact would have ensured the use of local labour. People felt part of the process. In the Isle of Dogs that probably is still not so. And, notwithstanding a 1991 announcement that 45,000 jobs have gone to the LDDC area in ten years, it is still too soon for any significant 'trickle-down' effects to have affected lives much beyond the LDDC boundary.

Who can foresee what this whole vast area of London's erstwhile docklands will be like in fifty years' time? Or twenty? Its future, like that of the nation, presents a minefield of imponderables. Yet, blinkered though we are, and in the full knowledge that posterity is bound to see it all differently, some sort of reckoning needs to be struck as this new-type agency, the LDDC, passes its tenth birthday. In the first place, who could fail to welcome wholeheartedly the amazing injection of investment which has taken place in what was the most desolate area in the whole of London? As has already been said, it has shifted the whole centre of gravity eastwards, and it is hard to believe that this could ever have been effected by the local authorities on their own. But it is no less possible, simultaneously, to see the first six or seven years of the unfolding saga as a graveyard of missed opportunities. As so often throughout history, quality and long-term objectives were sacrificed to speed and expediency. *Why* this should have been so is clear enough to us; to have achieved so much in so short a space of time is a triumph in itself. The trouble is that in twenty, fifty, eighty years, no one will be the least interested in *why* things were done in this way. They will only know that the end product is not what it should have been.

People tend to equate the LDDC with the Isle of Dogs and when they speak in these terms it is usually of the Isle of Dogs that they are thinking. In fact, of course, the Corporation has worked through two different sets of rules. In Wapping and Surrey Docks, and in the Royals when there is movement there again, it has traditional planning powers at its disposal, and has used them. In the Isle of Dogs the *laisser-faire* permissiveness which is the cornerstone of the Enterprise Zone concept has meant much less control over gung-ho developers. Nonetheless, this does not wholly absolve the absence of any overall strategic idea or structural balance between development and open space; the absence of adequate design guidelines; the failure to establish even a notional infrastructure framework before development was well advanced. Criticism of the Light Railway is easy in retrospect; at the time of its inception an expenditure of £77 million on something for which there was then no demand represented a real act of faith; greater expenditure would have seemed madness. Even so its refurbishment and improvement will now cost far more than if it had been got right at the outset. When the economy picks up, the Isle of Dogs will face a 'second wave' of regeneration – replacement of some of the first wave by more substantial redevelopment – but it is hard to believe that this part of Docklands will ever become the coherent city quarter that it might have been.

It is now clear – as it should have been all along – that renewal on this scale calls not only for a considered physical infrastructure but a comprehensive social infrastructure as well: of medical centres, schools, police stations, shops and so on. Such concerns have not been the prerogative of left-wing councils. In 1991 a private report commissioned by Olympia and York, no less, was leaked to the press. It was stated to slam LDDC neglect of health, social and educational facilities and to call for future development to include schools, colleges, hospitals and sporting facilities. The New Towns Corporations had of course, by comparison, *tabulae rasae* on which to draw their plans. The UDCs of the eighties were presented with the far more complex problem of dealing with existing urban frameworks, existing populations. The New Towns had the power to make plans, build, construct roads; the UDCs cannot make statutory plans (hence the conflicts with the existing planning authorities). They can package land for others to build on but are not normally in a position to build themselves (hence the problems over the lack of social housing and community facilities). They are under political pressure to produce results quickly (hence their reluctance to turn down even the most banal proposals), but, because they are so largely dependent upon private-sector initiatives, they are overwhelmingly vulnerable to wild pendulum swings in the economy.

It goes without saying that there is another side to the coin. Greenland Dock, for example, was subject to most careful consideration and planning before work began on the ground. Here a proper urban design framework was evolved; spaces, infrastructure, density and broad massing were established. Within these constraints developers and their architects were allowed freedom to work out the detail and adopt their own styles. One section, Greenland Quays, a site surrounded on three sides by water, was in fact designed with skill and sensitivity by David Price and Gordon Cullen – who has thus finally left his distinctive mark upon London's Docklands after all. And of course there are good and interesting developments to be found over the LDDC area as a whole, from the brio of Tobacco Dock (which will surely come to life again when the necessary 'critical mass' of demand has been reached) to the several very successful housing developments by self-build co-operatives. Altogether nearly thirty design and similar awards have come to the Docklands area.

A mixed picture, then, and one which is all the time changing. The LDDC itself is not the same organisation that was created in 1981. Can one, nevertheless, in the light of these first ten years, make any valid assessment of what the development corporation mechanism has to offer as compared with the traditional planning system? We have seen the views of Southwark Borough Council. For another I turned to Barry Shaw, LDDC's Head of Urban Design. Shaw, before joining the Corporation, led Southwark Borough's Surrey Docks team and has therefore seen the problem from both sides.

'I see this organisation,' he said, 'as in the forefront of planning change. The planning system – very public sector-oriented and possibly over-politicised – had reached a watershed. Radical solutions were required. Consensus planning, which is where the London Boroughs were in the late seventies, isn't going to give you radical solutions. The LDDC accepted that the public sector alone could not generate growth, particularly in the cities. We have broken away from the overweening nature of inflexible "master" planning. We are project-oriented. I see what we are doing as creating a stepping stone back towards the more strategic direction of planning – back to the long view, transport planning, regional strategy. We are changing the focus of the public sector, concentrating on the areas we need to focus on, not attempting to do everything everywhere in every detail. Out of that will come more freedom of choice, greater opportunities for smaller groups to have a stronger say in where the environment is going. I think now we are halfway through that process.'

But how is the long view to be equated with the kind of standstill forced upon LDDC in the Royals? Shaw admits to finding it very frustrating. 'The value of an organisation like this is its ability to tackle problem-solving in an unbiased way. The public sector has become much more innovative in its thinking, much better able to work creatively with the private sector but we are not getting the central government support needed – in strategic thinking for the South East, in transport, in environment and the public realm. I can think of many strategies that would enable us to go forward in this dead period if we had a little bit of funding, *or* if the pressure was taken off us to achieve maximum land values.* We need to be thinking, not just of next year and the year after that, but thirty, fifty, sixty years ahead.'

The LDDC, one must assume, will have left the scene long before that. At the Southwark end of Surrey Docks the Corporation reckons it has done about as much as it can, and there could be a certain logic in handing those areas back to Southwark in the early nineties. Looking at the rest, things like the new Tube stations will take maybe ten years and LDDC coordination will still be necessary for most of that time. The Royals, too, in the light of present inaction, must be expected to need ten years for their full development – which will take the Corporation well beyond its originally envisaged life span. Not everyone sees it that way. The end of 1990 produced a spate of departures from the Corporation, most significantly that of Michael Honey, its Chief Executive, who was replaced by Eric Sorensen (he of Heseltine's Merseyside Task Force in 1981 and subsequently a 'mandarin' of the DoE's Inner Cities Directorate). Developers began to bay that the Corporation was not marketing its land with sufficient vigour. Hackles were raised when LDDC's Chairman failed to attend an agreed meeting

* A fresh marketing effort to bring investment to the Royals was resumed in 1991 – through, conversely, as we have seen, the second half of Canary Wharf was mothballed indefinitely.

to discuss the Jubilee Line extension. The cry was heard that the Corporation was overstaffed, ineffective, that it was time to shut it down. Prematurely to disperse the talents assembled by LDDC, to reduce the organisation to a sort of glorified estate agency with some transport responsibilities, would be short-sighted indeed. Somewhere around the turn of the century, however, the whole eight square miles/21 sq. km. of LDDC territory will once again have settled into the general fabric of the capital. Then, and only then, will the significance of the whole great experiment begin to become clearer.

Beyond Southwark and Tower Hamlets and Newham lie Brent, Greenwich, Hackney, Hammersmith and Fulham, Haringey, Islington, Kensington and Chelsea, Lambeth, Lewisham, and Wandsworth: thirteen Programme authorities in all. As such they can apply for City Grant. In 1988/89, as we have seen, nine of these thirteen received nothing. Within Greater London there are currently three Task Forces; they have between them about £2 million spending money a year. Docklands by the turn of the century will, we may hope, be a humming, thrumming, wealth-producing city embedded in the greater city. But the ills of the greater city will not be overcome by Docklands on its own.

5

MERSEYSIDE

LIVERPOOL IS a gutsy city. Liverpudlians are tough, often bloody-minded, not given to kowtowing to authority – but warm-hearted, funny, proud, always ready to have a go in their own way. It is, or has been, home ground to the Cavern and the Beatles, Bessie Braddock, Militant, the Boys from the Black Stuff, and, by reason of its religious divide, two cathedrals and two famous football teams. A short list but it gives something of the flavour. And it accorded with the image that, for the rest of the country, Liverpool stood, in the seventies and eighties, as *the* symbol of the inner city. Most people probably do not now recall the exact whereabouts of the St Paul district, or Handsworth, or Broadwater Farm, but Toxteth burnt its way into folk memory as an enduring reference point. Other local authorities have thrown up party leaders of the radical left but none, unless it be Ken Livingstone, has reached the status in the demonology achieved by Derek Hatton.

Here, on Merseyside, as laid bare in newspaper article after newspaper article, television programme after television programme, seemed to be concentrated all the elements of large-scale decline. Coupled with the city's back history of splendours and miseries, they have fired a passion of frustration which has made itself felt all the way to the football terraces. Liverpool is the archetype of the city which grew furiously to meet a particular need, and, that need having disappeared, has collapsed in on itself. In 1700 the population was 7,000; a century later 80,000; by 1831 it was 205,000, and a century on around 803,000. In the single decade of 1967 to 1977, however, the city lost over 30 per cent of its population. Small wonder that the Merseyside Develop-

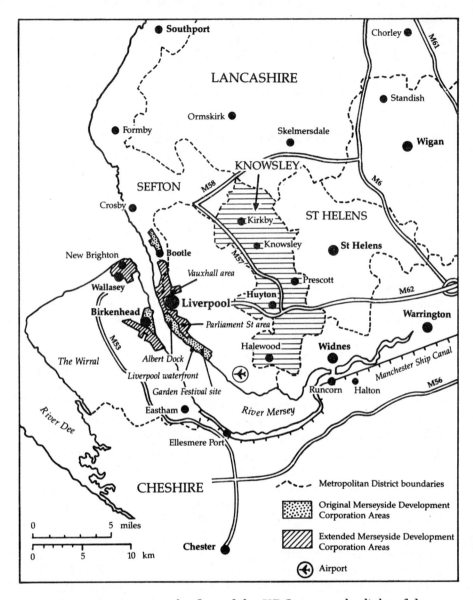

Southport

Chorley

LANCASHIRE

Standish

Ormskirk

Formby

Skelmersdale

Wigan

KNOWSLEY

SEFTON

Crosby

M58

Kirkby

ST HELENS

Knowsley

St Helens

New Brighton

Bootle

Vauxhall area

M57

Wallasey

Liverpool

Prescott

Birkenhead

Parliament St area

Huyton

M62

Warrington

The Wirral

M53

Albert Dock

Halewood

Widnes

Liverpool waterfront

Garden Festival site

Manchester Ship Canal

Eastham

River Mersey

Runcorn

Halton

M56

River Dee

Ellesmere Port

CHESHIRE

Metropolitan District boundaries

Original Merseyside Development Corporation Areas

Extended Merseyside Development Corporation Areas

0   5 miles

0   5   10 km

Chester

Airport

ment Corporation was the first of the UDCs to see the light of day, in March 1981, beating London, bogged down with a Select Committee of the House of Lords, by four months.

In London the Isle of Dogs lies not far east of the geographical centre of the whole metropolis. It not only touches the pulsing prosperity of the City; it is embedded in a great international power-house which, whatever its many problems, remains immensely rich, powerful and diversified. From this proximity the regeneration of London's Docklands has drawn its strength. Merseyside can look to nothing but itself.

The city lies on a continuous slope, sometimes steep, down to the sludgy and polluted waters of the Mersey. Nine miles of these shores were covered, in their heyday, by twenty-four miles/39 km. of quayside. It was from these that the area drew its sustenance, its confidence, its power. Sprightly privateering in the second half of the eighteenth century, coupled with the attractions of the slave trade (by the end of the century five sixths of the trade was based on Liverpool) laid the foundations. In the following century commerce with North America and the Indies reached unprecedented proportions, and the extension of the docks, from 1843, to the Birkenhead side of the estuary, served only to augment that growth. The tonnage entering Liverpool in 1800 was 450; by 1922 it was nearly 31,650,000, and the city had become the largest milling centre in the world. Through these docks flooded immigrants (300,000 near-destitute Irish in the single year of 1847); through them flooded emigrants to the New World (400,000 or so in mid century). Many hoping to pass through – in either direction – failed and remained to swell the already appallingly overcrowded slums.

A boom or bust city. A city of extremes. In the nineteenth century, along with those slums, among the nation's most horrendous, Liverpool laid claim to the biggest concentration of millionaires in the country outside London. That affluence is reflected in civic monuments of flamboyant confidence: the Pier Head buildings, St George's Hall (for Pevsner the most important nineteenth-century classical building in Europe) and a multitude of smaller ones from Oriel Chambers to the gates of the Philharmonic Hotel and the splendid Vines public house. Even today, when so much has been lost, the city retains many echoes of its past grandeur. Its listed buildings number no fewer than 2,300.

On the darker side, as early as 1790, a survey revealed 7,000 people living in 2,000 cellars with little or no sanitation. In 1849 alone 5,000 died of cholera. Inner-city problems are not new to Merseyside. Always, it seems, as nationally, they have grown faster than the capacity to deal with them. It is not that efforts were not made. In the mid nineteenth century no town in England had obtained for itself greater powers. It was the first, as we have seen, to appoint a Medical Officer for Health. After 1864 slum clearance and the first municipal housing in Britain were put in hand (St Martin's Cottages in Sylvester Street). But the muscle was lacking. Although 18,000 dwellings were declared insanitary and scheduled for demolition, by 1914 only 10,000 had gone (plus some pulled down by private enterprise) and only 2,900 families had been rehoused. The pace quickened between the wars – in all, 65,000 families were then rehoused, over 38,000 of them by the Council – but it was still not enough. The awful backlog grew.

World War II enormously intensified the problem. In 1941 the city was savagely bombed for seven nights in succession – Liverpool's 'May Week' – before the Reichsführer, with his inflexibly intuitive approach to strategy, switched the Luftwaffe to other targets. Apart from the loss of fine buildings like the Customs House and the Gorea Warehouses, over 6,000 houses were destroyed, 125,000 damaged. From then on there could be no question as to the city's social imperative.

With the coming of peace a tremendous effort was mounted once and for all to clear the slums and rehouse everyone decently. By 1955 the City Architect was able to report with satisfaction that 110 tower blocks were built or building. Two New Towns, Skelmersdale and Runcorn, were started. A smaller municipal equivalent was put in hand in Kirkby, which was in fact across the boundary in Lancashire (Liverpool then being an all-purpose County Borough). By 1965, 50,000 people had moved in, thrilled with their new kitchens and bathrooms and central heating – the fastest-growing community in the country, claimed the city.

In the early sixties the Council braced itself for the radical reshaping of the city's 'obsolete' heart, together with the whole of the twilight 'inner crescent' – much of the land being already in its ownership. Nudged by the government the City appointed Graeme Shankland as its consultant and set up a new Planning Department under Walter Bor – both architect-planners of distinction. As we have seen, all the indicators of the day were, to put it mildly, misleading. Steady growth of the economy was forecast. It was predicted that the city's population would reach almost a million by 1981, with additional *immigration* from elsewhere as likely (in fact, by 1981 the population was under 517,000 and, with continuing *emigration*, sinking steadily).

Up to 2,000 acres/810 ha it was suggested, should be reserved for new industry, and a minimum of 3.5 million sq. ft./325,000 sq. m. for office use. To service this new throbbing heart of a booming city, an elaborate system of motorways was going to be needed. In the light of the information then available Liverpool's brave plans were less foolhardy than they appear in retrospect (the 'clearances', as they were known, began before the arrival of Shankland and Bor). But the plans were built on sand and unimagined tides were to sweep them away.

Street after street continued to fall to the wrecker's ball and the bulldozer. Local anchor points like pubs – always a big feature of seaports – disappeared. Communities were scattered. Yet, in the twenty years between 1945 and 1965, the city had gained only 56,400 new homes – considerably fewer than in the comparable period between the wars. The industrial estate at Kirkby could not compete with Runcorn, and languished. Within a decade the housing there was to become notorious even among problem areas, degenerating into slums more danger- ous than those they had replaced. In the centre of the city chunks of motorway were built, to the destruction of townscape values; the upper-level deck system for pedestrians failed to come together. Georgian and early Victorian terraces were allowed to moulder. The great complex of Albert Dock stood empty and forlorn at the centre of the whole rotting docks system. In 1975 there were 1,235 vacant acres, or 500 ha, in the city, more than half of them publicly owned. Of Liverpool it began to be said, as of so many other cities, that its self-inflicted wounds were greater than those inflicted by the Luftwaffe.

Eastwards the nation's industrial heartlands slid into decline. Jumbos replaced the great transatlantic liners. Trade routes shifted from the north-west to the east and south-east. Unemployment rose and rose, to the point where, in some districts, among the black population, it was said to stand at 80 to 85 per cent. As unemployment soared, frustration turned to despair. A 1978 report[1] described tenants' reactions to an attempt to civilise a group of 'walk-up' flats in Angela Street. Trees were pulled to pieces, entry phones ripped out, doors 'nicked', the repainted walls smothered in graffiti. Embittered and antagonistic, the tenants, it stated, 'were prepared to be against anything remotely connected with Liverpool Corporation' ('the Corpie'). By the early eighties the industrial buildings were coming down too, like the vast, century- old Tate & Lyle refinery, symbol of the city's sugar trade. That particular closure meant the loss of 1,700 jobs. For more and more the future seemed without hope. In the summer of 1981, Liverpool 8 – to be better known as Toxteth – boiled over.

*

If you are in London and wish to go to Liverpool on a Friday evening, people in London will tell you not to take the train around six o'clock because it will be crowded with drunks, there will be fights, and you will get your luggage ripped off. But if you take that train anyway, you will find a lot of people who work in London during the week and commute home at the weekends. And you will find the train full of wit and humour and joy and passion.

Councillor Keith Hackett
Liverpool City Council, 1988 [2]

The perception problem is very real. 'There is a voyeuristic element in the way people come to look at cities in decline,' says Councillor Hackett, with truth. Changing the image has to be the first objective of any regeneration strategy anywhere. For Liverpool, the impression of a city in deep disarray was greatly magnified by the political feuding of the mid eighties, centred upon Militant Tendency's three years in control of the City Council. The end of Merseyside's long haul is not yet in sight, but the picture which greets the visitor today is markedly different from that which faced Michael Heseltine in 1981. Indeed, it is markedly different from that of even three or four years ago. All the usual indicators – investment, number of jobs, development applications – are positive once more. Even the port, after a traumatic period of rationalisation, is expanding its trade and its profits. The city is beginning to reclaim credibility as a centre for relocation, a place for new initiatives, and, to its own surprise, as a tourist attraction. Hotel occupancies are rising. By 1989 no fewer than 3.5 million people were visiting the Maritime Museum each year and, with 4.2 million visitors, Albert Dock was claiming itself to be the second most popular free tourist attraction in the country.

Some of the change has been effected from the top down (the Task Force is a conduit for injecting some £200 million a year), some from the bottom up, with a whole range of official and unofficial agencies in the middle, coaxing, assisting, pointing the way to new possibilities. Just as, in the Middle East, it seems almost impossible to scuff up the ground anywhere without uncovering layer upon layer of endeavour through the millennia, the moment you get below the surface of any big city, you begin to uncover groups of people beavering away, in a multitude of different directions, to the general betterment. Liverpool is particularly strong in this respect. Nonetheless the main engine of recovery – how could it be otherwise in the light of its powers and resources? – has unquestionably been the government's Merseyside Development Corporation.

The Corporation inherited, in 1981, a forlorn territory, of limited area. The Metropolitan County of Merseyside embraces not only Liverpool itself, but the Districts of St Helens, Knowsley, Sefton and, across the water, Wirral. The population of the whole area is about 1.5 million. Of all this the new Corporation's remit ran, until spring 1988, only to the rotting riparian belt south of the Liverpool city centre; to a much smaller strip in Bootle to the north, and to part of Birkenhead in Wirral – in all, 865 acres/350 ha. This patchy portfolio amounted to a mere half of one per cent of Merseyside County. In 1988 the Secretary of State announced a near-trebling of the Corporation's area by adding to it another 1,500-odd acres/610 ha on both sides of the water, comprising a substantial chunk of northern Liverpool (including the North Docks), western Birkenhead, and part of Wallasey at the north-eastern tip of the Wirral.

MDC has not suffered local authority antagonisms to the extent that they existed in London's Docklands. The same resentments exist, however, and for the same reasons. Its original area had a resident population of only 400 or so, and in its derelict state played little part in the life of the city. 'The entire social facilities for the area,' Dr Ritchie, the present Chief Executive has said, 'consisted of one public toilet and two telephone boxes.' Community protest was therefore less evident. The District Councils of Liverpool, Sefton and Wirral made no objection to the formation of the Corporation (though total deadlock existed with the City through the Militant years). On the other hand the malaise hanging over Merseyside was even more deep-seated than that in London's Docklands, and has proved more draggingly intractable. Until the very end of the eighties there was an obstinate refusal of capital values to rise commensurately to the costs of reclamation, construction and completed development. Of the £120 million of public money spent by the Corporation up to spring 1988, £80 million had had to be spent on reclamation and infrastructure – on fitting wasteland for development, removing derelict structures, building roads and river banks, installing essential services, etc. For each acre bought for £6,000, the Corporation had had to spend £100,000 on reclamation – to make it worth, at the end, no more than £40,000 on the market. The basic economics of 'getting rid of the negative value' can be daunting.

MDC's first phase lasted for seven years. It turned upon two 'flagship' projects: the reclamation of 125 acres/51 ha to the south of the city for the 1984 International Garden Festival, and the triumphant restoration of the great Albert Dock complex. Both were put in motion by the Corporation's first Chief Executive, Basil Bean, a man of vision and enthusiasm. The Festival – the first of its kind in this country – succeeded to an extent the inadequate lead time gave little hope for. Levi Tofari, the black Liverpool poet, wrote:

81

Heseltine proposes a garden full of roses, £30 millions down the drain.

Yes, we are the flowers in this concrete garden, we are withering away from political pollution.[3]

But the Liverpudlians who had scoffed at the notion initially – 'We want jobs, not trees' – took it to their hearts when it actually happened, and were really rather proud of it. Attendances were nearly 3.5 million, and at peak periods it took twenty minutes to get through the main gate. Then people began to beef again when they realised that not all of it was going to be permanent.

The follow-through was in fact dogged by ill fortune. The area is now bisected by the £2.6 million Riverside Drive, which provides an immeasurably improved link between the centre of the city and development sites to the south. Inland of Riverside Drive the land was designated for housing, but it was only after four years or so that any substantial progress was made in sales for this purpose. (A general criticism by the National Audit Office in 1988 was that the Corporation had only managed to achieve one tenth of its projected 1,400 houses.) The other section of the original site, to the west, is to be kept as public parkland for leisure uses. But the original agreement by the City to take it over collapsed when Militant demanded the funding necessary for maintenance; arrangements for a public-sector company to run it came to naught when the company ceased trading; the Corporation has continued to maintain the gardens and to open them up from time to time and for special occasions, but six years later the area's future was still not certain, and MDC was demanding a commitment within twelve months. The up side is that one of Merseyside's worst eyesores – a monstrous refuse tip, 70 ft high, unstable and active, producing large quantities of methane, together with a disused oil terminal and a blighted shoreline – has been turned into a positive asset, the value of which can only grow steadily as the surrounding area is brought increasingly to life. No less important, the Festival's success validated the emphasis increasingly to be given to the tourism element in the Corporation's planning.

A good start, moreover, has been made at this, the 'Herculanaeum' end, of the 2.5 mile/4 km. esplanade which will eventually run all the way to the Albert Dock (and probably beyond), providing Liverpudlians for the first time in more than a century with continuous access to the river. The Dock itself, a complex of 1846 warehouses, forms Britain's largest group of buildings listed as Grade I architectural or historic interest. It lies immediately south of Pier Head and close to the centre of the city. Designed by 'Big' Jesse Hartley of brick and cast iron (this was sometimes known as 'the iron coast'), it consists of five blocks round a rectangular water space, separated from the shore by more water (Salthouse Dock) and from Pier Head (which was built on infill) by Canning Dock. Meant for sail, Albert Dock saw little commercial activity after World War I; in 1972 it closed completely. There followed, at intervals, a number of tentative scenarios, from proposals for its total demolition to reuse by the University, to office development with all the water filled in for parking. Its daunting scale proved too much. Albert Dock, gaunt, blackened by the years, continued to moulder until acquired by the Development Corporation in 1982.

The whole complex was officially reopened, on a grey day in May 1988 when a brisk wind brought rain across the leaden river from the Wirral, by the Prince of Wales, emulating the example of his forebear the Prince Consort (who first opened them) in approaching the Dock by water. By then a vast dredging operation had cleared the sludge which had built up over the years; the Maritime Museum had moved into Block 'D'; the Tate Gallery was in its £7 million refurbishment of part of the largest block of all; Granada Television had taken over the handsome old Dock Traffic Office; the Old Pump House had become a pub-restaurant. Most of the quayside shops and eating places were operating and, despite the rain, Liverpool flocked that evening to a sort of son-et-lumière across the water of its new showpiece.

Albert Dock today offers 250,000 sq. ft./23,000 sq. m. of shopping, 450,000 sq. ft./42,000 sq. m. of office space, and includes 120 apartments. When the first twenty flats were put on the market at £50,000 to £70,000, they were sold within forty-eight hours; a further eighty 'off the board' within two weeks. A hotel was in the offing. Southwards to the Festival Garden site stretch the next phases of the whole enterprise, in various stages of completion. Housing includes 114 flats in the Wapping Warehouse and the rented housing of Mariners Wharf. The demand for space in the Brunswick Business Park outstrips availability. By 1989 nearly 520,000 sq. ft./48,000 sq. m. had been let to 120 firms employing between them over 1,000; a further 300,000 sq. ft./ 28,000 sq. m. were approaching completion. As part of the plan to open up some 70 acres/over 28 ha of waterspace between Canning and Brunswick Docks, a marina now provides 114 berths at Coburg Dock; so successful is this that a 100-berth extension is under way in Brunswick adjoining, the nearby grain silos and transit sheds having been demolished. Plans for the Waterfront area include the 'Arena', with indoor seating for 10,000; an 80,000 sq. ft./7,400 sq. m. shopping concourse; Multiplex and IMEX cinemas; and a 160-bed 'economy' hotel. In all new work the linking riverside walkway is incorporated.

Overshadowed by these headline-catching operations, work went on elsewhere. In Bootle and Birkenhead the Corporation had continued to assemble and dispose of land, draw up development briefs, to reclaim, undertake road and dock improvements, provide workshop space, assist training programmes and area promotion. By 1989 it could claim, among its achievements, to have cleared 655 acres/265 ha of dereliction – leaving only 86 acres/35 ha of the original designated area still requiring treatment. Nearly 2.6 million sq. ft./240,000 sq. m. of floorspace had been built or refurbished since 1981. Some £100 million had been injected into the local economy through engineering and construction work. Training opportunities were running at about 7,000 a year. The 430 people living in the area in 1981 had risen to 1,300 and was likely to be 5,000 by 1993. With the extension of the Corporation's designated area, however, a new chapter opened. New factors had to be taken into consideration. The immensely protracted negotiations – which had lasted no less than seven years – to acquire a vitally important 100 acres/46 ha of waterfront land in Birkenhead from the Mersey Docks and Harbour Company had finally been resolved. Overall, the hard slog of the previous years was beginning to pay off. Continuing government commitment had been demonstrated. A new buoyancy was in the air. In 1981 rental values were about 15 pence a square foot, and 'hardly worth collecting'. In 1985/86 it was still virtually impossible to interest buyers in particular sites, but by 1988/89 the number of enquiries for land – 433 – was up 44 per cent on the previous year, with an upsurge of interest by housebuilders particularly evident. Land values were between £7.5 and £10 per square foot.

The Corporation does not expect to become the major landowner in its new territories that it was in the original. It will seek rather to play the role of enabler/catalyst – 'stimulating, supporting, assisting private investment'. It will also be facing new types of challenge. The North Docks in Liverpool do not differ greatly in their problems from those of the South (a development application was quickly granted for mixed uses on the Pier Head–Princes Dock–Waterloo Dock section). But in other areas the MDC will find itself for the first time having to deal with a resident population (in all about 31,000) and therefore more intensive consultation;

and too with places which scarcely fit the media picture of the 'inner city'. New Brighton in Wirral, for example, is a tired little seaside resort – charming in parts but nonetheless typical of so many English coastal resorts which, since the war, have drifted down-market, failed to reinvest, and finally lost out to the Benidorm package. To how many such could MDC's description of New Brighton not be applied? Its problems include 'jaded leisure facilities, a dowdy exposed promenade, unfit dwellings, inefficient and unattractive car parking, an underused marine lake, crumbling and boarded-up properties . . . a run-down bathing pool and sporadic eyesores which imprint the hallmark of a "faded resort" on the whole area'. Try to compete with Blackpool? Let it die a natural death?[4] New Brighton 'has been blighted for too long by a series of unrealistic "mega-schemes".' Or take a modest mid-course that will ensure simply an adequate critical mass of leisure interests? Here the Corporation faces a situation familiar to local authorities and independent environmental agencies – such as the Civic Trust, which has worked sucessfully in, for example, Ilfracombe – in all parts of the country. Decline is not confined to metropolitan slums; how MDC deals with New Brighton could have lessons stretching far beyond the 'inner city'.

'What are the main blocks now?' I asked Dr John Ritchie, the Corporation's Chief Executive. 'Resources?' 'In twenty-five years on Merseyside,' was his reply, 'I've never known resources to be the problem. At this moment it's conservationists. They're coming out of the woodwork. That and the number of hours in the day. Right now I have to write eleven development strategies [for the newly designated areas], I've got three public inquiries – and staff of sixty-one. [The City has almost 130 in its Planning Department alone.] I've been trying for three years to get a £17 million hotel for Albert Dock. They want £1 million put in. Everyone's lined up – except the Treasury. I just can't give any more time to it. They'll have to go to Manchester or somewhere.' Other authorities envy the UDCs their financial clout; they do not always appreciate the accompanying pressures.

At the other end of the spectrum from the government's lead agency are Merseyside's community groups, spontaneous expressions of the local character. It was indicative that when the BBC launched a nationwide competition in 1989 for the best community projects aimed at improving the quality of local life – 'It's My Town' – more entries were received from Liverpool than from any other city.

It was here that desperation, and that deep suspicion of municipal authority we have already noticed, fuelled a powerful drive by groups at street level to achieve their own better housing. Housing associations are no less active on Merseyside than elsewhere, renovating early Victorian terraces, building new houses and maisonettes for rent. But the particular form of association on Merseyside which has attracted wider attention – and Royal approval – is the Housing Co-operative, pioneered there by the Weller Streets group in Liverpool. Their story has been well documented in Alan McDonald's blow-by-blow account[5] of the five years it took this tough and tenacious band in Liverpool 8 to bring into existence their own new 'village' of sixty-one homes. In 1976 the 'Corpie' had a list of fifty-seven clearance areas, which it was thought would take ten years to deal with. The Weller Streets – a pocket of intensely unsalubrious streets bearing Dickensian names – were said to be fifty-seventh on the list. With no experience, but unfailing determination, and learning as they went along, they formed themselves into a co-operative, battled for land, for finance, for planning permission, for the sort of houses *they* wanted in the layout *they* wanted. It was a roller-coaster operation but, sustained by a bloody-minded idealism, they got there. McDonald quotes a retired member-tenant as saying, after the move, 'It's a little bit of heaven, this . . . this is the best time of my life.' When the Prince of Wales visited them in 1984, he confessed himself 'electrified. I hadn't come across anything quite like it before'.

The prime movers in the Weller Streets operation, like Billy Floyd its chairman, saw themselves as 'beating the system' and were anxious to help others follow the same path. Other co-operatives had tended to concentrate on the conversion and upgrading of existing property. Where the Weller Streets example proved crucial, and infectious, was in its hands-on self-help approach to *new* building, running the whole project themselves from start to finish. A whole surge of new co-operatives followed. There are now fifty or so on Merseyside, of which around thirty – and the number grows steadily – are concerned with 'new build'. Between them they control upwards of 2,000 homes, of which perhaps 900 are in new development.

Most, by far, are in Liverpool 8, or originated there, though ten or twelve are to be found in Knowsley. For most the Housing Corporation has been the prime funding agency; for others, at times, their District Council. (During Militant's reign in Liverpool, Council policy was against 'queue-jumping' by co-operatives and half a dozen found their operations taken out of their hands and municipalised.) Most commonly the co-operatives represent a particular community, but there are co-operatives for the elderly, for one-parent families, for particular ethnic groups, and specifically for multiracial occupation. The size of their operations has varied greatly, from fewer than twenty homes comfortably into three figures. Not surprisingly, the style of their developments has varied no less. The Weller Streets fixed hard upon a tight layout of ten small courtyards – so tight in fact that the Council refused to 'adopt' the roads on the grounds that they did not meet normal public requirements in terms of turning circles and so on. Leta/ Claudia and Southern Crescent opted for curving terraces, which likewise serve to break up the area so that it is never seen as a whole. Thirlmere consists of terraced blocks around a central landscaped area. And so on.[6]

From all these the Eldonians demand special attention. They originated in 1978 as a Community Association for Eldon, Bond and Burlington Streets, together with Limekiln Grove, all in Liverpool 8, when the Council threatened them with dispersal all over the city on the demolition of their homes. They demand special attention because of the scale to which their operations have grown, and because of the wider thrust of their concerns. They see housing, jobs and social and health facilities, as part and parcel of a single process – their motto: 'We Do It Better Together'.

From the Association sprang the Eldonian Housing Co-operative. Its first scheme, at £3 million, was for 106 homes in Portland Gardens, north of the city centre. Its second called for even greater tenacity. When the giant Tate & Lyle sugar refinery in the Vauxhall area of north Liverpool closed down in 1980, the site was acquired by English Estates, the government agency charged with stimulating and building advance factories in declining areas. An ideas competition was announced for its future use. On a technical misunderstanding the Eldonians were disqualified – but were nonetheless offered the site for their project of housing and community use, if they could raise the money. The Militant City Council, however, ever doctrinal, refused them planning permission. The case went to appeal. In 1985 the Secretary of State granted permission. Sixteen months later the Department of the Environment agreed funding of £6.6 million, through the Urban Programme and the local Task Force, for land reclamation and building 145 homes; an extra grant was promised for another fifteen units for a Senior Citizens' Co-op. Completed a couple of years later, the scheme has received widespread acclamation and several awards.

Ten years on, the Community Trust and the Housing Co-operative have given birth to the Eldonian Development Trust, and received 'enterprise agency' status, which gives them added clout and leverage. Their first business project, a wholesale market garden, opened in 1987 (with £42,000 from the European Social Fund to put to training purposes). They then set their eyes on 120 acres/49 ha adjoining the Tate & Lyle site and the Leeds and Liverpool Canal. This whole area now falls within MDC's extended remit, and the Corporation is giving the Development Trust assistance to 'develop ideas for mixed tenure housing, enterprise and training activities and commercial trading possibilities, and to prepare a business plan'. What seems to be emerging is a £12 million scheme embracing, besides its other elements, 370 houses. The Eldonians, now said to be the largest co-operative in Europe, have become a significant factor in the regeneration of the Vauxhall area.

For smaller and younger groups the self-help route is booby-trapped at every turn; professional skills are essential, however independently minded the protagonists may be. To assist and service the housing co-operatives in what is inevitably for them strange territory, a range of 'secondary' co-operatives has come into existence. On Merseyside two in particular call for mention: Co-operative Development Services (CDS), dating from 1977, and Community Technical Services Agency (COMTECHSA), formed a couple of years later. The former concentrates on housing; the latter ranges more widely – for example into new uses for vacant land. According to the needs of its client organisation, CDS will educate it in the realities it faces, suggest approaches to design alternatives, provide or advise on the technical/professional services required, manage an estate, if necessary, once it has been built. COMTECHSA, offers its services free to its member associations if they are without funds, reclaiming its fees if later funding becomes available. To meet the special problems of maintenance on reclaimed sites, it set up an associated agency, Community Maintenance Limited. And its Director, Leslie Forsyth, played a lead role in 1983 in setting up a nationwide association of Community Technical Aid Centres (ACTAC), which now has a membership of over 100 such organisations.

It is tempting to overplay the significance of such community enterprises. With notable exceptions, they have been too limited in size, to date, to make appreciable inroads into the inner-city problem at the macro level. At the very local, or micro, level, the gains are obvious – the bypassing of official inertia, the creation of houses not as abstract units but as homes tailored to the desires of the users, the provision of social facilities which the community itself knows it most needs – and indeed an enormous strengthening of community bonds in a general climate of increasing alienation. These are things strenuously to be welcomed and encouraged in any city lucky enough to harbour the stirrings of community effort. There is yet something more: the release into the service of society of energies and skills which would most probably otherwise go unremarked and unrecognised. Chairman of the Eldonians, to take but one example, is Tony McGann, a sturdy bespectacled figure who was for twenty years, until his job folded under him, a fork-lift truck driver. To ask in which of these two capacities his contribution to Liverpool has been the greater is rhetorical.

For fifteen years the city has been haunted by its *Doppelgänger* – the all-pervading image held of it afar. Tucked into a substantial *Strategy Review* by the City Council in 1987[7] occurs the statement: '. . . there is often a disproportionate glare of publicity placed upon the City's problems, while its many strengths, attributes and achievements are largely ignored . . . The bridging of this gulf between image and reality is vital to the City's future prosperity – particularly in the fields of commercial and industrial investment.' All those who are labouring to turn the city round are acutely aware of the problem. A stream of promotional literature and marketing briefs flows from a dozen different sources. 'Liverpool today is a vibrant, exciting city in which to live and work,' proclaims a Council brochure. 'Merseyside – Boom City', 'Docks Report Profit Boost', 'Wirral's Year of Optimism', 'Freeport Makes Its Mark In City', are the sort of headlines which punctuate the *Merseyside & Cheshire Business News*. Indeed, the private sector has itself been active in working to re-establish confidence. Business Opportunities on Merseyside – BOOM (surely one of the better acronyms) – was set up by private enterprise in the eighties, with initial funding from the Task Force, specifically to spread awareness of the area's potential. BOOM has combined seminars in London for the capital's institutional investors and property companies with fairly intensive site tours for them on Merseyside. The Merseyside Tourism Board and Conference Bureau, dating also from the eighties, is now getting into its stride with a range of information packs, information centres, booking services and so on. The Merseyside Enterprise Board, set up in 1983, provides support for business and in particular, through its Small Firms Fund, for starter ventures. The original staff of six has grown to twenty-five, its initial funding of £2 million per annum to £5.5

million – with hopes of £10 million by the 1990s. To combat the skills shortage likely to be encountered by new and incoming companies, Merseyside Education and Training Enterprise Limited – METEL – yet again started in the eighties, offers training facilities to between 6,000 and 7,000 young people every year.

What would have looked like promotional hype only a few years ago is beginning to gain greater credence. There are real success stories to point to. The Docks, the Freeport and Wavertree Technology Park are all expanding. It is true that since 1980 the number of working dockers has dropped from 6,000 to around 1,300, but, since the low point of the early eighties, new deep-water facilities have been created for carriers of up to 75,000 tonnes; more than a dozen new shipping services were attracted in 1986/87 alone; and the export of scrap, a mere 2,000 tonnes in 1982, rose to 750,000 in 1987. The Freeport, of 600 acres/240 ha and expanding, handled about £200 million's worth of goods in its first five years. Perhaps most important of all, in relation to the commonly held image: while in 1972 the port lost 250,000 man days in strikes, between 1984 and the national strike called in 1989 hardly a day was lost.

Wavertree, two miles from the city centre, until 1983 was a 64 acre/26 ha wasteland of long-dead railway yards. 'It was an appalling eyesore,' wrote Michael Heseltine of his first visit.[8] 'You drove through Liverpool; you looked at this terrible place and you drove on.' Today, their buildings screened and softened by 62,000 trees and 150,000 shrubs, over forty companies, employing between them around 1,500, have settled there. The original plans looked to full occupation and 2,000 jobs by 1995; that target is likely to be achieved four years ahead of schedule and plans are well advanced for expansion. Wavertree Technology Park sprang from one of the shotgun public/private partnerships engineered by Heseltine on Merseyside (as we shall see, there were others). The government agency English Estates, the City Council and the Metropolitan County (the latter having since been wound up) were put into harness with Plessey, one of whose plants overlooks the site. Sir John Clarke, Plessey's Chairman, took on the chairmanship of the new Park company, and seconded a number of his senior staff to manage its creation and development. Wavertree became to Liverpool what the first private-sector users were to the Isle of Dogs: a pledge of faith in the future.

All the while the centre of the city changes. Most obvious of the transformations as yet, of course, is Albert Dock and the Water-front, but the wider image changes too. Stone cleaning and floodlighting have dramatically improved appearances. There is a sizeable traffic-free zone which works well. The St John's Shopping Centre has been completely done over and freshened up. There are forty-two new shops in the new Clayton Square Centre. Lime Street Station has had a major refurbishment. Plans are afoot to reopen St George's Hall to the public. The City has a £100 million plan for the Duke Street area. The windy and rather desolate space in front of the 'Three Sisters' at Pier Head is going to be turned into a tree-lined square in time for the arrival of the Tall Ships in 1992 . . .

If the changes seem piecemeal, it is hardly surprising – and perhaps healthier than the grandiose visions of a generation ago. Until 1974 the City of Liverpool was a 'unitary' authority, managing all its affairs like other County Boroughs. Today, things are more complicated. First, it lost much of its power to the new Metropolitan County of Merseyside, and became one of the five District Councils within the County boundary; then the Development Corporation came into existence; then the County Council was abolished; then MDC's remit was extended to take in, amongst others, chunks of North Liverpool. In the middle of all this the Militant left gained control of the City Council and – just when Glasgow was proclaiming itself 'Miles Better' – found itself at loggerheads with more or less everyone: central government, the Metro County, the Development Corporation, the private sector, even the non-profit co-operatives within its own boundary. It made so much noise barking at shadows that the more positive side of its reign tended to go unheard. On the one hand it busied itself with such antics as the forging of fraternal links with Chile and Nicaragua; on the other it pushed along what was claimed to be the largest housebuilding programme in the country. It knocked down ten tower blocks and got rid of 1,700 unfit flats, created neighbourhoods with private gardens, better lighting, improved recreational facilities, and fostered local management. Its efforts brought praise from Dr Alice Coleman.[9] 'Liverpool,' she said, 'has got it right.' But it all had to be paid for. The new housing cost nearly £260 million, and the debts incurred as a result have dogged Liverpool ever since. Militant was conscious, too, of the Council's position as the largest single employer in the city and sought to follow a no-forced-redundancies policy. In 1984 it had something like 80,000 on the payroll; by 1987 this had dropped to 31,000, but still around 15 per cent of Liverpool's jobs, and the Council has remained reluctant to privatise any of its services. The city's uncollected rents were piling up and at the end of the decade were running at about £23 million. It was in 1987, with the city to all intents and purposes bankrupt, that the Council's elected members were held by the District Auditor to have been guilty of mismanagement and made personally responsible for the Council's debts. Forty-seven councillors were accordingly surcharged and disqualified from office until 1992.

The new Labour Council, under the leadership of Keva Coombes, sought to bring things under control. Intensive effort was made to thrash out a coherent set of policies. The year 1987 saw a flurry of policy documents and initiatives – an appraisal of MDC's performance and the City's relationship with the Corporation; an economic development strategy; a tourism strategy; an arts and cultural industries strategy; and a major planning strategy review covering not only general policies but the problems and opportunities of eighteen specific areas of the city centre. There followed a detailed study of poverty in Liverpool, new forward projections of population trends and prospects, and a steady flow of planning briefs for the redevelopment of specific sites. The City is required (since the abolition of the Metro County Council) to produce its Unitary Development Plan, but lags behind the other Merseyside Districts in this and depends in the meantime on these individual development briefs. Responsibilities are divided; the Planning Department has lost a lot of its traditional functions to 'Environmental Services' and the 'Urban Regeneration Strategy Unit' which deals with the Urban Programme and Priority Areas. It may well be, however, that this apparently untidy approach in fact offers a more flexible and responsive mechanism for fostering regeneration than the older, slower and more cumbersome type of development plan.

Taken together, these various policy initiatives reflected a substantial turn round of the Council's mid 1980s strategies. Cooperation with the Development Corporation became more positive. At officer level, relations had always remained 'cordial', and of 250 planning applications determined by the Corporation up to 1987, only three had proved matters of serious disagreement with the City. Now, however, the Leader of the Council joined the Corporation Board and became party to its deliberations; with much of North Liverpool now within the Corporation's expanded area, that clearly made good sense. From 1987 a new note of realism likewise began to colour the City's relations with the private sector. Partnerships were sought actively, and all forms of economic enterprise encouraged.

The Council remained, however, in a Laocoön struggle with its debts and deficits, which it sought to cover by the disposal of land

and assets. In 1989/90 these produced some £64 million. The target for the following year was set – unrealistically in the economic climate of the day – at £88 million, but was in fact expected to produce a shortfall of £30 million, resulting in a predicted Council deficit for the year 1990/91 of £4 million. All the old familiar storm signals had once again been hoisted.

Liverpool lies at the heart of Merseyside, but Merseyside's problems spread far beyond Liverpool. The five Metropolitan Districts which made up the old County have very different characteristics, but none can be said to be wholly at ease with itself as the century enters its last decade. None of the others has the pulling power of Liverpool. The thrust of the MDC, though now spread more widely, is unfelt in substantial areas where deprivation sours every aspect of day-to-day life. 'What would you say has been the effect of the Development Corporation on your own District?' I asked one Chief Executive. He replied crisply: 'None.'

In some parts the problems lie thick upon the surface, self-evident to the most casual eye; in others they remain curiously hidden. One example of this is to be found in Kirkby, in Knowsley. The long avenue is flanked by two-storey suburban houses, tidy enough, unremarkable. 'You might not think it,' said my guide, 'but this area has one of the worst crime records of all.' Elsewhere in Kirkby burnt-out buildings, new as well as old, are not uncommon. There are iron bars to all new shopping developments. Security has become a main factor in design – in 1989 a new school in Kirkby achieved national attention by reason of its impregnable defences. Car thefts are an almost hourly occurrence, by joy riders, thieves after radios, vandals; police chases a daily event. I spoke to a Council planning officer. He had had deadlocks fitted to his car, but that had not stopped the windows being smashed a couple of days before and £500 worth of damage done. Not the sort of thing one puts in the appointments column to attract professional staff of calibre.

Knowsley District is not a longstanding local authority unit. The communities making it up came, until 1974, under Lancashire County Council. From Liverpool it inherited 26,000 properties. It is a dispersed area of more than 37 sq. miles/96 sq. km., running some 13 miles from north to south, immediately to the east of Liverpool – into which it is locked by the road system and history. Many of its elected members and officers live in Liverpool; Derek Hatton, conversely, while prevailing over Militant's phase in the city, was concurrently employed by Knowsley Council. Its component towns and villages, as might be expected, are pretty different in character. Halewood, at the southern end, is dominated by Ford's 356 acre/144 ha site and overspill from Liverpool. Huyton and Roby, together with Prescot, lie across the middle. The former, consisting largely of earlier and better built municipal housing, are attracting some industrial development and are probably in reasonable balance; Prescot has the most traditional feel – it is a real place. Northwards lie Knowsley itself and Kirkby (the 'new town' of the sixties which didn't come off); here lie the 2,000 acres/800 ha of the Knowsley Estate, home of the Earls of Derby since the fifteenth century, but here too are concentrated the District's worst housing problems.

'Knowsley,' says the official guide, 'is an area which successfully combines the old and the new and provides all the facilities for a full and healthy life.' In Kirkby 'on Tuesdays and Saturdays people from far and near flock to the open-air market where farmers and traders compete for customers in a happy country village atmosphere.' Well ... stirring stuff, but such apple-cheeked jollity is unlikely to be recognised by those who actually live there. In 1988 Knowsley was placed bottom of 459 district authorities in a 'living-standards' table prepared by CES Limited, an independent research centre. Its unemployment figures are more than twice the national average. Its population decline is forecast to be greater than that of any other metropolitan district. The rise in the number of empty properties over the five years 1983 to 1988 meant a decrease in rateable values of some £432,600. In much of the district, as we have seen, crime is endemic.

Heseltine came to Cantril Farm, a single-tenure overspill estate adjoining Knowsley Village, in 1981. At that time about 9,000 people lived there, 'slum cleared' originally from the streets around 'Scottie Road' in Liverpool on to land purchased by the City from Lancashire County Council. The surroundings were not even paved. Shocked almost into silence by what he saw, Heseltine could only say, 'Who did this?' His more considered response was to cajole Sir Lawrie Barratt (the house builder) and Clive Thornton (of Abbey National), two of the businessmen he invited to Merseyside to see for themselves, into responding to a suggestion made by Tom Baron, a housing developer on the new Task Force. Baron's proposal was that the estate should be transformed into a mixed-tenure area by privatisation, new-build for sale, demolition and general upgrading of the environment. The total estimated cost was £21 million, half of which would come from the public sector. Today the programme is substantially complete. Cantril

Farm has become Stockbridge Village. The former estate was sold by the Council to the newly formed Stockbridge Village Trust in 1983. The extensive remodelling which was undertaken in fact cost about £40 million (split between the Council, the Department of Environment, the Housing Corporation, Barclays Bank and Abbey National). On the spot where Michael Heseltine stood in 1981 now stands the £4.5 million Stockbridge Village Leisure Centre.

At the time it was all something of an experiment, an act of faith, though it chimed in well enough with the research on hard-to-let estates done by the DoE's Housing Development Directorate in the mid seventies – and of course with the privatisation ethic of the Thatcher government. Since then the elements it embodied have become more formalised, first through the 'Right to Buy' legislation and the widespread disposal of council housing; secondly through the Department of Environment's Estate Action programme.* It is thus largely under the latter banner that further estate improvements have been carried out – for example on the Tower Hill, Hillside and New Hutte estates in Kirkby. Here three gaunt tower blocks are coming down, houses have been given porches, front gardens given walls and so on, while road systems have been extensively altered to create 'hammerheads' and cul-de-sacs. Knowsley District receives the highest *per capita* aid from the government's Urban Programme funds of any Programme Authority in England, with special allocations to Stockbridge and for security measures in Knowsley Industrial Park. Nonetheless progress remains grindingly slow. Improvements to the Ravenscroft estate (a part of Tower Hill) have been achieved only by putting *all* the Council's available resources for the period into this one scheme. How does one explain that to those living on the other side of the main approach road, as yet untouched? When I asked Richard Penn, then Knowsley's Chief Executive, what were the main blocks to further progress, his unhesitating answer was the reverse of Dr Ritchie's, of MDC. 'Resources,' he said.

Penn himself, with a degree in Economics and Psychology, and earlier experience in setting up (with Maurice Howell of Swansea) a Home Office Community Development Project in the Upper Afan Valley, understands well that solutions cannot be imposed on a community. Failure actively to consult and involve those concerned in what was being proposed on their behalf he sees as the root cause of the failure of the 1960s rehousing schemes. 'Can

* See pages 233–4.

we be sure,' he asks, 'that we are not doing again what Liverpool did twenty-five years ago? That in three years' time it will not all have been vandalised? Unless people feel they have a stake in the place, in the decisions and the objectives, it's hopeless.'

His Council, in fact, makes exceptional efforts to communicate. It operates no fewer than sixteen neighbourhood and maintenance offices as local 'embassies'. Knowsley produces by far the best annual report I have seen from any local authority. It sets out clearly and fully its policies and progress in every field, costs (broken down), employee analysis (under every heading), comparative figures for other District Councils on Merseyside and elsewhere (again under every heading) and much else. It is an object lesson in a sphere which has often in the past been subject to deliberate obfuscation. In the same spirit, Knowsley claims one of the best ombudsman records. Complaints, and they are not numerous according to Penn, are invariably acted upon speedily, unlike a good many other authorities – including some on Merseyside – which have had repeated referrals because of failure to take appropriate action.

At the end of 1988 a report undertaken for the Council by the Bristol School for Advanced Urban Studies was presented to the Policy Review Sub-Committee. The two overriding objectives for the Council were seen as, first, ensuring the survival of the Borough; secondly, the preservation and improvement of its services to its citizens. Within these broad objectives, the report identified six main strategic issues and suggested eighteen possible areas for action. It may be worth setting these out here, for, though in some ways unremarkable, their general thrust has a significance for many other areas in similar plight.

The essential issues, the report suggested, were at least the maintenance of, if not an increase in, the size of the population (otherwise estimated to drop from 165,000 now to 136,000 by 2001); increased access to jobs; an increase in community confidence; improved use of buildings; the development of policies for the 1990s; and improved communications and image (the image of Knowsley as an 'abandoned' district).

Its suggestions for action were as follows:

- To review what is known about the reasons for which people leave the Borough.
- A feasibility study of 'high-cost' development in the south of the Borough.
- Application of the Council's strategic thinking to central govern-

ment processes of developing guidelines for Merseyside, and subsequently to the preparation of Knowsley's Unitary Development Plan.

– Development of a local employment strategy.
– Continuation of a modest, cost-effective economic development programme aiming to attract to Knowsley such jobs as might be available.
– Establishment of a corporate community development strategy, aiming at a higher level of community participation and involvement.
– Continued pursuit of external resources for a housing renewal programme aiming to radically improve the state of the housing stock.
– Establishment of a corporate approach to the management and use of vacant/derelict buildings.
– Continuation of budget management to provide a stable financial context for programme development.
– Generation of commitment to and cooperation with organisations winning tenders for Council service provision from the Trade Unions.
– Move towards further corporate and integrated systems of local service 'delivery'.
– Establishment of formal meetings of Council Committee Chairmen to discuss strategic issues.
– Reduction of the number of Members on Committees.
– The Council's Chief Officer Group to discuss strategic planning.
– Establishment of a Borough newspaper and staff newsletter.
– Establishment of arrangements for regular formal meetings between Elected Members and Trade Unions to discuss strategic issues in a non-negotiating environment.
– Setting up a timetable and programme for Member and Officer meetings on monitoring progress on strategic planning actions.
– Preparation of a Charter, or Compact, between the Borough Council and the Borough residents.

To those not habituated to the language, such matters – skimmings, of course, from much fuller arguments – may seem self-evident, arcane, bureaucratic, or of small significance. But this is how the fate of the inner city comes to be dealt with at local level, by a Council's elected members and officers. Knowsley has no Development Corporation to help it, no County Council back-up. There is the Merseyside Task Force to coordinate government inputs, but basically Knowsley is merely one of the fifty-seven Programme authorities – with which it has to compete – recognised under the Urban Programme. This certainly gives it a head start over those authorities with similar problems which are *not* so recognised; as we have seen, however, more and more of the Urban Programme funding available is being channelled into the UDCs, while older forms of assistance – such as the Rate Support Grant and the Housing Subsidy – are being scaled down or phased out.

A number of the report's recommendations are in fact current practice in Knowsley. For example the Policy Review Sub-Committee, to whom the report was presented, exists specifically to consider strategic issues. Others, such as that for a Charter or Compact to be established between the Council and its citizens, raise fundamental questions of political accountability. Could such a local 'Compact' be introduced except in conjunction with a national 'Bill of Rights'? Some of the recommendations are lightly coded. People well placed to view Merseyside's problems objectively told me that Union attitudes here and elsewhere constitute the area's biggest single obstacle to better progress – in relation to Council work, Council contracts, in relation to industry generally. It would be wrong to paint a totally black picture: apart from the continued presence of such major names as Barclaycard, BICC, Birds Eye, Delco Electronics, Ford, Lucas Aerospace, Rentokil and the largest privately owned company in Europe, Littlewoods, new industry *is* being enticed into the Borough. But the line on the employment graph zig-zags up and down too erratically for comfort. It somehow seemed symptomatic that on the very day in 1989 the Prime Minister chose to visit the Borough, a major closure was announced, on grounds of union intransigence, with the loss of 1,000 jobs.

If ever an area was in need of an overall regeneration strategy it is Merseyside. Liverpool and Knowsley, after all, are but two of the five Metropolitan Districts, and to these Halton, to the south of Liverpool, could be added as another Programme authority covered by the Merseyside Task Force. The latter, and the Development Corporation, can here and there promote the long view, but basically each Council is charged with producing its own Unitary Development Plan. In this they are required to take into account the strategic guidance provided by the Secretary of State for the Environment. What this means in practice is that the Planning Officers of the Districts meet in conclave to agree, as far as they can (and in fact on broad issues the extent of agreement is considerable) matters of common concern and what they want from the government (for example 'a balanced, integrated transport system' – and, of course, resources). In the fullness of time the Secretary of State issues his 'guidance', which more or less lobs the ball back into the Districts' court. This may be likened to the consensus situation existing in London's Docklands in the seventies. It is not a situation, as Barry Shaw said of that, from which radical solutions can be expected. Greater urgency perhaps attaches to the cooperation forced upon the Districts by the need to produce joint 'Integrated Development' proposals for any bid for European Community funding, if only because of the hope of attracting additional cash. With the enlargement of the Community, however, a smaller proportion of such funding is to be expected for Britain.

There *are* some long-term collaborative programmes, of which the twenty-five-year Mersey Basin Campaign to deal with the gross pollution problem is probably the most significant. This covers an area of over 1900 sq. miles/5000 sq. km. and some 1060 miles/1700 km. of rivers and streams; it receives EC funding, the last contribution being more than £130 million. There is talk, not only of extending the Underground system and adding new stations, but of further links across the water to ease communications between the Liverpool side and the Wirral. The long-awaited proposals by a twenty-four-firm consortium for a hydro-electric Mersey tidal barrage were published in autumn 1989 and the debate attaching to this is accordingly hotting up. With the completion of the Channel Tunnel in sight, there is at least the *possibility*, if enough pressure can be brought to bear, of creating a fast freight link from the port to continental Europe (should we fail in this, movement is likely to be in the opposite direction, *from* France *to* Britain).

There is unquestionably a new feeling of confidence abroad on Merseyside, at least in certain areas, and for Inner Merseyside the prospects are probably brighter than for thirty years. The kinds of developments we have noticed are already having their effect, and, as they spread, their cumulative impact will increasingly step up momentum overall. But hard facts remain. Regional unemployment is still the third highest in the United Kingdom and one of the highest in the European Community. New jobs have been created – but the jobs gain since 1983 was the second slowest of any United Kingdom region (1 per cent compared with 6 per cent in the South East). Regional depopulation has been the highest in the United Kingdom and is among the highest in the Community. Housing? Much has been done to improve the housing stock – but the number of houses under construction in Liverpool is less than half the estimated number required. Liverpool is active in the

European 'Healthy Cities' campaign – but the mortality rate remains one third higher than that of the United Kingdom average. Fewer than half the households in Liverpool have a car – and the figure in the outer estates, where this becomes significant, is estimated to be less than a quarter. Muggings, arson, vandalism, drug abuse persist. An independent Inquiry, set up by Liverpool Council under Lord Gifford, reported racial discrimination in 1989 to be at crisis proportions, blamed the police for 'unacceptable' attitudes and stated that Liverpool's black population were denied access to jobs 'more systematically and comprehensively than in any other major city or black settlement'. The police, not surprisingly, refute the charges.

Perhaps it is not to be wondered at, then, that opposition attitudes continue to bubble up over wide areas of Merseyside, from Wirral to St Helens. Bitter sectarianism is rife within the left. 'There seem to be more factions *within* the Labour Party,' someone said to me in Liverpool, 'than there are other parties.' Coalitions come and go in Council chambers. One Council was described to me as not merely 'hung' but *extremely* hung – 'they hardly know who their chairmen are'. As the Weller Streets group set out to 'beat the system', so perhaps in a totally different way the radical left hopes to beat the system. Policies sometimes seem to be based on the assumption that the area's needs are so exceptional that society will have to bail it out eventually. Wirral, most recently, in 1990, was warned by the District Auditor that it faced a £5 million deficit by the end of the year. Yet, conversely, what looks to an outsider like Merseyside pig-headedness sometimes stands in the way of accepting the money. The Transport and General Workers Union on Merseyside, which has radical affiliations, opposes local training programmes and in 1988 a local MP accused Liverpool City Council of turning away £30 million of government grant aid for this purpose. After Liverpool's forty-seven councillors were removed from office, and ten Militant supporters (including Derek Hatton) had been expelled from the Labour Party, that might have been expected to be that. But the influence of Militant and Socialist Organiser (another Trotskyite group) on Merseyside is pervasive. Among its various manifestations it has been evident in Birkenhead, where Militant has seven full-time staff, and where strenuous and long-running efforts were made over 1989/91 to 'deselect' the middle-of-the-road Labour MP Frank Field. A few months later, back in Liverpool, the press began to run stories about the part played by Derek Hatton (now a public relations consultant) and Keva Coombes (until May 1990

Leader of the Council) in the Council's land disposals. By summer 1990 the Liverpool Fraud Squad had launched an investigation into these transactions and the Catholic and Protestant archbishops had come to London to appeal to the Labour and Liberal Democrat leaders, and the Environment Secretary, to intervene in the Council's tangled affairs – again threatened by takeover by the District Auditor. In 1991, to escalating accusations of political thuggery, strikes and open warfare between Militant and the Labour Party, the moderate Labour Council began to take the hard decisions necessary to bring the city's finances under control. With what success remains to be seen.

One records these things without pleasure. As has, I hope, been made clear, great things have been achieved on Merseyside during the past ten years. Concurrently with all the 1990 political carry-on, the Merseyside Development Corporation reported its most successful year to date, with around £87 million secured from private investment and business. Nonetheless, upon the outcome of Merseyside's political strife and the stability of its municipal finances must turn the manner in which the UDC divests itself of its assets, property, institutions, programmes, when the time comes. To this extent Merseyside's example could colour government policy in respect of the UDCs generally. The message from Merseyside is one of hope – but hope that has to be tempered with appreciation that deep-seated decline and deprivation, attitudes and practices, are not to be changed quickly. The timescale over which regeneration strategies have to be designed and implemented is one of thirty and more years rather than ten to fifteen years. Can we keep alive over such periods the enthusiasm and political will required to sustain them?

6

GLASGOW

As the crow flies it is about 170 miles from Kirkby to Castlemilk, but quite a bit further as you and I travel. Yet, taken to one or the other blindfold, we might not quickly know for certain at which we were looking. Here are the same boarded-up windows, the same forlorn monotony of unkempt wasteland, the same desperate sense of a no man's land from which life has ebbed away. Over 86 per cent of these stained and forbidding buildings – three- and four-storey 'walk-up' flats, interspersed here and there with high-rise blocks – are without central heating; condensation affects 28 per cent of them; 88 per cent have kitchens which are below standard;* insulation is way below anything that would be acceptable in any new flat today; security leaves much to be desired. The annual turnover rate of tenants, at 18 per cent – in some parts well over 30 per cent – is the highest in the city. Tenancies sometimes last only weeks, even days, and in some parts there is simply no demand for houses at all. The 'void' rate – the percentage of empty properties – is, but only just, the second highest in the city, and the population is falling by 1,000 a year.[1]

The city is Glasgow, and Castlemilk covers an area of nearly 800 acres/323 ha on the north-facing slopes (bleak in winter) along the southern boundary, about four miles from the city centre. About 24,000 people live there. Like Glasgow's other peripheral estates it was put up – one building block in a heroic vision – speedily, but as is now apparent shoddily, as part of the great post-war clearance programme. As in so many other places,

* The government's Bulletin 1 standard.

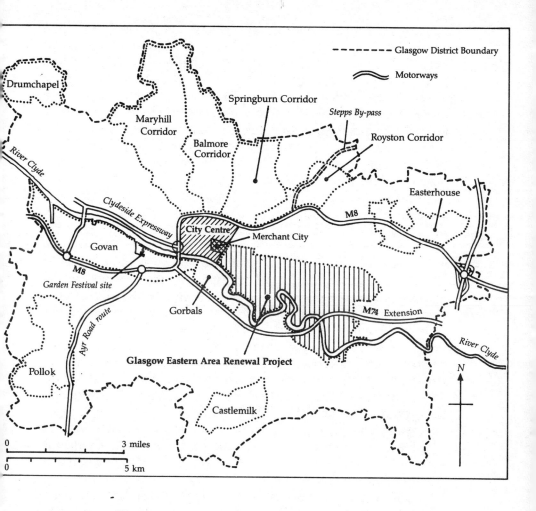

and other cities, it never quite came together. Houses, schools, churches were thrown up here and there around a road system; there is still no proper centre and promised facilities failed to materialise. The area is without rail or Underground services. Castlemilk today is more hated by its inhabitants than any of the other peripheral estates, unless it be notorious Easterhouse.

Unlike the Kirkby estates, Castlemilk remains within the city boundary. Those who built it remain responsible for it. In 1989 the City Council published a Strategy aimed at reversing the area's apparently inexorable decline – *The Castlemilk Initiative*. The essence of the Strategy is that improvements to the housing stock, crucial though they be, cannot alone hold the shrinking population or ensure for the area a viable future. It recognises that the relationship between housing availability and demand is now so 'out of kilter' that, without much wider changes, the Council can have little influence on the type of community which develops there. As the young and the more experienced – the natural 'contributors and leaders and organisers of the community' – seep away, 'they are being inexorably replaced by people with little or no real attachment to Castlemilk' so that 'an essentially unstable situation prevails'. 'The perception of Castlemilk solely as a "housing" problem *must be avoided*,' says the Strategy, 'otherwise the mistakes of the past could easily be repeated.'

To turn the area round, what is proposed is really no less than the creation of a new town, or township. A structure of six new neighbourhoods will be based on a township centre having a wide range of shopping, commercial, civic and leisure uses. Two subsidiary centres will also be built. Additional job opportunities will be created, and greatly improved transport access provided to the wider jobs market elsewhere (for example, East Kilbride); there will be a much wider range of tenure options for tenants and home owners ('a self-sustaining housing market which will meet the needs of all the stages of a family life cycle'); and overall environmental improvements, including the creation of several new parks. Quality becomes the leitmotif. 'For too long,' states the document – and it makes refreshing reading in an official publication – 'there has been the willingness to accept mediocrity. Poor-quality housing, poor-quality shops, poor-quality services and facilities. This will no longer be acceptable . . . the image of Castlemilk must be one of quality, of a quality place in which to live and as a quality place in which to invest.'

Valiant words, reminiscent of so many planning documents, from so many cities, over so many years. Can Glasgow pull it off? The city has been struggling with such problems for a century and a half.

> In the very centre of the city [it has been said] there is an accumulated mass of squalid wretchedness, which is probably unequalled in the British Dominions. There is concentrated everything that is wretched, dissolute, loathsome and pestilential. These places are filled by a population of many thousands of miserable creatures. The houses are unfit even for styes . . .

The Prince of Wales, last year? No, the City's Chief Constable, addressing the British Association in Glasgow in 1840.

From the splendid Victorian Western Necropolis, hard by the

mediaeval cathedral and presided over by a huge John Knox, 'the chief instrument under God of the Reformation in Scotland', the city spreads below one – grey stone in the very centre, with a red, pink and brown stone fringe, and, beyond, vast areas of brick and concrete housing. From here one can look across the Clyde as it winds through the city to the silent docks and shipyards of Govan and beyond, whence came the *Queen Mary* and the *QE2*, across the battered wastelands, across what was once the Gorbals, past a sombre miscellany of the city's 140 tower blocks, starting at one's very feet, towards Castlemilk and the outer estates to the south and east. Northwards and westwards lie Loch Lomond and the Trossachs, a bare half-hour or so from the City Chambers. Was it from here, the heart of the original settlement, that Defoe, in the early eighteenth century, decided that Glasgow was 'the beautifullest little city I have seen in Britain'?

Growth came, with industry, a couple of generations later, but it was in the mid nineteenth century, when trade with the Indies and America burgeoned mightily and the second wave of industrialisation brought heavy engineering to Clydeside that the 'beautifullest little city' lost its earlier character for good (though to this day it has a wonderful heritage of parks). The new suburbs coalesced. The surrounding villages, swollen into burghs by earlier expansion, in turn found themselves engulfed as the city's spreading boundaries washed over them. During the nineteenth century Glasgow grew in extent from 2,000 to 12,500 acres/800–5,000 ha. After the Union it had had the status almost of a city republic; now it was 'the Second City of the Empire'. And, carried forward by its own momentum, between 1925 and 1938 it more than doubled its size again, while local government reorganisation in 1973 added even more to its territory. Yet, by the same mid seventies, this great thrusting metropolis, the economic capital of Scotland, seemed to have no discernible future. Its citizens were leaving at the rate of 20,000 a year. Its decline was thought by many to be terminal.

Uncontrolled growth, as we have seen over and over again, brings uncontrollable problems. Glasgow has always been prepared to 'think big'; its history is punctuated by heroic gestures, by efforts to cleanse and renew itself, to meet its great social problems. They have almost always been overtaken by time. Its City Improvement Act of 1866, giving the Council powers to purchase and clear slums and to build houses, was the first big municipal intervention of its kind in Britain – but although by 1914 some 16,000 houses had been demolished, the City Improvement Trust, created in the wake of the Act, had built only 2,200 houses. Another Improvement Act in 1897 resulted, it has been written, in the eviction of 3,000 poor, but no new housing 'on the grounds that there were plenty of empty houses'. Densities in the tenements were staggering. The Gorbals became a national byword. A 1901 investigation by the *Glasgow Daily Mail* revealed 200 brothels and 150 shebeens in an area adjoining the University no more than about 450 yards square. It all seemed inexorable. An estimated housing need of 5,000 after World War I had grown to 90,000 by the start of World War II. The urge to renew reached its orgiastic peak in Robert Bruce's 1948 proposals totally to raze and redevelop the entire centre of the city so that little more than the Clyde remained (the then Lord Provost quoting D. H. Burnham's 'Make no little plans; they have no power to stir men's minds'). This was a gesture too heroic even for Glasgow (though more clearance areas were declared than in any other city in Britain), but as it came to naught great tracts of land on the periphery were bulldozed and flattened for four new 'townships': Castlemilk, Easterhouse, Drumchapel and Pollock, in which were colonised between a third and a quarter of Glasgow's entire population. The City came to own some 170,000 houses, or more than 56 per cent of the entire housing stock, thereby becoming Europe's biggest municipal landlord. After the initial euphoria engendered by fresh paint, bathrooms and proper kitchens, the peripheral estates rapidly became synonymous with multiple deprivation. The notorious Hutchestown estate on Crown Street was built in 1970; within eight years all 759 flats had been abandoned. By the mid 80s some 45,000 houses were below 'tolerable standard' and the repair bill was estimated at double the actual expenditure for the *whole* of Scotland. Among the confirmatory indicators that things are seriously wrong may be instanced Glasgow's mortality rate, which is about 12 per cent above the Scottish average – itself higher than the average rates for England and Wales. Deaths from lung cancer are no less than 40 per cent above the Scottish average. Castlemilk is just one part of this deeply shadowed picture.

Yet ... join those sauntering through the glittering conservatory of the St Enoch Shopping Centre. Or take one of the wall-creeper lifts for a dram at the airy bar of the Penguin Café at the top of Princes Square. Or revel in the indoor–outdoor feel of Britain's (then) first new art gallery for goodness knows how many decades, the Burrell Collection. For there is, at the same time, a totally different Glasgow – buoyant, brashly confident, busy throwing off the past, bouncing into the future. Tribal loyalties have ever been strong here; Glaswegians have always held to a strong sense of corporate identity and fundamental certainties about their city's role and status. When, in 1983, the then Lord Provost, Michael Kelly, coined the tag 'Glasgow's Miles Better', no one smirked. It simply expressed what everyone knew; it was aimed, not at Glaswegians, but at everyone else. Could any other great city in similar straits have got away with it? Fuelled by heady excitements like the Garden Festival of 1988 and nomination as European City of Culture for 1990, the hype is stronger than ever today. 'I always feel, when I go to Glasgow,' a city planner in England told me, not without envy, 'that I'm being brainwashed.'

By the quirks of the British planning system Glasgow, like Liverpool or Knowsley, is a District Council. Glasgow has great underlying strengths – it has two universities, a major airport, many business headquarters, and is the third largest shopping area in Britain. It has, moreover, a long tradition of large-scale civic administration denied a fairly new authority like Knowsley. Glasgow lies within the strapping Strathclyde Regional Council area – home to half the population of Scotland – but Merseyside Metropolitan County is no more. The thrusting Scottish Development Agency has an altogether wider remit than the Merseyside Development Corporation. North of the Border there are other official agencies unknown in England, like the Scottish Special Housing Association (now Scottish Homes), which can be brought into the picture. The partnerships thus made possible can bring considerable fire power to bear upon chosen targets.

But partnerships demand a degree of common motivation, of mutual respect, of give-and-take. Glasgow, like Liverpool, suffers a Protestant/Catholic divide (its two football teams, as in Liverpool, guarding their loyalties fanatically). Glasgow has long been a city of radical politics and 'hard men'. It was the birthplace and main stamping ground of the Independent Labour Party, the ILP. In the aftermath of the great 1919 strike, on the morrow of 'Black Friday', tanks, artillery and machineguns were deployed in George Square. Over fifty-seven years there have been only five when Labour did not control the City Council (and today many of its councillors are unemployed). Glasgow, however, never went the way of Militant in Liverpool. The Council seems to have had no problems in its dealings with a Thatcherite government (Margaret Thatcher in turn lavished praise on the city's achievements), or with the private sector. In another direction, so far from working *against* local housing co-operatives as did Hatton's Liverpool, it has coordinated them fruitfully into its housing programmes. There are around 150 Glasgow associations, thirty of them full-blooded co-operatives. Since the mid 1970s, they have refurbished well over 10,000 Glasgow homes.

One comes back to Glasgow's sense of destiny. In 1979 Michael Kelly suggested that the city link up with Liverpool, whose history and problems are so similar, to share ideas and expertise. It was not to be. In Kelly's words, 'One of the Liberal Councillors [there] said the idea of twinning with Glasgow was a suicide pact. I think that illustrates the difference between the two cities. They saw their problems as insoluble. We didn't. We thought, We believe in this place. Things are going to happen here.'[2]

To date, the most comprehensive drive to make things happen was GEAR. GEAR is also the trail-blazing exemplar of the consortium approach in Scotland. The letters stand for the Glasgow Eastern Area Renewal project, and over its ten-year life span, from 1976 to 1987, it was responsible for one of the biggest regeneration programmes of its kind in Europe. The area covered was 6 square miles/nearly 1,600 ha, or 8 per cent of the City of Glasgow, stretching from Saltmarket, on the edge of the city centre, to Sandyhills on the east. The population at the outset was 45,000, having fallen from a peak of about 150,000 in 1952. One fifth of the area lay vacant – and largely derelict; 12 per cent of its buildings were empty and unused.

By the early 1970s it was all too clear that housing construction could not keep pace with the clearance programmes (five of the city's twenty-nine areas designated for comprehensive redevelopment were in the East End). The shadow of recession fell across the Clyde, as elsewhere, and the great ironworks began to close. Studies undertaken with the Scottish Office made it clear that the East End *must* receive priority treatment. A series of local plans was put in hand by the City Council; the Scottish Office ditched thoughts of another New Town and decided rather to put the money into Glasgow itself; in 1976 the Scottish Development Agency was brought into being and found itself (once, it is said, its initial reluctance had been overcome by its Chairman, Sir William Gray, an ex Lord Provost of the city) the lead partner in the GEAR project. With it were the still-new Strathclyde Region, the City, and Scottish Special Housing – to which came to be added later the Housing Corporation, the Greater Glasgow Health Board and the Manpower Services Commission. It is tempting to see the thrust of many of the SDA's subsequent programmes elsewhere as having been forged in its experience with GEAR. It is interesting, too, to compare this comprehensive partnership approach with that of the Urban Development Corporations in England.

Groups were set up initially to look at population implications, employment, education, environment, transport, community care, leisure, shopping, housing and health. GEAR's first moves were then concentrated on packages for environmental improvement (including air pollution and traffic management); on housing programmes; and on the acquisition of land for new industry.

Ten years later *all* old tenement homes – 4,000 of them – had been renewed by housing associations; 8,000 inter-war houses had been modernised by the City and Scottish Special Housing; 4,000 *new* houses had been built, half by the private sector (which had not previously put up a single house there for fifty years). Special arrangements ensured that a proportion of the latter were offered for sale to those on the Council's housing list. (The Council could to some extent call the tune because it was, to all intents and purposes, giving the land away.) The bill – over £86 million to the City; over £41 million to Scottish Special Housing; nearly £79 million to the housing associations through the Housing Corporation, and £87 million to the private sector.[3]

Some 150 sites – covering nearly 250 acres/100 ha – had been landscaped at a cost of £8 million plus. New parks and sports facilities had been created (notably the complexes at Helenvale and Crown Point Road). Sixty per cent of all tenements had been stone-cleaned, most backcourts had been given a face-lift, Bridgeton Cross has been given a new coherence by the townscape improvements there, including the diversion of through traffic, and extra 'weight' by the new supermarket. On the site of Parkhead Forge, which once had 40,000 workers making big guns for the Navy, now stands another new focal point – a £25 million shopping centre of 344,000 sq. ft./32,000 sq. m. with parking for 1,500 cars. The glass pyramids of its roof structure (shades of I. M. Pei at the Louvre) signal the promise of a changing future to a wide, wide catchment area. Cambuslang Investment Park, a green-field site of 400 acres/160 ha, is being developed as a main employment and living area for the 1990s and beyond; already about eighty companies are operating there. Templeton's one-time carpet factory, grouped around the splendid 'Doge's Palace' on the edge of Glasgow Green, has been transmuted by the SDA into the Templeton Business Centre – a new base for electronics and telecommunications development, and very successful. Two training schemes deserve note – 'Workwise', private-sector led, and GEAR's Training and Employment Grants Scheme. The latter, administered by the SDA, was so successful that it has been incorporated in all the Agency's other subsequent 'integrated area projects', as well as more than half a dozen other special initiative areas. On the health front, three new Health Centres were set up in the GEAR area – indeed all targets set for health and social facilities were met.

Of course, all is not yet right. 'You can see that money was spent here,' says James Rae, the City's Planning Officer, of some 'improved' housing, 'but it hasn't worked.' Many parts of the East End – Dalmarnock, for example, and Camlachie and Barrowfield – need urgent attention. But, overall, it is already difficult to remember quite how awful eastern Glasgow was fifteen years ago. The private sector is investing in areas that nothing would have induced it to look at then. Land values which stood at £1,500 an acre ten years ago now reach maybe £30,000. An expenditure of some £300 million of public money during the life span of GEAR has so far led to £200 million private investment – and the story is as yet but half told.

GEAR came formally to an end in March 1987. But if GEAR is dead, long live the East End Management Committee, set up by the City and the Region, and the East End Management Unit! The area covered by this successor agency has been doubled from GEAR's six square miles to twelve square miles. And underpinning it is a public 'Declaration of Continuing Commitment' by each of the former GEAR participants – in addition to the two local authorities themselves and the new Management Committee, the SDA, Scottish Special Housing, the Housing Corporation, the Greater Glasgow Health Board, Manpower Services Commission, and Glasgow Opportunities. These now comprise the East End Strategy Group. 'We, the undernoted and our successors,' states the Declaration, 'accept responsibility for providing continual support for the regeneration of the East End and its social, economic and environmental development. A vital element in the achievement of these tasks is the active support and participation of both the local business and residential communities. Such support will be sustained by the establishment and development of new management structures.' One of the first such initiatives has been the creation of a development company, the East End Executive Ltd, to spearhead the creation of jobs and appropriate training for them. In the words of a recent brochure, GEAR was not the end of the East End story, but 'offers a springboard to future heights of achievement'.

*

GEAR represented a new, single-minded concentration of effort upon a defined area. Subsequent programmes in the city have followed the same pattern. Two years after the start of GEAR, the 'Maryhill Corridor', one of the main approaches to the city from the north-west, was defined as a distinct project – in this case by Strathclyde and the City jointly. Here the clearances had begun in the 1930s, and had been stepped up after World War II, until a once dignified 'boulevard' and its hinterland had collapsed into decay. In the mid 70s nine out of ten houses were considered unfit to live in. The 'Corridor' project was based on a sort of planning opportunism. By identifying openings for improvement at any point in this particular swathe of land – for new housing, for rehabilitation, for playing fields or a park, for new shopping – it was hoped gradually to eliminate the spatial chaos left by the demolitions, to reassert townscape values, to strengthen community confidence. In the Maryhill Corridor over the past ten years over £100 million has been spent by public and private sectors. Of 5,500 unfit houses, 2,500 were demolished, 2,000 completely refurbished; and 1,200 new homes built. Around 160,000 sq. ft./15,000 sq. m. of industrial and workshop space have been provided; and 215,000 sq. ft./nearly 20,000 sq. m. of new or renovated shopping.

Not far to the west is the 'Balmore–Saracen Corridor', another such initiative, and west of that Springbush, where the SDA, the City and the private sector are in partnership. Between Maryhill Road and Saracen Road meanders the Glasgow branch of the 1780 Forth and Clyde Canal, closed since 1963. Here the British Waterways Board, in conjunction with the local authorities and the SDA, is labouring to bring back into the city's life a twelve-mile stretch from Anniesland in the west to Kirkintilloch in the east. The £2.6 million scheme involves not merely the improvement and redevelopment of the land adjoining the Canal, but the raising of bridges to make it fully navigable for sailing craft.

And so on. The big Eastern Area; Castlemilk, Easterhouse; Maryhill and the similar Special Project Areas; other stress areas like Govan; opportunity areas like Partick–Kelvin – gradually the big jigsaw begins to join up, held together at the centre by a whole series of key sections from Woodlands to the Merchant City. Of course there are highlights and focal points, from the West of Scotland Science Park at Garscube to the rebuilt Rangers' Ibrox Stadium (all covered seating and a model, say Glaswegians, to the rest of Europe); the Exhibition and Conference Centre across the

111

river from the Garden Festival site; the 9-acre/3.6 ha Broomielaw development and Carrick Quay, the balconied and rather liner-like new tenement block on the Clyde.

But what is only fully apparent to those who knew the city fifteen and more years ago is the sustained improvement which has taken place across the board throughout the wider city centre – the immense stone-cleaning programme which has newly revealed the pink and buff sandstone from under the grime; the careful efforts to fill gaps in a manner and scale that is consistent with the character of the area; the conversion of old industrial buildings (for example the bonded warehousing overlooking the Canal at Spiers Wharf, or the commanding Bell Street warehouse on the edge of the Merchant City, both to housing); restorations too numerous to mention, but including such set-pieces as the Great Western Terrace and majestic Carlton Place overlooking the river, to smaller buildings like Mackintosh's Willow Tea Rooms and the Ca d'Oro. Add in the exclusion of traffic from Buchanan Street and a fair chunk of Sauchiehall Street, which has returned dignity to what had become a near slum; add in the steady extension of the riverside walkway which is opening up the water afresh to the people of the city; add in the floodlighting of forty or fifty buildings which brings magic to the streets and skyline after dark, and you will see why Glaswegians exclaim, 'It's all different now. The city's shining.'

The centre of the city has had its own priority area – the eighteenth-century Merchant City. This lies between the Cathedral and the river, and formed the first significant extension to the mediaeval settlement. In 1969 the Fruit Market at Candleriggs was moved away to relieve congestion, which nonetheless remained a problem. The eastern edge was blighted by the uncertainties attaching to major road proposals. A domino effect led to a number of businesses moving out or shutting up shop altogether. By 1980 one third of all property in the quarter was vacant or underused.

The City, however, owned about 40 per cent of it (60 per cent of the vacant property) and, encouraged by the resolution of the road-proposals problem, began to look at housing as the means of bringing the area back into use. After testing the temperature of the water in one or two pilot schemes, and receiving confirmation of their acceptability to the public – if the economics could be sorted out – the Council evolved a number of different financial packages with the SDA and the private sector which have led to the substantial revitalisation of the Merchant City. The largest individual schemes have been the Ingram Square project – a whole street block, 239 homes, six shops and car parking space for 120 – which includes new building as well as conversion; what is to be the 'Italian Centre'; and the 'fortress-like' Bell Street Warehouse mentioned above, 482 ft./147 m. in length and said to be the largest single building project of its kind in Scotland. One eighteenth-century church is now in use by the Glasgow Theatre Club as the Tron Theatre; the John Street Church has been turned into offices with a restaurant at ground-floor level; while one of the most heartening rescues has been the conversion of a Georgian mansion in the now pedestrianised Blackfriars Court into a café-bar-restaurant-hotel: the Babbity Bowster.* From breakfast until midnight here the animation of the new-style Merchant City ebbs and flows. Not everything has worked. The city's old Fish Market, the Briggait, was turned, quite stylishly, into a galleried shopping and eating hall, but – for much the same reasons as Tobacco Dock in London's Docklands – languished and had to close. As other parts of the jigsaw fall into place around, it must assuredly – as Tobacco Dock – be relaunched successfully.

Glasgow's drive to jack itself up has intensified over fifteen years or so. Eight hundred weeks, say, and *something* new happening in every one of them. Statistics mask the complex struggles, the tortuous twists and turns – legal, financial, social, psychological – by which every small advance has been made. Nor do they, of themselves, give much sense of the range of organisations and agencies involved – the civil servants, the politicians, the local authority departments, the builders and developers, the trusts and associations and community groups, the architects and planners, the banks and the businesses, the individual owners and tenants . . .

'It doesn't matter in Glasgow where you look,' says James Rae, 'you'll see something to do with regeneration. Every person in our city is an element in regeneration, every site. As an officer, I want to get involved in everything – and a whole lot of citizens have the same feeling. They think they have a right to come in and tell me how to do my job. It's something that's accepted in this city in a way in which perhaps it isn't elsewhere.'

This sense of partnership, and participation, starts at the top. It is a reiterated principle of the SDA, 'one of the enduring aspects of [our] approach'. Strathclyde Region, with a massive annual budget

* The name comes from a traditional wedding dance.

of around £1.3 *billion,* has channelled powerful resources into Glasgow's regeneration.

> Strathclyde [states one of its documents] has within its boundaries many of the most severely depressed areas in the country. Since its inception in 1975 the Council has made tackling that problem its principal policy objective . . . To have any hope of success, attempts to regenerate these areas must be genuine partnerships, drawing together the efforts of government, local authorities, other public agencies and the private sector. Crucially, any initiative must ensure the active involvement of the communities themselves. Imposing solutions on the shattered parts of Britain is doomed to failure. Rebirth must ultimately come from within . . . Lasting change will not be achieved quickly. As our experience in the first phase of the GEAR programme . . . demonstrates, such initiatives must be long-term commitments. And long-term means a minimum of ten years.

Reports and promotional literature flood out from all directions – it is part of the image building. Inevitably the same successes appear in most of them, but rivalry is for the most part kept well under control. Any initiative, says Strathclyde categorically, 'should become identified with the area and not any one partner'. Rae is laid-back about the whole thing. 'You've got to allow for organisations taking credit. There's nothing wrong with a bit of morale building.' I asked him how the City got on with the SDA. 'I say thank God for the SDA,' was his answer. 'It's been a blessing having their headquarters in Glasgow. If it hadn't been so we could never have progressed as far as we have done. They're just a step along the street. We're on first-name terms. And with day-to-day contacts you get an insight into an organisation. The more you get to know them the more you can use their system – and vice versa. You interrelate. In fact we've been accused by the rest of Scotland, until fairly recently, of regarding the SDA as our own personal property.'

This identity of purpose, however, goes far beyond national and local government, and softens the organisational and administrative boundaries which, elsewhere, so often lead to a shrug of the shoulders and an 'it-can't-be-done' attitude. As we have seen, corporate relations with the private sector have been good, and increasingly productive. An additional bridge between the two sides is provided by 'Glasgow Action', which brings together leading figures from the business and industrial world and from local government. Its origins lay in a study undertaken for the SDA by

McKinsey & Company in 1985 on the potential of Glasgow's city centre. This argued strongly for a service industries base, strong enough to stimulate the economic regeneration of the city as a whole. David McDonald was seconded from the economic side of the SDA to be the new organisation's Director; Sir Norman Macfarlane became its Chairman. Glasgow Action is essentially a promotional body. It has focused on three things for future development: headquarters activity, exportable services, and visitors. To these were added three other dimensions: the city centre environment, consumer services, and image building; and four principles: a commitment to *quality*, emphasis on *projects* rather than masterplans, the need for *private-sector leadership* and fourthly – which I find in many ways the most interesting – 'a sustained commitment to the vision'. As we have seen elsewhere, economic and environmental change are not susceptible to quick fixes. Recent history – including that of Glasgow – is studded with heroic efforts which have faltered and then collapsed because the political will that initiated them collapsed. Whether an organisation like Glasgow Action is the most appropriate 'guardian of the vision', as it hopes to be, can only be proved by time, but there can be no doubt of the need, everywhere, for long-term objectives to be stated and restated constantly.

Another vital strand in the public–private-sector mix: the housing associations and community groups. In Glasgow, as elsewhere, they have developed greatly over the past fifteen years – though virtually unknown before the late sixties. A Scottish Federation of Associations was formed in 1976 with seventy members; today there are at least 150, and they have refurbished between them maybe 15,000 homes. Glasgow, however, decided in 1977 to form its own Glasgow Forum of Housing Associations, which operates with specialist staff groups on development, housing management, and finance and maintenance. Encouraged by Lord Goodman, its then Chairman, the Housing Corporation in 1974 set up a sub-office in Glasgow (which subsequently became one of the partners in GEAR) and elsewhere. Working closely with the City's Housing Department, the Corporation set out to stimulate new approaches to community housing, and the City Council's strong support for the movement has been in marked contrast to attitudes in some other cities.

In the mid 70s prospective tenants on the housing list were offered the option of managing – with a budget – part of a new estate at Summerston. They not only jumped at the suggestion, but other parts of the estate asked to be included. The Council set up a special committee to foster the movement, within which three main forms of community group have evolved in Glasgow. There are Tenant Management Co-operatives, set up by the Council as in Summerston, which involve residents in the management and maintenance functions previously undertaken by the Housing Department. There are 'Par Value Co-operatives', made up of tenant members who collectively own the houses in their area, but without any individual share in the equity. This enables them to seek finance from sources normally restricted to private-sector properties, and is the main form of community ownership being most strongly promoted currently by the Council. (The Calvay Co-operative, which took over 366 houses, has been lauded by Prince Charles.) Thirdly, there are Community Trusts, set up as companies limited by guarantee, with the wider objectives of environmental redevelopment and improvement, job creation and cultural activities.

The trail-blazer here has been the Woodlands Community Development Trust, set up in 1985. The Woodlands area, consisting of twenty-three late Victorian tenement street blocks, lies close to the city centre and a stone's throw from the University. When Mrs Dorothy Henderson brought the Trust's predecessor, the Woodlands Residents Association into being in 1975, the area had deteriorated to the point where its life expectancy was quoted as five to seven years. In fact, only four years later, the redoubtable Mrs Henderson, her neighbour Mrs Angela Petrie and some thousands of other owner-occupiers and tenants, with the help of the City Council and financial assistance from the European Community, had dramatically turned the whole near-square-mile of it round. Decay had been arrested, all the main frontages cleaned, front gardens reinstated, model schemes for the redesign of internal courtyards – which had mostly become cheerless and filthy dumps – had been completed. Traffic management measures had improved the streets themselves. By 1980 nearly £2 million had been spent and Woodlands was unrecognisable as the place it had been so short a time before. House prices had jumped about nine times. No less marked was the change in the community spirit. Woodlands houses about 4,500 people, a substantial proportion of them immigrants. As a result of all the new contacts made during the improvement programme, a range of local groups and organisations came into being; a new friendliness was evident. 'Nothing else could have brought us all together as this did,' says Mrs Henderson.

*

116

Effectively, Glasgow's big policy switches date from 1975. The new District, shorn of many of its previous powers but even bigger in extent and population, ditched the clear-fell ethic and began to feel its way towards more organic forms of change. It was in that year* that the Merchant City was designated as a Conservation Area. (The city now has twenty-one.) Since then significant markers have been raised at ever more frequent intervals. In 1976, GEAR; in 1978, the Maryhill Corridor; in 1979, Woodlands; in 1980, the reopening of the refurbished Underground (its use has increased by 40 per cent); in 1984, the big Exhibition and Conference Centre on the river, and the opening of the Burrell Collection (which, overnight, became Scotland's third biggest visitor attraction); in 1988, the National Garden Festival (with over 4.3 million visitors – and 'it would have been over 5 million but for the weather'); in 1989, the opening of the St Enoch Centre; in 1990, in time for the city's crowning as 'European City of Culture', the great new concert hall, and the creation at last of a proper setting for the Cathedral. Ahead lies the new potential offered by direct transatlantic flights from the airport.

These are some of the visible peaks. No less important have been the invisible successes. One example: commercial pressures to build out-of-town shopping centres in the corridor between Glasgow and Edinburgh have been, as might be expected, tremendous. If allowed, these would have put paid to the shopping improvements which are helping to bring life back to the stress areas of the city. It is only because Strathclyde and Glasgow – and indeed Edinburgh – have joined strategic forces against such development that St Enoch's, the Italian Centre, Parkhead Forge and others have been made possible.

Again, tourists do not beat a path to your door, lemming-like, without good reason. 'Ten years ago,' Eddie Friel, who heads Greater Glasgow Tourist Board, is fond of saying, 'the definition of a tourist in Glasgow was "someone who has lost his way".' Yet in six years the number of tourists multiplied sixfold (in 1982, 700,000 visitors; in 1987, 2.2 million; in 1988, 4.3 million). There are three or four new hotels and occupancy rates have soared. The runaway success of the Burrell offered a pointer to the potential role of the arts in the area's regeneration. In 1983, the three District Councils of Glasgow, Strathkelvin and Renfrew jointly set up the Greater Glasgow Tourist Board, and since then policies have become much more sharply focused. When Councillor Pat

* Was it fortuitous that 1975 was also European Architectural Heritage Year?

Lally, Leader of the City Council, says: 'We didn't go out to get nominated as European City of Culture (we knew it already – the trouble was that others didn't)', he is being economical with the truth. Glasgow got the nomination because it was Glasgow that had got its act together. 'Originally,' Lally has said,[4] 'much of the cultural life of the city lay dormant from April to September each year. Now festivals and other arts events have begun to change that. Audiences have increased ... Life in the city has become more active. While the initial incentive was [and is] to improve the quality of life in Glasgow, we came to realise that the arts and culture were tools that could be used in the economic regeneration of the city. At the outset there was no official cultural policy, but the city now plans ahead to seek out new opportunities.' People speak of Lally's strong political leadership in this. He is seen as entirely responsible, for example, for the new concert hall. 'It's really a bit of a miracle,' said James Rae in 1989. 'A £28 million programme for completion in two years. But it *will* be finished. Full stop.' And of course it was.

The year itself, 1990, was an unceasing cultural bonanza, possibly to the point of surfeit, from the moment in the Kings Theatre that M. Jacques Chirac handed over the torch from Paris, the previous 'European City of Culture'. It included a dozen different festivals, 125 exhibitions, forty world premières in music and theatre, sixty sporting events. Glasgow's annual Mayfest is always a firework display in itself. Among the special exhibitions mention has to be made of the vastly ambitious (and expensive) 'Glasgow's Glasgow', a thought-provoking multi-faceted portrait of the city, housed in the arches beneath Central Station. The year's permanent legacies range from the opening of the old/new McLellan Galleries to provide the largest air-conditioned space for temporary exhibitions outside London, to the Tramway Theatre, the enormous Victorian structure that once housed the city's 385 tramcars and 4,000 horses, but more recently provided the space for Peter Brook's epic *Mahabharata*; from a sparkling new front for the Citizens Theatre to the great concert hall sitting at the top of Buchanan Street. Home for the Scottish National Orchestra, its 'modern' lines were received by Glaswegians with mixed feelings – but glee that Edinburgh, after several decades, is still chasing its phantom opera house. And £3 million was invested on behalf of the city's art galleries, the interest from which will be available for new purchases. Traditionally wealth produced the arts. Glasgow sees it the other way round. Proof will emerge in the 1990s.

*

So, once again, two stories. Lots of hope, lots of hype. More than £2 billion of new construction, it is said, built or in the pipeline since 1985. But a 1988 Inquiry headed by the greatly respected Sir Robert Grieve found the city's housing problem to be increasingly horrendous. Marked growth in the professional and financial sectors. But Ravenscraig is to be closed down, and with it steelmaking in Scotland. The flight from the city has slowed, but it has not stopped. If in the black spots unemployment has dropped from 40 per cent to 38 per cent, that is no big deal for the communities concerned. (In the second half of the 80s half the unemployed had been out of work for a year or more.) Plans for Easterhouse, Castlemilk, Drumchapel and Pollock promise hope – but the peripheral estates are so vast that they soak up effort and money like blotting paper. How are the enormous sums required to be found?

Glasgow is actively analysing the factors that might be expected to shape the needs and form of cities in the twenty-first century – what it is that will make them 'tick' – and hosted an international conference on the subject in 1990. Because confident, thrusting Glasgow is determined to be *the* European city of the twenty-first century. At the end of the eighties it is all best summed up in the title of a brochure produced by five local housing associations (with help from the Council itself): 'Miles Better, Miles To Go'.

7

SOUTH WALES

Swansea – Cardiff – the Valleys

FROM THE valley of the Wye, and Offa's Dyke, a massive range of Old Red Sandstone rock stretches westward for more than fifty miles, first as the Black Mountains, then as the Brecon Beacons and, beyond, the high moorlands of the Carmarthenshire Fans. The highest points of the Brecon Beacons rise to 2,900 ft./830 m. and, to the north in particular, the slopes are very grand. Southwards to the coast, run the Valleys, close, deep cut, infinitely intricate, choked for generations with the grimed paraphernalia of mining and iron working, the sprawl of vast spoil heaps, and the snaking terraces that were home to those who toiled in the pits and at the furnaces. Scarcely a square yard of this terrain, from the bleak uplands to the coastal plain, has not been worked, one way or another, at some time during the past two hundred years. Down the Valleys clattered the trains bearing the coal, the iron and the tinplate to the ports – Newport, Cardiff, Barry, Port Talbot and Swansea. Here there was copper smelting, and later steel. In the 1920s nearly half the male working population of Wales – which meant more or less half the working population, for the women were not expected to set foot in what was a man's world – worked in mining, steel, shipping or on the railways, so that this whole area once held three quarters of the entire Welsh population. Two thirds still live there.

Coal and steel; steel and coal. With such a narrow industrial base Wales was cruelly exposed to the vicissitudes of world demand. Nowhere was the impact of the great Depression more harshly felt. In 1920 over 270,000 were employed in the coal industry – one in three of the male Welsh workforce; ten years

1

2

3

4

1–4) London, Glasgow, Merseyside, the North-east? Scenes like these are to be found in scores of towns and cities the length and breadth of the country; decay has no one address. These are places which seem to have no future, where no one wants to live. Sometimes, to expunge them totally is the only answer. Below (5), eight unloved tower blocks in Salford bite the dust in 1990 – the biggest demolition of its kind to date.

6

The Isle of Dogs in London's Docklands:
Canary Wharf (6) as it looked in May
1988 and, opposite (10), thirty months
later – eventually to produce, it is hoped,
20,000 jobs. Docklands housing takes
many forms, much of it indifferent; some,
as here in Shadwell Basin (8), has greater
character. The Light Railway (9) is being
extended and augmented. In Southwark
Hays Galleria (7) has been created on a
filled-in dock between warehouses.

8

7

9

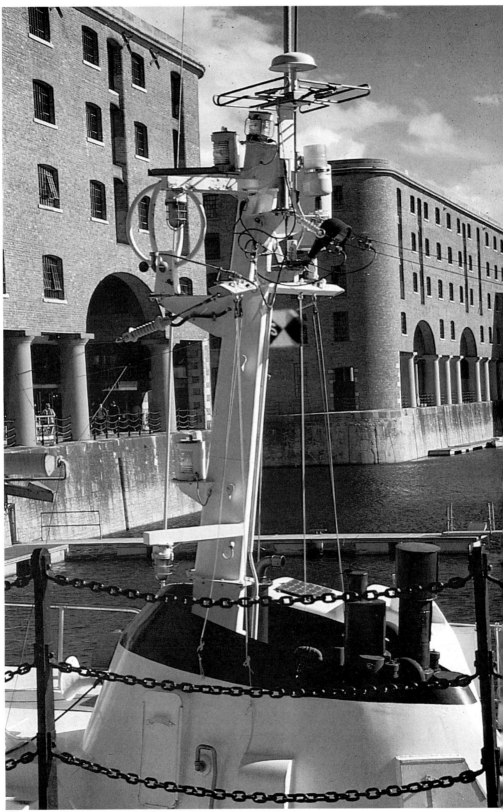

Merseyside saw the other of the first two Development Corporations. The crowning achievement of MDC's initial phase was the massive restoration of Albert Dock (11), now housing museums, shops, restaurants, apartments and TV Studios.

On this page, Glasgow: the giant crane (12), across the Clyde from the site of the Garden Festival, symbolizes the city's past; three shopping centres its present – St Enoch's (13); the Briggait, the old fishmarket (14), adapted but for the moment empty; and Princes Square (15), an ingenious and elegant conversion of what had been a glorified back yard, choked with an infill structure.

13

12

14

15

16

17

18

19

Left, Swansea's Maritime Quarter (16–19): old ships, moorings for 600 boats, 1,000 new homes, well-designed car parking and, on the Bristol Channel, for the first time an esplanade. Fifteen years ago all this was derelict and deserted.

21

20

On this page, Cardiff Bay: mud flats for much of the day (20, 21), soon to become a big water area retained by a barrage across the mouth. At Penarth Head, seen on the far side beyond the blackened timbers, new housing (22), with a big comprehensive scheme to follow.

22

23

24

The mining valleys of South Wales were choked, until very recently, by the hardware and spoil of the coal, iron and steel industries – now almost entirely vanished. Massive reclamation is greening them once more. This was the old Ogilvie Colliery in the Rhymney Valley (23) – and how it looks today (24).

later 100,000 of those jobs had gone. The pay of those still in work was all but halved. Thousands fled the Valleys, and Wales. It was but a foretaste. When the industry was nationalised after World War II there were still 214 active pits in South Wales; today the number is not even in double figures (Maerdy, the last pit in the Rhondda, closed at the end of 1990), and only one in a *hundred* works in coal. Steel, too, plummeted. A mere twenty years ago the industry employed 70,000 in Wales; today, worldwide overproduction and improved methods have cut the number to about 3,000. Inevitably, in the wake of the main industries, the ports, built so expansively and confidently in the nineteenth century (and indeed into the twentieth), have shrunk – in some cases almost to nothing. About all that passes through Barry today, some wit has had it, is bananas.

The effect upon the appearance and physical fabric of the area was shocking. Even at the zenith of the Industrial Revolution, Wales was never rich. Individual coal owners, ironmasters, shipping magnates and dock owners made fortunes, but the Principality as a whole remained modest in civic display, chapel-going in its ethic, and at once radical politically yet curiously resigned to the harshness of its labours. Towns for the most part remained small and workaday, grimed and grim in the Valleys, shaped by the contours and the lie of the land, tending to spread monotonously in the coastal plain. Some focal points expanded in the nineteenth century at breakneck speed. The one-time hamlet of Merthyr Tydfil became, for a while, the biggest town in Wales. On the coast Newport, Cardiff and Swansea grew steadily into the three big cities of the Principality – though big is a relative term; Cardiff and Swansea together, the two largest, account for less than 60 per cent of the population of a city such as Leeds. Cardiff, through its acquisition of Cathays Park from the Third Marquess of Bute in the early days of the present century, has been able, as befits the capital city, to clothe itself with a civic centre of some grandeur. But decline cannot be disguised. Almost everywhere in Wales one is close to the most ravishing countryside. Northwards from Newport stretches the Usk valley; minutes from Swansea is the Gower peninsula (the country's first Area of Outstanding Natural Beauty); westwards from Cardiff and into the Valleys long vistas and hidden dells open up everywhere before one. Yet, interwoven with the beauty of the landscape, through the thirties and forties and fifties and sixties, was the accumulating evidence of decay: a confusion of rusting industrial detritus and dereliction, the shabbiness of the towns. When the Luftwaffe had finished with Swansea,

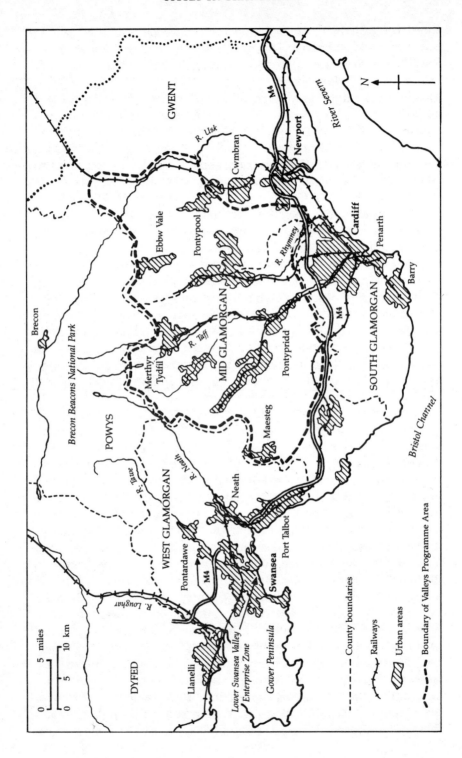

the street pattern of the centre had disappeared under the rubble; but the rebuilding was without charm. When Tiger Bay in Cardiff, the old area between the docks and city centre, was swept away by war and post-war clearances, what was left was mostly wasteland. And the 4,000 caravans that disfigure the coastline at Porthcawl represent the holiday that poverty can afford.

Some of this is hard to remember at the start of the 1990s. The M4 and the Severn Bridge have driven a direct link to England. New double-carriageway roads have opened up the Valleys, so that journeys which once took fifty minutes now take fifteen. Massive reclamation schemes have swept away the worst of the industrial scars. Intensive diversification into new manufacturing industries has been effected, and Wales now consistently gains 20 per cent of all inward investment into the UK (though representing only 5 per cent of the UK population). One quarter of the UK's oil is refined in Wales. Swansea has created an impressive new 'Maritime Quarter' and a 'Swansea Bay Partnership' of the public and private sectors is promoting the whole sub-region. A Development Corporation has been brought into existence to deal with the regeneration of 'Cardiff Bay' – the big area south of the city centre. Ebbw Vale is to be the site of the 1992 Garden Festival, and a 'Valleys Programme' of regeneration is in hand for an area that still has about 180,000 people living in it.

A success story then – if as yet half told – and, as in Glasgow, a corporate one. There has been no single fairy godmother in Wales, unless it be the Welsh Office, which presides over all the Principality's affairs. In Swansea, reclamation and renewal has been municipally led, though aided extensively by other agencies. Cardiff's exceptionally bold strategy for the Bay area is being masterminded by an Urban Development Corporation – the only one in Wales and set up, as we shall see, slightly differently from its English counterparts. The Valleys Programme, involving no fewer than twenty-one local authorities, stems directly from the Welsh Office with detailed planning largely devolved to the Welsh Development Agency, an almost exact equivalent of its Scottish counterpart ('almost' because Scotland and Wales never do things quite the same, and Wales, for example, has an additional organisation, the Welsh Land Authority, for the assembly and disposal of land). As in Scotland, however, a tighter social and administrative network – compounded perhaps with a whiff of nationalism – makes communication and partnerships a touch easier than in England, at least in the south; and nowhere in Wales have left-wing politics, though staunchly held, hindered

123

relations with government or the private sector. Job creation is seen everywhere as paramount.

Nowhere in Britain was industrial dereliction more appalling than in the Lower Swansea Valley. The Valley runs north-eastwards from the city, following the line of the River Tawe, through Pontardawe to Ystradgynlais in the mountains. A big swathe of the lower end, around Llandore, grew into the biggest copper-smelting centre in the world, with other kinds of metal processing developing as the copper trade faded. At its zenith, in the last century, more than 300 chimneys blanketed the landscape with their smoke and fumes. In clear weather the black pall could be seen as far as fifty miles away. Not only was the air thick with pollution; the ground was impregnated with toxic wastes. Gradu-ally, after World War I, the various works died, one by one, the last two giving up in 1980. But long before that the ground too had died. In that whole grotesque, sulphurous panorama of crumbling buildings and black and yellow and orange waste, no living thing could exist. It was a legacy, clearly, which fell to the public sector somehow to deal with – but how? The problem was so daunting that some thought it insoluble.

In 1966 an abandoned coal tip slipped and engulfed a school in Aberfan, a few miles south of Merthyr, in a smothering, suffocating black slurry. Over one hundred, mostly schoolchildren, died. The shock waves of the disaster unlocked, as never before, resources and determination. Government Derelict Land Grant, 75 to 85 per cent of the cost of reclamation work, was extended to the whole of England and Wales – and in 1975 increased to 100 per cent. In Wales, within months, a special Derelict Land Unit was created by the Welsh Office, and this – absorbed ten years later by the Welsh Development Agency – transformed the whole situation in the Principality. The level of grant aid available was no greater than in England but the existence of a centralised unit, with its concentration of technical know-how, plus the decision by the Welsh Office not to claw back the after-value of a reclaimed site from the promoting local authority until redevelopment of the site had actually taken place, produced an explosion of activity. Over the following ten years the Welsh Office grant-aided around 280 projects, at a cost of £29 million, resulting in the reclamation of nearly 7,000 acres/over 2,800 ha.

In this changed climate, what had previously seemed impossible in the Lower Swansea Valley began to look as though after all it might be possible. In 1968 the City Council began to work towards an ambitious programme that would cover the whole five-mile stretch – 2,000 acres/over 800 ha – from Pontardawe to the city's docks. Much of the thinking had already been done. Some years earlier, as a joint initiative with the City and the Welsh Office, the University College of Swansea had put in hand a four-year fact-finding study of the problems of the area. At the end of this, by 1966, a whole range of technical studies had been completed, a comprehensive photographic record undertaken, and the Territorials called in to blow up and clear some of the rotting structures. Now the Council began to acquire the land. In 1964 it owned less than four acres; by the beginning of the eighties it had possession of nearly all and was negotiating for whatever was left. Land assembly on this scale during the seventies was, to say the least, very bold. 'The very marked achievements in [Swansea's] Enterprise Zone and Maritime Quarter,' the WDA's Director of Land Reclamation and Civil Engineering has said, 'will be a lasting tribute to their courage and foresight.'[1]

What the city now proposed was the transformation of this grisly landscape into a string of five distinct but linked parks: at the northern end a big Enterprise Zone (in fact, because plans were ready, the first and at 775 acres/314 ha the largest in Britain); in the middle a Leisure Park, a Riverside Park and a City Park; and, to the south of the city itself, a Maritime Quarter. The City's then energetic Director of Planning, Maurice Howell, saw the traditional process of formal plan-making as altogether too slow and restrictive. The Council resolved to base its programmes on informal 'Interim Planning Statements' – for all parts of the city, not just the Lower Swansea Valley – which would enable major proposals to begin immediately.

Over the following years, with government grant aid flowing more readily, seven million tons of waste were removed from the Valley, great areas of soil treated and grassed, hundreds of thousands of trees planted (the first living trees to be seen there for generations). The Enterprise Zone has brought development; centre-piece of the 240 acre/100 ha Leisure Park is the big athletics stadium, first phase of a Commonwealth-Games-standard sports complex; the damming of the River Tawe by a barrier at its mouth, to obviate a thirty-foot tidal rise and fall and thereby bring its mud-flat banks into use, is in hand; the Maritime Quarter, around the old South Dock, is a runaway success. Financial help has come from the Welsh Office, the WDA and the European Community, but the essential push in all this has come from the City Council itself – and it is worth noting that the decisions relating to the creation of the Maritime Quarter predate most of those for the numerous waterside developments now springing up in all parts of Britain.

The South Dock closed in 1969. The Borough Council acquired it and began to fill it in for a proposed inner relief road. The proposal was dropped and in 1974 the new (District) Council, created by the local government restructuring of that year, adopted a plan to unpick it and restore the dock as a marina and residential area. In 1977 an impressive Leisure Centre was opened hard by. In 1978 work began on removing the silt from the Dock. In 1981 work began on the first forty-eight homes. In 1982 the 'Yacht Haven' opened; by 1986 there were 365 berths available and today the number is 600. In the early eighties the big Quadrant Centre shopping complex was opened, pushing the city's shopping area further towards the Maritime Quarter. The Maritime and Industrial Museum was in being and growing, with several ships of interest at the quayside alongside. Between 1983 and 1989 half a dozen housing schemes, by the Council, commercial developers and housing associations, completely enclosed the South Dock marina with some 1,000 housing units for sale and rent. Some shops, a pub and a wine bar are included. A sizeable hotel has arisen between dock and sea. A splendid seaward esplanade has been constructed. Overall, between 1973 and 1990, net city expenditure on the Maritime Quarter was £16,634,900 (nearly £19.2 million, less nearly £2.6 million in grant aid from various sources), with some £2.6 million further public sector expenditure on housing association work. Private investment completed or under construction in 1990 amounted to over £29 million with development estimated at £30.5 million between 1990 and 1995.

The essential infrastructure (dock walls, paving, bridges, etc.) was well executed at the outset. What is impressive, now that the bulk of redevelopment is complete, is the interlock of the layout, more especially in the south-eastern corner where walkways, courtyards and integrated parking create a pleasant sense of shelter while still allowing glimpses through to the water on either side. On the seaward side, where the new promenade sweeps round the once forsaken foreshore, in the fullness of time to link the land east of the Tawe with Mumbles to the west, the houses remember the Regency terraces of so many seaside resorts. Those facing the marina bear echoes of dockside warehouses and structures. Both are maritime in character, but gain from these additional nuances. Further cohesion and character is given to the whole area by the Council's extensive programme of public sculpture. Some of this is

126

free-standing; more is in the form of hardwood or stone reliefs, designed by a Special Projects Team working with the architects and artists to be intrinsic elements of the buildings. All such features relate to historical, geographical, cultural and social links with the city.

Control over development generally has been effected by the Council through detailed briefs for each section, worked out with care to ensure variety of roof line, interesting pedestrian routes, proper parking provision and so on. These briefs, with deemed planning consent, are then, as it were, put out to auction, tenders being invited from developers. Details are approved as work progresses, and on, or near, completion, the Council grants the developer a lease (mostly of ninety-nine years). In the result, the Maritime Quarter has become the most desirable residential part of the city, and house prices have doubled and trebled over five or six years.

Swansea is one of those cities – we have noted Glasgow in Scotland, and shall see others in England – exemplifying how much can be achieved, if the will be there, by 'traditional' means; without, that is to say, the superimposition of additional machinery by Whitehall. It turns upon attitude. 'Local authorities must move from merely producing land-use plans and waiting for something to happen. They must move into several new functions – functions where they begin to understand the economic problems and potential of their area.' By the 1990s such a statement[2] has become a platitude. In 1982, when Maurice Howell made it at a Council of Europe conference in Swansea, Swansea was ahead of the game – and even government thinking at that time. For he went on to point out that a then current draft memorandum of the DoE specifically insisted that 'non-land-use matters, e.g. financial support, subsidies, etc., and matters arising from the non-planning functions and powers of the local Planning Authority . . . should not be included in statutory or local plans as policies or proposals'. 'It is incredible,' said Howell, 'that on the one hand authorities are being persuaded to take a dynamic business approach, while on the other hand they are being told to restrict their thinking to something which is . . . largely irrelevant on its own.' Well, as we have seen, other authorities – such as Liverpool – have come to the same conclusion, and, like the UDCs, now place more reliance on flexible and market-responsive development briefs than on cumbersome 'master' planning. But Swansea was one of the first to show the way.

At a conference in 1988 Trevor Osborne, Swansea's Director of

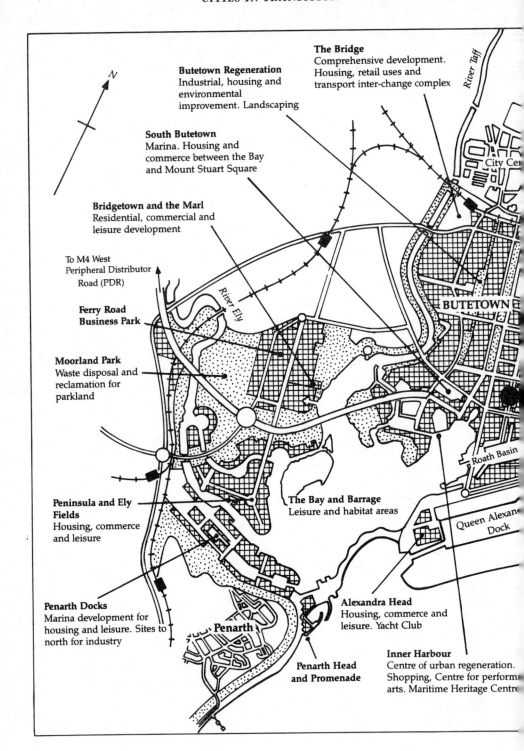

N

The Bridge
Comprehensive development.
Housing, retail uses and
transport inter-change complex

Butetown Regeneration
Industrial, housing and
environmental
improvement. Landscaping

River Taff

South Butetown
Marina. Housing and
commerce between the Bay
and Mount Stuart Square

City Ce

Bridgetown and the Marl
Residential, commercial and
leisure development

To M4 West
Peripheral Distributor
Road (PDR)

River Ely

BUTETOWN

**Ferry Road
Business Park**

Moorland Park
Waste disposal and
reclamation for
parkland

Roath Basin

**Peninsula and Ely
Fields**
Housing, commerce
and leisure

The Bay and Barrage
Leisure and habitat areas

Queen Alexan
Dock

Penarth Docks
Marina development for
housing and leisure. Sites to
north for industry

Penarth

Alexandra Head
Housing, commerce and
leisure. Yacht Club

Inner Harbour
Centre of urban regeneration.
Shopping, Centre for perform
arts. Maritime Heritage Centre

**Penarth Head
and Promenade**

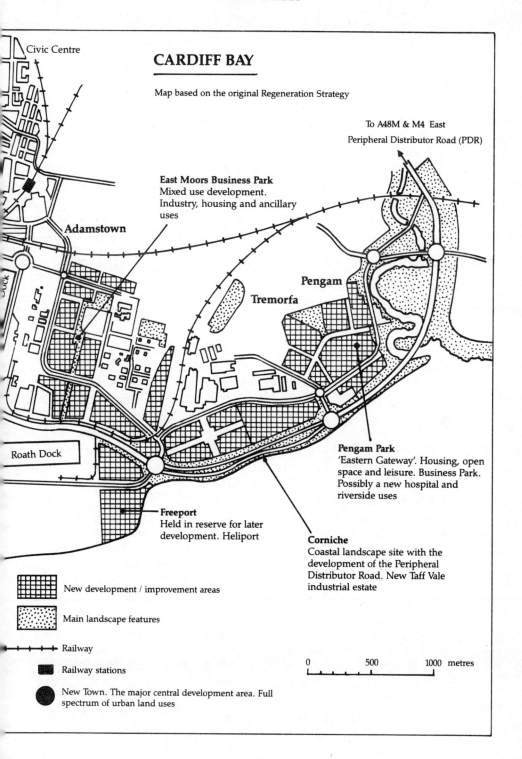

CARDIFF BAY

Map based on the original Regeneration Strategy

To A48M & M4 East
Peripheral Distributor Road (PDR)

East Moors Business Park
Mixed use development.
Industry, housing and ancillary
uses

Adamstown

Pengam

Tremorfa

Roath Dock

Pengam Park
'Eastern Gateway'. Housing, open
space and leisure. Business Park.
Possibly a new hospital and
riverside uses

Freeport
Held in reserve for later
development. Heliport

Corniche
Coastal landscape site with the
development of the Peripheral
Distributor Road. New Taff Vale
industrial estate

Civic Centre

New development / improvement areas

Main landscape features

Railway

Railway stations

0   500   1000 metres

New Town. The major central development area. Full
spectrum of urban land uses

Planning in succession to Howell, following someone from the Cardiff Bay Development Corporation, remarked: 'We're not *talking* about plans and strategies. We've *done* it.' Justifiable pride. However, the Corporation was at that stage still assembling staff and not even properly into its HQ offices. It is of interest as one of the 'second-generation' corporations, but set up slightly differently from its English equivalents; and its genesis is indicative of the kind of way in which the UDCs come into existence.

The strategy outlined at that 1988 conference was ambitious. It needed to be. The Corporation's designated area covers 2,700 acres/1,100 ha of South Cardiff – that part stretching south to the docks from the city centre, and east and west to embrace the wide stretch of coastline from the bluff of Penarth Head on one side to the River Rhymney and to the cheerless flatland of Pengam on the other – in all, about one sixth of the built-up city. Into the Bay proper two more rivers empty themselves – the Ely and the Taff – their mouths considerably complicating the shoreline which is anyway subject to the thirty-foot to forty-foot tidal rise and fall that affects the South Wales coast, and here leaves extensive areas of mud flat at low tide. Jutting out in the middle of the Bay are the great docks of yesteryear, largely but no means wholly closed now and deserted. There are no great warehouse complexes here, as in London or Liverpool or Bristol, but here and there a fine building remains in isolation – the Pierhead building for example – and Mount Stuart Square stands as a fairly complete monument to florid Victorian confidence. Astride the centre of the Square sits the Coal Exchange, abortively done over in the seventies to be the home of the intended Welsh Assembly and now being adapted to other uses. Some yards away, National Westminster Bank in the 1920s put up what is said to be their tallest building outside London. This was the grandest part of Bute Town. From here northwards to the city centre, on either side of the straight road driven through to his docks by the second Marquess of Bute, lay, until after World War II, 'Tiger Bay' – cosmopolitan, pretty squalid and raffish, sometimes though not often dangerous, typical of such port areas the world over. Tiger Bay has gone now. Demolition has left in its wake some sad council housing, wasteland, small industrial uses hanging on by their eyelashes and considerable areas of tipping. Sixteen thousand people live there, but in the middle eighties only 3,000 worked there.

The centre of the city not only has its castle and its grand Civic Centre; much has happened throughout in recent years. Queen Street is now the main artery of a sizeable traffic-free network (its arcades were always one of the pleasures of Cardiff). There are several new shopping complexes and new office blocks betoken a new commercial vitality. St David's Hall, the 1982 concert and conference hall, is a splendid addition to cultural life. Streets and buildings everywhere have been spruced up. South Cardiff, however, cut off from all this by the main railway line, has remained forlorn, forgotten by the rest of the city because after the closure in 1978 of the East Moors steelworks, which had once employed 9,000, there was no longer any reason for anyone to go there.

By the planners and politicians, of course, it was far from forgotten. In the City Council, the County, the Welsh Office, the Welsh Development Agency and elsewhere, there was a total consensus that South Cardiff had somehow to be brought back to life. Some fairly uncoordinated moves were in fact made. The WDA cleared the East Moors site and put up some advance factory units. The Welsh Land Authority assembled land for a housing development by Tarmac. South Glamorgan County Council showed its commitment by earmarking a site for its new County Hall. Work began on a marina village at Penarth Head. Better access was necessary, so the Welsh Office and the County started to plan – and build – a coastal road that would totally bypass the city centre. The thought began to be mooted that maybe a barrage across the narrow neck of water between Penarth Head and Alexandra Dock could transform the featureless mud flats of the Bay into something altogether more attractive. All very well, but who would pull it all together? The area was too big, and the stakes, it was beginning to be realised, too high for hit-and-miss initiatives.

In 1986 the then Secretary of State for Wales, Nicholas Edwards (now Lord Crickhowell), commissioned Messrs Jones Lang Wootton to study and report on the subject in a four-month 'fast track' exercise. They were surprised by the amount of material already existing (though no less by its uncoordinated nature). They looked at all the main regeneration programmes in comparable areas elsewhere. They consulted widely in Cardiff, seeking creative ideas and opportunities, and finished with a rip-roaring brain-storming weekend. In their two-volume report to the Secretary of State they concluded that the increase in land values stemming from the construction of a barrage would be somewhere between £145 and £195 million; that opportunities would thereby be created to bring to Cardiff a 'new pride, new wealth and a totally new image in the outside world' – but that all-party support would be needed for the necessary programmes, which would last twenty years or more. Their proposals for 'New Tiger Bay', as they tagged it, they saw as

... in the historic traditions of town planning as practised immediately post-war ... where ... the emphasis was more on creating the vision of the environment rather than on a mass of detailed figures and statistics usually relying on historic data. The fact that many of these schemes turned out to be disappointments had more to do with lack of quality in execution than in the vision.

The vision they offered was of 'a superb environment which will have few if any competitors in Great Britain'.

So far, so good. It would be worth having a go. But by what mechanism? A third report from the consultants, in November 1986, considered the organisational options. Among the criteria, they suggested, by which alternatives should be judged, were

- the need for a mechanism by which the Secretary of State could set the organisation's strategic goals;
- the ability to attract the best staff, and obtain the services of any other person or body to achieve the organisation's aims;
- the need to be close enough to the private sector to encourage its involvement in the area, yet capable of working with local authorities and public bodies;
- the organisation must have control over at least two of three factors (if not all three): land, planning and money. It must command direct ownership or compulsory purchase powers, to be in a position to make land available for development as and when necessary. It should have development control and plan-making powers. It should have the financial resources to ensure development of essential infrastructure, etc.

The report then went on to consider four possibilities:

- a consortium of land owners (but would their public responsibilities be compatible with their duties to their shareholders? A single organisation, with sole ownership of the land, might work, but there was no precedent for such a thing on this scale);
- a private-sector development company (subject to the same objections, and would lack planning powers);
- an Urban Development Corporation created by consensus (and with delegated powers. Again, there was no precedent – and what guarantee would there be of its stability and continuity?);
- an Urban Development Corporation created by government.

Next, the claims of the existing organisations were examined: the City Council, the County Council, the Welsh Land Authority, the Welsh Development Agency and the Welsh Office. Having then looked at some of the arguments *against* UDCs (an agency in *partnership* with the existing organisations may improve the general quality of public administration more than one which simply u.urps the powers of local authorities; a UDC may tend towards excessive secrecy; the imposition of a UDC may be resented by the local population), the report nonetheless came down in favour of a government-sponsored Development Corporation for South Cardiff. However, it suggested that, in the light of experience in London and Merseyside, it would be helpful to consider changes in the format for Cardiff, and recommended a period of local consultation to agree on *principles*.

Some gentlemanly posturing by the organisations most concerned took place over the next few months in relation to their respective roles, but, basically, a consensus existed. The creation of the Cardiff Bay Development Corporation was announced in April 1987 with the blessing of all. In the event its 'format' did differ slightly from the English model. On its Board sit two County Councillors, two from the City Councillors and one from the Vale of Glamorgan District Council – nearly half the total, and an augury for cooperation. Most importantly, the potential for friction between Corporation and planning authorities was reduced by allowing the latter to retain their planning powers – though the Corporation in effect has power of veto over development applications it considers inappropriate or of insufficient quality. In practice, matters are ironed out by constant liaison and regular meetings between officers; should agreement prove impossible (it has not yet happened) the matter must be referred to the Secretary of State for determination. Secondly, *no* land was vested in the Corporation. All land has to be negotiated, purchased and assembled openly from scratch – time-consuming, but reducing any sense of ruthless imposition by an official bureaucracy. Most basic of all, as we have seen, agreement already existed on the three infrastructure essentials: the need for the barrage; for a peripheral distributor road (the outer lengths of which, indeed, had already been constructed); and the need to link the area strongly with the main city centre a mile to the north.

A convergence of views then – but if that 'superb environment with few if any competitors in Great Britain' was to be achieved, much more intensive thought had to be given to those 2,700 acres as a whole. The new Corporation quickly decided that 'regeneration should be undertaken against a far-sighted strategy, prepared after much research, consultation and thought, rather than solely against the imperative of the market'. For reasons

133

previously made clear the job was put out to consultants – in this case Llewellyn-Davies Planning. Their suggested 'Regeneration Strategy', an impressively full study, replete with maps, diagrams, photographs, and perspective drawings, all in full colour, was presented exactly a year after the announcement that the Corporation was to be set up – another 'fast-track' exercise. This was in no sense a 'master plan'; it rather offered a vision: a flexible framework within which to develop and refine more detailed briefs for different sectors of the designated area. The new fundamentals were for a 'new town' – on the scale of Edinburgh New Town – through which would pass the axial avenue to the city centre; for the undergrounding of the peripheral distributor road (PDR), as it passes through the dockland area, so as to avoid severing that all-important axial link to the city centre; an indication of the possible major uses which might be envisaged around the Bay and the Inner Harbour (the latter in fact an almost exactly equivalent area to Baltimore's much-acclaimed, and reclaimed, Inner Harbor); an eastern 'gateway' of mixed development on the Rhymney Estuary; and a strong, coherent urban design concept to bring all elements into a cohesive whole.

Ideas and words take on a life of their own. 'Superb environment,' said the Jones Lang Wootton report. The words reappear as the first of the objectives laid down for the Corporation by the Secretary of State (followed by an injunction to 'achieve the highest standards of design and quality in all types of investment'). They reappear – sometimes with the stakes raised to 'superlative environment' – in almost every piece of paper produced by the Corporation, and represent a stronger formal commitment to environmental quality than that of any of the other UDCs. The realisation of the commitment is another matter. As London and Merseyside discovered in their first few years, when you are responsible for thousands of acres of run-down land which no one is interested in, the pressures to allow any sort of development at all, whatever the quality, are very great. In the case of Cardiff Bay the problem is compounded by the scale of the infrastructure work envisaged. Bringing the PDR across the waters of the Bay, and tunnelling it underground for an important stretch, is itself a considerable project; the construction of the barrage, when finally approved, no less an engineering undertaking. Neither can be completed quickly, but until completion dates are firm, developers cannot be expected to stampede into Cardiff Bay.

So what steps has the Corporation taken in the direction of quality? The tone has to be set at the top. On the Board, other than those already mentioned, are Honor Chapman, main author of the Jones Lang Wootton reports of 1986, and an architect, Professor Richa.d Silverman of the University of Wales, in succession to Sir Alex Gordon, a distinguished Past President of the RIBA. Chairman is Geoffrey Inkin, already Chairman of the Welsh Land Authority; his Chief Executive is Barry Lane. Both the latter are military men (some amusement was caused by the fact that Lane retired with the rank of Major-General, but Inkin – who retired much younger – had only reached Lt.-Colonel. After the interviews for Chief Executive, a Welsh Office man is quoted as saying: 'You've got a good chap, but I think there'll be some problem in knowing which is which'). Both believe in the concept of planning. As someone put it to me: 'It's only natural, the Army *have* to plan.'

One of the Board's first moves was to appoint a 'Design and Architecture Review Panel', on a part-time basis, to advise on planning applications and other design matters. Among those on the Panel (several of them past and present members of the Royal Fine Art Commission) are, or have been, Paul Koralek, John Lyall, Richard Rogers and Sir Peter Shepheard (architects, Sir Peter being not only a Past President of the RIBA but also of the Landscape Institute); Audrey Lees (planner); David Carter (industrial designer); John George (the Building Centre); and two respected environmental writers, Tony Aldous and Judy Hillman (who had worked on one of the JLW reports). The Panel is linked to the Board through its Chairman, first Sir Alex and now Professor Silverman. This was the first initiative of its kind among the UDCs; it has since been emulated elsewhere, as in London's Docklands.

Following acceptance by the Board of the Regeneration Strategy, formulation of more detailed area-planning briefs for nine individual sectors of the designated area was put in hand. These refine the infrastructure needs, land-assembly priorities, design of the public realm, programming and phasing. Two of these were entrusted to Llewellyn-Davies Planning, who had undertaken the main Strategy; two were handled by the City Planning Department; the crucial Inner Harbour area went to Benjamin Thompson & Associates of Boston, responsible for the Rouse Company's developments there of Quincy Market, of Harborplace in Baltimore and of South Street Seaport in New York, amongst others. All these have shown imaginative flair but Thompson's grasp of realities was never less than firm. In the initial planning of Quincy Market, it will be recalled by some, he told the Boston Redevelopment Authority: 'You've got to *get* people there. You need at least fifteen to twenty eating places for a start.' To the BRA that seemed a bit over the top. 'One, perhaps,' they said, 'or two?' So strongly did Thompson hold his view that, in the event, he financed four himself. (Fifteen years later, of course, the eating places probably outnumber the retail outlets.) For Cardiff's Inner Harbour he started with a model and colour-coded bricks for different uses. Only after much moving around of the bricks ('we need something bigger there', 'why not put the opera house here?') and a good deal of Polaroid photography, were concepts formalised into an outline framework. The 'plans' were still notional, the uses market-responsible, but they provided the sharpened context within which development briefs for particular sites could be established. By 1990 things had moved on. Benjamin Thompson & Associates, now working to the agreed developers, Grosvenor Waterside (a subsidiary of Associated British Ports) had produced, with the Cardiff architects Holder Mathias & Alcock, more detailed proposals for 160 acres/65 ha in the Roath Basin area (bounding the north-east of the Inner Harbour), and, working to Tarmac, for the area immediately north of that. Public debate centred on the siting of the hoped-for Welsh National Opera House.* Should it stand proud, rather like Sydney Opera House, at the water's edge as a marker and a symbol, or should it be more closely integrated into the bustle of the surrounding area in a less 'elitist' way? How the dilemma is resolved will be important for the whole 'feel' of the Inner Harbour.

On the ground, land assembly and the relocation of small businesses progresses. Small-scale landscape improvements have been effected. The new County Hall (with 1,000 staff) is built and in use. Housing around two sides of East Bute Dock is well advanced, and a warehouse block recycled into a new hotel. The Penarth Head marina village is complete and proposals for a much bigger development adjoining it are well advanced. Much cleaning up and improvement has taken place in and around Mount Stuart Square. A Taff Community Park of 11 acres/4.5 ha has been agreed, and a nature reserve on the Taff Saltings. Studies have been completed on the heavily polluted Ferry Road peninsula, where much waste needs to be removed and backfilling undertaken. A comprehensive strategy for public art has been commissioned and adopted.† Land values are rising . . .

Overshadowing all else has been the question of the Barrage. From the outset it had been clear that ecological and wildlife objections were likely to be raised against it. So it proved. In

* A substantial injection of cash by the Welsh Office and the Arts Council in 1991 restored WNO'S faltering finances.
† See page 242.

distant parts of the world, I found, even in 1988, the one thing that was known about plans for Cardiff Bay was that they were going to destroy a feeding ground for migrating waders.

First, the nature of the Barrage itself. It is planned as a curving structure, 1,300 yds./1,200 m. long, and 25 m. wide at its crest, between Penarth Head and Queen Alexandra Dock. Armoured on the outer side to resist the elements, it will have a 'softer' edge on the inner to provide gentle visual containment for the new lake. Along the crest will run a promenade and a service road; there will be no upstanding structures and no through traffic. The Barrage will impound some 500 acres/200 ha of freshwater and create a waterfront of 7.5 miles/12 km.; the water level will be equivalent to an average high tide. Ancillary works include sluices, the modification of fourteen sewer and storm-water outfalls, three sea locks and a harbour of refuge on the seaward side, and a fish pass. The cost of the structure itself is currently estimated at £89 million; the total, with all associated works, at £125.5 million (1989 prices). Because the Barrage will affect existing navigation rights, it was necessary to promote an enabling Parliamentary Bill, the passage of which became increasingly sluggish.

Opposition centred upon several issues. The docks company, Associated British Ports, wondered about the effects of the Barrage upon their operations. Local people were worried about the effect of the raised water level upon their houses (with stories of possible flooding doing the rounds). There were queries about the purity of the water to be impounded. Naturalists, headed by the Nature Conservancy Council and the Royal Society for the Protection of Birds, expressed total opposition to the loss of the mud flats used by migratory wading birds.

The first three concerns could be dealt with. Flooding could be discounted. Indeed, the Barrage would obviate the existing threat posed by spring and storm-surge tides from the sea. Where there could be any danger of increased basement damp from a raised water table, the Corporation promised remedial works directly and without formal claim, with safeguards for the following twenty years. The purity of the impounded water, according to expert advice, posed no serious problem, though the Corporation pointed out that this turned, to a considerable extent, upon the standards set by the National River Authority and the water company, Welsh Water, for the Taff and the Ely. Conscious of the need for single, coordinated management of the total water environment proposed – and especially to safeguard standards after the Corporation has ceased to exist – the Corporation have created a special company – BAVCO – for this purpose. Directors include representatives of the local authorities; on the dissolution of the Corporation, its controlling interest will pass to a successor local authority or statutory undertaker.

There remained the ecological objectors. For generations a gentle melancholy has attached to the estuarial flats of Cardiff Bay. The silence, the wide skies, the absence of human intrusion, the gulls overhead and the hopping waders exploring the mud – these offer for some a refreshment to the spirit that cannot possibly survive the introduction of – in their view – yuppie waterside housing and quayside pubs, motorboats and waterskiing. But there was more to it than that. An important matter of principle was at stake.

Much of the land around the Bay has been man-made since 1800. Dredging ceased in 1978, with the closure of the inner docks, since when siltation has increased rapidly. Without dredging, and without the Barrage, the Bay would eventually fill in. The mud flats created by this process attract over-wintering wading birds – mostly dunlin, redshank and curlew – in numbers sufficient to have led to the area's designation as a Site of Special Scientific Interest in 1980. A much larger SSSI, of 39,000 acres/15,800 ha, has more recently been designated in the Severn Estuary. The Nature Conservancy Council view the two as a potential Special Protection Area under the European Community Directive of 1979, and, under the Ramsar Convention, a possible 'Wetland of International Importance'. It should perhaps be noted that Cardiff Bay is but one of nearly 4,850 SSSIs registered in Britain by the NCC, covering between them over 5,500 square miles/1,430,000 ha, in addition to 214 National Nature Reserves.

In the scales, therefore, were two disparate sets of values. Conservationists can point to the steady erosion of natural habitats as Britain becomes more and more built up, and the need to protect every scrap of the natural ecosystems still remaining to us. To be weighed against this were the building of 6,000 homes, 3 to 4 million sq. ft./300,000–400,000 sq. m. of commercial development, the creation of 30,000 new jobs, new leisure opportunities and a new role for the City of Cardiff. The Welsh Office Circular of 1987 on Nature Conservation advises that planning permission for development in any Special Protection Area under the EC Directive should only be granted if the disturbance to migratory birds or damage to habitats will not be significant in terms of the survival and reproduction of the species, or if any such disturbance or damage is outweighed by economic or recreational requirements. The Cardiff Bay Development Corporation has been advised that the number of birds disturbed by the Barrage will in no way reach levels to threaten their survival or reproduction. It proposes, by way of amelioration, the creation of a new inland lagoon of some 55 acres/23 ha about four miles to the north-east, which, it is believed, will attract at least a proportion of the birds 'displaced'. And it looks to the creation of a new habitat for wildlife in the new landscape that will be created in the wake of the Barrage.

In the spring of 1991, having wended its way through select committees of both Houses, the Barrage Bill was filibustered to a halt after thirteen hours of debate in the Commons – whereupon the Welsh Office accepted parentage and announced its intention to introduce a government Bill to the same end. Since the construction period is likely to be four years, the Barrage is now unlikely to be opened before the tenth birthday of the corporation and a dozen years or more after it was was first mooted.

I have dealt with these first years of the Cardiff Bay Development Corporation at some length because it seems to me that they may have lessons for our planning system generally in the future. The Corporation has not been imposed upon the local authorities but in all important respects – as with the Scottish and Welsh Development Authorities – works alongside them. The Corporation is formally committed to the very highest environmental standards. It has based its programme on the work of an army of consultants – geotechnic engineers, economists, ornithologists, hydrology experts (from Holland), historians, university research teams, and many others. It could be said to have investigated its territory, and the impact of its proposals, to an almost unprecedented degree. Finally, it has gone further to meet its moral obligations than is legally required – offering, for example, those in any way affected by its proposals more generous compensation than the minimum required. In a period of intensive change, these seem important points.

It must have been a man from the Valleys who coined the phrase: 'Cardiff is, because the Rhondda was.' Cardiff prospered because it was the main gateway through which the mineral wealth of the Valleys passed to the rest of the world. Now one hears the hope expressed that maybe a freshly rejuvenated Cardiff will be able to repay some of its historical debt to the Valleys, and that a new prosperity will trickle *up* to the communities to the north. This belittles what has already been happening. The extent of the changes wrought in these communities over recent years can only be appreciated by those who knew them in their grimy past. Truly the Valleys have shown, in the words of the Director of the Welsh CBI, 'an astonishing will to live'.[3] But the redevelopments, the rescue operations, the clean-ups, have been somewhat piecemeal – which is not surprising since the South Wales valleys are covered by no fewer than twenty-one different councils (sixteen Districts and five Counties), each its own master and used to doing its own thing.

It was to pull all the effort together in one coherent package that the Welsh Office launched its 'Valleys Initiative' (to become the Valleys Programme). The framework was announced by the Secretary of State, Peter Walker, in 1988. 'It is a very considerable programme,' he wrote, 'that will create a far greater diversity of opportunity than has existed throughout this century. A programme to eradicate the scars left by the industrial past and replace them with elegance and beauty, new places to work and better homes in which to live.' A reduction of 25,000 to 30,000 in the ranks of the unemployed; 10,000 new homes and 32,000 improved; 2,500 acres/over 1,000 ha of dereliction cleared; new and enhanced programmes in education and training, health and social services, music, the arts and recreation – these were some of the broad objectives at which the fifty or so 'firm actions' listed were to be directed over the following three years (the period has in fact been extended, and Peter Walker's successor, David Hunt, has announced his own four-year £14 million campaign to improve the environment in Wales). Within this framework all the major agencies – the Land Authority, the Welsh Development Agency, Tai Cymru/Housing for Wales, the Wales Tourist Board, the Training Commission, the Enterprise Agencies, the Voluntary Sector and not least of course, the local authorities – had important roles to play. 'The building blocks of a new future,' stated an explanatory brochure from the Welsh Office, 'are already in place.' The Valleys programme aims to add a new dynamism to a process already in train.

Until perhaps ten or fifteen years ago, such an initiative would have been impossible. The settlements straggling up and down each cleft in the hills had each its own history, its own characteristics, its own problems. Towns and villages in the next valley might as well have been on the moon. Improved communications have transformed all this. 'We regard the area covered by the Valleys Programme,' a WDA man told me, 'as one conurbation with a population of 700,000.'

If regeneration was already in train, Nicholas Edwards, the respected Secretary of State from 1979 to 1987 had done much to bring it about. He strengthened the machinery, spoke widely about the Valleys' problems, directed people's thoughts towards what had to be done. His successor Peter Walker, as it was put to

140

me, on his arrival thought, This is something I can make my mark with, picked it up, and with his strong political flair added a potent PR element which gave identity to the whole exercise.

The Valleys have for generations presented a confused visual image. The intricacy of the terrain compounded the disorder of the Industrial Revolution. There is little flat land on which to build. Shafts were sunk wherever access to the seams below demanded; the spoil spilled over in great conical or ridged tips which redrew the skyline and overshadowed the villages at their foot, or else flowed along the valley bottoms like monstrous streams of black lava. Reclamation here means not just the re-greening of the Valleys but the creation of sites on which job-providing development can take place. Reclamation has had to be the essential precursor to the realisation of anything and everything else.

Following the 1966 Aberfan disaster, as already noted, the Welsh Office set up a Derelict Land Unit, which was subsumed a decade later by the WDA. The WDA built the work into a rolling programme, shaped around their maximum technical capacity for five or so years ahead, major additions to the programme being fed in every two years. The Agency is empowered to give 100 per cent grant aid to projects within the public sector, 80 per cent to private reclamation, but submissions for assistance – from all parts of the Principality, not just from the Valleys region – considerably outweigh its capacity to respond. Its criteria in the selection of proposals, in order of priority, are: removal of hazards, development potential, suitability for formal recreation, and agricultural, afforestation and general amenity uses. Additionally it seeks to concentrate effort to maximum effect in support of other parallel initiatives. In practice, of course, these objectives are seldom wholly distinct but overlap. By the late eighties, over twenty years, the Welsh Office and the WDA had between them cleared 16,000 acres/nearly 6,500 ha. The WDA's overall reclamation budget for 1989/90 was £25 million, the rate of clearance of the order of 1,500 acres/610 ha a year. The programme for the Valleys, however, has been significantly stepped up as part of the Valleys Initiative. Expenditure was increased from £8 million to £12.5 million in 1988/89, with a further £30 million earmarked for the following two years. Over the three years of the Valleys Programme 2,500 acres/over 1,000 ha were scheduled for clearance. In the Valleys context this is substantial, for the physical effort involved is great. A site of 700 acres/280 ha at East Merthyr, near the Heads of the Valleys road, on which work is beginning, is likely to take seven to ten years to complete. What is heartwarming is that those close to the problem in the Valleys are now beginning to talk of the end of the programme being in sight – of the day when all essential reclamation of derelict land in South Wales will in fact have been achieved.

What goes on to this 'new' land? Industry first and foremost, housing, schools and playing fields, even tourist attractions ... The WDA is the largest industrial landlord in Wales, with a portfolio of about sixty sites totalling over 9 million sq. ft./836,000 sq. m. in the Valleys alone. Over half the Agency's 1989 budget of £52 million for property development went into the Valleys and it is aiming at providing an extra 800,000 sq. ft./74,310 sq. m. in the area over the following two years. It provides advance factories, ready to move into; will build to a company's own specifications, either for rent or purchase; it will provide land for companies wishing to build their own premises. Where the terrain permits it creates industrial estates, among them Rassau (bare mountainside in 1977, and recently enlarged by a second phase), Hirwaun, Llantrisant and the Rising Sun Estate (so named even before the Japanese came). Treforest, dating from the 1930s, has been updated and extended (160 tenants, 140 investment clients), and now boasts, among other facilities, a quality enterprise and design centre. Companies are wooed by every conceivable means. Detailed surveys are commissioned, and published, of firms' industrial relations and assessment of their workforces. A fat *Facts for Industry*, setting out all the basic information a company locating in Wales could wish for – history and culture, political administration, incentives, taxation, labour relations, company formation, work permits, environmental and pollution controls, customs and excise, patents, and much else – seemed to me a model of its kind.

Housing problems in the Valleys centre, not upon absolute shortages, for overall the population is still declining, but upon poor condition and the fact that accommodation is often today in the wrong place. Improvement has therefore figured as largely in housing programmes as new construction. 'Enveloping'* and 'Block Improvement Schemes' have given a new lease of life to older terraces – 2,600 homes in 1988/89. The nine housing associations in the Valleys can claim 5,000 new or improved homes in seventy Valley communities between 1980 and 1988, and have raised their annual target from 1,000 in 1987/88 to 1,500 in each of the Programme years. Increasingly now private developers are moving in – Barratt, for instance, have built on part of 280 acres/113 ha of reclaimed land in Clydach Vale which

* For an explanation of the term, see page 180.

142

looks across a new man-made lake, fed by a falling stream. Indicative of the changing nature of the Valleys and the growing demand for 'executive'-type property is the fact that these houses, snapped up in 1987 for £45,000 to £50,000, are now going for £75,000 to £85,000.

Hand in hand with all this goes a wide range of other initiatives. In nine designated 'Action Areas' town centres are beginning to be given a bit of a face-lift: streets are being pedestrianised, shopfronts improved, workshop training in marketing offered to shopkeepers. Afforestation is here and there reclothing the hills with the woods that covered them long ago but were cut down for pit props or eaten by the ubiquitous and insatiable Valleys sheep. The 1983 closure of the Lewis Merthyr and Ty Mawr collieries led to moves by the local community, by the County, the two Borough Councils, the WDA and the Wales Tourist Board to create the Rhondda Heritage Park – opened summer 1991 as the major, haunting reminder for future generations of what coal meant to South Wales for the best part of two centuries.

Dwarfing all else at the Heads of the Valleys, is the preparatory work for the 1992 Garden Festival at Ebbw Vale. The site is a mile and a half long, 240 acres/97 ha in extent, running along a valley bottom between steeply rising hillsides. This will differ from its predecessors in offering magnificent views downwards from above, as well as upwards from the valley. Here stood one of the big steelworks and a number of mines. Eleven pit shafts have had to be capped, 1.5 million cubic metres of slag and shale shifted (one sixty-foot mountain of slag will be turned into a feature). A major river culvert, sixty feet down, has had to be strengthened; railway sidings moved; and several companies moved out and relocated. Already drifts of alder and ash, poplar, maple, larch and willow are well established on the bare, steep slopes of the hills – hundreds of thousands of them, with hundreds of thousands more of shrubs and bedding plants. A ski lift is proposed on one hillside. Opposite, an existing farm prepares for its five-month life as a 'demonstration' farm. To the south there are plans for a new bypass – 'the road through Cwm is diabolical and we'll never get the people in otherwise'. They are reckoning on an attendance of two million, and though the local community were probably sceptical in the early stages, if the Festival brings the estimated £56 million into the economy of Ebbw Vale, they will doubtless come to love it – and perhaps even its proposed after-uses of housing, commerce and parkland.

I have concentrated upon the role of the WDA because it seems to me the most important single agency at work in the Valleys. At

143

the same time this is less than fair to all those others labouring, in their diverse ways, to similar ends. It omits the twenty-one local authorities. It omits the private sector. It omits those magical individuals who emerge from the shadows to light beacons for whole communities. Let Blaenau Gwent stand as one example. Factories, says Peter Law the Mayor, tend to be capital intensive. 'It takes a lot of little factories to make up for the loss of a steelworks or coalmine, which is labour intensive.' Fifteen years ago the [Labour] Council took a deliberate decision that everything it did should be directed towards job creation. It has stuck to that policy steadfastly ever since. 'I hate to think what the place would have been like if the Council had taken a different line,' says Allen Williams, until recently the WDA Valleys Director. 'They don't really care what they do so long as it's bringing jobs.' Or take Bill Morgan, one-time miner, economics graduate and founder of the St John's Industries self-help training schemes through which more than 10,000 young people have passed. As the Revd William Badham Morgan he was for eleven years leader of the Methyr Council. 'He gets himself disliked,' I was told. 'He says what he thinks. Makes me laugh sometimes to see him in the pulpit, when I think of what he was saying an hour ago. But when you've created four hundred jobs, probably more, then you've got to be a hero.'

Among the Valley authorities generally a certain scepticism attaches to the Valleys Programme. The Counties had long argued for a less *ad hoc* approach to South Wales's problems by the Welsh Office but, while welcoming any additional assistance, they point out that funding within the Valleys Programme forms only a small part of total local authority expenditure. Indeed, it has been suggested that, since the official figures show no significant increase in funding for Wales above the usual government formula, and make no mention of the Valleys Programme, it can be presumed that there are in fact no special moneys for the Valleys. Councils' every aspiration is tempered by the availability of resources – and always the relationship between capital-account and current-account spending. The Rhondda Heritage Park attracted £2 million in government grant, but its maintenance and revenue funding becomes a problem for the local councils. Mid Glamorgan County is responsible for ninety-nine pre-1903 primary schools. To replace these would cost about £1 million each, but the 1989/90 capital programme is sufficient only to tackle two, leading to an ever-increasing maintenance burden, so that the current account – of about £9 million – can do little more than keep the rain out and allow some warmth. The County's Land

144

Reclamation Unit, a thirty-strong team of engineers, has as many schemes approved for clearance as it has achieved in the last eighteen years – but is hampered by lack of resources because the 100 per cent grant available for the physical work does not cover all the on-costs of administration and staff (the solicitors, planners, surveyors, engineers). 'You can't *spend* money,' says J. R. Lewis, Assistant Planning Officer and Head of the Economic Policy and Research Unit,[4] 'without the people to spend it. Local authorities haven't the funds to make available the necessary staff resources.' He extends the argument to the wider field. 'Current private-sector interest does not reduce the need for public resources. On the contrary more resources are needed to reap the true benefits of the interest, to achieve an economy that will be more self-sustaining.'

Regeneration in the Valleys, then, is a patchy process, based on incremental improvements, many quite small-scale, scattered over a big area. Great differences still exist between the communities. Of the sixteen District Councils only eight are designated Programme areas. Not all the Valleys are coming up at the same speed. The Cynon Valley, for example, remains one of the most deprived. Although its potential for development is great (it is broader than many and offers flatter land on which to build), depopulation from here, with the Merthyr and Rhondda Valleys, is the highest in the UK. The Rhymney Valley, too, remains hard hit, save at its southern end. Overall, the drop in unemployment figures compares badly with other parts of the country. Between 1987 and 1989 unemployment dropped by 30 per cent in the South East of England; by 18.9 per cent in Britain as a whole; by 14.3 per cent in Wales; by 10.7 per cent in Mid Glamorgan. District Councils estimate the necessary repair bill on their housing to be of the order of £300 million and have made clear their belief that the Valleys Programme does not really address the housing issue. In all parts of the Valleys, landscape and townscape detailing and quality are variable to say the least. Development is utilitarian, rather than uplifting. Sometimes authorities and agencies find themselves pulling in different directions.

The Programme is a matter of opportunist planning rather than integrated 'master' planning. There are those who deride it as a skilful piece of public relations – useful for image building to encourage inwards investment, but not much else; a repackaging of previous policies rather than a new vision. But, as we have seen in London and Liverpool and Glasgow, and shall see again elsewhere, that in itself is no negligible thing. Peter Walker was wont to claim that Wales's industrial recovery has dramatically outstripped that of the rest of Britain. Certainly at the last count – to take but one example – Japanese companies alone in Wales employed nearly ten thousand people. That did not happen by chance.

One cannot but be aware, both in Scotland and in Wales, of a subtly different climate of opinion from that to be found in the English regions. One senses a greater unity of purpose, in part tribal, springing from a shared sense of identity and a 'We'll show them' attitude; but in part also from the greater physical proximity of everyone concerned, with the easier communication and relationships which that makes possible. It is interesting to note that one of the reasons given by Sony, for example, for locating in the Valleys is that 'It is possible to have access to top government officials, both in business and socially, on an almost day-to-day basis. Good relations can be built up very easily.'[5] In England the Secretary of State for the Environment, or the Secretary for Trade and Industry, is likely, during his year or two in office, to visit Salford Quays, or Dean Clough in Halifax, or the Gateshead MetroCentre, but he remains a remote presence compared with his colleagues in the Scottish and Welsh Offices. 'I have personally monitored progress,' said Peter Walker when he was Secretary of State, 'on every item in the Valleys Programme, and I intend to publish regular statements on that progress.' No one doubted that he meant it.

When Walker was 'banished' (as the press had it) to Wales, it was likened to a refusnik being packed off to Siberia. Wits recalled Sir Thomas More's line in Robert Bolt's play *A Man For All Seasons*: 'A man might sell his soul in return for the world, but for Wales . . .' But when in 1990 he resigned his office the President of Plaid Cymru[6] called him 'the most effective Secretary of State Wales has ever had'. Walker subscribes to the 'one nation' creed of Disraeli Toryism. The hardships of the 1930s, it is said, are as real to him as they were to Macmillan. 'Social justice' are words which come easily to his lips. He is interventionist by temperament; Wales provided him with a test-bed on which to try out his theories in relative freedom. His predecessor set up the machinery, and oiled it, and trained people to use it, but Walker revelled in revving it up. He marketed Wales as no one else had done. 'I could not do this,' he told the Tory Reform Group, 'without government intervention.' 'I think that this policy,' he said on Channel 4 in 1989, 'must be applied to all the bad regions of the United Kingdom.' No English region has a voice in Cabinet like that.

8

THE NORTH EAST

Tyne and Wear – Teesside

AFTER LONDON and Merseyside came four 'second-generation' Development Corporations in England: Tyne and Wear, Teesside, Trafford Park and the Black Country. These differed considerably in their nature, not only from the first Corporations but among themselves. Three are very big, the two in the North East alone accounting, between them, for over 45 per cent of all the territories covered by all ten English UDCs. Teesside's area covers about 11,260 acres/4,560 ha; Tyne and Wear's embraces riverside corridors totalling some 27 miles/43 km. in length. They are here considered together.

The North East has been likened to a kind of English peninsula, thrusting north to the Cheviots and Scotland, bounded on one side by the Pennines and on the other by the sea. Northumberland is open, bleak, and was brought to cultivation, in historical terms, but recently. In County Durham mining, iron and steel, heavy engineering and, more recently, the very big-scale manufacture of chemicals and associated products, have overlaid much of the countryside (though pretty little villages, like those on the Raby estates, and much else remain). The rivers and their estuaries were for long marked by all the paraphernalia of massive shipbuilding and port facilities. Three big rivers run from the Pennines to the sea – the Tyne (into which flows the Derwent), the Wear and the Tees. In its upper reaches the Tyne turns sharply southwards until it almost touches the springs of the Wear. It is in the area thus enclosed that the industrial North East is to be found – and its inner-city problems.

Oversimplification has to be avoided. The terrain south of

147

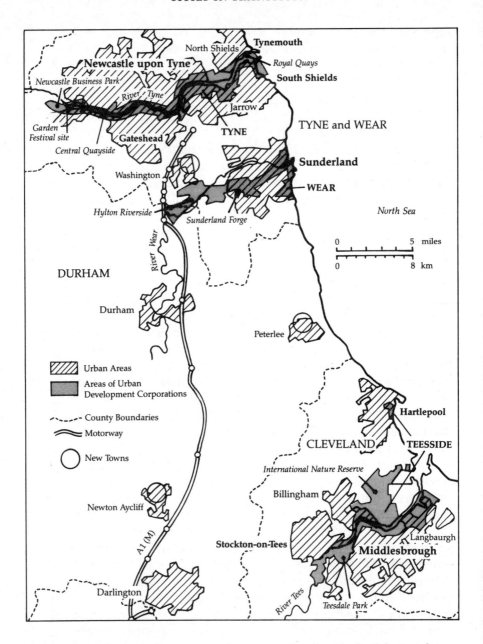

Hadrian's Wall embraces attractive moorland, wonderful stretches
of coastline and, among its monuments, what is for many the
finest cathedral in England. But it includes, too, great sprawls
of industry which developed, and coalesced, unplanned, un-
structured, into what are now continuously depressing vistas of
decay. So also with the towns and cities: the temptation to

generalise has to be resisted. Newcastle has always been robust, can still boast many fine buildings, shows real nobility in parts and is capable of springing numerous vernacular surprises. It shares with Gateshead that succession of five bridges which, once seen, is impossible to forget. Gateshead, across the Tyne, is by comparison a nondescript mess (even a couple of hundred years ago it was, for Dr Johnson, no more than 'a dirty lane leading to Newcastle') though tribute must be paid to its energetic public art programme. North Shields is more or less derelict; South Shields, which used to handle the iron ore from Consett, attempts a show of seaside gaiety with chips kiosks and funfair razzmatazz – its main asset the mile-long swathe of turf along the coastal bluff which faces the white rollers sweeping in from the North Sea. Sunderland is really three towns – the original settlement ('sundered' from monastic lands and now the focus of 'inner-city' decay); the present commercial centre to the west; and Monkwearmouth on the north side of the river. Tynemouth has splendid sands. Stockton is famous for the width of its High Street. There are two New Towns: Washington and Peterlee ... Great variety then. Nonetheless, collectively, all these places, with Hartlepool and Middlesbrough and Langbaurgh and the rest, for long conjured up for those in the South little more than an image of cloth caps and whippets.

Decline occurred over a long period. It was the 1933 closure of the Palmers Shipbuilding Company yards that caused Jarrow – 'the town that was murdered'* – to set off on its march to London to draw attention to its plight. Already by 1956 Japan had supplanted Britain as the world's major shipbuilding country. In Hartlepool the last yards closed down in 1962 (when Lord Hailsham, then Mr Quentin Hogg, became for a short time 'Minister for the North East'). At intervals support operations were attempted. In 1936 the Team Valley Trading Estate was opened in Gateshead. After the war the two New Towns were created. Between 1960 and 1974 T. Dan Smith campaigned forcefully to re-establish the importance of, first Newcastle, then the whole region. During the five years of the Wilson administration, 20 per cent of all industrial investment in the UK went to Teesside. This produced a short-lived boom in growth, but it was to little avail. The undertow of world trends was inexorable. Within a year or two the cuts and the closures were renewed. From time to time

---

* The phrase was 'red-headed Ellen's' – Ellen Wilkinson, Jarrow's MP, who marched with her constituents.

yards changed hands, flickered briefly to life again, even through the eighties, but the harsh reality was that, as far as big-scale shipbuilding was concerned, Tyneside and Teesside had slipped, with Clydebank and the rest, into the maritime history books. British Steel remained; ICI's massive installations, silvery by day, twinkling by night, still employed many thousands; the ports continued in operation (ICI bring in 1,000 ships a year). None of these remained unaffected, however, by the whirlwind of the early eighties. Unemployment soared. There was anger and frustration – how could it have been otherwise? – but in general attitudes were determined and pragmatic rather than bloody-minded and obstructive. The Japanese, headed by Nissan, have been welcomed, and have pumped in something like £1.3 billion. And when the two Development Corporations came into being they seem quickly to have established a good understanding with the local authorities concerned.

It is inevitable that there should be common threads running through the strategies of both Corporations for their main areas share rather comparable backgrounds. There are industrial and trading estates (a number of them established well before the Corporations came into existence); Enterprise Zones with their fiscal advantages and relaxed planning controls (two in Teesside and the most recent – and probably the last of its kind – in Tyne and Wear); pushes to exploit the experience gained in the region's offshore industries (200 companies or so, employing some 20,000 are engaged in North Sea oil and gas); and – yes – marinas. Work has started on the 300 houses of 'Warrior Quay' in Hartlepool's South Dock, the first phase of a £150 million scheme (boosted by a massive £51 million government grant) which promises 'a marina and much more'. On Tyneside the £200 million 'Royal Quays' development, around the old Albert Edward Dock between North Shields and Wallsend, promises, in addition to its marina, 1,500 new homes and an expectation of up to 2,500 jobs. 'We are *not* a plan-led organisation,' the Tyne and Wear Corporation stated at the outset. 'Our job is to respond to the needs of the marketplace – locally, nationally, internationally – within broad guidelines.' Teesside would probably not disagree. Nonetheless, concepts have to be given shape before they can be floated in the marketplace; priorities in phasing and financing have to be established. In practice the strategies of the two Corporations, as they have evolved, show the variations to be expected from differing terrains and differing teams.

Tyne and Wear had little option but to go for a 'necklace of waterfront developments' along the narrow strips of its river edges: its 'string of pearls' at intervals of a mile or so. Starting at the western end of the north bank is the 60-acre/24 ha Newcastle Business Park on the old Vickers-Armstrong site – optic-fibre cable network throughout and 'now, the best business address in the North East,' claims the Corporation, 'if not the country.' They are justifiably pleased with this: by 1990 investment was three times that forecast; 80 per cent of the 670,000 sq. ft./over 63,000 sq. m. had been pre-let; and British Airways alone was expected to create up to 1,000 jobs with a £36 million sales and software development centre. A public/private sector investment ratio of 1:12 is claimed. Moving downstream, towards the city centre, a 156-bed Copthorne Hotel was, by 1990, well on its way; and the city's central quayside, for so long neglected and down at heel, is pulsing with new life. There are handsome buildings here, mostly cleaned up now (like the Exchange Building, refurbished at a cost of £5 million), and additions like the new Law Courts. Pubs and wine bars and restaurants are thronging (where else can you drink with an electric model train circling above your head?). On Sunday mornings the open-air market is crowded – but on any day of the week the quayside is becoming an attraction in its own right. The East Quayside, hitherto a non-event and requiring intensive land acquisition (fought by two of the landowners), is seen by the Corporation as its eventual 'jewel in the crown' – a mixed development which could bring up to 3,000 jobs. 'Inland' a science park is foreseen in conjunction with the University and the Polytechnic.

And so it continues towards the coast, from St Peter's Basin through an offshore development park to Royal Quays and North Shields. The south bank, 'Catherine Cookson Country', has proved more obdurate, largely because of difficulties encountered in acquiring land. However, Jarrow is promised a 60 acre/24 ha industrial park. In Sunderland, plans long thwarted by uncertainties attaching to the shipbuilding and repair yards appear now to have been resolved, and even in the meantime clean-up operations have been effected at a number of sites like Pann's Bank. (The Corporation bought more than 500 specimen trees and 40,000 other trees and shrubs from the Gateshead Garden Festival site at the Festival's conclusion.) At Hylton Riverside, a long swathe on the north bank of the Wear, a £45 million business park is under construction, with other major developments at St Peter's Riverside, Deptford and Sunderland Forge on the south bank. Among related initiatives by the Corporation are its proposals for a free bus system on the

Newcastle Quayside, using cable-in-the-ground auto-guidance, to relieve the traffic pressures generated by increased activity; and its creation of community monitoring panels in different districts for consultation and participation purposes.

Teesside's nearly 19 square miles/50 sq. km. called for a pretty broad-brush approach. It was to Teesside that Mrs Thatcher elected to come in 1987, a month or two after the second-generation UDCs were born. It was here, bounding about an area of wasteland, that she proclaimed: 'Within four years I am going to be photographed on that site full of buildings, and that will just show you what we can do in Teesside.' 'We are setting out once again to be ahead of our time,' she declared. 'Where you have initiative, talent and ability, the money follows.' The Corporation took that on board as its motto and has used it ever since: *Initiative. Talent. Ability.* For most of the other UDCs land assembly and reclamation for packaged release to developers has had to be a major preoccupation. It would be false to suggest that this has not been necessary in the North East. For example, Teesside had to remove two million cubic metres of spoil as part of the reclamation of the Teesdale Park site (as Tyne and Wear had to remove 80,000 tonnes of spoil from Hylton Riverside). Nonetheless, the very size of its territory has meant that Teesside could scarcely embark upon land-acquisition programmes throughout; it has opted rather for a high-profile role of intensive promotion – of identifying potentials and selling them hard. Full- and half-page advertisements in the 'quality' press are frequent. The area is put forward as 'the UK's biggest new urban development project'. The very word Teesside is always split by a pound sign through the middle. Initiative. Talent. Ability.

The Corporation's main developments include the Teesside site, already mentioned, of 250 acres/over 100 ha in Stockton. Here will be built a weir and river crossing, the former to create new amenity areas for leisure activities, the latter to link Stockton with the other side of the river. On the old Stockton racecourse, Warner Brothers are part of a consortium creating an £80 million leisure and retail complex. Billingham and Wilton are dominated by ICI; how natural, then, to propose a European Chemical Centre within easy reach of them on land at Seal Sands – but less than obvious to propose, between there and Billingham and residential areas, a substantial International Nature Reserve: a world wetland park, to which might be joined a seal centre. Unexpected, too, the Langbaurgh project for a motor-sport centre, the first of its kind in Britain since the war. Like Tyne and Wear, Teesside is setting out to attract companies associated with offshore activities. To the Offshore Base in Langbaurgh has now been added the Ocean Technology Centre, where research and development of subsea systems can be undertaken in two huge converted dry docks, once part of Smiths Dock. Among other forward-looking ventures are the CAD/CAM* Business Park claimed to be the largest in Europe; the Research and Development Campus at Riverside; and the Belasis Hall Technology Park.

It is easier thus to list some of the projects backed and initiated by the two Corporations than to bring into focus the labour of all the local authorities in the region – let alone the diverse workings of the private sector, upon which the main burden of investment rests. Any appraisal of the North East must take account of Sir John Hall, the miner's son who built the Gateshead MetroCentre on 115 acres/46 ha of marshland previously used for dumping ash, and then moved to Wynyard Park which straddles the Co. Durham and Cleveland boundary. The MetroCentre claimed, at the time of its opening, to be the largest covered shopping area in Europe. Since then later additions – warehousing, a 150-bed hotel, an office block – have taken its value to some £300 million. Its effects upon other local shopping have yet to be properly gauged; so too the effects upon the Centre itself of the ending of the Enterprise Zone fiscal concessions in the early nineties. However not only was it visited by 25 million people in 1990, but in Newcastle Eldon Square/Eldon Gardens claimed 30 million. Once the MetroCentre was up and running, John Hall sold it to his main backers, the Church Commissioners, and started over again at Wynyard Park, the one-time Londonderry family mansion set in 6,000 acres/2,400 ha to the north-west of Billingham. Here he aims, over the nineties, at another £300 million development including a business centre, with conference facilities, two big hotels, a 400 acre/160 ha business park, championship golf courses and doubtless much else. Final approvals for all this were hoped for in summer 1990. Sir John, with his oft-stated belief in 'provincial regeneration', has inevitably come to be seen as having the King's touch for the cure of all enterprise-deficiency ills, and is to be found amongst the board members and trustees of quite a few local bodies.

Hall is a one-off, but many of the big property companies and volume housebuilders are investing heavily in the North East.

* Computer Aided Design/Computer Aided Manufacture.

Lovell, for example, say that the 'Hartlepool Renaissance' is the biggest urban regeneration project they have undertaken. Self-interest and social imperatives can become indistinguishable. ICI, for example, have joined with English Estates in the creation of Belasis Hall Technology Park. The Port Authorities, as major landowners, find themselves partners in a wide range of ventures. In Redcar, British Rail and Langbaurgh Borough Council have joined hands to turn the greater part of the station (which is listed) into managed workshops. This perhaps is worth a second glance as an example of the many smaller projects to be found in all parts of the country but which never make the national headlines. Stemming from all sorts of sources, their cumulative value is considerable.

British Rail's Community Unit was set up in the early eighties to encourage, among other things, partnership arrangements with local authorities, whereby environmental improvements on or near railway premises and land could be undertaken jointly. During the eighties British Rail made over £8 million available for this purpose, to match an equivalent input by local councils. Latterly the Unit's activities have been extended by BR's Urban Renaissance Initiative which aims at carefully targeted schemes to assist economic regeneration.

There are at least ten managed-workshop schemes in Cleveland, more than half of them in Middlesbrough – but none in Redcar (a priority area for Urban Programme support within Langbaurgh). British Rail's feasibility studies (by Rock Townsend, who have much experience in this field) chimed in with a County study of 1988 and the Borough's own Regeneration Study in demonstrating the worth of such a project. The proposal, published in 1990, was to adapt that part of Redcar Station which is surplus to British Rail's requirements (much of it under a glazed canopy) for use as workshops and a small-business centre. Once established, such a centre should pay its way as far as running costs are concerned, but could not be expected to recover the conversion costs. British Rail therefore proposed to grant a long lease on the premises, and to provide half the £467,000 cost of the first phase, which should create about 4,740 sq. ft./440 sq. m. of workspace and about thirty-five jobs. The centre would be run by the Langbaurgh-on-Tees Development Agency Limited, originally set up by the Borough Council to manage the South Bank Business Centre on the edge of Middlesbrough.

Here the blurring effects of the 1980s upon traditional demarcation lines become apparent. On the one hand we find ourselves confronted by 'private-sector' companies set up by public authorities; on the other by charitable agencies set up by the private sector. One of the local organisations pledging support (possibly in kind) for the Redcar Station operation was 'Teesside Tomorrow'. Teesside Tomorrow is typical of the private-sector groups which sprang into existence so widely during the eighties. Here it was in 1988 that several local businessmen met to consider how best their businesses, and they as individuals, could assist the regeneration of Teesside. From this sprang a larger group of thirty or so, from which in turn sprang Teesside Tomorrow, set up as a limited company. ICI seconded the chief executive for eighteen months; Middlesbrough Enterprise Partnership offered secretarial help; core funding came from membership fees (initially £500) and company donations (British Telecom were generous). Funding, all of it from private sources, was thus secured for the first two or three years.

Objectives are foreseeable: to help identify and promote a clear vision for the area's future; to identify opportunities for investment in the area; to encourage public- and private-sector co-operation and generally to act as a forum and focus for those concerned with the economic and social development of Teesside. One of its first moves was to pump-prime the creation of the Middlesbrough Botanic Centre with £10,000, which levered a further £40,000 from Inner Area Programme funding.

Comparable, but a year older, is The Newcastle Initiative (TNI), launched with glossy publicity in June 1988. First sponsors were (again) British Telecom, John Hall's Cameron Hall Developments, National Westminster Bank, Newcastle Breweries, Northern Rock Building Society, and the *Newcastle Chronicle and Journal*. Directors included the Chairman of the CBI's northern region, the Chairman of Business in the Community (BIC) in Tyne, Wear and Northumberland, Sir John Hall (of course), the Director of the Polytechnic, a Professor from the University, and the Managing Director of the *Chronicle*. Chief Executive is Bill Hay, seconded from British Telecom.

A high-powered team, then, but what can such organisations actually do? They are without powers, own no land or property, and do not themselves command the enormous resources demanded by any substantial development today. They *can*, however, beat the drum for local achievements, and publicise possibilities in ways which would be more difficult for public authorities. They can involve the local business community more closely in municipal affairs. They can attract commercial funding for specific projects. They can play an important role in local enterprise

155

agencies and in training programmes. One example of support activity which it is hard to see coming from any other quarter is TNI's aim to strengthen local links with Japan both commercially and culturally.

To get to grips directly with physical regeneration is more difficult. Their small offices are unlikely to be able to come up with fundamentally new strategies; it may be possible, however, to direct attention to matters which seem to have been overlooked or forgotten by others, and to bring additional support to particular official policies and programmes. TNI, for example, have taken under their wing the promotion of certain concepts for that area in western Newcastle now referred to as Chinatown and Theatre Village. The possibility is seen here of bringing into being a new community based on the arts, the media and leisure, all centred on the recently restored Tyne Theatre and Opera House, with an important pedestrian square and 'necklace of pedestrian courts'. To open up the factors involved, an intensive four-day brainstorming event was laid on in autumn 1988 by a 'CUDAT' – or Community and Urban Design Assistance Team – not in the hope of coming up with definitive solutions but of stimulating thinking in the city and suggesting some of the more exciting potentials. By January 1990 TNI had carried this forward by the creation of the Westgate Trust (set up as a limited company) especially to further regeneration in this part of the city. An additional link in the process of developing partnerships.

Another kind of approach is offered by a body like the North East Civic Trust, born in 1965 as an associate to the parent body in London. All the Civic Trusts have experience of mounting cooperative improvement schemes and NECT, among its other activities, has long been concerned with the enhancement of industrial sites on Tyneside. Such work is generally undertaken in conjunction with local authorities, or, latterly, the Development Corporation. As we have seen, the Corporation's territory is extended; its main projects, even when complete, will be some way apart. For years to come, unless otherwise dealt with, there will continue to be between them long stretches of shot-up sites: abandoned or down-at-heel buildings, unused wasteland. Lack of faith in the future does not encourage generous maintenance. Conversely, the improvements that can be effected at a relatively superficial level, at a relatively small cost, can be striking – and their psychological impact enormous.

One recent study by the Trust was concerned with the area between Tyne Dock and Wapping Street in South Shields. Its purpose: 'To determine ways in which the present industrial environment can be improved, upgraded, smartened and brightened.' Its maps, drawings and colour photographs covered the area in sections, and detailed ninety-eight premises – some large, some quite small – on sixty-one principal sites. Ninety site owners or occupiers were interviewed as to their current plans and requirements, future intentions, particular problems, and willingness in principle to participate in a cooperative upgrading exercise (a process complicated by takeovers and changes of owner-ship as it proceeded). The resulting report identified specific problems and opportunities associated with particular uses, partial use, underuse and non-use of buildings and land; proposed action both for individual sites and for the area as a whole; and suggested likely costs. The design approach covered such things as the uses made of existing buildings and land, opportunities for reuse, or for new development; the external appearance of buildings; signing, graphics, lighting – either for security or its relevance to the site; fencing, boundaries, security; hard and soft landscape treatments; car and lorry parking; storage of materials, waste and waste disposal. Several nuclei or node points were identified, the character and potentials of which could help to articulate the structure of the area as a whole (in this case, for example, Mill Dam and the Wapping Street fishermen's boat sheds – both recognisable 'places'). The reinforcement of area identity through colour and lighting was proposed. All this was shown on the maps as 'urgent' or 'desirable'. The schedule of cost estimates ranged from £1,000 to £160,000, but figures generally were modest. Costs would be split fifty-fifty between owners and the sponsoring body – in this case the Tyne and Wear Development Corporation.

What then? In any such project the Trust takes over the whole operation. Having secured approval – and a firm budget – from the sponsoring body, new approaches are made to owners and tenants to discuss the range of work and costs they will accept. With their approval, formal applications are made on their behalf for grant, for Building Regulations and Planning Permissions; contractors are invited and tenders obtained, based on the Trust's detailed drawings; work is supervised and certified. On completion the owners pay the contractors and the sponsoring body then makes the grant payments to the owners. The Trust is paid for its services by a 10 per cent fee from the Development Corporation, or, in the case of a local authority, by an annual retainer. Where private architects and designers are employed directly by the owners, the Trust's role is merely to approve the work.

'It is a simple – if lengthy – process to relieve site owners of all the tasks involved,' says Neville Whittaker, Director of NECT since its inception and himself an architect. 'Their chief role is to approve, or not approve, and pay when required. We find this infinitely more effective than mere exhortation, which either produces nil results or dire effects.' It is another illustration of the sustained effort required, at whatever level it may be, to lift the environment in areas of decay. There are no quick fixes in regeneration, though the *third* generation of UDCs have been given only five to seven years – rather reminiscent of the 'short, sharp shock' approach to young offenders. At three of these we take a look in the following chapter.

9

LEEDS – SHEFFIELD – BRISTOL

THE THIRD-generation UDCs were set up in 1988 in Leeds, Central Manchester, Sheffield and, after a struggle, Bristol. They were smaller, given a shorter lease of life than the earlier corporations – five to seven years – and their task was a little different. The cities in which they found themselves, though having quarters which were run-down and even derelict, were by no means in total decline. Their economies, on the contrary, were tending to strengthen, and the Corporations' job was seen as providing an extra boost to enable them more speedily to reach their potential – pacemakers, if you like, for the civic heart. To the extent that the four Corporations found themselves responsible, not for vast areas of thinly populated wasteland (Sheffield was perhaps the exception to this), but sectors of living cities, possibly hard-hit but still active, they were the more obviously alien implants and the less welcome to the local councils.

Manchester lifted an eyebrow when the proposal was made, and there were those locally who maintained that the object of the exercise was to enable central government to get in on Manchester's act and be in a position to take some of the credit. Leeds started warily but came to terms with its UDC fairly speedily.

'Our relationship with the City Council is an interesting one,' says Martin Eagland, the Corporation's Chief Executive. 'Certainly from both points of view it's a pragmatic one. Both sides realise there are advantages in working together. They do quite a bit of planning control work. Many of the current improvement schemes are on the City's land. And we work together on transport matters. It's a relationship which can blow hot or cold on individual issues – and there are issues on which we differ. The Corporation is still seen as representing the government.'

159

Sheffield, too, perhaps more reluctantly, has come to terms with the advantages of cohabitation, though the City's initial opposition – certainly as far as individual councillors are concerned – has by no means totally evaporated. Sheffield has been ruled by Labour for sixty years. Towards the end of the seventies it took the title of the 'People's Republic of Sheffield', and at the end of 1985 the Council sent hampers to the striking steelworkers. Since then the rapprochement with the private sector has been marked and today any form of partnership which helps the city is welcomed.

It was touch and go at the outset whether the City would do battle and push its opposition to a Development Corporation to the top. At the last moment it cried off. Bristol did not. Bristol was so incensed that it petitioned formally to be left alone. The petition was heard by a Parliamentary Select Committee, which made certain changes to the Corporation's proposed terms of reference (to the City's advantage) but turned the petition down. Because of the delays incurred by all this the Bristol Development Corporation started its working life the best part of a year later than the others.

Leeds, with a population of more than 700,000 and covering 217 square miles/560 sq. km., is England's third biggest city after London and Birmingham. Like Manchester and Bristol, Leeds has had no particular 'image' problem. There are complaints that it has no conference centre, no trade and exhibition centre, no modern concert hall. But it has both a university and an important polytechnic; it has Temple Newsam and the Henry Moore Centre; it has the new, two-auditoria Playhouse complex, the enterprising Opera North, the Leeds Piano Competition and an international film festival. Its representatives at the Palace of Westminster have included Hugh Gaitskell, Denis Healey, Sir Keith Joseph, Merlin Rees and Sir Giles Shaw. And though the rebuilding of the sixties was crude and insensitive, it has its seven Victorian arcades,* linked by considerable pedestrian areas; the Market, where you can buy everything from flowers to bacon, greetings cards, socks, china and glass, and Yorkshire oven cakes (and where Michael Marks set up his first stall in 1882); and plenty of imposing monuments from the past, from the newly restored and adapted Corn Exchange, its interior rendered doubly spectacular by the hole punched by the architects, Alsop and Lyall, in the main floor,

* Two by Frank Matcham have been elegantly restored as part of a new shopping centre, and added to by glazing over Queen Victoria Street. Here the architect Derek Latham, has introduced some dashing new stained glass, mosaics and sculpture.

to the amazing 1878 'Arabian Saracenic' St Paul's House. In recent years it has developed rapidly as an important financial centre. Loss of population has slowed as more people have come to live there.

What, then, was the need for an Urban Development Corporation here? None of those I asked had much of an answer. 'Any UDC starts as a political initiative' was the nearest I got to it. 'Maybe a local MP floats the idea. Maybe the Regional Director within the DoE/DTI. Not from the local authority, that's for sure.' Martin Eagland, who was previously with the West Yorkshire Metro County and then, as Chief Executive, at Kettering, is bullish about things. 'As far as we are concerned the object is to show that a lot can be achieved in the period we've been given and we are working to achieve the optimum possible. A lot depends, of course, on how the market behaves generally.' Clearly 1990, he foresaw, was going to be difficult.

The Leeds UDC covers two distinct areas: the South Central, 940 acres/380 ha, extending southwards from the city centre, across the River Aire, to and beyond Hunslet; the other, of 380 acres/150 ha, in the Kirkstall Valley a mile and a half to the west of the city centre. Between the two, and through the city, run the River Aire, the Leeds–Liverpool Canal and the Aire–Calder Navigation. To deal with these areas the Development Corporation has been allocated £15 million spread over its five to seven years, with perhaps an equal sum available through City Grant. (By way of comparison, to bring the funding into perspective, the City estimated in its housing investment programme submission to the DoE, 1989/90, that £600 million was required to bring its housing stock to 'a reasonable standard of repair'.)

In Leeds the development pressures are commercial rather than industrial. The conventional wisdom would have been for commercial expansion westwards, where the existing commercial quarter lies, but City and Corporation determined rather to open up the somewhat cut-off and long-neglected area southwards – South Central – and to channel development in that direction. The barrier created by the main railway line on its long viaduct approach through the city to the central station, and by the river, once the heart of the community but for long years lined by decaying warehouses, has been both psychological and real. Now waterside development is proceeding fast in the Calls area (a headquarters building for ASDA giving 1,200 jobs is the biggest single development to date), and a development competition has been launched for 20 acres/8 ha around Clarence Dock (where a new £35

161

million national museum will receive half the Royal Armouries from the Tower of London in 1996). The arches of the railway viaduct are being unpicked to provide new through routes, as well as shops. A new pedestrian bridge is planned.

Further to the south pulses raced and hearts sank at a proposal which promised to be for Leeds what Canary Wharf will be to London's Docklands. This was a £3 billion scheme by Canadian developers Triple 5, embracing 3.2 million sq. ft./300,000 sq. m. of office space, 200,000 sq. m. of shopping, and much, much else. Although four fifths of the 100 acre/40 ha site was on Development Corporation land, the deal was done by the City and its commercial arm, the Leeds City Development Company – LCDC – (formed in 1988 with the City as main shareholder) before the Corporation was fully operational. However, when the drawings began to come in the following year, the City took fright at the sheer scale of the scheme and its further implications, and pulled out. Feelings were mixed. 'It could have taken Leeds out of the Second Division into the First,' Mel Burrell, Chief Executive of the LCDC, was quoted as saying. 'It could have changed the whole economy of the city and changed Leeds' role in the British economy.[1] On the other hand one can imagine a certain relief within the Development Corporation at not having a hundred acres tied up in a single speculative development, with all the imponderables inevitably attaching to that – though Martin Eagland admits that the scale of the Corporation's thinking may have been raised by the bravura of Triple 5's ideas. At all events the Corporation is planning a 50 acre/20 ha Business Park in South Central, and has launched another development competition for a further 50 acres at Hunslet Green, to include a new village. A £100 million office development at Centre Gate, hard by the access road to the motorways, is due for completion in 1992. To the south of the city the local Groundwork Trust is embarked on a three-year programme of regeneration for five mining communities – the Five Villages Project.

Westwards, two thirds of the Kirkstall Valley area is due for comprehensive mixed development. The Corporation has published a strategy for improving the whole of the waterways corridor, and has undertaken a range of environmental improvements, from the planting of 100,000 trees to the stone cleaning (with the City and British Rail) of the imposing twenty-three-arch Kirkstall viaduct. The City itself has Terry Farrell drawing up proposals for the 18 acre/7.2 ha Quarry Hill area (site of the famous 1930s flats, which were demolished in the mid seventies), where Dutch developers have

Leon Krier working on a masterplan for the same area. Both City and Corporation are cooperating on proposals for an inner relief road, and for a £38 million light railway (which is not welcome to all those through whose streets it would run). The housing problems remain. Design quality remains a question mark until there are some spanking modern buildings and effects of the urban landscaping can be judged. But commercially Leeds is booming.

So what are the blocks? I asked Martin Eagland. 'Time,' he responded instantly. 'UDCs are not given much in the way of delegated powers. Everything they do is "shadowed" by Regional Office or the Department in London. That not only slows down the momentum but stops Corporations acting in a truly entrepreneurial way. My own view is that the planning system is far too complicated – too detailed and not sufficiently market responsive. It is easier for us than a local authority, but even so, though we have less to *prove* in, say, a Compulsory Purchase Order Inquiry, the time taken to reach the decision is no quicker. The Department of Transport may promise to "fast track" a scheme, but I don't see how they can while they're trying to satisfy everyone. We need a little more emphasis on progress and a little less on the democratic process. They seem to do things better in France. One way to approach this would be to offer people more generous compensation when they are disadvantaged, rather than the absolute minimum.'

If this sounds authoritarian, it has to be said that Leeds Development Corporation tries to be not only market responsive, but community responsive (it was one of the first of the UDCs to open its meetings to the public). To an outsider, the working relationships between Corporation and City Council, City Action Team, Inner City Task Force, Chamber of Commerce, two Enterprise Agencies, British Waterways Board, the voluntary organisations – and the list is far from complete – seem always workmanlike and at times almost cosy. Interestingly, the City set-up in 1990 a Leeds Development Agency, a little on the lines of the SDA and WDA, to carry forward long-term strategies beyond the life of the Development Corporation.

In Sheffield there was undoubtedly an 'image' problem to overcome. And for quite a time things were far from cosy. Sheffield: the Steel City of South Yorkshire, one third of which yet lies in the Peak National Park. The 'dirty picture in a golden frame'. Industrial problems might pile up elsewhere, but recession, decline, it seemed, were for others. The Council's first Draft District Plan for the

Lower Don Valley zoned much of the land for *expansion* of the steel industry. When the collapse came at the beginning of the eighties, it came, for Sheffield, almost out of a clear sky. One after another the great steel mills shut down, and with them went 40,000 jobs. An unemployment rate which had been half the national average shot up to double the national average. (Even in 1988 the central ward, Hyde Park, had a 90 per cent rate of youth unemployment.) The city was in shock. Communications between left and right broke down. Public slanging matches were common. 'If you had to go to the City Hall,' Peter Cormick, President of the Chamber of Commerce in 1989, has been quoted as saying,[2] 'you practically needed a minder' ('escort' was the word he actually used). But Yorkshire common sense prevailed. Some have pinned the beginning of the change of heart to the time when, as part of a civic delegation to China in 1983, Clive Betts, the then and still Council Leader, and John Hambridge, then newly appointed Chief Executive to the Chamber of Commerce, were forced to share a car for several days. In practical terms it was a move by the Chamber of Commerce, all too well aware of the damage being done to the city by open tumult, which began the partnership process. The Chamber, in 1986, formed an 'Image Working Party', which led later in the year to the setting up of the Sheffield Economic Regeneration Committee, with Councillor Helen Jackson in the Chair. Nudged by government, the Committee commissioned consultants (Coopers & Lybrand) to examine and report on the problems of the Lower Don Valley, which was where the steel masters had congregated. While this was going on the City, on the initiative of one of its officers in the Recreation Department, had the crazy idea of putting in a bid for the 1991 World Student Games (or Universiade, to give it its international name) – and, almost to its own surprise, at Zagreb, won it. Then came Coopers & Lybrand's report, which recommended the creation of a private-sector development authority for the Lower Don Valley. This the government refused to accept; it would have to be a proper UDC. As we have seen, that rankled, but it happened. The Development Corporation is in existence and three City councillors sit upon its Board.

The Lower Don Valley runs north-east from the centre of the city, to and across the M1, culminating in a big downward-pointing axe-head. Three miles of this constitute the Corporation's designated area. The population dropped from about 10,000 at its peak to a mere 300 or so in 1989; almost half the area lay derelict or unused; nonetheless there were still 750 small firms there, employing between them around 13,000 people. The problems facing the Corporation were thus the familiar ones of creating and opening up sites for redevelopment by means of land assembly, reclamation and improved access. It did not, however, have to start from scratch. Since 1983 the City had been evolving, and putting into practice, a strategy for the lower Don Valley, elements of which – for example the big Meadowhall shopping centre, which received planning permission in 1987 – have since come to fruition.

Within its boundary the Corporation has identified ten areas, each of which is planned to have its own uses, its own identity. At the south-east corner lies the site earmarked for a new airport (Sheffield is said to be the largest city in Europe without its own airport). This is within the biggest of the sub-areas: Tinsley Park, seen as the major concentration of specialised large-scale steel production, with other industrial and business uses. North of this is Meadowhall, gateway to the Valley from this direction, and claiming to have overtaken Gateshead's MetroCentre as Europe's largest shopping and leisure complex – a £400 million development with parking for 11,000 cars and offering jobs to 9,000 people. Initiated by a local entrepreneur, Eddie Healey, Meadowhall (with a distinctly better exterior than most) got off to a cracking start in 1990, attracting one million shoppers in its first ten days. Strung out between here and the city centre sites have been earmarked for housing (it is hoped that 1,000 new homes will have been provided by 1993), for industrial and commercial development, for small workshops, for leisure purposes. The Valley is threaded through by the River Don and the Sheffield and Tinsley Canal. These are being restored, and their potential developed as the main focus for the Valley's new landscape structure. A 'supertrain' route is envisaged from the city centre to a major interchange at Meadowhall; running through the Games area in the Corporation's southern boundary in the heart of the Valley.

A big package; a bold, courageous vision. The Universiade alone, making provision for 6,000 athletes from 160 nations and 250,000 spectators, has involved the largest sports-facilities construction programme ever seen in Britain. Of the half-dozen new facilities, attention has focused first upon the £52 million Ponds Forge complex in the heart of the city and the £27 million athletics stadium, seating 40,000, in the Don Valley. But at the end of 1989 the sky was dark, there were rumblings, and in mid 1990 the lightning struck. The company set up to organise the event by the Council, a Council concern called Health for Sheffield, and the British Students Sports Federation, was forced to wind

165

itself up with debts of nearly £3 million. Total cost of the Games had been estimated at around £180 million. Of this, construction of the new facilities accounted for nearly £150 million, with £27 million or so required for the running of the event itself. Most of the construction was being underwritten by the Council, though one £34 million arena was being funded by an American group. Three million was promised by the Sports Council; corporate sponsorship was looked to for £12 million; a sizeable fee was hoped for from television coverage. However, by mid 1990 only £500,000 had been raised and, with the death of the organising company, the Council's only options were to pick up the tab or cancel the whole enterprise. 'The student games should be sent back to Duisberg,'* said *The Times* – hardly a realistic course with construction of the stadia and arenas well advanced. The Council's loan charges from 1992 would already amount to £8 million, and Councillor Betts admitted that further losses could only fall on the community charge payers of Sheffield (raising the spectre of further government capping). 'If local democratic accountability means anything,' *The Times* had no doubt, 'more fool them.' Lightning, they say, never strikes twice. But concurrently with these problems the proposed light railway, originally intended to be completed in time for the Games, was put in jeopardy by the government's refusal, notwithstanding Parliamentary approval, of funds, and a refusal to let South Yorkshire Passenger Transport Authority, the main sponsoring agency, apply to the European Regional Development Fund for assistance. At the end of 1990 the DTp, perhaps persuaded by the congestion resulting from Meadowhall's success, seemed to be weakening. Conversely, the City were preparing to appeal to Michael Heseltine to come to the rescue of the Universiade – though, as it transpired, without joy.

It is too soon to foretell the end of the story, but in September 1990, the Don Valley stadium hosted its first major athletics event. Peter Elliot there broke the UK all-comers record for the 1,500 metres before a crowd of 22,000, the largest number of spectators at a UK athletics event since 1963. Encouragement for a council faced, on the one hand, with the exhortations of the enterprise culture to act entrepreneurially; on the other with the view that local authorities should restrict their activities to things like rubbish collection and certainly never put public money at risk. The final verdict is likely to be a familiar one: if you pull it off you are courageous and far-sighted; if you don't you are foolhardy

* Where the 1989 Games were held.

and lacking in probity. Deciding a city's course of action in such matters becomes wrenchingly harsh because the stakes are so high. Can our cities ever be rescued by timidity? Sheffield has initiated innovative projects at a number of levels, from a pioneering district heating scheme to 40 acres/16 ha of urban forestry in Stocksbridge. However, the Games and associated developments, tying in closely with the strategy and plans of the Development Corporation, relate to the achievement of that critical mass which will alone make other developments possible. What has been at stake here is not just the Student Games as such, but the future of much of the Lower Don Valley.

Most contentious of all the UDCs since London's Docklands has been that for Bristol. To catch the full flavour of the dispute it is necessary to go back a little. Since John and Sebastian Cabot set out in 1497, with eighteen sailors, to reach Newfoundland, Bristol's history has been continuously vigorous, adventurous, thrusting, entrepreneurial – but its prosperity went hand in hand with the most civilised civic virtues. 'All ship-shape and Bristol fashion' came to stand for more than nautical propriety alone. Here one finds not only a cathedral, but England's most splendid parish church. Here is the oldest (1766) theatre in the country. Here, still, are 3,600 listed buildings – and more listed Georgian buildings than in Bath. Here Brunel left evidence of his railway building, his bridge building, and his shipbuilding.

The Luftwaffe took out the centre of the city on 24 November 1940. The main shopping area and a quarter of the mediaeval core went that night and Bristol was never to look the same again. Post-war reconstruction was dominated by grandiose road building and coarsely impoverished architecture. Up the hillside to the west of the city centre, the backdrop to so many views, are now piled, unforgivably, multi-storey car parks, crudely reductive office blocks, and the banal science buildings of the university (which should have known better). This must stand as one of the bigger disasters of British urban design in the past half-century. No less horrific were the City's proposals, at the end of the 1960s, to close the docks and fill in the greater part of the Floating Harbour and the Feeder Canal,* an enabling Bill for which was – successfully –

---

* Bristol's maritime power was made possible because the Rivers Avon and Severn were navigable. The Avon was linked by a diversionary cut to the natural basin, once fed by the little River Frome, which became known rather curiously as the Floating Harbour. This runs into, and through, the heart of the city, and, with the river and Feeder Canal, gives to Bristol much of its character.

presented to Parliament. Distinguished consultants were appointed to draw up proposals for the redevelopment of the docks area but the nature of their suggestions was greatly constrained by the macho scale of the then City Engineer's road planning. Unsurprisingly, between the mid sixties and mid seventies, a proliferation of local amenity and conservation groups sprang into being to express the public's disquiet at what was happening to their city. To this day, Bristol probably has more such active groups than any other city of its size.

In the restructuring of local government in 1974 the city lost its all-purpose County Borough status and became a District Council within the new and artificial Avon County – a bitter pill for so historic a city to swallow. However, though its powers were slashed, the ensuing shuffle of officers and elected members not only gave Bristol a new Council but made possible a total turnround in its planning policies. Its new planning officers were determined to salvage and, if possible, enhance what was left of the city's character. The coincidental crash of the property market at the end of 1973 gave the Council a breathing space in which to formulate its new approaches. For the next fifteen years conservation and urban design were to colour, if not to dominate, all its planning decisions. A new rapport was established with the amenity groups (which should not be seen merely as negative protesters: in the fifteen years to 1988 the Civic Society planted 1,800 street trees; the several preservation trusts acquired and restored a considerable number of buildings; and between 1974 and 1977 the Bristol City Docks Group produced seven reports, the quality of which has been described[3] as 'quite outstanding . . . their analysis and prognosis will remain relevant for the foreseeable future'). The Council made it known that its Docks Act, though safely through Parliament, would not be implemented; the docks would not be closed. Indeed, the docks were given first priority in the series of local plans, envisaged in 1975. A working group produced an 'Opportunities Report' in 1977 which, of course, aimed at regeneration, but also recommended that the whole area be designated a Conservation Area (which was quickly done). The main report was accompanied by a 'Townscape and Environment Topic Study'. 'This extraordinary document,' one commentator, John V. Punter, already quoted above, has written, 'must be one of the most comprehensive and intelligible townscape studies ever undertaken in British planning.' Bristol at last seemed to be in good hands.

Not everything went smoothly. It never does. There were tensions within the Council. Once development pressures built up again there were cries – from the real-estate world, from some architects – that the Council was being too restrictive. (A main policy plank, over this period, has been the maintenance of a balance between industrial and office development, between blue-collar jobs and white-collar jobs; speculative development, how-ever, is almost entirely in offices.) Some are said to have found the committed, determined Chief Planning Officer, Iain Patterson, too outspoken in his dealings. Social problems remain – are even in some respects, notwithstanding the city's bouncing prosperity, more acute. In 1986 no fewer than 83,000 people moved *into* Bristol. However, by that same date the 1,600 who, in 1976, had been unemployed for more than a year had grown to 10,000. One in five of the city's population live in areas of multiple deprivation; rioting, it will be recalled, broke out in 1980 in the badly decayed St Paul's district.

As in most places, then, a confused picture, but with much on the positive side. Overall, confidence was higher in 1985 than it had been in 1975. The conservation programme has been enormously successful. Today, nearly 90 per cent of the city's historic buildings in disrepair have been restored, with exceptionally generous assist-ance from the Historic Buildings Council and its successor English Heritage – and others.* Colourful corners like Christmas Steps have been rejuvenated. Substantial new buildings have gone up at many points. Much work has taken place around the Floating Harbour, with new housing around Bathurst Basin and westwards towards Cumberland Basin. The strip between Prince Street and Narrow Quay has been redeveloped, with the Arnolfini building and the Watershed Media Centre across the water giving new life to the heart of the city. The longstanding log jam of the Canon's Marsh promontory has been broken by the construction of the vast crescent of Lloyds Bank's Bristol headquarters. There are proposals – as yet rather notional – for a private-sector light-rail system to help counter the undoubted problem of Bristol's very high car ownership.

If it had been irksome since 1974 for a Council which had 'done its own thing' for centuries to have to accommodate the views of a higher-tier authority – the new County – its reaction to the government's proposal to impose upon it an Urban Development Corporation, and at a time when the city was riding the crest of an economic wave, can be imagined. The announcement was made

---

* Between 1977 and 1987 public funding of £3.65 million resulted in £28 million investment by the private sector.

on 7 December 1987. The Corporation was to be responsible for the segment of the city running eastwards from Temple Way to the city boundary – in effect, the industrial valley of the Avon. As one of the third-generation UDCs its life was foreseen as only five to seven years; as with the others its funding for that period would be £15 million. The Council immediately repudiated it, on the grounds that a large number of planning approvals had already been given in the area (in fact around 538,000 sq. ft./nearly 50,000 sq. m. of industrial space had been built there during the previous five years and planning permission given for over 800,000 sq. ft./74,000 sq. m. more); that, if not lovely, the area nonetheless contained 'backyard' industries vital to the city and gave work to 20,000 people; that if land values were forced up by massive office development, these activities would have to leave and the jobs disappear. Underlying everything, of course, was the familiar – but no less fundamental – objection to the granting of extensive powers to an undemocratic body answerable only to the government.

The arguments on the other side were not strong. Most substantial was that of inadequate accessibility (the important area around Temple Meads in particular needs to be opened up). Other reasons were stated as fragmented ownership (though there were only 150 acres/60 ha of unused land); contaminated land (though the Corporation itself gives the amount of derelict land as only 26.5 acres/less than 11 ha); and 'one of the poorest environments in Bristol' (a junior Minister was quoted as having said it looked 'untidy from the train'). There were uncharitable souls who suggested that the UDC proposal resulted merely from a vague bureaucratic wish to have one somewhere in the West Country; from a desire to be associated with a boom in being; or simply that the DoE had made a mistake. At all events, at the end of March 1988 the government announced an extension of the UDC boundary westwards, to give the Corporation several additional prime sites for office development near the very centre of the city.

One or two meetings, doubtless acrimonious, were held between the Council and the DoE. They were to no avail. In June 1989 the Council voted to petition against the Bill in the Lords, on the grounds that it injuriously affected the authority by prejudicing planning permissions already given or under discussion. The petition was heard before a Select Committee in October, and the Committee reported at the end of the following month. It accepted the government's general argument (though rejecting much of its accusation of planning neglect), but proposed the exclusion of four key areas bearing directly upon the city centre. The Select Committee's recommendations were accepted by the Secretary of State and the Bristol Development Corporation Order came into effect on 20 February 1989.

A difficult birth, then, and not an altogether easy household to grow up in. One cannot but sympathise with those charged with responsibility for the success of the Corporation and its works. The UDC's 'corporate plan' appeared in July 1989: its main goal 'to create a visionary but achievable strategy'. In truth it read as somewhat generalised in its proposals, somewhat repetitive in its presentation, but its objectives were ambitious to say the least. Having set out three options for the city – the document tends to speak for the city as a whole – of low growth, high growth and international growth, the Corporation opts for the last. Some wonder whether in this it may have overreached itself. Specifically in its own area it foresees private-sector investment of £1,300 million over ten years, based on a private to public gearing of 30:1 – a figure more than seven times the government's rule of thumb for these things and higher by far than anything achieved in London's Docklands. This scenario forecasts the creation, over the same period, of 23,000 jobs (including the secondary jobs brought into being by the 'multiplier factor').

Central to the strategy is the construction of a north–south link road running through the area to connect with the A4 to the south. A weir is proposed to regulate the tidal range of the Avon as it runs through the city, and thereby to eliminate the mud-banks which line its course for much of the day. In land-use terms three key projects in particular are put forward. Temple Meads Station and the surrounding area are to be redeveloped as 'a triumphal entry to Bristol' which will alter the whole perception of the city. First proposals, in fact, proved controversial. Linked with this, across the Feeder Canal, the existing largely residential neighbourhood will be revitalised as 'Kingsley Village'. Secondly, St Philip's Marsh is seen as offering the major opportunity for industrial improvement. Thirdly, the site of the former St Anne's Board Mill in the Avon valley, at the eastern end of the UDC area, is put forward for a new village fronting the river. Needless to say there is much else – on the environment, on housing, on training, on consultation, on marketing. The title of the illustrated consultation document is *A Vision for Bristol* and the tone – how could it be otherwise? – is uniformly upbeat. The Urban Development Area will be 'an economic powerhouse for the city'. 'The Corporation will inspire a new spirit of enterprise in the city as a whole' and its 'intention is to transform the image of Bristol to [sic] one of the great citics of Europe'.

The City Council continues to see things differently. When the Deputy Leader of the Labour Group agreed to join the Corporation Board, he was promptly relieved of political office by his party. It is early days yet, and far too soon to guess at how the final balance sheet will look. On the one hand there is evidence already of the steep rise in values which the Council feared. Punter cites the sale, a week before the UDC was announced, of the St Anne's Board Mill site for £7 million (itself 30 per cent above the value put upon it by the UDC consultants); the site was sold on six months later for £13.75 million, and changed hands again four months after that for £30 million. On the other hand the UDC has levered an additional £39 million out of the government – primarily to help with the £55 million spine road, which has been given the official go-ahead. It is questionable whether this would have been so readily forthcoming except to the UDC. The central question, to which as yet there can be no answer, is: what exactly would have been gained if Council and Corporation had been in greater harmony? What may have been lost as a result of the present state of affairs? The differences between them, and the manner in which such differences might be reconciled, are significant, not only for the future of Bristol, but for future forms of national and local government partnership elsewhere.

What happened in Central Manchester, the last of these third-generation UDCs, is touched upon in a subsequent chapter.

10

THE WEST MIDLANDS

Birmingham – the Black Country

BRISTOL STRUGGLED but failed; Sheffield tried the private development agency card but was trumped; Birmingham – big, bold,
brash Birmingham – got away with it. In 1988 a redevelopment
company comprising the City Council and a private-sector
consortium, Heartlands, was formed with government blessing to
tackle the area between the city centre and the M1 to the north-east.
Beyond the city on the other side, in the Black Country, a second-
generation government UDC, born in 1987, was already in place.

Until 1986 the whole conurbation, stretching northwards and
westwards from Coventry to Walsall and Wolverhampton, with
Birmingham the great sprawling heart, formed the West Midlands
Metro County. The country is generally flat, until it meets the
green hills of Shropshire and Worcestershire. There are flashing
vistas of agriculture and park-like stretches; the area is criss-crossed
with canals; to the south particularly (where was once the Forest
of Arden) it is well wooded. For the most part, however, it is all an
unlovely muddle of power lines and cooling towers, long sheds
with ventilators astride their roofline, great piles of rusting scrap,
uniform streets of houses, and random pockets of scrub and
wasteland: a dour landscape left by a century and a half of
intensive metal-bashing and manufacturing,* from motorcars and
quality engineering to jewellery making and glass blowing.

The picture painted by Disraeli in *Sybil* was appalling:

---

* 'Chainmaking,' said my taxi driver, 'the small work was done at home. And
when you see some of the local ladies you can see it all. They're big ladies. Not to
be tangled with.'

... on mounds of ashes by the way side, sheltered only by a few rough boards or rotten pent-house roofs, strange engines spun and writhed like tortured creatures. Men, women and children, wan in their looks and ragged in their attire, tended the engines, fed their tributary fire, begged upon the road, or scowled half native from the doorless houses ... behind ... was the same interminable perspective of brick towns, never ceasing their black vomit, blasting all things living or inanimate, shutting out the face of the day, and closing in on all those horrors with a dense dark cloud.

His description of 'this dreadful spot' by night builds into a veritable *Walpurgisnacht*, a Dante/Doré vision of hell. The Black Country.

The Black Country was always an idea rather than an area with a line round it. It is maybe sixteen miles across but ask a local where it is and, like as not, he will point and say 'That way. Over there.'* Through the sixties and seventies, outside the South East, the West Midlands was the fat-cat part of England, smug in its prosperity. The shake-out of the early eighties, the collapse of steel and the decline of the motor industry were therefore doubly traumatic. Dole queues were a new experience. But the West Midlands is resilient and energetic; its present generations were never ground down into apathy by long decades of poverty and deprivation. The entrepreneurial spirit is alive and well in people like the Richardson twins, the local developers currently considering throwing up the world's tallest tower (at over 2,000 ft./610 m.) on wasteland in Dudley.

The Development Corporation's annual reports are sprinkled with rather *recherché* quotations in the same spirit: 'A wise man will make more opportunities than he finds' (Bacon); 'You can never plan the future by the past' (Burke); 'When a thing ceases to be a subject of controversy, it ceases to be a subject of interest' (Hazlitt); 'Progress is not an accident, but a necessity' (Herbert Spencer); and so on. When they set up shop they wondered whether they should not find some catchy new name for the area. To their credit they decided against it. One of their promotional tags now runs 'Black Country, Bright Future'.

In 1988 the Corporation's original seahorse-shaped area was enlarged to include 620 acres/250 ha in Wolverhampton, giving it responsibility in all for some ten square miles (nearly 2,500 ha).

---

*In 1986 the four Borough Councils commissioned a Gallup Poll to try to establish the perceived image of the area, both nationally and locally. Among local people, only two thirds thought they lived in the Black Country.

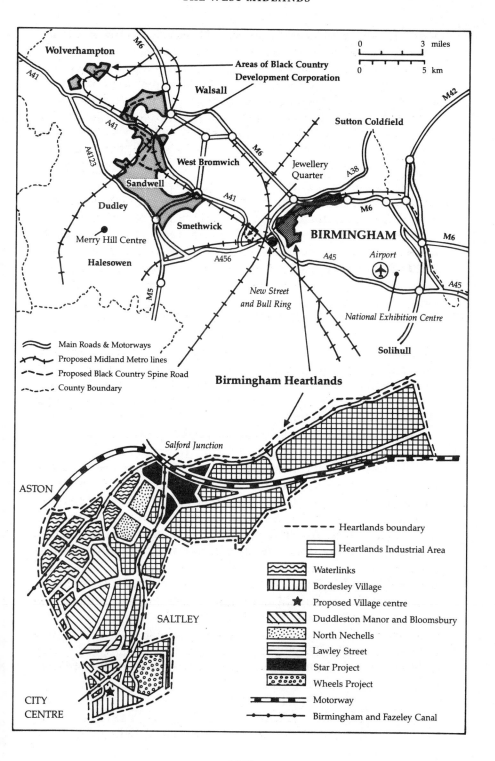

Wolverhampton

M6

Areas of Black Country
Development Corporation

0   3 miles

0   5 km

A41

Walsall

M42

A41

Sutton Coldfield

A4123

M6

Jewellery
Quarter

A38

West Bromwich

Sandwell

A41

A41

BIRMINGHAM

Dudley

M6

Smethwick

Merry Hill Centre

Airport

Halesowen

A456

A45

M6

A45

M5

New Street
and Bull Ring

National Exhibition Centre

∿∿ Main Roads & Motorways

Solihull

⪢ Proposed Midland Metro lines

Proposed Black Country Spine Road

County Boundary

Birmingham Heartlands

Salford Junction

ASTON

Heartlands boundary

Heartlands Industrial Area

Waterlinks

Bordesley Village

★ Proposed Village centre

Duddleston Manor and Bloomsbury

North Nechells

Lawley Street

SALTLEY

Star Project

Wheels Project

Motorway

CITY
CENTRE

Birmingham and Fazeley Canal

175

Of this 1,500 acres/over 600 ha was officially classified as derelict. This total, however, was made up of 200 sites, only four of which were mo e than fifty acres, many of which were less than twenty acres. Unlike, say, Teesside, land assembly thus became BCDC's biggest concern. In sixteen months it had acquired 400 acres/160 ha with an equivalent amount in process of acquisition. Hardly less important was the question of access. From the outset the Corporation's strategy turned upon the creation of a new dual-carriageway spine road, joining the already proposed Black Country Route to link the M5 with the M6, open up the heart of the area, and give access to 400–500 acres/160–200 ha which were otherwise hard to get at. It sounds easy, but the attendant problems illustrate how difficult it is to restructure an existing urban area. The estimated cost, when the road was first mooted, was £40 million for 4.7 miles/7.6 km.; that had risen to £140 million by the time the government had to approve it (that it *was* approved was taken as an indication of government confidence); by mid 1990 the figure had gone up to £210 million and the Secretary of State was calling for a review. Why such an increase? Earlier mineworking has created difficult ground conditions, so that the engineering aspects pose greater problems than expected. To deal with just *one* marl pit is going to cost £11 million. The local authorities have sought as minimal an impact as possible upon housing areas; the Corporation will therefore have to put massive resources into relocating something like 110 companies – on land, says Ian Page, Director of Marketing and External Affairs, ruefully, which could have gone to new development. 'In other words, we're just shuffling jobs around, not creating new ones.' Yet no one can doubt the long-term necessity of such a road.

The Corporation's broad objectives were the creation of some 5.4 million sq. ft./500,000 sq. m. of new industrial space; 1.1 million sq. ft./100,000 sq. m. of shopping (creating between them 20,000 new jobs directly); 4,000 new homes; and over 280 acres/ 160 ha of parks and open space. In operation is the formless £230 million (or £300 million or £400 million?) Merry Hill Centre of the Richardson twins on the old Round Oak Steelworks site in Dudley, fighting it out with Gateshead's MetroCentre and Meadowhall in Sheffield for the title of Europe's biggest. But coming up is yet another: the 4 million sq. ft./370,000 sq. m., £300 million Sandwell Mall proposed for a site that was opencasted until 1989 – that is, unless Birmingham, Wolverhampton, Dudley and Walsall, who fear its impact on their own shopping areas, contrive, notwithstanding the UDC's approval, to block it. Black Country

Quays, a 1,000 acre/400 ha site, is the subject of plans by the Corporation and a consortium of eleven property and construction companies. There will be housing here, offices there. The Black Country Museum is a success. If all goes well a new, 110-mile light railway, Metrolink, will run from Wolverhampton to the Birmingham Exhibition Centre. It is a kit of parts that has a familiar ring. One or two aspects of the Corporation's programme, however, warrant further attention.

The first stems from the fact that 35,000 live in the Corporation's area, and 56,000 work there, which means that community relations has to be an important part of the programme. The second is that, to a greater extent than has been done in many other parts of the country, the Corporation has embarked on an overall landscape strategy to give a landscape structure to the random development of earlier years.

'We see regeneration in three ways,' says Ian Page, 'though the government probably sees it in one – economic. Of course the economic is important – and not just the big schemes which get the headlines but, just as important, the encouragement of existing firms. Sixty-five per cent of work in the Black Country is still in manufacturing – well above the national average. Secondly, there's environmental regeneration: the canals, the design of the new roads, planting and urban forestry. Third, there's social regeneration. If after seven years or whatever it is, we pack up our tents and leave, and no one knows we've passed by, we shall have failed. So we have a community programme – working with local groups, forming them where they don't exist, acting as liaison between them and the official world. Often there has to be physical disruption of one kind or another; with a liaison committee local people know what is happening, know where to address their complaints. As a result we've had no problems. There's a £1 million budget for community schemes; £300,000 going to schools for community use.'

BCDC's landscape strategy is planned at two levels. Extensive 'woodland cores', major focal points, will re-establish the balance between the natural landscape and the built-up areas. 'Woodland spines' will radiate out from these, along road, canal and open-space corridors, to create a linked landscape network. By early 1990 the Black Country Urban Forestry Unit was operational, with two whole-time staff and two part-time staff. The long list of its sponsors includes Dudley, Sandwell, Walsall and Wolverhampton; the Development Corporation; the Countryside Commission and the Forestry Commission; Esso; the Black Country

Groundwork Trust and Bourneville Village Trust. The scheme is distinct from the Countryside Commission's proposed 'Community Forests',* but as one of the first initiatives of its kind its progress will be watched with interest.

Confuse a Black Countryman with a Brummie and you will be in trouble. It is the ultimate insult. The way the stories of the government-sponsored BCDC and the private-sector Heartlands initiative in Birmingham unroll will have a particular piquancy.

Birmingham. Powerful in metalworking, strong in Nonconform- ism, it was made famous by the Chamberlains a hundred years ago for the firm far-sightedness of its municipal management. Its first great 'improvement' scheme, which laid low the centre of the city, took place between 1876 and 1882. Birmingham has been at it ever since. It is now engaged on its third reshaping in half a century. After the emergency work occasioned by the bomb damage of World War II, the 'big thinking' of the 1950s and 60s – symbolised by the road system, the 423 tower blocks,† the Bull Ring and the Rotunda – gave the city the generally unloved character it has shown for more than a quarter of a century. Its main buildings, mostly large and undistinguished, bump one another in the spaces left over from the highways like unwieldy mastodons. Now, struggling back after the loss of 200,000 jobs in the seventies and eighties, the city is in the middle of a development boom that will change its character yet again.

From its past as the manufacturing 'city of a thousand trades', Birmingham is now rushing headlong towards the goal of inter- national business centre. 'Forward' is the injunction on its coat of arms. 'A city in a tearing hurry, addicted to instant success, biggest, first, pragmatic, profitable, confusing, incoherent and monotone' – this was the view of a symposium group in the late eighties of the image presented by the city centre.[1] 'A concept of natural development,' it continued, 'seemed to have been swept away. There was neither time for people to participate in city development, nor time for the city landscape and its people to absorb that development. Collaboration with time,' it suggested, 'is important.' Birmingham has become used to this sort of comment, but it hurt when Prince Charles slated its cherished new conven- tion centre – the City's flagship development, completed in the spring of 1991 and bearing the highest of municipal hopes as the

* See pp. 227 et seq.
† Over fifty have been converted for use as sheltered accommodation.

natural complement to the enormously successful National Exhibition Centre – as 'a concrete silo' and 'an unmitigated disaster'. Intense controversy has attached, too – how could it have been otherwise? – to the Council's proposals totally to redevelop the whole 26-acre/10.5 ha Bull Ring area, possibly including New Street Station. In fact, whatever feelings may be about the main convention centre building, the concert hall is admired and Centenary Square, the big new space that holds the whole thing together and links it to the centre of the city, has received nothing but plaudits. This has much to do with Tess Jaray's paving and street furniture – made possible by the City's per-cent-for-art policy. One hopes that the Bull Ring redevelopment may have something of the same quality.

Any big city has many faces. Birmingham's include, at random, apart from its 1960s buildings and roads, leafy Edgbaston, Bourneville, an elaborate network of canals, its Exhibition Centre and airport (a new £60 million terminal in 1991), one of the most comprehensive reference libraries in the country, and an accelerating commitment to the arts – once dependent upon its pre-Raphaelites and the Birmingham Rep, then upon Simon Rattle, now too upon companies like the Royal (erstwhile Sadlers Wells) Ballet and D'Oyly Carte which have been persuaded to relocate there. A 'convention city', which it hopes to become, must have its cultural sideshows. Birmingham was one of the first cities to embrace the per-cent-for-art ethic.

Another aspect of its municipal *persona* is to be seen in its long-standing commitment to the decentralisation of its services. Some years ago it set itself the target of 39 neighbourhood offices, possibly reflecting the city's wards. By 1990 it had established 38 – though *not* tied into the ward pattern but rather set up in the areas of greatest need, so that sometimes a ward may have two or three. By 1991 there should be 46, with six more coming into operation every year until they total about 61 to 63. These neighbourhood offices were originally seen as representative of all council departments; more recently they have been centred on one particular department, which supplies the core staff. Nonetheless each acts as an 'embassy' for the whole Council and will deal with all problems and queries. Beyond this network, though only at the moment 'a twinkle in the eye', is the eventual objective of setting up urban parish councils throughout the city, which would have some powers and some funding. This policy, it has to be added, represents the views of the present Labour majority, but not of the Conservative opposition.

The city is pushing ahead with various environmental improvements and rehabilitation schemes. Birmingham is always said to have more miles of waterway than Venice, for it marks the meeting point of the Birmingham Canal Navigation (which was started in 1767), the Worcester and Birmingham, the Birmingham and Fazely, and the Grand Union Canal. Until fairly recently all this was a hidden world, cut off from the life of the city. First moves to open up the system for wider public use were made around 1970, with the improvement of James Brindley Walk, right in the centre of the city. There followed some piecemeal work on the towpaths, but it was in 1982 that the real push began with a collaborative effort by City, British Waterways Board and the DoE, which brought £1.25 million to bear upon the problem. Today about 6 miles/9.5 km. of canalside walkway exist through inner Birmingham, and a 14 mile/22 km. length of cycleway is proposed all the way from Birmingham to Wolverhampton.

It was Birmingham which pioneered the concept of neighbourhood 'enveloping' – giving a lift to run-down areas by the exterior restoration and redecoration of whole streets at a time, thereby giving owners and tenants an incentive to take on further work themselves inside. Enveloping became widely copied elsewhere. Birmingham, conversely, has adopted from elsewhere – it was first tried out in Rochdale – the 'Industrial Improvement Area', of which there are now four in the city: in Digbeth, Moseley Road, Tyseley and the Jewelry Quarter. Here grants are available up to £10,000, on a pound-for-pound basis, for the comprehensive refurbishment of workshops and industrial premises.

In the Jewelry Quarter, for example, £1 million in grant aid has produced investment totalling £3 million from the private sector. The Jewelry Quarter has been the subject of particular study. In 1987 URBED,* with consultants Segal Quince Wicksteed, was commissioned to propose a strategy for its revitalisation. The area is somewhat cut off from the central business district – to which it is close – by the road system and one of the canals. Though there are still between five and six hundred firms there, employing maybe 4,000 people, foreign competition and bulk buying by retailers have rendered many of them vulnerable. Many properties are empty. The report nonetheless considered that the Jewelry Quarter, though rather diffuse and too down-market, has the potential to be the commercial centre of the industry outside London. As such it could be developed as a training centre and, as

* See p. 302.

part of a wider industrial Heritage Park with new transport links to the upgraded retail area of the 'Golden Triangle', for visitors and tourists. Improvements occur incrementally. The Duchy of Cornwall has recycled one building to provide seventy-nine managed workshops; St Paul's Square, the only remaining Georgian square in Birmingham, has been transformed (the down side of which is that it has become too expensive for the jewellers, who have moved out).

The City, therefore, has in hand a wide range of work, from the very big to the quite small. It is against this background that the Heartlands programme has to be seen. Birmingham Heartlands covers 2,500 acres/over 1,200 ha at the confluence of the Rivers Rea and Tame and Hockley Brook, lying astride the M1 (close to Spaghetti Junction) and extending inwards almost to the city centre. Not much is visible from the motorway because of the sound baffles on either side. Overhead the powerlines dodge to and fro, and only a group of big gasholders provide a reference point for the motorist. At ground level most of the area is a familiar muddle of housing and industry and public utilities and disused land, cut by railway lines and two canals. Nearly 13,000 people live there, but in the spring of 1989 unemployment ran at 32 per cent (compared with a national average of 9.3 per cent) and there were 140 vacant sites ranging from 60 acres/24 ha to a mere couple of acres or so. In the mid 1980s it had become clear that only a coordinated thrust could bring the area back to life.

Somewhere around 1986/87 the City got to hear that it might be on the government's 'post-Docklands list' for a UDC. 'But Birmingham,' I was told, 'has a long tradition of being pretty interventionist and doing without central government involvement. The response was to go to Nicholas Ridley (the then Environment Secretary) with a package, saying we will meet you halfway with a private-sector agency within the local-authority framework. It would be untrue to imply that the Council alone was taking the initiative. The Chamber of Commerce pushed hard. You have to remember there are still a number of benevolent entrepreneurs around who want to be seen to be doing something. Ridley obviously warmed to the notion of a private-sector initiative of this kind.' They got away with it and Birmingham Heartlands Ltd was formed – so far the only body of its kind.

The shareholders are Bryants, R. M. Douglas, Galliford, Tarmac, Wimpey (i.e. both national and more-local names), the City Council and the Birmingham Chamber of Commerce. The Company 'coordinates and stimulates action; markets and promotes the area; aids the assembly of land and development packages; promotes new development projects; supports training and community development'. The Council retains all its statutory powers in the consideration of planning applications, the construction of highways, the compulsory acquisition of land, the provision of housing and social services, training, etc. Heartlands Ltd has a small office of seven or eight people. Policy is set by the Board, in the light of reports from a whole number of working groups (on which sit officers from Company and City Council). The initiative is expected to cost £1 billion in all, and take ten to fifteen years to complete. The government has committed £70 million to the initiative, on condition (a) that this will not be the only money put into it; (b) that no further funding from the government will be available (other than through City Grant, Estate Action and so on in the normal way). The Regional Office, I was told by the City, 'has bent over backwards to see that we get as much as possible within the rules. They've probably pushed their City Grant formula as far as it's ever gone.'

The first move was to commission a study of the area from consultants Roger Tym and Partners. Their report, *A Development, Marketing and Investment Strategy*, was published in January 1988; it included, in a separate volume, ten detailed appendices on such things as housing, land ownership, ground conditions, highways and public transport, and so on. Following three months of public consultation the strategy was revised, and adopted by the City's Planning Committee in July 1988.

Heartlands as a whole has been subdivided into a series of smaller initiatives, each having a distinct character and each having a separate development framework. First off the ground has been 'Waterlinks', 320 acres/135 ha, straddling the Birmingham and Fazely Canal. This it is hoped will 'set the tone' for the whole venture. It is close to Aston Science Park and fairly close to the city centre; new basins off the Canal will provide an opportunity for imaginative mixed development, especially for medium- and high-technology firms and professional uses. The first phase of Aston Cross is finished and occupied. A new residential community, Bordesley Village, is proposed to the south. Pushing up against the M6 is the 'Star Project', an as yet vague but ambitious proposal for a major 'marker', centred on a prominent high building of exceptional design, which is intended to raise the 'profile' of the whole area. Possibly here could be sited the proposed 450,000 sq. ft./42,000 sq. m. retail centre which it is thought Heartlands needs. Provision is made elsewhere for local shopping, recreation, open space, additional housing; running in a long swathe on the eastern side of the whole is the Heartlands Industrial Area. Here will be the city's first Simplified Planning Zone. Allied with all this the Strategy foresees a new spine road from the M6 to Nechells Parkway and an improved link from the latter to the Aston Expressway. Public transport is recognised as important. Extensive environmental improvements will be made throughout. Job training and stimulus for new initiatives is given great weight ('very much the key issue' was the view expressed to me on more than one occasion; 'perhaps we haven't been doing as much as we should have in the past'). When all this is put together, it is hoped that Heartlands will create 20,000 jobs.

So far, so good. Rhetoric or reality? The same can be asked of many of the development briefs emanating from the government's Development Corporations, but in an operation of the Heartlands type there are additional problems. There is no reason to doubt the general commitment of any of the partners but inevitably the weight each feels able to give to the commitment is likely to vary with changing circumstances. The essential 'keeper of the vision' is the tiny Birmingham Heartlands Ltd team. Its chairman, Sir Reginald Eyre, as an ex MP, knows local needs and has the ear of important potential supporters. Alan Osborne, its chief executive, ex Tarmac, was described to me as 'ideal – very sharp, very scrupulous, straight as a die'. Among his staff are an ex Assistant Director from the City Planning Department and an ex Assistant Treasurer, now Heartlands' Finance Manager. Their job is to keep things moving, create opportunities, match executant capabilities to priority needs. They stand in relation to the consortium members much as the European Commission does to the member nations of the European Community. As in Europe, not all members of the consortium are equally concerned about all parts of the programme. Different partners take the lead in different areas. Life being what it is, they will tend to want to move – or not – as market conditions dictate, rather than as a master plan may require. Serious recession can knock the stuffing out of the best intentions.

On its side the Council, too, has problems. Chief officers meet quarterly (it used to be monthly) to discuss Heartlands, but they too are beset by other responsibilities and may have differing priorities. In a city the size of Birmingham departments are large. To what extent, one wonders, does the Heartlands commitment filter down to more junior officers? What happens, conversely, if the latter's enthusiasm outweighs that of their superiors?

Finance raises political and technical problems. Because so much of the funding (through City Grant and so on) is not 'new' money, political decisions quickly come to the fore. The Council could not contribute to work throughout Heartlands on the scale it has done to the first big scheme without reducing its input elsewhere in the city. How can that be justified politically, and what then will be the attitude of the private-sector companies? Again, the interface between public and private funding can produce situations which are, to the uninitiated, bizarre. For example, the proposed Heartlands spine road had to be included in the Council's rolling road-development programme for government approval. Approval, when it came, included a requirement that £15 million of the estimated £70 million cost be contributed by the private sector. This City and Heartlands are working to achieve. However, legal opinion is that any such receipts will not affect the Council's capital budget under the terms of the 1989 Local Government and Housing Act, which requires (a) 50 per cent of such capital receipts from 'barter' to be reserved to meet credit liabilities; (b) that any such barter capital value be considered in fact as a capital receipt, even though no money may have changed hands. A Heartlands developer has suggested that he build part of the road, at an estimated cost of £4.5 million, as part of his overall development scheme (which, apart from all else, would allow earlier completion than could be managed under the Council programme). Should this happen, £2.5 million will have to be set aside from the City's capital account, even though no money has actually accrued to the Council. In other words, the Council will have had to pay a sizeable premium for having got something done by the private sector.*

These may seem arcane details to which to devote space, but it is probably on how scores, hundreds, of such matters are resolved over the next few years that the outcome of the Heartlands experiment turns. And this is important. Partnerships are seen everywhere as essential to the way forward. However, if they are to work, not only are clear objectives needed but the right corporate machinery to give effect to the corporate commitment. If Heartlands can get things right, it will offer lessons for towns and cities all over the country.

---

* This formula, it would seem, has been abandoned in the case of Olympia & York's contributions to transport access to Canary Wharf.

11

GREATER MANCHESTER
Manchester – Trafford – Salford

THE MANCHESTER Ship Canal, started in 1887 and opened in 1894, was the last epic achievement of Victorian engineering. It runs for thirty-five miles/56 km., across the Lancashire/Cheshire plain, through Warrington and Runcorn to the Mersey at Eastham. It brought ocean-going ships of up to 12,500 tonnes into the heart of the city; in the middle 1920s it was carrying some 6,360,000 tonnes a year; the inland city of Manchester, in fact, rated as the third busiest port in the country.

The genesis of the Canal lay in a period of local decline no less savage than that which was to hit the area a hundred years later. Manchester, and the West Midlands, formed, in the second half of the last century, the most dense concentration of manufacturing in Britain. But its products had to flow westwards to Liverpool for export. The handling charges, rail costs and dock dues became ruinously prohibitive; industrial profitability for many collapsed; factory closures in 1893 alone resulted in the loss of 12,650 jobs. Many of the working population – as too their descendants today, a hundred years later – were forced to flee the city. By 1881 over 18,600 houses were vacant. How familiar it sounds. Against this background, the creation of the Ship Canal had an epic dimension, not merely by reason of the scale of the concept (and the obstacles and disasters its construction had to overcome), but because of the scale of the opposition it aroused. Inevitably it was fought by every possible interest in Liverpool and enabling Bills were twice thrown out by Parliament. Nonetheless it was seen through, and for sixty years or more transformed the economy of Greater Manchester (in the first dozen years after its completion

185

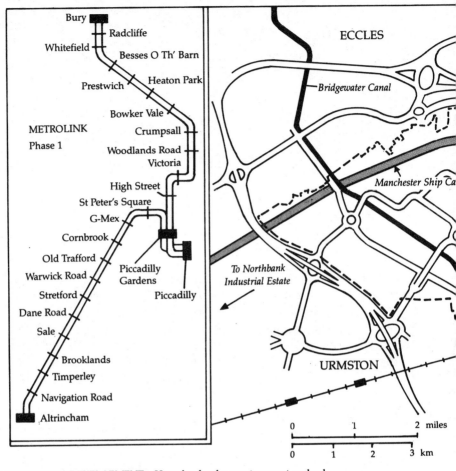

METROLINK
Phase 1

To Northbank
Industrial Estate

SALFORD QUAYS DEVELOPMENT: How the development concept evolved

1. The site as it existed

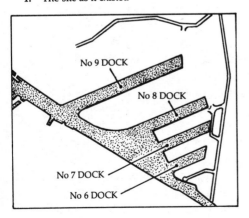

2. Construction of dams and new canals

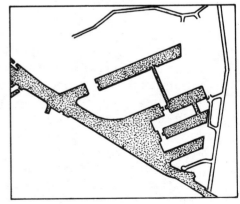

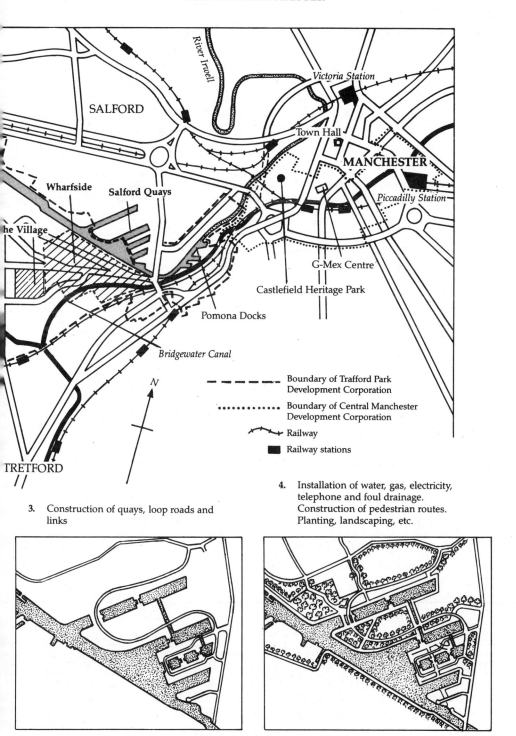

River Irwell

SALFORD

Victoria Station

Town Hall

MANCHESTER

Piccadilly Station

Wharfside

Salford Quays

he Village

G-Mex Centre

Castlefield Heritage Park

Pomona Docks

Bridgewater Canal

N

- - - - - - Boundary of Trafford Park
Development Corporation

• • • • • • • • • • Boundary of Central Manchester
Development Corporation

Railway

Railway stations

TRETFORD

3. Construction of quays, loop roads and
links

4. Installation of water, gas, electricity,
telephone and foul drainage.
Construction of pedestrian routes.
Planting, landscaping, etc.

the rateable value of the area had more than tripled).

By the same token, for obvious reasons, it was here in the areas around the docks, shared by Manchester itself, Salford and Trafford, that the inner-city problems of the 1980s were most acute. The economic health of the ten authorities making up the conurbation varies considerably. Manchester has never exerted over it quite the degree of dominance that, say, Birmingham has over the West Midlands, or Liverpool over Merseyside. Several of its towns – for example Bury, Stockport and Warrington – have *increased* their populations over the past fifteen years, and Stockport, in 1989, had an unemployment figure, 5.6 per cent, which was the lowest in the county. Nonetheless, overall, the North West lost in the eighties 34 per cent of the manufacturing jobs it had had at the end of the seventies (around 333,000 of 971,000) and the saddest single area of all was perhaps that at the eastern end of the Manchester Ship Canal. It was there that the government inserted, first, in February 1987, a 'second-generation' UDC: the Trafford Park Development Corporation; and then in 1988, a 'third-genera-tion' Corporation: Central Manchester. But it was here also that the third local authority concerned, Salford, independently pushed through, during the second half of the eighties, the remarkable redevelopment of what are now known as 'Salford Quays'.

Trafford Park, not much more than a mile west of Central Manchester, is the oldest and largest industrial estate in the country – indeed the world. It came into being in 1896, as a direct result of the completion of the Ship Canal, and was an instant, runaway success. It covered 1,200 acres/486 ha, included housing for 600, and within five years had forty firms located there. By the mid 1930s 35,000 were working on the Estate; during World War II the figure rose to 75,000. By the eighties, however, it had dropped to 24,000 and, although 600 firms were still there, it was obvious that major investment was needed if the Estate was ever to resume the role it once had. Trafford Council were having to spend between £1 million and £2 million a year – 10 per cent of their capital budget – simply on maintenance; wider assistance had to be sought. The Council, with the major companies on the Estate and support from neighbouring authorities, first lobbied the government for 'assisted-area' status; then, jointly with the main employers, commissioned an 'investment strategy' from consult-ants. This proposed the formation of a UDC. A month after its publication the creation of a Development Corporation for Trafford Park was announced by the government. Here at least the UDC and the local councils (Trafford and Salford) seem to have got off on the right foot.

The Corporation covers over 3,100 acres/nearly 1,270 ha lying mostly between the Ship Canal and the main Chester road to the south, and westward to the M23. Within this remit, but as a distinct enclave five miles away, are 250 acres/100 ha at Irlam, site of the former British Steel works (closure of which meant the loss of 4,500 jobs). The Corporation has been allocated £160 million upon which to draw during its life; its tasks are the familiar ones of land clearance, upgrading the environment, and improving transport facilities. Apart from roadworks the latter includes new bus services, support for the proposed Metrolink transit system and, possibly, a Greater Manchester freight terminal for Channel Tunnel traffic; the Corporation has also helped to ensure the long-term navigability of the Canal through a £2.75 million contribution to the Canal Company's improvement programme, now costed at £27 million.

The Corporation early identified four main areas for development and improvement: the Irlam site, now the Northbank Industrial Park; Hadfield Street, a finger pointing into Manchester along the main A56 road; the 'Village', a revived, 55 acre/22 ha, mixed-use focal point in the centre of the Estate (site of the original housing for 600); and, as the 'flagship' project (flagships are *de rigueur* in the UDCs), Wharfside, a swathe of 89 acres/36 ha lying between the Ship and the Bridgewater Canals. This latter (many of the firms being displaced are offered sites at Irlam) holds major possibilities, facing as it does the redevelopment of Salford Quays across the water.

When Rosehaugh Trafford, with the Canal Company, emerged as preferred developers, Wharfside was promoted as 'the largest single redevelopment scheme outside the South East'. There were general protestations of faith and goodwill. The Corporation was 'delighted by both companies' outstanding enthusiasm and commitment'; Rosehaugh Trafford proclaimed themselves 'dedicated to the comprehensive development of Wharfside as an environment of the highest quality'. This was indeed a 'big' scheme of tree-lined avenues, park, lake and other water features. Alas, the dedication did not survive the 1989/90 property collapse. By the end of 1989 Rosehaugh was gone from the stage (as too, as we have seen, from its involvement in the Royal Docks in London) and the Corporation was negotiating with others for development 'on a more phased basis'. Nonetheless 'the concept behind the Wharfside Masterplan remains firm', Mike Shields, Trafford Park's Chief Executive, states unequivocally. 'It is a marvellous opportunity which is being firmly grasped.' Let us hope so.

By 1990 some developments were in fact to be seen on the ground here – most notably Quay West (80,000 sq. ft./7,435 sq. m. of office space) and the Samuel Platt restaurant/pub (with its projection out over the water). Elsewhere the big White City retail complex had been completed; work was in progress on the 530,000 sq. ft./nearly 50,000 sq. m. of Exchange Quay and (with £3.9 million from the Corporation) on the 22 acre/9 ha Centre-point site. There are half a dozen business parks. Environmental improvements had been undertaken at a number of points, notably near the Barton Swing Aqueduct and in the Ordsall area in Salford. By 1990 the Corporation could claim the reclamation of 620 acres/250 ha; 1 million sq. ft./93,000 sq. m. of new development completed, with 2 million more under construction; the creation of 2,000 jobs; and an investment in Trafford Park of over £380 million, for an input by the Corporation of £43 million. It could claim, too, to have recognised the importance of getting the infrastructure right before allowing development to rush ahead – but then its Chief Executive is a planner. And it seeks to write into its agreements (now becoming general among the Development Corporations) a formula which will enable it to benefit from any 'super profits' arising from development – which will of course strengthen its budget for further initiatives.

Manchester's industrial base was always much broader than that of Liverpool at the other end of the Canal. Notwithstanding the great shake-out of the early eighties, the city soon showed its mettle in a range of positive initiatives. It has so far failed to attract the kind of investment from abroad that the Japanese have brought, for example, to South Wales and the North East, but recent years have seen a marked resurgence of financial and commercial activity. Four elements can perhaps be singled out in particular as reflecting Manchester's changing image in the eight-ies: the expansion of its airport; the creation of the Castlefield 'urban heritage park'; the transformation of the old Central Station into the G-Mex exhibition centre; and the steady upgrading of the city centre by stone-cleaning and the refurbishment of its older buildings, the introduction of some lively new ones, and the exclusion of traffic to create pleasant pedestrian areas.

The airport claims to be the fastest growing in Europe. A new £57 million domestic terminal opened in 1989; a second, inter-national terminal, at £600 million, is due to open in 1993, with a second phase to be completed by 1997. The new facilities will give the capacity for doubling the ten million presently using the

190

airport. The Castlefield 'heritage park' includes the country's largest industrial museum, housed in the world's oldest passenger terminal – the old Liverpool Road Station; the Air and Space Museum in the old Victorian Lower Campfield Market; and the remains of the city's Roman fort. It is hard by the main Granada Television Studios, which now take hundreds of thousands annually in organised tours through the world of *Coronation Street* and much else. G-Mex now offers 100,000 sq. ft./9,300 sq. m. of uninterrupted exhibition space, seating for 9,000, and extensive parking. New dignity has been given to the city centre by the restoration and refurbishment of such Victorian splendours as the Albert Memorial, the Barton Arcade and the Midland Hotel (now clumsily renamed the Holiday Inn Crown Plaza Midland Hotel).

Manchester, too, has its freelance 'think tanks' and enterprise agencies. In the eighties a group of architects, businessmen and union leaders formed the 'Phoenix Initiative' to float ideas and stimulate action in specific quarters of the city. They started with a banana-shaped strip of land, south of the River Irwell, running from Piccadilly to Deansgate Stations. Here was conceived 'Granby Village' – 200 flats and houses to be built by Wimpey Homes in the Whitworth Street corridor, with the help of £3.3 million City Grant – perhaps the first new homes to be created in the heart of the city for generations, and a foretaste of the 2,000 which the Council would like to see bringing 6,000 people back into an area which has in recent years numbered its residents at fewer than 150.

This was the broad context into which the government introduced the Central Manchester Development Corporation in 1988 – the first of its kind to so wholly embrace the heart of a city. Its area of 470 acres/187 ha covers very much the same ground that was the subject of Manchester Phoenix's first study and first initiative. To the west the Corporation to all intents and purposes touches fingers with the Trafford Park Corporation like Michelangelo's God and Adam. Within this area are to be found the city centre, the Town Hall (surely, with Glasgow's, the apotheosis of nineteenth-century civic grandeur), G-Mex, the Castlefield area, Piccadilly Station, the housing site conceived by Phoenix – in fact most of the city's central assets. It will hardly occasion surprise, therefore, that the imposition of the UDC created suspicion and ill feeling – suspicion that central government was positioning itself to take credit for the achievements of others; ill feeling because the Corporation would be taking over responsibility for projects already in the pipeline.

The City swallowed its pride. Phoenix moved on to another area

191

(around the Cathedral and former Royal Exchange Station). The Corporation proclaimed its desire for dialogue and partnerships all round. (It is worth noting that the Corporation's Chief Executive, John Gle ter, was previously with the City's Environment Department.) The existing pattern of land ownership, and the excellent state of the city's existing infrastructure, absolve Central Manchester, unlike the other UDCs, from massive land assembly. The Corporation seeks rather to engage the further interest and investment of the private sector directly, stimulated where necessary by City Grant and environmental improvement. There is talk of something between £500 million and £1 billion investment by the second half of the nineties, leading to the creation of maybe 6,000 jobs.

The two Development Corporations sit along the south side of the Ship Canal; on the northern side lies Salford. The docks here are at an angle to the line of the Canal, creating between Salford and Trafford a big triangle of water which was the turning space for ships heading back to the Mersey. From this, four long fingers of water formed the docks on the Salford side. By the end of the 1970s the quays were deserted, derelict and rat-infested. The water stank on sunny days. Closure of the whole Canal east of Runcorn was being considered by the Canal Company. In 1981 150 acres/about 60 ha in the neighbourhood, in the ownership of the Company, were designated as an Enterprise Zone – a straggling, irregular area, looking on the map much like what is left when the man doing the paper-tearing act has finished. Part of it abuts No. 9 Dock, and part includes No. 6 Dock, the smallest.

Several things now occurred. As the result of an Enterprise Zone exhibition in London Peter Hunter, of the architect-planners Shepheard Epstein Hunter, met a councillor from Salford, who invited him up ('but you won't come'). He did, and decided to take a chance on preparing a development scheme for No. 6 Dock for presentation to Salford Council and the Ship Canal Company. A large developer showed initial interest, but in the light of a very adverse report from market research consultants, decided that the area had altogether too much against it and, in 1982, withdrew. In the autumn of that year, however, a local entrepreneur/developer, Edward Hagan, entered the stage. He would, he said, try to put together a series of development packages with other interests on a risk-sharing basis – but, before that could happen, funding had to be secured to ensure the removal of the area's 'negative values'. Salford Council approached the DoE for Derelict

192

Land Grant with which to purchase and reclaim Dock 6 and adjacent land. The £10 million grant obtained enabled a certain amount of work to be put in hand, but it rapidly became clear that this wou.d in no way cover provision of the essential infrastructure. After a certain amount of haggling – essentially over the point that here in Salford private investment could not be expected until the infrastructure had been completed – it was finally agreed that Urban Programme funding could be used to cover the on-site works (i.e. the quays) and Derelict Land Grant the 'off-site' works (i.e. essentially, the basins).* This funding enabled the Council, urged on by Councillor L. Hough its Leader, to purchase the *whole* of the docks at a cost of £1.6 million: 160 acres/65 ha plus 75 acres/30 ha of water space. Dock 6 and adjacent land, it was agreed, would be transferred to the company Mr Hagan had set up, Urban Waterside Limited, on condition that they secured at least £4.5 million of development (which, with DLG, would make £9 million in all), within three years. This part of the saga had a nail-biting finish. Hagan tramped the banks and pension funds and big builders. It was only, however, with hours to spare and a £500,000 mortgage on his own house thrown in, that he just made it on New Year's Eve three years later. Regeneration does not come easy.

It was clear by 1984 that Dock 6 would not be a viable proposition on its own. A comprehensive plan for the whole docks area was essential. The Council asked Shepheard Epstein Hunter to prepare an overall strategy, with Ove Arup and Partners as consultant engineers. By then the huge grain elevator at the head of Dock 9 had been demolished. Apart from mounds of rubble, reflected in the stretching puddles, the site was flat and desolate – so characterless, in fact, that a visitor was unaware, until he reached them, of the great fingers of water dividing it; but then, faced by their extent, would become awed by the intimidating scale of these three miles/4.8 km. of waterfront. The development plan, when it was published in the following year, covered four main matters: water quality, roads and services, public access and landscape. Its real achievement, as subsequently followed through, is to have given so strong a character to what was so vast and featureless an area.

Dams were constructed across the dock entrances to exclude

---

* This was possibly the first time that DLG had been used in this way to cover water areas. 'After all,' the argument ran, 'if we filled them in and covered them with topsoil you'd give us the grant – so what's the difference?'

most of the heavily polluted canal water. Bunds were thrown out from the sides of the quays to vary and humanise the scale of the water areas; new canals were cut through the quays to link the basins. A 'vocabulary' of design elements was established to give order and consistency to the whole. Great granite keystones form the docksides; red clay bricks the walkways. All water edges are lined by trees and lampposts in a continuous rhythm (three trees, one lamppost, three trees, etc. – in time, the two outer trees will be removed, leaving the fully grown centre one). Every opportunity has been taken to create changes of level and to create vertical emphases where none existed. Many of the quaysides are at two levels; walking, in time to come, at the higher level, one will still be under the canopy of trees planted at the lower level. Steps combine two rhythms, a 'full' size and a half size; there are long ramps for the disabled. Bridges offer different vistas of the water; the lower-level quayside walk as like as not passing beneath them. There are obelisks, incised quaystones on edge, bollards. Two giant cargo cranes have been relocated. A disused 300 ft./90 m. railway swing bridge weighing 640 tons was jacked on to pontoons and moved three quarters of a mile to cross Dock 9 where, resplendent in red, white and blue, it now provides an important focus. Small details, most of these things, in themselves; cumulatively they spell quality. Salford's decision to complete all infrastructure in advance of development only serves to underline the opportunities thrown away in the Isle of Dogs.

A word has to be said here about water quality. The Ship Canal is foully polluted and although the bunds prevent any significant entry of its waters into the impounded basins it was clearly vital to improve quality in the latter to the point where they not only looked attractive but were safe for water sports. Intensive testing and sampling established that, without treatment, stratification of the water would occur, leading by stages to anoxic conditions – the absence of oxygen – which in turn would lead to the production and release of methane and hydrogen sulphide gases from the decayed silt at the bottom. To overcome this helixors were installed in the basins, by means of which compressed air produces cones of bubbles which circulate and oxygenate the water in a steadily purifying process. Already quality has markedly improved and a fish growing programme will introduce tench, bream, rudd, perch, chub and carp.

The first buildings began to go up on Hagan's Dock 6: a £3.5 million eight-screen cinema, which was a success from the outset; a four-star Copthorne Hotel – for which, one is told, bookings have to be made well in advance; a pub; and then 200,000 sq. ft./ 18,600 sq. m. of office space. Elsewhere 400 houses have been built, offices, and mixed developments of various kinds are in hand, including 'Harbour City' at Basin 9 at a cost somewhere between £100 and £200 million. At the beginning of 1989 investment in Salford Quays by the private sector had reached about £65 million; committed development amounted to more than £260 million; total investment envisaged was of the order of £350 to £400 million; it was expected that by 1991 something like 4,000 jobs would have been created.

In August 1988 a Development Strategy Review was published, with, inevitably, further amendments since then. Essentially, however, the original concepts have remained in place. Ingenuity has been shown in many quarters – in 'massaging' grants, in business deals, in political decision, in water engineering – to make this possible. The success of Salford Quays, however, springs above all from the courage and vision of three people: Councillor Hough of Salford City,* who pushed through the purchase of the docks, even though the Council had no money with which to develop them, and who braved local criticism that too much of the Council's resources was being diverted into the Quays; Peter Hunter and his team, who first saw the potential of the area, 'sold' the idea, and masterminded the detail of its execution; and Ted Hagan, the local man who put his own house and overdraft on the line to ensure that development did in fact take place.

Salford is an enlightened authority. It was the first to have gas street lighting. It was one of the first industrial cities to go smokeless. Its landscape group in the Planning Division, with a staff of twenty-two, must be one of the biggest in the North West, if not, for District Councils, in the country. (The group has won a couple of contracts for work in Trafford Park.) Indeed, a 1988 survey by the *Architects' Journal* found the City of Salford to be the authority spending most on conservation and the environment. However, though the Quays made the cover of Mrs Thatcher's launch brochure for 'Action for Cities' in 1988, great problems remain elsewhere. Dr Alice Coleman has described Salford's Pendleton flats as one of the worst estates in the country. Unsurprisingly therefore, pride in the Quays is mixed with resentment in some quarters that disproportionate effort has gone into that quarter of the city. It should not be thought, however, that the Council is unmindful of its wider obligations – its programmes in

* Who sadly died in 1987.

Trinity (a £30 million project spread over five years), in the Barracks area (where housing partnerships are showing results) and the Ordsall area (another five-year initiative, with support from Trafford Park) are indicative of its concerns.

In greater or lesser degree, all the authorities of Greater Manchester have successes of one kind or another to point to. What hits the outsider forcibly is the absence, since the demise of the Metro County, of any kind of overall strategy for the conurbation as a whole. Ten local authorities, two Development Corporations, a couple of Task Forces and a CAT, do not make up a recipe for coordinated effort. Stir in the big landowners like the Manchester Ship Canal Company, assorted agencies like INWARD (the North West's body for the promotion of inward investment), a sizeable clutch of enterprise agencies (there are seven in Manchester and Salford alone), Phoenix and others, and it is hardly surprising that progress is patchy.

Of course togetherness is by no means totally absent. There is the Association of Greater Manchester Authorities. For ten years, until it was closed down in 1989, there was Greater Manchester Economic Developments. The airport is run by a local authority consortium (though Manchester dominates by matching the nine directors nominated by the other councils with nine of its own). Metrolink, the 'supertram' initiated by the Metro County before its death, which will link Bury in one direction to Altrincham in the other, and part of which should be running by 1992, is supported by the Development Corporations as well as all the councils concerned. There is the Mersey Basin Campaign (aimed at solving the gross water-pollution problem). There is the North West Channel Tunnel Group. Manchester, Salford and Trafford come together to formulate joint bids for European Community funding. And they financed an English Tourist Board planning study, *A Framework for Tourism Development*.

Nonetheless, these are *ad hoc*, single-purpose groupings. Will it not seem odd to subsequent generations that Salford Quays, Wharfside, and Central Manchester's proposals for Pomona Docks, for example, all facing one another across the same sheet of water, could not be handled as a single project? Here, surely, was an opportunity for grandeur of vision which most other countries in the western world would have exploited to the full. Perhaps, should Manchester gain nomination as the host city for the Olympic Games in 2000, an embracing vision could yet arise.

12

WEST YORKSHIRE

Bradford – Calderdale

YORKSHIRE HAS many faces. Think only of York itself with its Minster, of Fountains and Rievaulx, of Swaledale, of Flamborough Head and Whitby and Humberside. But it is in what was once the West Riding, and is now West Yorkshire, that its industrial heart lay. Two million people live in this great sprawling conurbation which includes the cities and towns of Leeds, Bradford, Huddersfield, Wakefield and Halifax. We have already glanced at booming Leeds, and, to the south, at Sheffield – both accorded third-generation Development Corporations. In between these, in the Metropolitan County of West Yorkshire, the communities are having to use their native ingenuity to combat the aftermath of the collapse of the textile industry on which they were built. This is how two of them are doing it.

Wool, weaving and dyeing. Clogs and cobblestones. Vast mills, each employing many thousands of Lowry figures. Forests of belching chimney stacks, blotting out the day and blackening the gritstone terraces. So indeed it was and the image has great staying power. It was the most insidious of the problems faced by Bradford and Calderdale, when, in the eighties, they set out to find new ways of earning a living (though 95 per cent of the British wool industry is still to be found within twenty miles of Bradford). 'In 1980 people's idea of Bradford was a place where the sparrows woke up coughing and pigeons flew backwards to keep the dirt out of their eyes' – so says the city itself, looking back to the year it launched, to general guffaws, a *tourism* programme.

The initiative stemmed from Ian Page of the Black Country UDC, formerly Director of the Council's Economic Development Unit*. Initially the purpose was as much to flaunt the notion as leverage for changing Bradford's image as actually to make a direct impact on the local economy. But it was so ludicrously improbable, and was nonetheless promoted with such energy, that it got a lot of publicity and it worked. Two thousand short-break holidays ('In the Footsteps of the Brontës' and 'Industrial Heritage') were sold in that first year. Today six million visitors come to Bradford annually; the number of hotels has increased from twelve to thirty-one, the number of restaurants fourfold, the number of settings for conferences from eight to twenty-six. More than £56 million a year is generated by tourism, and, it is estimated, 7,000 jobs. Glasgow was Miles Better. The tag from West Yorkshire was 'Bradford Bounces Back'.

Here one is already in the foothills of the Pennines. From Leeds the railway sinks dramatically to the centre of the city in a long rock-lined slide. It is still a tough and gutsy place, cosmopolitan (with the largest Asian community in Britain), and takes in several smaller towns and villages around. Bradford played merry hell with its rich Victorian legacy during the redevelopment years after World War II, but a good deal remains. It is all much cleaner now and real efforts have been made latterly to restore areas like the so-called German Quarter, Southfield Square (which ten years ago seemed doomed) and even the spacious Undercliffe Cemetery. The clock tower of the Town Hall, modelled on the Palazzo Vecchio in Florence, still stands as symbol of the heyday of civic building; St Blaise, patron saint of woolcombers, still looks down on Market Street from the Wool Exchange; Manningham Mill remains an awesome reminder of the sheer scale of the industry that was. Within the city boundary is the Brontë village of Haworth, where over 200,000 a year pass through the Parsonage, buy clogs and eat Brontë Burgers. Not far away lies the charming model village of Saltaire, created for his workforce in the mid nineteenth century by Sir Titus Salt (in the Aire Valley), where a local entrepreneur, Jonathan Silver, is currently turning Salt's Mill itself into an arts and leisure centre.

If one thing served above all else to put Bradford on the wider map in the eighties it was, however, the arrival of the Science Museum's offshoot, the National Museum of Photography, Film and Television. Not without reason this has been spectacularly successful, drawing over 800,000 visitors a year, and at a stroke

* Claimed as one of the first of its kind in Britain; now the Bradford Enterprise Service.

changing public perceptions of the city. Already there are plans to double its size. It is to be followed by the Victoria and Albert Museum's Eastern Collections, destined for part of Manningham. Manningham, listed Grade II✻ for its architectural and historical importance, was the biggest mill of its kind in the country, sitting on a 14 acre/5.7 ha site and boasting a 250 ft./76 m. campanile. In reality it is two mills, the north and the south, separated by a road. The north mill is to be retained by the owners, Lister, as a continuing textile works. The south mill will be ingeniously recycled, at an estimated cost of £70 million, to provide premises for the V & A, serviced business apartments and an up-market hotel. The architects, Shepheard Epstein Hunter, propose to make it more manageable by removing some of the roofing to create a series of internal courtyards, around which the new functions will be grouped. It is hoped that these will produce 3,000 new jobs.

Bradford must not be seen, however, as simply a heritage/ museum city. Bradford claims the UK's second-most-successful business park, into which a five-year programme will pump £200 million. There are plans to create a £25 million 'computer village' of 27 acres/11 ha – a centre for software expertise and component manufacture, together with conference facilities, which will be the first of its kind anywhere. There is a big 'West End' project, costed at £180 million, for the area around the Alhambra and the Museum of Photography. Overall, at the end of the eighties, £400 million of investment was said to be committed in the city.

Headlines have been created in recent years by, inside the Town Hall, the coming and going of Ernest Pickles, the Conservative Party's most extreme municipal hardliner; and, outside, by the burning of *The Satanic Verses*. But in more ways than these the eighties proved a remarkable decade for Bradford.

In an arc to the south of Bradford lie Wakefield, Dewsbury, Huddersfield and Halifax, sprawling across the landscape in untidy confusion. Into the Pennine chain, westwards from Halifax, cuts the Calder Valley, half a dozen towns strung out along it like so many beads. It is dramatic terrain by day; by night, from the tops, the running lines of lights interweave from valley fold to valley fold into magically twinkling carpets below one. Straddling this area, with Halifax as its 'capital', is the Metropolitan Borough of Calderdale, a creation of the mid seventies' restructuring of local government.

The population is about 190,000, of whom half live in Halifax, the rest in the townships of Brighouse and Elland (which almost touch Huddersfield), and, in the other direction, past Halifax,

Sowerby Bridge, Hebden Bridge and Todmorden (which actually sits astride the Yorkshire/Lancashire border). Here, too, are the smaller settlements of Mythelmroyd and Heptonstall. Unemployment in Calderdale is not far from the national average. The Borough does not figure among the government's 'Assisted Areas'. It certainly does not conform to the 'inner-city' image in its crudest sense. Nevertheless the problems to be encountered in an area such as this are of the same kind, if not of the same intensity, as those on Merseyside or Tyneside or Clydebank. The urgent need for regeneration stretches far beyond these and Calderdale's experience may thus be of interest to the rest of the country.

Looking down upon Halifax as one turns the corner at Pule Hill, or from Beacon Hill, over which ran the mediaeval packhorse route, the Magna Via, the town still speaks of its industrial past. Gone now the forest of great chimneys which once blackened everything with their grime. The soot-encrusted buildings have been cleaned. But big mills remain, and most of the Victorian monuments to past prosperity. Halifax today – though its history goes much further back – is essentially a nineteenth-century town and, though Pevsner was rather sniffy about it, one of the most coherent remaining. It has a Town Hall by Barry; the mighty All Souls Church which Gilbert Scott reckoned to be his best; the splendid covered market and Russell Arcade. Two competing families strove to leave their mark upon the place. The Ackroyds left the model estate of Ackroydon (including All Souls); the Crossleys not only the People's Park but the vast Dean Clough mills complex which once employed 6,000.

Predating all of these, however, is the astonishing Piece Hall of 1779, surely one of the most remarkable 'industrial' buildings in Europe. Built around an arcaded hollow square on falling ground, it accommodated 315 cloth merchants in the days when weaving was still a cottage industry and a central outlet became necessary for the sale of their 'pieces'. Piece Hall and Dean Clough epitomise the chequered history of Calderdale. The former became redundant within a mere decade or two of its construction as the textile industry was mechanised; the latter, a temple of that mechanisation, became redundant in the early 1980s with the all but complete collapse of the industry. Neither can any longer serve its original purpose.

For, threading through townscape and countryside is a darker picture. Employment in textiles in the Calder Valley dropped by over 60 per cent during the 1970s (one month alone in 1978 saw three firms with household names announce their closure).

25

26

27

A handful from the north: in Newcastle (25) the Quayside is being brought back to life; across the river the Gateshead MetroCentre (26) attracts around 20 million people a year. In Leeds (27) new buildings and skilful adaptations are changing the heart of the city. In Sheffield great new stadia (29) are changing the image of the Lower Don Valley. And Wigan Pier (28) is no longer a music-hall joke but an immensely successful multi-purpose local amenity which also attracts visitors in great numbers.

28

29

31

Salford Quays, at the eastern end of the Manchester ship canal, have been impressively redeveloped (30,32) for housing, industry and leisure. On the near side of the water, in the aerial view (31), can be seen Trafford Park's Wharfside; to the bottom right, off the picture, lies Central Manchester.

Opposite – Calderdale. Part of the vast Dean Clough complex in Halifax (33), now humming with a multitude of different activities; beyond in the distance, the spire of Gilbert Scott's favourite church. Inset (34), white-water canoeing at Sowerby Bridge, against a backdrop of restoration.

30

32

35

36

37

38

Lea View House, in Hackney (35–38), became a benchmark in the redesign of run-down housing estates when it was radically improved, in collaboration with the tenants, between 1980 and 1982. Elsewhere, on other estates, total demolition has replaced the gaunt blocks of the fifties and sixties with more homely and friendly houses – as below, for example (39), here in Glasgow.

40

Quality is grounded in the overall concept, but comes through no less in the detail. Some random examples: a cornershop in Halifax (42, 43), taken over by the Calderdale Project team as office and information centre. Very different, but how splendid, the bravura half-dingy fascia sported in Glasgow, (40). The sturdy structural details of Hays Galleria (41) accord with the Victorian buildings and look, not half-hearted, but as though they were really meant.

42

41

43

The very simplicity of the Cardiff Bay Visitor Centre (44), hard by the Pier Head building, creates a visual drama as it looks out across the bay. The waterfall (45), part of the Liverpool Garden Festival (and so far still in being) reminds us that water features need not be as boring as they so often are. And the detail below (46) is proof that small industrial buildings can be as well designed as more obvious showpieces.

47

48

49

Public art can take a multitude of forms – strident, decorative, abstract, figurative. The ribbed globe (47) is a sundial in Swansea's Maritime Quarter. The brick Shakespeare (48) is on a flank wall in Newcastle. 'Lightwave' (50), on the BR station in Wakefield, lit sequentially from within, casts wonderful shadows after dark. Within the inner city, events and happenings which directly involve local people can do much to recreate a sense of community – as here (49) in Barrow-in-Furness' Town Hall Tattoo.

50

Churches and chapels, mills and warehouses, theatres and almshouses bit the dust. One 1983 survey estimated that 40 per cent of the South Pennine mills had disappeared or were in ruins; another reported 10 million sq. ft./about 930,000 sq. m. of industrial floorspace to be vacant in West Yorkshire. Notwithstanding the supremely confident air of the Halifax Building Society's big new headquarters; notwithstanding the enlightened restoration of Piece Hall; notwithstanding the sprucing up of the town centre, Halifax's economic health was precarious. And what was true of Halifax was doubly true of the other townships. Todmorden lost nearly 16 per cent of its population between 1961 and 1981. Dereliction and decay marked each one of the towns. Approaches to the countryside, still marvellous when you reached it, were marred by eyesores of one kind or another. Housing estates of the sixties and early seventies remained unlandscaped and looked increasingly down at heel. Trade continued to slip away to Huddersfield and Bradford and Leeds. The railway gateway to Halifax symbolised it all. The station entrance, and a muddy expanse around, presented a picture of total squalor; across the road the 1772 Square Chapel, one of the town's few remaining Georgian buildings, was mouldering into a state of ruination that was considered unsafe.

Halifax hit bottom in 1982. Crossley's, after more than a century in Halifax, announced the closure of Dean Clough. Suddenly, 1.25 million sq. ft./116,000 sq. m. of industrial floorspace in the town became vacant; silence fell upon the big mill buildings. 'It was the most traumatic moment in the town's history,' says Michael Ellison, himself appointed as Calderdale's Chief Executive only two months before; 'people couldn't believe it.' Yet 1982 was also a turning point. Five years later, but a few hundred yards away, Calderdale was hosting a Council of Europe conference on 'Heritage and successful town regeneration'. What had happened in the meantime? Two events in particular stand out. The Council called in the Civic Trust from London; and the local press announced 'Mystery Buyer for Dean Clough'. The one gave Calderdale a vision, and a strategy for realising it. The other demonstrated triumphantly that enterprise regeneration could be more than a wistful dream.

Michael Ellison is a native of Halifax; it had always been his hope to return there. Soon after his arrival in the Town Hall he reported to the Council on the need to make more of Calderdale's historic character if the area's image was to be changed. The demolition tide had perhaps been turned when in 1979 the Secretary of State disallowed an application to pull down the oldest buildings in Halifax, an ancient group in the Woolshops, for redevelopment as a shopping centre. (The centre was built, but in modified form.) Now Ellison, with one of the Council's planners, John Lockwood, approached the Civic Trust with the thought that a central street in the town might be restored to its full Victorian splendour (and even named 'Quality Street' after the chocolates made in Halifax by Rowntree Mackintosh!). The Trust at that time had a remit from the Department of the Environment to encourage the putting together of conservation packages for grant aid through the Historic Buildings Council, and had been in touch with Calderdale in this connection.* Independently, in 1982, it had already suggested to the Minister then responsible for tourism that the real challenge facing tourism development was to realise the potential of unrecognised places like Halifax (on which it based its case). The Trust responded to Ellison and Lockwood that, to make any significant impact on Calderdale's image and economy, action would have to embrace, not just a single street, but the whole district, and gave them the paper prepared for the Minister. By the end of the year, 1983, Calderdale had asked the Trust to prepare a full report on its proposals for Halifax.

This, in fact, became the first of two reports. *Halifax in Calderdale – A Strategy for Prosperity* was published in June 1984. It dealt with the architectural treatment of three blocks, including the bringing back into use of hidden courtyards and ginnels; and with the landscape treatment of the whole central conservation area, as well as the town's wider setting. The report was not, it stated, 'a magic formula for instant results' but set out 'certain guidelines for policies and programmes stretching, we venture to hope, far into the future. Only long-term commitments will bring about long-term change.' This was followed, in January 1986, by a second report, *Calderdale: the Challenge – A Strategy for Prosperity*. It dealt with the townscape qualities of the other five main townships and opportunities for their improvement; with the reuse of empty buildings and revitalisation of industrial areas; with the canal system, derelict land, and the enhancement and better use of the countryside; with the tourist potential and fuller interpretation of the area's past and present.

The aims of the Strategy were set out as being: 'to improve the quality of life for all those who live and work in the area; to make

---

* It was indeed at the suggestion of Mrs (later Dame) Jennifer Jenkins, then Chairman of the HBC, that the Trust first made contact with Calderdale.

the area more attractive to new industry; to stimulate tourism as a significant contribution to the District's economy'. It dealt, in outline, with finance (suggesting that a gearing of 1:7 public/ private investment should be possible); with phasing the programme over ten years; with partnerships; and, in particular, with the need to create a special team to oversee the programme's implementation. The report concluded:

> We believe that the Strategy ... offers the possibility of a great District-wide campaign in which all who love and seek to serve Calderdale can find common ground; an objective which transcends all short-term differences; an opportunity deliberately and steadily to reshape their surroundings and their way of life in a finer, more prosperous form. The magnitude of the concept may at first seem daunting, but we have always to recall that our environment does not happen by chance. It is shaped by us, and if the will to change it be strong enough, all is possible. The goals these two reports sketch in are totally realisable – provided only that all the Calderdale communities, all sectors of society, all citizens of goodwill, make them their own. If the people of Calderdale can grasp this opportunity, they will not only be working for their own and their children's future, but lighting a beacon of hope whose rays will reach all corners of Britain – and beyond these shores.

A little high-flown, perhaps, but not so far from the truth. Since then, needless to say, there have been setbacks and disappointments, but much has been achieved. The Council set itself to a ten-year 'Heritage Decade' programme (since renamed). The special team was set up (under Lockwood) in an empty shop in the centre of Halifax, nicely restored and doubling as an information centre. To this the bigger local companies seconded staff (even the DoE Regional Office lent a planner). A 'travelling circus' took the proposals to every township in the District; local groups were set up through whom dialogue with the communities could be carried on; newsletters were issued. Funding, though not reaching the levels hoped for, outstripped the gearing suggested as possible by the Civic Trust.

Concurrently with these developments another engine of renewal was turning: its creator – a maverick developer named Ernest Hall. Hall, by any account, is a remarkable man. He started in the milling business. He is a concert pianist. He is a millionaire. Ernest Hall it was, the 'mystery buyer', who acquired Dean Clough and within five years or so had put into its echoing spaces 200

203

companies, creating 2,500 jobs and a £3 million turnover. There are 1,000 telephone lines to the site, and 'we now feel short of space' says Hall. Dean Clough is thought, in fact, to be Europe's largest wholly private regeneration scheme.

Back in 1983, Hall originally had somewhere else in mind for an initiative of this kind. He came to Calderdale not because the Council was in a position to offer him any financial inducements but because it was more forthcoming and cooperative. He came with the intention not of leasing the great white elephant through estate agents but handling the whole process himself. To smooth the way for small enterprises, everything was kept as simple as possible. People could move in on two weeks' rental: easy in, easy out. Its infinite flexibility of space meant that Dean Clough lent itself to a multitude of different uses. Here is a conference centre, here a wholesale health foods company; here a small high-tech engineering workshop, here a theatre group. There are architects, photographers, silk-screen printers, people making mediaeval doors, people working on computer graphics. Many of Dean Clough's tenants are first-time ventures. They are helped with advice, with assistance in getting grants, in getting technological training. And because Hall is the sort of person he is, there is not only a wine bar, a hair and beauty salon, a crèche, but a design centre, an offshoot of the Slade School of Fine Art, an artist in residence, a substantial collection of paintings. And – of course – there are concerts.

Many of these things link Dean Clough directly with the wider community. From the outset Hall saw the enterprise as a tool of social engineering as well as of economic regeneration. He believes passionately in the individual. 'The qualities in people that produced the nineteenth century,' he says, 'are still there waiting to be released. I believe *everyone* can be an entrepreneur.' At the same time he can say: 'I think simply making profits is a shallow view of life.' He admires the Dartington ethic, the concept of a practical utopia in which work and leisure are one; in which the individual and the community are one. 'I set out,' he says, 'to unite the community. We meet on a three-weekly basis to decide what we can do to help the community.' He is perhaps the late-twentieth-century equivalent of Titus Salt, building his community only a few miles away over the hills 130 years earlier. With success has come widespread interest. Visitors come to Dean Clough from far and wide. The Prince of Wales and government Ministers have given it their blessing; it is a favourite of the media.

In the other towns other agencies were at work on other mills.

204

In Hebden Bridge David Hutchings, of the lively Pennine Heritage Trust, with great courage was restoring Nutclough Mill for use as small industrial units. In Sowerby Bridge the West Yorkshire Metropolitan County, before its demise, had commissioned a report from URBED on the substantial group of decaying buildings lining the River Calder, and put in motion a programme for their restoration and adaptation to create a new waterside centre for the town. The abolition of the Metro County Council in 1986 created financial problems. The County had costed the scheme at £1.2 million, but could only pass on half that sum. Nonetheless Calderdale are carrying forward the work – albeit probably more slowly than would otherwise have been possible – and the completed scheme will transform Sowerby Bridge.

Partnerships of many kinds multiplied during the second half of the eighties. Early in 1987 Business in the Community* announced a joint Calderdale Partnership with the Council, and, for a year or two, put in place a local director. From this several new initiatives developed. At the suggestion of the Prince of Wales sixty senior executives from top companies were shown the area and some of its potential. Rowntree Mackintosh established a £200,000 revolving fund to provide low-interest loans to assist the improvement of prominent buildings. The Department of the Environment announced a pilot scheme to assist the improvement of neglected land in private ownership. The trustees of EUREKA, a proposed £8 million interactive learning centre for children, were introduced to Halifax and decided to locate there next to the railway station.

Across the District all sorts of small, but incrementally valuable, things were happening (many arising directly from the Civic Trust's reports). Victorian shops in Todmorden were being improved. St George's Square in Hebden Bridge was repaved; British Gas donated land for a new pedestrian route into the town centre; a major face-lift was proposed for the run-down station approach. In Brighouse the Trust's proposals for a new canalside walk and improved open-air market were put in hand. And so on. In Halifax itself British Rail reconstructed the approach to the station. Square Chapel is being restored. Upper George Yard, one of the 'secret' interior spaces within a central block, was brought to life by a pub extension, with exciting further developments in the offing on the lines of Princes Square in Glasgow. The new and much-needed bus station was built by the West Yorkshire Transport Authority with especial care (parts of three older

* See page 279.

buildings were incorporated, one, an old Sunday School, being dismantled stone by stone and re-erected in a new position to provide a travel centre and café). The private venture 'Museum of the Working Horse' was established. Northern Ballet decided in 1990 to make Halifax their headquarters. And in fact a Glasgow University survey in 1989 put Halifax/Calderdale second for quality of life in a national listing of thirty-four medium-sized towns (Exeter came top).

An undoubted success story then. Between 1983 and 1988, Halifax achieved a 46.5 per cent reduction in its unemployment figures (from 13 per cent to 7 per cent), better than anywhere else in the North – which is perhaps why, in 1987, it was struck off the government's Urban Aid list. Nonetheless its economy remains fragile. Its unemployment figure is still above the national average. Closures continue, and are expected to go on. (When United Biscuits KP factory went in the late eighties, and with it 1,000 jobs, not a few noted that Business in the Community's chairman was also United Biscuits' chairman.) The essential point is that the demoralisation and inertia of a decade ago have been killed; the image of the area has been transformed; it now has a base from which to operate which simply did not exist at the end of the seventies. In early 1983 the Civic Trust met a phalanx of civil servants from several Ministries, together with representatives from a number of quangos, to press upon them the potential of Calderdale and suggest ways in which the District might be assisted. The reaction was one of incredulity. *Halifax?* 'If you feel that way,' someone said, 'you'd best pick up the ball and run with it yourselves.' That the Trust did so is the ultimate justification of the voluntary organisation.

Many people, then, and many more than have been mentioned here, have been involved in the turnround in Calderdale's fortunes. In the last analysis, however, that turnround must be a tribute to the Council and its officers. To the fact that Calderdale is the poorest of the West Yorkshire Districts, and had its finances further depressed by the death of the Metro County Council,* has to be added the fact that for the greater part of the eighties it was 'hung' politically.†

At one time the chairmanship of the Council and its committees passed from party to party, on a six-weekly basis – scarcely a

---

* County Councils, up to a point, can exert a redistributive function; Calderdale received more from the Metro County than it put in.
† Labour gained control in 1990.

formula for decisive action. There were those who hoped that the 'Inheritance Decade' would wither on the vine, so that the Council's housing and social responsibilities could again be seen to be paramount. One of Calderdale's councillors acknowledged that 'the Project has been successful beyond our wildest expectations', but nonetheless expressed his doubts about the priorities it embodied. For these reasons the programme was almost brought to a halt in 1988, but was reborn as the 'Fair Shares – Inheritance and Community Development Project' with a *second* team concerning itself primarily with the social effects of change on those disadvantaged by other developments. Since then political differences have diminished and, notwithstanding community-charge capping in 1990, the momentum built up since 1983 seems certain to carry the programme forward at least to the end of the ten years originally foreseen. Expressed as a graph, the private sector and external resources attracted show a steady increase year by year, but really take off – much as in London's Docklands and elsewhere – from the fifth year on. In 1990, cumulatively, other investment in the Project amounted to some fourteen times the Council's expenditure.

John Lockwood feels that the holistic approach developed in Calderdale has lessons for other towns everywhere. The aim: a self-sustaining process of economic regeneration. The means: audit, strategy, and then three interlinked campaigns: partnership, exemplar projects, and promotion – all of which should include community development. He sees 'the distinctive feature of the holistic approach to be its emphasis on processes rather than projects', on people, on the opportunity given to all sectors of the community to have a say in the overall scheme of things, and to improve their circumstances and quality of life in the process.

Which, I suppose, is what this book is all about.

PART THREE

PROSPECTS

We have to ... fight our way back. We will do so decision by
decision, and we will succeed over a long period of time only to
the extent that we all want to, and try to achieve results that for
whatsoever reason and for whatsoever fault escaped us in the
past. It is now the duty of those who hold positions of leadership
in our society, whether locally or nationally, to build on [our
existing] strengths ... for the implications of failure go way
beyond the boundaries of Liverpool.

Rt Hon Michael Heseltine, MP,
speaking in Liverpool in 1982

In a highly urbanised society, urban problems may be the
problems of society itself.

Managing Urban Change: policies and finance, OECD, Paris, 1983

13

A CHANGE OF PERSPECTIVE

Derelict Land – Community Initiatives –
The Role of the Arts – The Pursuit of Quality

FROM THE air the landscape of Britain stretches into the blue haze, predominantly, even surprisingly, green and rural. From the Orkneys to the Isle of Wight, from St David's Head to Lowestoft, it covers some 89,000 square miles – more than 94,000 if you include Ulster. Of the total, 12 per cent is built up. In the north and west, in the Highlands and Snowdonia, spreading landscapes unroll where the human settlements are few and far between. But also, splashed and spattered across this canvas lie the great conurbations, the grey and gritty imprints of the passage of the first Industrial Revolution. Greater London covers more than 700 square miles. The regional metropolitan districts of England encompass about 2,200 square miles. Clydeside accounts for another 320 or so. Boundaries oscillate with the purposes for which they are drawn, but, in all, the conurbations cover, say, 3,250 square miles. Not all this land is in ruins; not all of it is even built up. It includes very grand areas – civic centres and historic quarters – parkland, and pockets of ravishing countryside. Nonetheless it is here, in the metropolitan boroughs and districts, and in Strathclyde, that populations are at their densest and that the problems of the 'inner city' are most acute. It is here that eleven Development Corporations have been introduced to spearhead the government's regeneration efforts. But of those 3,250 square miles the UDCs cover maybe sixty-five. And if this alone suggests a very sharp concentration of resources, it must be remembered that social and economic malaise, though concentrated in these areas,

211

spreads far beyond them across the rest of the country. Outside this particular net are scores of other towns and cities – for example Blackburn, Corby, Dundee, Hartlepool, Kingston-upon-Hull, Leicester, Northampton, Nottingham, Preston, Scunthorpe, Stoke-on-Trent, Swansea, Warrington, to name but a baker's dozen – few of which are without 'inner-city' problems in some measure. The need for change and renewal spreads nationwide.

Across this spectrum the 511 local authorities are central to everything.* In England 69 of them – the London Boroughs and the Metropolitan Districts – are 'unitary', all-purpose authorities, responsible for a wide range of activities and subject only to the government's overriding constraints. The rest – the Districts, the Counties and, in Scotland, the Regions – are part of a two-tier system in which, though to a decreasing extent, strategic planning is done by the 'higher' authority and local planning by the District. Both, of course, are subject to current government constraints. The point should perhaps be made that these councils vary enormously in size and wealth. Strathclyde Region, admittedly exceptional, commands a budget of around £2,000 *million*; a Metropolitan District like Salford a little over £32.6 million. Birmingham's population is just under one million; South Tyneside's 156,000. Doncaster covers 143,000 acres/58,000 ha; Wolverhampton less than 17,000 acres/6,900 ha. It is hardly surprising that, in this context, the 'Action for Cities' campaign sometimes looks pretty hit or miss.

Sixteen 'Task Forces' – small teams of six to eight – have been set up by the government to act as catalysts at very local level (their locations change from time to time). The ten regional offices of government, though an intrinsic part of the Whitehall machine, nonetheless play an important part in the two-way jockeying that goes on between local authorities and London. The chief regional officers of the departments mainly concerned additionally come together in ten 'City Action Teams' (CATs) to coordinate the government input into those particular areas. As we have seen, a range of government quangos stands ready to offer further assistance in their special fields of interest. If there are broad patterns in all this they are not easy to descry. What is clear, however, is that the sixty square miles covered by the UDCs have been increasingly favoured financially, at the expense of the rest of the country. Expenditure within the 'Action for Cities' programme rose from

* There are a further 28 District Councils in Northern Ireland, and nine Area Boards.

just over £3 billion in 1988/89 to some £4 billion in 1990/91. Through the eighties Urban Programme spending on social problems declined by 25 per cent; that on 'economic' projects rose to 45 per cent of the whole. Of particular significance to the great mass of local authorities, however, is the fact that funding for the Urban Development Corporations now greatly outstrips that for the *whole* Urban Programme, Derelict Land grants and grants for urban development combined (with funding for the LDDC nearly equalling that for all the other English UDCs combined).

In the absence of any regional strategy – save perhaps in Scotland and Wales – as towns and cities and regions jostle to stake out their claims to new investment and a place in the sun, near-identical projects and programmes are being put in hand, copycat patterns are emerging, the assertions of superiority are becoming indistinguishable. 'Forward to 1991' (Tyne and Wear). 'Nottinghamshire Naturally'. 'Boom! Boom! Boom! (*Scunthorpe Evening Telegraph*). 'Bringing success to Sheffield'. 'Your very own motorway . . . with the Lake District thrown in' (the West Lancs Project). 'A place for people, progress and prosperity' (Cardiff Bay). 'Teesside is for living, living, living' (the UDC). 'The envy of Europe' (the Mersey Waterfront). Thus the brochures and press advertisements, as each place flaunts its notional catchment area.* Partnerships sometimes come into collision. It is not unknown to come across separate billboards on the same site proclaiming different parentage for the scheme concerned. Several areas make claim to 'the biggest urban renewal project in the UK' – or 'in Europe'; at least two to the most inward investment in Britain. Which is *really* the biggest out-of-town shopping centre? But if the public sector's promotional efforts sometimes seem interchange-able, those of the private sector can become quite hallucinatorily similar. The housebuilders have discovered water. So it's 'Come home to your waterfront heritage' and 'the magic of waterfront living'. 'Miles from the City and close to perfection'. 'You'll have time to enjoy the delightful style in which modern design elements are combined with columns, beams and other original features from historic buildings.' Your address, wherever it be, is likely to include 'Mariners Wharf', 'Chandlers Wharf', 'Prospect Wharf', 'Free Trade Wharf', or maybe 'Timber Wharf Village', 'Merchants Landing', 'Mariners Steps', 'Admiral's Jetty', 'Clippers Quay' – or, of course, 'Quay West'. It will offer secure parking, video entry,

---

* One city, having reached for the dictionary, claims the first 'integrated symbiotic leisure and shopping experience of its kind in Scotland'.

resident porterage, sauna, whirlpool spa, fully fitted gymnasium and cable television.

It is not just the housing which comes to a pattern. The regeneration menu, as already hinted at, is likely everywhere to include, with a light rail or tram system (some forty are in hand or under consideration), at least one vast shopping centre, a marina, a 'business park' and/or a 'science park', large-scale conference or exhibition facilities, coupled with which will be at least one new hotel; there will be a new museum or two, a multiplex cinema or two, a new or restored theatre or concert hall, a sports complex – and of course, apart from the 'parks', office space galore. These buildings will presumably be seen by future generations as equally redolent of the last quarter of the twentieth century as the town halls and libraries, railway stations, covered markets and shopping arcades, warehouses and mills are redolent to us of the second half of the nineteenth.

The lemming-like rush to water in all its forms is curious. Why now? At least since the end of World War II amenity societies had been pressing for canals and rivers to be recognised as potential assets, to be restored, improved, brought into wider use, and better integrated into the urban fabric of the towns through which they pass. Yet as late as 1980 the docklands boroughs in London, for example, were still aiming to fill in those dock basins which had not already received attention. Ten years later, however, seventy or more marinas had come into being around the country, with more under construction or planned, offering berths for 20,000 boats and more.* Most included residential, shopping and leisure elements. Some were very big – Brighton has 1,800 berths – and most were pretty expensive (like £200–£300 million). Not all of them show much design flair, but Swansea, and Hythe on Southampton Water, two of the first 'marina villages' in Britain, have received thought and care. Most of the nation's dock-lands areas – Birkenhead, Cardiff, Chatham, Hartlepool, Kingston-upon-Hull, Liverpool, London, Manchester/Salford, Preston, Southampton among them – now have waterfront developments in hand. Some of these were canal-served, and most towns and cities on the canal system are now belatedly seeking to exploit what is at last seen as an asset. British Waterways is looking to the potential of its 1,860 miles/3,000 km. of canal with a new urgency; rivers, too, are being studied with a new eye. Where water does not exist, it is being created – after sand and gravel

* There are now said to be approaching 160,000 pleasure craft in British waters.

extraction for example; and by the creation of new lakes (Cardiff, Swansea and Merseyside have put in hand, or proposed, estuary barrages to this end). For water, it is said, can increase values by 50 per cent.

Shopping centres, it seems, are irresistible. Stores give way to superstores, supermarkets to hypermarkets, to shopping malls, retail markets and retail parks. To the customer – if aware of them – the distinctions are unimportant. What is obvious is that the places where he or she shops are all the time getting bigger and bigger. In the familiar supermarket one retailer brings a wide range of goods under one roof; it is likely to be a local, or district, convenience, often quite small, sometimes more sizeable. More recent is the fast-growing trend towards 'speciality' shopping, in which a number of retailers offer a range of more up-market lines – often in a 'themed' setting, maybe newly designed, maybe in an old building of character converted for the purpose. Normally towards the edge of the town are the 'retail parks', originally no more than big sheds dealing in bulky goods, like furniture, requiring a lot of cheap storage space, but now covering much else. Proliferating garden centres could almost fit this category. And then, finally, there are the leviathan complexes, always out of town, which draw upon regional or sub-regional catchment areas, offer a vast number of retailers, the widest possible range of goods, and all sorts of other facilities as well – filling stations, restaurants, multi-screen cinemas, play areas for children, and of course parking for maybe 1,500 cars.

The spread of greater affluence has produced an astonishing, and still growing, expansion in all of these forms of shopping. Some 4.5 million sq. ft./418,000 sq. m. of new town-centre floorspace was completed in 1989; out-of-town growth is even faster. Refusals of planning permission (eleven refusals or withdrawals took place in 1989 – sixteen remained) have slowed the construction of regional shopping centres on green-field sites, but retail parks – defined by Messrs Hillier Parker as out-of-town complexes with over 50,000 sq. ft./4,650 sq. m. of gross lettable space – currently account for 60 per cent of all shopping centre proposals. The first – in Britain – opened in 1982; by 1987 there were forty-five; twenty-one opened in 1988; by the end of the following year there were approaching ninety in all. Together they provided 11 million sq. ft./over 1 million sq. m. of shopping space. Completions dropped a little in 1989, but there is said to be little diminution in the further 50 million sq. ft./4.6 million sq. m. reputedly on the drawing board.

These glitzy temples of a consumer society, modelled on American precedents, are a far cry from the dispiriting stained concrete of the shopping centres of the sixties. For some, their regulation atria, their cascades of escalators, their wall-creeper lifts, going up and down like yo-yos, their trees (sometimes real), fountains and anodyne background music offer an escape from the humdrum much as the luxury of the art-deco cinema offered their parents release in the 1920s and 30s. For others their sheer size induces panic. 'How d'you like the new MetroCentre?' I asked the little old lady on the pavement outside the Gateshead Metro Station. 'Oh it's too big for me,' was the reply. 'I still go over the river.' To those charged with finding new uses for idle wasteland the attractions of these sprawling developments, cocooned in their vast, desolate areas of parking, are obvious. However, as the United States quickly found, they can suck life from the traditional shopping areas in the centre of the city and thereby make central-area regeneration more difficult. It is for this reason, of course, that such developments are so often opposed. New forms of shopping are here to stay; the real challenge lies in relating their siting to requirements for the renewal of the city itself.

'Parks' have become part of the marketing vocabulary. Joining the 'retail parks' are now the 'business parks', the 'technology parks' and the 'science parks'. Together they all crossed the Atlantic in the mid seventies, and really took off in Britain during the eighties. In a nutshell, business parks set out to provide purpose-built accommodation, with the complex wiring systems and sophisticated trunking demanded by today's information and computer technology, in a more or less park-like setting which is more attractive to the white-collar worker than are the hectic pavements of the city. There were estimated, in October 1989, to be 575 sites in the UK calling themselves 'business parks', with maybe four more coming into existence *every week*. Most of the growth is now to be found in developments of 50 acres/20 ha and above. The 40,000 acres/16,200 ha covered by these sites is about equivalent, it has been pointed out, to half the area of the Isle of Wight; the potential floorspace they offer is some 224 million sq. ft., or getting on for 2,100 ha. Of this, 40 per cent is in the South East, but over 20 per cent in the North, and perhaps 13 per cent in the Midlands.[1]

Apart from the intrinsic attractions it offers for business network-

* Not generally welcomed by planning authorities in their efforts to stop inappropriate uses in particular buildings and quarters in their towns.

ing in an attractive environment, the concept of the business park was given a big boost by the new freedoms offered by the Town and Country (Use Classes) Order 1987.* This brought within the 'business-use' class of the planning control system a much wider range of uses than previously; this in turn made possible greater flexibility in the design and use of buildings, and thereby encouraged developers to invest in them more readily. In keeping with this general movement, a number of older industrial estates have refurbished themselves to meet today's higher expectations – for example, on a big scale Trafford Park; on a smaller Kembrey Park in Swindon. A good many of the new parks form essential elements within wider renewal strategies. The Clydebank Business Park, by the Scottish Development Agency, is on the site of the old Singer Sewing Machine Company's factory, once the largest works in the world, with 11,000 employees. Four parks in Birmingham aim between them to offer 5.7 million sq. ft./530,000 sq. m.; Barking Reach in London aims at 2 million sq. ft./93,000 sq. m.; Warrington likewise 2 million. Two of the most impressively designed are Bristol's Aztec West (one of three in the city) and Stockley Park in Hillingdon, London. The former, an early one, got a second wind a year or two ago and in the *élan* of its buildings has shown a vitality greater than most of its competitors. Stockley Park, more recent, is probably the most successful to date, particularly in its rich and effective landscape design. Until 1985 the site was a rubbish tip; now the 100 acres/40 h of commercial building is threaded through by a string of lakes in 250 acres/100 ha of parkland. Facilities include a championship golf course and a children's day-care centre.

To some extent similar, but more specialised, is the 'science park', designed to facilitate technology transfer from academic research centres to knowledge-based businesses and industries. Linked formally to a university or other higher-education centre, a science park provides a fruitful framework for research development, prototype design and production, and intelligence networking for companies involved at the sharp end of technical innovation. There are already forty in this country which fit the UK Science Parks Association's definition, with perhaps another twenty under consideration. Heriot Watt and Cambridge were early examples – the latter is the largest and held by many to be the most successful to date; of the more recent, Glasgow's well exemplifies the type of development which is off the campus but indeed embedded in parkland and surely conducive to this kind of work.

These are some of the things, then, which have come to form the common currency of promotional literature wherever regeneration is afoot. They are not the only ones. There are the twenty-six Enterprise Zones, the Freeports. There are the convention centres, the international sports arenas, the new opera houses and concert halls, the new museums and nostalgia centres (mining, football, cooking, local poets, comedians, trains, trams, childhood toys, the Blitz, hunting, old shopfronts). Everyone is in love with Baltimore's aquarium, and most have pencilled 'aquarium' on their list, though so far none has pulled this one off. 'Flagship' projects are so ubiquitous that all the little boats of the fleet tend to be overlooked – those thousands of smaller developments which are taking place every day of the week: the new school, a sheltered-housing scheme, improved streetlighting, a little park on what used to be a waste lot, a new traffic-free zone, a better training centre.

None of it happens totally by accident. It may be that a chief officer in the city hall, with part of his budget unspent at the end of the financial year, deflects his surplus to an unexpected quarter. Or an elected member successfully stakes a claim for a new amenity in the ward he represents, or in an area he remembers with affection from his childhood. For large-scale area regeneration, however, strategies have to be agreed, plans made, briefs issued, organisational structures established. The detail will vary infinitely, but the framework will always be similar, for it represents the commonsense, step-by-step approach to similar sets of problems.

First, the constraints and assets of the area have to be analysed. What are its weaknesses and difficulties? What are the strengths, actual or potential, on which to build? For example, does it enjoy good access by road, rail, air, water? Or will improved access have to be provided before proper use can be made of the land? How coherent are the ownership and use patterns, the neighbourhoods? Are they severed by railway lines, canals, above-ground piping? Have plots been so chopped up, and become so oddly shaped, that nothing short of their acquisition and re-parcelling into bigger units will make them useful to new investors? If so, what will be the problems of relocating the present users, and what is it likely to cost? What is the area's track record in labour relations? What are its working traditions and the job prospects of those whose only experience has been in industries which have disappeared from the scene for ever? What sort of retraining programmes will have to be instituted if the local workforce is to benefit from the new activities introduced by the regeneration process? What is the environmental quality of the area? Can it offer companies an address of which they will be proud; surroundings in which their employees will feel at home and happy? Does it offer housing of the kind their staff will want to live in? Are there adequate shopping and leisure facilities? Schooling and health provision? If not, what is the catchment area and on what scale do they need to be provided?

In the light of all these things the potentials of the area have to be weighed in relation to what other parts of the city, neighbouring towns, the region, the country, maybe other countries, can offer. Is local expansion more likely than inward investment? If not, what are the activities, the industries, the businesses for which the area is likely to have the most attraction? Might the transport network attract the distribution industry? Might high-tech firms be attracted by the university? Might tourism be developed on the basis of the sporting and cultural attractions within the city and the landscape beyond? The demand for office space seems to grow everywhere – but what *kind* of offices would be right here? Financial services? The media? Regional HQ for national or inter-national companies? These are only some of the questions that have to be asked. Then a physical framework has to be evolved which will meet the criteria that have been established, and a realistic time frame. Redevelopment and improvement of a big area cannot all be done at the same time; programmes will have to be phased, cash flows worked out. And then finally, having brought all this into some sort of resolution, a marketing strategy will have to be drawn up; bankers, developers, building firms brought into the team; the financial and other inducements that can be offered must be publicised to potential investors, assistance given to them in all sorts of ways. Running through the whole process like a *leitmotif* has to be sensitive, open-minded, continuing consultation with the local communities and organisations – on objectives, on what *they* want and need; on options available; on means to be employed; on progress and timing. As we have seen, 'partnership' has been *the* buzz word now for fifteen years and more. Sometimes the reality has proved wholehearted, sometimes no more than a glibly expressed aspiration. If one thing is certain amongst all the difficult complexities of renewing our cities it is that committed, and continuing, partnerships alone can fit them for the next century.

In all this activity it too often becomes a matter for relief and satisfaction that, in a problem area, any development at all has been achieved. That it could so easily have been better – which is how the future will see it – is dismissed as of secondary importance. In this chapter four themes are considered which bear very directly upon the question of quality.

DERELICT LAND

We live on a congested island. Britain's population is larger by a good many millions than that, say, of France, but we have to support that population on a landmass that is very considerably smaller. A good deal of it is remote and wild, but even if we include the uplands and the mountains, we have only about one acre, or less than half a hectare, per person in which to spread ourselves. The land is our basic resource and we squander it at our peril. Yet very large areas are permitted to remain derelict, underused, unsightly – to the detriment of the economy, the blight of communities and the loss of national and local self-respect.

Surprisingly, we have no accurate, overall, national picture of the extent of the problem. The official definition of derelict land – for government grant purposes – is 'land so damaged by industrial or other development that it is incapable of beneficial use without treatment'. For land of this kind we have official figures. The 1982 Derelict Land Survey showed more than 112,000 acres/over 45,000 ha of such land to exist in England.[2] However, extensive areas of wasteland, which fall outside the official definition, exist in nearly all parts of the country. In particular, all cities have numerous derelict sites in their central areas and on their outer fringes (in the latter case often even labelled as 'green belt'). Many of these urban sites – perhaps even a majority – are likely to be less than an acre/0.4 ha in extent (which until very recently put them outside the official figures). Cumulatively, however, their collective impact may be hardly less blighting than that of a single larger area. For a sense at least of the *order* of the total area thus immobilised we have to turn to various academic estimates. Bradshaw and Bart, in 1986[3], put it at 395,000 acres/nearly 160,000 ha for England. Chisholm and Kivett, for the Institute of Economic Affairs in 1987,[4] put it at nearly 520,000 acres/ 210,000 ha. What is indisputable is the *effect* of wasteland on this scale. A Civic Trust report published in 1988[5] suggested that over 60 per cent of such sites had been vacant for five years or more; and that over a quarter (in fact 28 per cent) had been vacant for more than twenty years. In that time a generation can have been born, and come to maturity, knowing nothing else. Let us look at these two broad categories – of 'derelict' and 'waste' land – in a little more detail.

In 1970 – which was European Conservation Year – the Civic Trust mounted a national two-day conference, on a coal tip in the middle of Stoke-on-Trent, on the reclamation of industrial dereliction. It was the first time that attention had been directed in this way to the problem nationally, and the occasion was seen by many as launching a drive to solve it once and for all. Indeed, at that conference the then Minister for Housing and Local Government, Anthony Crosland – it was a year before the Department of the Environment was created – firmly pledged the government to rid the country of all derelict land within ten years.

Alas, like other commitments before and since, it faded and was forgotten. In actuality, although much clearance has taken place, the collapse of manufacturing and heavy industry, coupled with inner-city decline, has increased the amount of dereliction faster than it has been dealt with. Although 42,000 acres/17,000 ha in England were reclaimed between 1974 and 1982 (the Northern Region, North West, West Midlands, East Midlands, Yorkshire and Humberside made good progress), total dereliction *grew* by nearly 6,000 acres/2,400 ha. In some regions the increase was enormously greater than the average: in the North West there were some 5,000 acres/2,000 ha more, or 25 per cent; in the West Midlands 1,120 ha, or 24 per cent more; Merseyside's dereliction increased by 22 per cent; the Black Country by 26 per cent; Greater London by more than five times. For various reasons since 1982 the area of land being reclaimed annually has declined and, without changes of policy, the amount of dereliction in Britain as a whole seems likely to increase indefinitely into the future.

How has this happened? Possibly the main cause has been a shift of policy which took place in 1982. Originally, reclamation work was directed primarily at open sites in the countryside which had been marred by workings of the big mineral-extractive industries – coal, ironstone, sand and gravel, brick clay – and by large dumps and rubbish tips. Heaps and holes. Increasingly, *new* workings were brought under effective control by the planning system: ironstone to start with, then open-cast mining, with the sand and gravel operators more and more being required to leave their worked-out sites as amenity water areas for boating and fishing. However, the backlog from a less-disciplined past was considerable and as, for example, the coal industry shrank, its erstwhile dominance over the mining communities was evidenced mainly by the great black tips which still overshadowed them. Much of the reclamation of the sixties and seventies was thus of the 'soft' type – grading and earth moving to restore more normal

221

contours to the land; treating the pollution of the ground; seeding for grass; maybe some planting of trees and shrubs. A frequent complaint was that these things were done without imagination, that the resulting landscapes lacked character. Often, however, the aim was only to make sites more acceptable to potential developers, in the knowledge that, without such short-term improvement, they would never be seriously considered.

In the years following the Aberfan disaster, as we have seen, a new thrust developed. Grant aid was extended and increased. Crosland's pledge seemed attainable. However, as the economy slid into recession and whole industries disappeared, new forms of dereliction began to proliferate. Square miles of urban and semi-urban land took on a ghostly aura of decay as abandoned mills and docks, warehouses and machine shops mouldered among the weeds.

At the end of 1981 the then Environment Secretary, Michael Heseltine, in the spirit of the 1977 White Paper, decided to 'bend' Derelict Land Grant more purposefully towards these new forms of decay – and in particular towards the inner city. Priority was to be given to schemes leading to industrial, commercial and housing development; in some cases recreational after-uses. In terms of inner-city policy this made the best of sense. However, the higher costs of dealing with urban land – higher acquisition costs and the greater complications of clearance and services infrastructure – have meant a reduction in the *amount* of land that can be treated for the same amount of money. It has been pointed out by Michael and Bradshaw, of the University of Liverpool[6], that the cost of dealing with such urban sites is, for most of the country, between twice and nearly four times that for schemes in the countryside (the exceptions being Wales, Eastern and South West England). The mean cost for England as a whole increased between the five-year period *before* 1981/82 and the five-year period *after* from £27,000 per ha (nearly 2.5 acres) to £65,000 per ha (figures at constant 1987/88 prices). As a result the national acreage of dereliction continues to grow rather than shrink, and, to effect the acreage of reclamation being achieved in the late seventies, government expenditure – in 1988 about £120 million for Britain as a whole – would need to be more than doubled. To honour that pledge of twenty years ago – and remember we are speaking only of land covered by the official definition of 'derelict' – the amount would have to be very significantly raised again. What is actually happening is the reverse. In autumn 1989 the DoE announced a reduction in Derelict Land Grant of about 13 per cent – from rather over £77 million in 1988/89 to rather over £67 million in

1989/90. But, as has been indicated, the full problem spreads much wider than that. Urban wasteland constitutes a major element in inner-city decay. It is often hidden – although sensed – at street level by hoardings and corrugated iron, as like as not themselves disfigured by flyposting and graffiti. From upper floors or the top of the double-decker bus its extent is distressingly evident. Unused sites attract fly-tipping on a revolting scale; they are often rat-infested. Like the paper-bag huddles of the homeless, they give the sense of having escaped the normal constraints of society and thus help to dissipate the sense of community. They speak of lost confidence in the present and the future.

There is a need – of course – in any city for a pool of uncommitted land as part of the stock-in-trade of an ever-changing society. It is a question of degree. Whether the total amount of urban wasteland in England is 500,000 acres/200,000 ha, or 400,000 acres, or 300,000 acres, is almost beside the point. It does not call for precision to know that dereliction of this order of magnitude is an affront to decent urban living.

The government initiated in 1980 – partly in response to an earlier Civic Trust report – a national register of unused or underused land (now including sites of a quarter of an acre) in the hands of public authorities.* (There has in the past been widespread criticism of the apparent hoarding of vacant land by such organisations without evident operational need.) Since then a good deal has been released. British Rail, for example, have noticeably stepped up disposals. However, probably more than half such land is in *private* hands. It remains undeveloped because the owner hopes that it will increase in value over the years; or because, being stubbornly unwilling to acknowledge that values have plummeted in the area, he can find no purchaser at the price he is asking; or because it forms part of a larger area he is seeking to assemble for a major development (which could take up to twenty years); or because, having demolished the perfectly usable building previously on the site, he has run out of money with which to redevelop. There are many reasons. Allied is the problem of vacant buildings – great empty-windowed warehouses, streets of breeze-blocked terraced housing shored up with baulks of timber, abandoned workshops. A Reading University team found, in 1985,[7] that 131 million sq. ft./12.2 million sq. m. of industrial and commercial floorspace lay vacant; official figures for 1986 showed 697,000 houses in England to be empty.

* Not to be confused with *derelict* land, as defined earlier.

How is action to be triggered on these things? Unused land – and buildings – *can* be acquired compulsorily by central government agencies (such as the Development Agencies and Corporations) and by local government, for reclamation and assembly into more desirable parcels. Grant aid is now directly available to the private sector as well. Some councils are more energetic than others: Bristol, for example, identified and published in 1985 a comprehensive survey of sites throughout the city, together with twelve policy and programme measures aimed at their priority treatment. Voluntary groups are active everywhere in finding both temporary and long-term uses for urban sites – small public gardens, ecological parks, city farms, adventure playgrounds, and much else. The problem is a national one, yet immensely fragmented, having to be dealt with piecemeal and *ad hoc*, yet calling for some bigger, overriding vision that will give coherence to our efforts.

All questions of land reclamation are tied up with land values, negative and positive, which lead quickly to the availability of land, the means by which it is allocated for different purposes, and the prohibitions upon development in designated areas – for example, green belts. Administratively, distinctions may be drawn between *derelict* land, *waste*land and *neglected* land, *dormant* land earmarked for future development, *operational* land which is part of an existing development but not realising its full potential; between urban and rural dereliction; between bigger sites and smaller. In real life such categorisation blurs at the edges. Green belt – at the urban fringes – is much of it not green at all but neglected wasteland. What happens in one type of area impinges on others. For example, the more development is permitted to spread outside the city, the more difficult it is to bring reclaimed inner-city land into use. Land, as such, is the basic resource. Short-term palliatives will always have their place, but, additionally, we need long-term strategies to maximise its value to society. How often is the opportunity grasped to use such work for a fundamental restructuring of public open space in the city, for the creation, say, of a network of green pedestrian routes threading the urban fabric and holding it together? The City of London has shown how much can be achieved, in very adverse conditions, by utilising every square yard, every square metre that ingenuity can win back from the concrete above ground and the snaking services below: a tree here, a patch of grass there, a group of flower boxes, a churchyard, a small hillside bombed site – nothing very spectacular in itself but cumulatively forming a green

224

framework because inventive opportunism has been married to an underlying vision.

On a larger scale the Garden Festivals represent one of the major efforts of the 1980s to carry through land reclamation strategically and with panache. They have demonstrated triumphantly what a transformation of big, far-gone sites can be effected by a concentration of skills. They have provided a psychological lift to the cities concerned, and a certain amount of temporary work. How far, however, has their real purpose been thought through? Is their achievement commensurate with the investment involved? Liverpool's, as we have seen, was repudiated by the City Council, fell victim to a private-sector financial collapse, and is still largely mothballed, having failed to attract the high-tech industry originally hoped for and only now seeing some new housing going up on part of the site. Stoke-on-Trent's succeeded in raising land values, but subsequent development has largely absorbed the landscape so carefully designed, (though whether this could have been achieved otherwise is a moot point). Glasgow's provided an immensely cheerful jump-up, and Laing Homes, who had previously acquired much of the site, are now getting on with the houses they all along intended; another stretch of riverside will have been civilised and an area of Govan, written off ten years ago, will have been brought back into use. Gateshead's, too, with its long, linear site meandering through the forlorn north of the city, may prove to have restructured a whole group of neighbourhoods. Gateshead renounced any grand design in favour of a hopeful opportunism. Nonetheless, 40 per cent of the site is to be kept as permanent parkland where before there were only gasworks and cokeworks, rail yards and wharfs.

The garden festival idea was born in Germany in 1951 as a device for dealing with war-damage reconstruction. There, much greater time has been allowed for preliminary work, attendances are about double those our own festivals attract, and the primary purpose is always to create permanent public parks. There is a greater commitment to ecological principles, and green 'lungs' figure purposefully in German planning in a way they do not in Britain. This drive to create permanent assets contrasts markedly with the way our own garden festivals are rushed into being – with enormous technical skill, let it be said – and as hastily rushed, more or less, into oblivion. The average cost of the investment in our own festivals has been of the order of £40 million each. The question that has to be asked is whether this investment could have achieved more if spread more widely through additional

Derelict Land Grant, or whether, used in this way, greater permanent benefit could not have been gained for the cities concerned. In 1987 the DoE commissioned an *Evaluation* of the first three festivals. Published only in early 1991, this found that they may not be 'powerful instruments' in isolation, but a useful additional element in a regional strategy. Officially, no decision will be taken until after Ebbw Vale, but, further government support seems unlikely during the nineties. It is to be hoped that the concept will not be allowed to die, but rather clarified, to the more lasting benefit of the areas thus so briefly adorned.

It is not easy, within existing administrative structures, to agree and implement comprehensive landscape strategies, to create new landscape on any scale. The big vision, which came so confidently to earlier generations, has faded. We play around with little pockets of land, tidy them up when we can (and like as not fail to maintain them so that in no time they have once more lapsed into litter-strewn eyesores). Urban space is 'greened' only when no other use can be found for it. Parks are seen as a worrisome drain upon the public purse, and, to all intents and purposes, no new parks of any size have been created in British cities since World War I. (The GLC's 133 acre/54 ha Burgess Park was perhaps the main exception.) Failure to encompass the idea of landscape as a major unifying element in our surroundings has impoverished much of the development of the 1980s.

Consider for a moment the case of the Welsh Valleys. It seems churlish to quibble when so much has been achieved over a quarter of a century, but as yet it is hard for the outside eye to descry that overall, coordinating vision which could in time restore the full grandeur and landscape integrity of the Valleys. There are still minor valleys which bear witness today to the beauties which once the whole region must have had. They constitute a sort of benchmark reminder, not so much of how things could look again, for the main valleys will never look like that again, but of the *scale* of thinking the terrain calls for. Many of the redeveloped sites – inevitably – are small. The big sheds which are all that light industry calls for nowadays lack the visual grandeur of the old pithead gear. Housing lacks indigenous character. Reclaimed land is green, but bland and gentle. Walls and fences and small detail tend to lack the robustness which was always part of the Valleys' identity. This is three-dimensional landscape. One is always look-ing across, or down upon, the valley bottoms; up at the skyline. To hold together the scattered disorder of housing and industry and roads an altogether larger vision of the landscape imperatives is called for: greater sensitivity to the drama of the changing levels, afforestation on the grand scale, and (in the right places) even a renunciation of development. Here, as elsewhere, such a framework exists – at least on paper. The County Council, Mid Glamorgan, published its approved County Structure Plan,[8] incorporating the Secretary of State's modifications, in September 1989. This deals, of course, with a whole range of matters, such as employment, transportation, housing and settlement, retailing, waste disposal and others. The section dealing with Landscape and Conservation sets out fourteen ground rules for the county, mostly in the form of presumptions for or against development in certain types of area. Thus:

> There will be a presumption against development which constitutes a significant intrusion into the landscape particularly on the side of the valleys in the coalfield and other areas that may be defined as having a particular landscape value.

> The County Council proposes that existing natural woodlands should be protected and effectively maintained and that the current stock of hardwood trees . . . should be increased.

> . . . There will be a presumption in favour of afforestation proposals unless such proposals would (1) lead to the establishment of isolated blocks of trees other than shelter belts; (2) involve clear or substantial felling of indigenous trees; (3) detract from the appearance of significant landscape features; (4) endanger the preservation of ancient monuments . . . ; (5) adversely affect nature conservation interest; (6) . . . or agriculture; (7) result in continuous tracts of coniferous trees.

This is how, normally, such matters are regulated. Principles, however, are not quite the same as offering a positive vision of how things might be – and in any case over the past ten years the powers of Counties to enforce them have been weakened. Lacking a common vision, authorities may simply follow what they perceive as their own interests. ('Look. Mineral extraction on the skyline. A great scar on the horizon just where we are trying to attract people.') That way there can be jobs, houses, leisure facilities, much that is excellent. Only the superlative will have escaped.

It is for the scale of the vision it offers that the Countryside Commission's proposal for the creation of a dozen new urban forests is so significant. Each forest, it is envisaged, will contain up to twenty-five million trees, cover between 25,000 and 50,000 acres/10,000 and 20,000 ha and cost something of the order of

£20–£25 million. By way of background it has to be remembered that only about 10 per cent of Britain is forested, compared with a European average of 25 per cent or so. Fields have been denuded of their trees and hedgerows in the interests of mechanised farming. Dead trees are not replaced. The great storms of the last few years laid low square miles of forest. At the same time farmland is having to be 'set aside' through European overproduction; the economic basis of the Forestry Commission is being questioned. (Although we import 90 per cent of the timber we need, the bill for which amounts to £6 billion, 9 per cent of the Commission's holdings are to be sold off by the end of the century.)

The three lead project areas of the Countryside Commission/ Forestry Commission initiative are the Great North Forest (32,000 acres/13,000 ha between and south of Gateshead/Sunderland); the Forest of Mercia in south Staffordshire (50,000 acres/20,000 ha); and Thames Chase (23,000 acres/9,400 ha between Brentwood, Thurrock and Dagenham). Nine more were confirmed by the government in Spring 1991 for Bedford, north Bristol, Cleveland, south Hertfordshire, west Manchester, east Liverpool, north Nottingham, Swindon and south Yorkshire. The Secretary of State for Scotland has announced proposals for £50 million planting in the lowlands between Edinburgh and Glasgow.

The forests will involve no change of ownership. Their achievement will turn upon the coordinated efforts of consortia of interests – the Countryside Commission itself, the Forestry Commission, the local authorities concerned; upon persuasion in the case of private landowners, and the use, wherever possible, of existing grant mechanisms. The forests are seen as including not only woodland but farmland, heathland, meadowland and lakes, providing a habitat for a rich variety of wildlife, but also leisure facilities – picnic areas, camp sites, riding centres, footpaths, cycleways, spaces for open-air concerts and the like. They will embrace derelict land, urban fringe and green belt – so often consisting only of scruffy, neglected, underused and undermanaged land, mothballed by over-rigid, do-nothing policies. It has been estimated that as much as 40 per cent of land designated as green belt in England and Wales is in fact derelict or seriously scarred by old mineral workings, abandoned works and farm buildings, refuse tips and the like. For such as this 'green' has long been a misnomer: 'brown' has sometimes been used instead. The re-greening of such areas, and the reintroduction of countryside pursuits, need in no way diminish their role as inhibiting the outward spread of the cities. They should be able, conversely, to give coherence as never before to the outer estates and the whole fringe sprawl of the great conurbations which already exists. A foretaste of what this whole initiative could mean is offered by the project, spearheaded by the local Groundwork Trust, to create a new urban-fringe Community Forest on the south side of St Helens in Merseyside: two million trees, on 1,300 acres/530 ha of previously derelict land, at a cost of £4 million. It will be a quarter of a century and more before such schemes begin to mature; this is the timescale on which fundamental improvement has to be considered.

Do these great projects seem to stray from the problems of the inner city? Not so. The problems of land utilisation everywhere are inextricably interlinked. Development, reclamation, improvement, conservation all turn upon land values, 'negative' in the case of wasteland, exaggerated in 'desirable' areas. Inner-city policies and green-belt policies are but two sides of the same coin. They need to be tackled in the same spirit, to a common purpose.

Free marketeers point to the fact that approved green belts in all cover a staggering 5.25 million acres/2.13 million ha – or 10 per cent of all England and Wales (indeed about the area of Wales). As we have seen, much of this is not green at all, and may in fact be heavily despoiled in one way or another. There is a constant need for more land for development. To prohibit all new construction in green-belt areas, runs the argument, runs counter to people's desires and further inflates land values within the city – thereby making renewal even more expensive and difficult. On the contrary, reply the planners. There is vacant land and floorspace galore in the cities, where the services infrastructure already exists. To allow development to spread outwards into the countryside unchecked is to condemn much of the inner city to perpetual decay, quite apart from the losses to our ever-diminishing countryside itself. Their case – either way – is seldom as black and white as the most strident make out. The pressures for urban dispersal arise from many different factors, and circumstances vary greatly from one part of the country to another. The green belt, however, is a simple concept which from its inception has been loved by most politicians, most planners, and most of the public. Whenever it is threatened, violent opposition is to be expected. So it was at intervals during the 1980s. Sensing a more permissive mood within the government, developers and housebuilders began to lodge increasingly bold applications for regional shopping complexes, big housing estates, new 'villages'. Consortium Developments, a group of the ten largest housebuilders in the country, proposed a series of such new villages, covering each perhaps a square mile or so: at Tillingham Hall, in Essex; Foxley Wood, in Hampshire; at Stone Bassett in Oxfordshire; and at sites in Kent and Cambridgeshire. Disquiet existed because of the number of applications, refused by local planning authorities, which were being allowed by the Secretary of State on appeal. 'If you argue,' said Michael Heseltine at this time[9], 'that a demand only has to exist for it to have a right to be met, then in the end, from the Weald of Kent to the Berkshire Downs, from the Chilterns to the Channel, you will go on building until you reach the sea.' By way of riposte Nicholas Ridley, the then Secretary of State, invented the Nimby ('Not in my Back Yard') syndrome as characterising green-belt residents, and raised the number of houses likely to be needed in the South East by the end of the century by an additional 150,000 (above an estimate of only two years earlier). Nonetheless he reiterated the government's general support for the green belts, and his successor, Chris Patten, subsequently disallowed a major appeal which Ridley (against the findings of his Inspector) had been 'minded to allow'.

It is a debate without conclusion, save in the most generalised terms. What we should be able to agree upon is the need for a degree of flexibility in our control system, coupled with a much more positive and imaginative approach. The Adam Smith Institute, for example, has suggested that 'the principle might be to permit development on ten acres of damaged land within green belt, if in return a further damaged ninety acres are restored to pleasant greenery . . . such a policy would increase by a considerable margin the total of green land and without cost to the public'.[10] Only by exploring this and every other possibility can we hope – perhaps by the year 2000? – to cleanse the nation of its derelict land.

COMMUNITY INITIATIVES

'Community architecture is a busted flush', was the proposition at a public debate in February 1989. On the contrary, claimed its proponents, reports of its death were greatly exaggerated. The tag had come into circulation in the middle eighties, promoted vigorously by a number of architects, notably Rod Hackney, soon after to become President of the Royal Institute of British Architects, with the enthusiastic backing of the Prince of Wales and the assistance of a handful of journalists.

At the heart of the idea lay the recognition that people wish to have a far greater say in the shaping of their surroundings; recognition that the gap between 'us' and 'them', the decision makers, has to be bridged more effectively and directly if the widespread sense of alienation which exists in our cities – in particular the inner-city areas – is to be overcome; recognition that, unless people feel they are in charge of their own destinies, frustration and despair can drive them to the point where whole districts and quarters become well-nigh ungovernable. 'Community architecture' was based, therefore, on the principle of meaningful consultation with and participation by the eventual users of any scheme of development or improvement, whether this came about from the top down (i.e. from a local authority or housing association) or from the bottom up (i.e. from a local community group).

Competitions, new trusts, royal visits, opening ceremonies, interviews, provided material for books, television programmes and newspaper features. If by the end of the decade the 'movement' seemed to be floundering somewhat rudderlessly, it was largely because it had sought to hijack a whole range of related but disparate concepts, to the point where its own identity had become blurred. (In some quarters 'community architecture' had come to be seen merely as the antithesis of 'Modernism' – the battle against which was being pursued by the Prince of Wales on a wider front.) However, if the tag itself has become restrictive and confusing, this principle can never be 'a busted flush'; it will remain even more potent in the future than it has in the past.

For the tradition of citizen participation in such things goes back, in this country, at least 160 years. It was in the 1820s that a group of citizens in York banded together – successfully – to stop the demolition of the city walls. Since then a great network of societies, trusts and associations has come into being – there must certainly be 2,000 or so, though no one knows the exact number – to work for the improvement of their own area. They have created housing out of derelict buildings, parks and playgrounds and urban farms out of wasteland; they have provided facilities for the young and the elderly; they have cleared and restored canals, brought about traffic-management schemes, organised anti-litter drives ... On a larger scale they have commissioned plans and reports for the redevelopment of their towns and cities, in some cases even obtaining the substantial financial backing required. The feasibility of projects undertaken on a cooperative basis was shown by the Civic Trust's improvement schemes in shopping streets at the end of the 1950s, and official approval of the need for wider public participation in the formative stages of planning was enshrined in the Skeffington Report of 1969.

In the 1970s a new thrust developed, powered by the urgencies of urban decline and the steady development of the housing association movement, backed as it now was by government funding through the Housing Corporation, created in 1964. That funding has fluctuated through the years, but by the eighties, as we have seen, housing associations had become the Thatcher administration's chosen instrument for the provision of social, or 'fair rental', housing as this was prised from local government. It was during the 1970s that the words 'consultation' and 'participation' began to be applied to housing developments. For the first time blue-collar communities in areas of deprivation were being helped to involve themselves directly in what was going on around them. Ralph Erskin based the big Byker redevelopment in Newcastle on the active participation of the existing tenants. Ten years later the total redesign of Lea View House, a big municipal block in Hackney, took the form dictated by the wishes of the residents. Elsewhere, as we have seen, small groups of tenants began to take matters into their own hands by banding into co-operatives to build houses for themselves. These were strands of participation which, in particular, became known as 'community architecture', with most of the attention – understandably – focused upon the heroic 'self-build' groups.

For the families concerned in most such co-operative groups the results have been spectacular. In relation to the national problem, however, the collective potential of their effort has been oversold. Rod Hackney, on becoming President of the RIBA in 1987, said:

> We can rescue 500,000 inner-city houses from dereliction by small-scale, locally based enterprises that give the people a chance to rebuild their own environment the way they want, and so create a land as safe and prosperous as Switzerland.

Over what sort of period? It has been implied that everywhere great reservoirs of creative energy need only to be uncapped to well forth into regeneration. The Prince of Wales has written:

> Many . . . seem to have found their plans thwarted by a potent concoction of official inertia, bureaucratic wrangling and financial setbacks.[11]

And on another occasion has said:

> We must sink our differences and cut great swathes through the cat's-cradle of red tape which chokes this country from end to end.

'Break the deadlock – release the energy' is the battle cry. Well . . . yes. But community architecture is anyway a slow process,

involving much persuasion, education in what is involved, guidance, encouragement. And the self-build co-operative stands or
falls by the personality and calibre of its leading spirit. In truth, if
significant progress is to be made in reducing the urgent housing
problems of the nation, we have to feel our way towards the
formalisation of community participation on an altogether bigger
scale: processes which are accepted and understood at all levels,
and have become the rule rather than the exception.

It is *beginning* to happen, though as yet fitfully. One of the
government's programmes, Estate Action, embodies many of the
lessons so painfully learnt at local level. Estate Action was formed
in 1985 – originally as the Urban Housing Renewal Unit. It arose
largely out of the findings of three 1980 papers from the Housing
Directorate on difficult-to-let housing [12] and a 1985 Inquiry into the
condition of the local authority housing stock in England, coupled
with the six years' experience gained in the Department of Environment's Priority Estates Project started in 1979.

The latter, following in the wake of the examples we have
already noted, confirmed that, if run-down and unpopular estates
are to be turned round, certain criteria *have* to be met:

- Housing management must be estate-based, with a local office
  which is able to respond directly to tenants' needs, and express
  firm commitment to the estate's future.
- Co-operatives and trusts are the obvious mechanism by which
  tenants can participate in, and control, the running and improvement of their estates.
- The diversification of tenure and the introduction of private-
  sector investment are vital (they tend to go hand in hand).

These things are interlinked and it is essential that all concerned
see the problem in a holistic way. [13]

Estate Action can assist local authorities in the pursuit of these
aims through 'targeted' loan sanctions which supplement the
annual allocations made by the Housing Investment Programme.
Such assistance has risen from £50 million in 1986/87 to £190
million in 1989/90. Resources are allocated on the basis of local
authority bids; during 1988/89, 190 new schemes were approved,
to join the 131 in the pipeline. Factors taken into consideration
when judging applications involve security (for example, by installing porter/receptionists), the provision of 'affordable warmth', the
improvement of external areas (perhaps the creation of individual,
walled, front gardens) – but also such matters as the social,
physical and economic factors in the area.

The estate office should have a local repairs team; should be responsible for local lettings; should have control over rent collection and arrears; should be responsible for caretakers and wardens, cleaning and open-space maintenance. A Residents' Forum should determine priorities, provide advocacy for the estate as a whole and individual tenants within it, and perhaps be responsible for local management decisions.

Clearly such a state of affairs can be reached by different routes. Glasgow, for example, among other cities, has set up Management Co-operatives to be responsible for functions previously the responsibility of the Housing Department. 'Responsibility', 'Accountability' and 'Choice' are words enshrined in each Management Agreement drafted in concert with tenants: 'Our intention will be to explain our philosophy on responsibility more clearly to our tenants, act more accountably – and offer more choice.'[14]

To strengthen tenants' power of choice was an objective of the 1988 Housing Act. Designed to speed the transfer of tens of thousands of council flats and houses to the private sector, the Act permits estates to opt for transfer to commercial control, to a housing association, or for the status quo under local authority control.

Many of the signals, then, emanating from the Department of the Environment's towers in Marsham Street are clearly designed to encourage greater local participation in housing and environmental improvement. Others are more conflicting. In July 1988 the Department announced its intention to set up a number of Housing Action Trusts in some of the most severely run-down areas. Eighteen estates would be bought by the government at 'market' value, their 25,000 properties renovated, and the tenants' views then sought on whether they should be sold to the private sector, to housing associations or – an unlikely possibility – back to the local authorities concerned. Predictably, this was seen by many as a further indication of the government's itch to centralise powers whenever it can. However, only eight months later, plans for the first six estates – all in Tower Hamlets, in London, were scrapped – the government having taken fright at the estimated costs produced by their consultants.

Another story from London – this time Waltham Forest. It concerns five large 'panel concrete' estates on 50 acres/20 ha, inherited from the Greater London Council, and housing in all some 2,500 people. They are windswept, forbidding, vandalised and hated. A first social survey established some main facts about tenants' attitudes and wishes. The Council called in Hunt Thompson, the architects responsible a decade before for Lea View

234

House in Hackney and leading advocates for – and practitioners in – 'community architecture'. Hunt Thompson came up with proposals for a phased rolling programme, within which the existing tower blocks could be demolished and replaced by low-rise houses with private gardens, with a minimum displacement of existing tenants.[15] Within the broad concept a range of options was provided (for two-storey/three-storey houses; maisonettes; two-, three-, five-person accommodation, and so on). More detailed consultation with tenants was planned before detailed design took place, but the broad objectives were to provide family houses on the ground; to give every house its back garden; and to break down the barriers, real and psychological, between the estates and adjoining streets.

The proposals were ingenious, as well as humane (they found a place in the Prince of Wales's *Vision of Britain* exhibition at the V & A in 1989). The estimated cost of the whole programme was in the neighbourhood of £315 million. This was way beyond the Council's means (its housing capital programme stood at £18.5 million a year), but the Council bit the bullet and proposed to 'sell' the estates, at nil cost, to specially formed Industrial Provident Societies; on the Board of each of which would be three Council nominees and five tenants' representatives. Of the new houses 20 per cent would have to be sold. 'It's not the road we wished to go down,' said Clive Morton, Chairman of the Housing Committee.[16] 'We wanted to redevelop the estates with people staying on as Council tenants. If anyone can come up with such a plan, we'll do it. But it looks unlikely. So we think it only fair to put to tenants the real choices before them. We are not advocating one or the other. We will give them all the information we can. And then it is up to them to choose. It is their future. They should decide.'

The whole project, then, seemed set to become an exemplar – of detailed consultation with those concerned; of architectural ingenuity; of a Labour council prepared to go against its own ethos by selling off a fifth of the properties and removing 2,500 from its tenants lists; in short a symbol of governmental aims achieved. It did not work out like that. In September 1989 the Council's officers were bidden to Marsham Street to be told that Waltham Forest would not be allowed (presumably as part of the government's efforts to keep down public expenditure) to borrow the crucial £175 million that would enable the scheme to go ahead. In effect, the scheme had been vetoed.

Confusing and conflicting signals, then, from Whitehall. Money is certainly being spent on many forms of community involvement – through the Housing Corporation, Estate Action, local authorities, and by means of 'enabling' grants channelled through trusts in this field (the Civic Trust, the RIBA, the Groundwork Trusts, the Gulbenkian Trust, etc.). Some say that, notwithstanding the government's claim to the more efficient targeting of funds, their use in fact leaves much to be desired. Reservations were expressed to me, for example, about Estate Action as, in the words of one professional, 'throwing money all over the place in small dribs, without ever enabling anything to be done properly'. Certainly it has been proved over and over again that improvements done on the cheap represent money down the plughole, since they are all to do again a few years later. Equally, it certainly often *appears* that, faced by the costs of doing anything 'properly' – the Tower Hamlets HAT estates and those described above in Waltham Forest both required the same order of expenditure – the government takes fright and shies off. Yet, such are the slow-motion convolutions of official policy that, two years later, a *tranche* of HAT money, won from the Treasury by the DoE but still lying unspent in the bottom drawer, was in fact offered to the Waltham Forest scheme, which once again went to ballot among the residents, for some then, infinite tenacity and infinite patience may produce hope. For thousands of others in desperate conditions, the opportunity to take a measure of control over their future continues to be denied them.

Let us briefly recap. Community action – or enterprise, or architecture – covers a sliding scale of activity, from local consultation, through local participation, to local responsibility and local control. It can cover housing, wider environmental improvements, area renewal and a range of social functions. However, land purchase, construction and continuing management and maintenance on any scale require resources far beyond those of any voluntary group unaided. If the energies of local communities are to be fruitfully released to make a significant impact upon the national problem, far greater resources have to be put at their disposal – or at the disposal of public and voluntary agencies working with and for them. No less is there a need to identify, and possibly train, more people for working in this sphere – people capable of rigorously analysing local needs, of monitoring and assessing results; above all with the experience, enthusiasm and commitment to make things happen.

THE ROLE OF THE ARTS
'Men come together in cities,' wrote Aristotle, 'in order to live; they remain together in order to lead the good life.' Culture, learning, recreation and social intercourse have always been es-

sential functions of the city; they are its life-style. 'Culture', however, is a compendium word which covers a vast spectrum, with the arts and sciences at one end, a host of popular concerns and activities – from watching television to playing bowls – at the other. These multifarious engagements impact on one another in patterns which, in their totality, are beyond the capacity of the human mind to grasp. Nonetheless their totality powerfully colours the nature of a society, the quality of life in a particular community and its attractiveness to others. Urban decay weakens it; prosperity can – though not always – strengthen it. But do the arts have to *follow* in the wake of economic wellbeing? Increasingly over recent years attention has been given to the potential of cultural activities as an *engine* to power urban regeneration and economic recovery.

The sheer scale of the economic role of the arts is only now beginning to be recognised. Their monetary turnover in Britain has been estimated at £10 billion, or 2.5 per cent of all spending on goods and services by UK residents and foreign buyers (this figure excluding expenditure in connection with the built heritage, libraries, books, architecture and design, the manufacture and purchase of 'tools of the trade', such as paints, musical instruments, etc.). The arts give employment to nearly half a million people – or 2.1 per cent of all those in work – and, significantly, the figure rose by no less than 23 per cent in the five years between 1981 and 1986. Attendances in 1984/85 totalled over 250 million: 73 million at museums and galleries; 59 million at cathedrals, castles and historic houses; 49 million at theatres and concerts; and 70 million at cinemas. (Omitted from these figures are attendances at parks and gardens, zoos, steam railways and other attractions.) A powerful ingredient in the balance sheet stems from the tourist industry. Tourist spending in Great Britain in 1986 was £12.5 billion, of which £5.4 billion was spent by overseas visitors; of this total over £3 billion, or 25 per cent, was arts related.

Small wonder, then, that 'arts-management strategies' began to be developed in the USA through the 1970s, and that interest in the economic potential of the subject came to the fore in Europe in the early eighties. I am indebted, for the figures above, to John Myerscough's splendidly comprehensive study *The Economic Importance of the Arts in Britain*.[17] In his introduction he writes:

There is a growing belief that the arts can bring a competitive
edge to a city, a region and a country, as a source of creativity,
a magnet for footloose executives and their businesses, and as a

237

means of asserting civic, regional or national identity through the quality of cultural life.

This message has been reinforced from several quarters. An international conference in Glasgow in 1988 brought together for three days 350 of those most closely associated with the subject, and gave an airing to a wide range of projects and programmes.[18] Richard Luce, then Minister for the Arts, blessed it with the words 'We must not look on the arts as just an optional extra; they must be an integral part of any strategy for urban regeneration.' In 1988 the Arts Council launched its own initiative aimed at increasing public awareness of the 'substantial contribution to the revitalisation of our cities' being made by the arts, and followed this up in 1989 with *An Urban Renaissance*, citing sixteen case studies from different parts of the country.

'Art', like 'culture', is a slippery word. In this context there are at least three quite distinct strands to be considered. Most obviously attractive to local politicians are the big prestige projects that will bring their city fame and the municipal coffers new revenue. Over recent years a range of new museums and galleries – public sector and private – has shown convincingly how great a draw such things can be if you get it right. The York Railway Museum attracts nearly a million people a year; the National Museum of Photography, Film and Television in Bradford, as we have seen, approximately the same figure; the Burrell Collection in Glasgow – 1.2 million in its first year (though down since then); the Yorvic Viking Centre in York – around 700,000. These have been followed by the Tate Gallery of the North in Liverpool (which anyway claims 1.25 million visitors to its *other* museums and galleries); the Museum of the Moving Image on London's South Bank; the V & A is coming to Bradford; the Yorvic team are setting up 'living history' equivalents in a number of towns and cities.

In music and the performing arts the story is the same. Simon Rattle brought new fame to the City of Birmingham Symphony Orchestra, which has now been given a fine new concert hall in the £120 million convention centre; Sadlers Wells Royal Ballet moves to the Hippodrome in the same city. Glasgow's £24 million concert hall opened in 1990. A new opera house for the Welsh National Opera is planned in the wasteland surrounding the inner harbour of Cardiff Bay. Swansea has lavishly restored the Grand Theatre, Belfast its opera house, Manchester two major theatres ... and there are many, many more. Festivals, if rightly tuned, can pack them in. Aldeburgh and Edinburgh are long established, but

Glasgow's Mayfest, Dundee's and other cities' more recent festivals, are triumphantly indicative of a potential now beginning to be tapped in many parts of the country.

All these things can directly assist the regeneration process in two ways. They attract visitors, whose expenditure circulates within and strengthens the local economy through the 'multiplier effect' (money spent in the restaurant goes, some of it, to the butcher and the greengrocer, who in turn use it to buy clothes, petrol, what-you-will, whence it is recycled in yet more directions). They can also exert a very positive effect upon the upgrading of the surrounding area as their success ripples outwards, encouraging new life and new forms of activity to take root there. In some cases whole cultural 'quarters' have resulted.

A second important strand in the regenerative role of the arts relates to their use in making cities fine places in which to live and move about. The partnership of art and architecture is a dream which waxes and wanes. In the Renaissance ideal the city, in its layout, its buildings, its monuments and sculptures, was itself seen as a work of art. Bitter such thoughts in the non-places of today's inner cities. Somewhere at the end of the eighteenth century painting jettisoned its decorative function and, with sculpture, began to seek autonomy as a language of personal expression. A century or so later architecture began to lust after a total, complete-in-itself rationality – and slid, for the most part, into a featureless anonymity. Only very rarely were art and architecture overtly on speaking terms. Today, as part of the reaction against the sheer boredom of so much twentieth-century development, the tide is moving strongly once more towards a new marriage of the visual arts with architectural and urban design – notably in the per-cent-for-art concept, which would have a percentage of the cost of all new development committed to the commissioning of original works with which to add distinction to buildings and urban spaces.

This is not a new idea. In America over twenty states and around one hundred cities have per-cent-for-art policies. In Europe nine countries have put their weight behind them. In Britain they have been adopted by counties (for example, Hereford and Worcester), by cities (Birmingham prominently in the lead), and several of the new UDCs (Black Country, Cardiff Bay and Sheffield). The Arts Council has lent its weight to the movement, and in 1989 appealed to all local authorities to make such a commitment part of their planning policy and to request developers to write it into their budgets and planning applications.[19] 'Good design,' says

239

Lord Palumbo, Chairman of the Arts Council, 'means good business. I hope that local authorities will look carefully at the advice we are giving.'

It is an attractive idea, but not without its pitfalls. It has produced such splendidly appropriate works as Calder's big (53 ft./ 5.4 m.) scarlet 'Flamingo' in Chicago's Federal Center Plaza. It has also produced meaningless afterthoughts pinned smugly to meaningless buildings, and bright murals which serve only to emphasise the squalor and decay they are meant to disguise. Corporate companies tend to opt for the prestigious (if they are feeling rich) or for 'safe' mediocrity (if they are not). Not all buildings *need* this kind of embellishment (think only of Richard Rogers's Lloyds building in London, for example); others might benefit from putting the expenditure into better-quality materials and finishes, rather than into covering up what they have in fact used. Heroic agit-prop murals of bare-breasted women marching into the future rapidly become tiresome. Maintenance of all exterior art poses problems.

Urban *spaces* tend to benefit more readily from the introduction of visual markers than the buildings themselves. However, the more imposing the space, the more important the quality and scale of what is placed there – over and over again one sees some miserably ineffective little piece of sculpture cheeping like a new-born chick where it should be roaring like a lion. A policy for public art requires the most sensitive appraisal of sites and potential; often a water feature, an obelisk, a big tree, or even an *objet trouvé* (like the great generator towers which stand like gigantic sculptures in Seattle's Gasworks Park) will serve more appropriately than sculpture as such. A good example of a considered programme aimed at lending distinction to an *area* is offered by Swansea's use of sculpture in its Maritime Quarter. At the last count just under fifty carved plaques and relief panels had been built into the new docklands buildings (apart from various freestanding pieces), many of them by the sculptor Philip Chatfield. A common thread of imagery relating to the city's maritime and industrial past runs through these decorations; individually unassuming, they build up incrementally to reinforce the area's sense of identity with tact and charm.

But there is yet a third way in which the arts can play a part in the regeneration process – a third strand: through community participation. Here is one example from many.

'You'll never see anything like this again in my lifetime,' said the town councillor to his small boy. 'Or in yours.'[20] The town was

Barrow-in-Furness, where we build our Trident submarines. The occasion was the centenary of the Town Hall's official opening in 1987. The 'Town Hall Tattoo', as it was called, ran from noon until 6 p.m. Buskers and clowns wove in and out of the clogdancers, pipers, jazz bands, stalls and 15,000 people. Three hundred kites, made under the guidance of two master kite-makers imported from Japan, were flown by schoolchildren. A 'cataclysmic firecracker crescendo' and a centenary choir of two hundred singing a specially composed oratorio of popular songs marked the arrival of the ghost of Queen Victoria (who, having been unable to make the journey in her Jubilee year, had graciously consented to concede her presence on this occasion a hundred years later). The Monarch amazingly rode the Great Elephant of History (eyes flashing, gigantic trunk waving), followed by an effigy Mayor perched on the town's coat of arms (an enormous bee, transfixed by an arrow) and a parade of gargantuan floats and vast mobile 'puppets'. At the appointed moment the Town Hall blew its top in a hundred plumes of coloured smoke. Mortar shells exploded overhead. Pin-striped bureaucrats abseiled down its walls while four miles of red tape and bunting cascaded about them. All the church bells pealed. Tickertape poems fell from the sky. And, for reasons best known to herself, Queen Victoria's outsize bloomers could be seen flying amid the smoke from the flagpole atop the Town Hall. A *Guardian* journalist described the whole event as 'possibly the biggest single artwork of the year in Europe, making *Aïda* at Luxor look like very fancy old hat'.[21] County Councillor Alf Horne placed the emphasis differently. 'It's community spirit,' he said, 'that's never been seen before.'

This civic extravaganza was mounted by Welfare State International, who like such tags as 'Engineers of the Imagination', 'Civic Magicians' and 'Guardians of the Unpredictable'. It was the culmination of a six-month programme of events in Barrow, itself only part of a continuing assault upon the sensibilities of a culturally isolated town carried out over about seven years. For Welfare State International's objective goes much deeper than just a few hours of fun. They seek to rekindle that sense of wonder we have as children, but so quickly lose as we adjust to the day-to-day demands of the world about us. They aim to bring art – in the widest sense – into the lives of the great majority, not as an elitist activity which someone else has decreed is good for our health, but something in which all can participate creatively. Their performances are the ultimate in mixed media, fusing painting, sculpture and music with traditions of carnival, music hall and

241

fairground. Whatever they do, be it a fireside story in a village hall or a 'metropolitan spectacular' like that at Barrow, is based upon detailed local research and bears directly upon the nature and potential of the particular community.

Welfare State International was started in 1968 by John Fox, its present artistic director. It is, in effect, a consortium of about fifty different talents, some whole-time, some more loosely attached. It has worked in Japan, North America, Australasia and East Africa as well as in all parts of Britain (including, almost inevitably, a region-wide celebration converging on Glasgow during its reign as European City of Culture). However, their aim is always to set up models, exemplars, which can be taken over or copied as self-sustaining activities, run by and for the local community. Barrow offers a good example of the changed thinking that can result from a continuing thrust by such an organisation. In 1983 the town's commitment to the arts amounted to £700 per annum; by the end of the decade that had risen to £22,000 and the Council had a full-time arts development officer in post.

The greater the expenditure of public money the greater the need for it to be structured. The spraying of money vaguely into 'the arts' will achieve little of lasting value. Increasingly, an arts management strategy is seen as essential if objectives are to be related to means and to financial support. This is fairly new territory in Britain. Let us take two examples.

The first is the 1990 *Strategy for Public Art in Cardiff Bay*,[22] commissioned by the Development Corporation from a special consultancy team – and believed to be the first comprehensive study of its kind in this country. The report addresses only questions relating to the use of the visual arts in public places, but does this very thoroughly. The document rehearses the usual arguments in favour of public art (cultural tourism, attracting inward investment, an improved quality of life, and so on); it sets out a suggested per-cent-for-art basis of funding (pooled for greater flexibility); deals with site selection (major landmarks, serial or linear works to aid orientation, gateways, enhancement of identity at street level, meeting places and spaces for live events – devoting about eight pages to possible sites for key commissions. It makes a plea for the inclusion of artists in design teams, for artists working 'live' on site, for studio and workshop provision; for a major international contemporary art gallery, and for a Community and [arts] Education Programme. The financial implications are examined, a funding strategy proposed, linked with the creation of a Cardiff Bay Art Trust Fund and a Cardiff Bay Art Commission as the principal focus for the whole programme. Staffing, administration and implementation are considered. The package as a whole is broken down into short-term and longer-term objectives. The principles set out in the Strategy have been endorsed by the Corporation; a Cardiff Bay Art Trust brought into being to handle the programme; and the first commissions placed.

This is one kind of document – admirable for its purpose. Another local authority policy document, but more wide ranging, is *An Arts and Cultural Industries Strategy for Liverpool,* approved by the City Council at the end of 1987.[23] This widens the activities considered by Myerscough and includes the promotion and distribution of books and printed material; broadcasting; the music industry; the film, video and photographic industry; advertising; and the performing arts. After emphasising the importance of existing facilities on Merseyside (those nearly 2.5 million visitors in 1986), it offers statistics indicating that 'home-based consumerism poses a threat to out-of-home activities' (98 per cent of the population own a television set and spend twenty-two hours a week watching it), and emphasises the need to develop alternative means of marketing and distribution if the patronage of local facilities and material is properly to complement the imported 'cultural products' of the major companies. Much, too, it states, will depend on whether the City Centre can be transformed so that residents feel that it belongs to them; sense that it is safe to visit, particularly at night; can visit it cheaply and easily; find it pleasant to visit because of the quality of its appearance and its 'street atmosphere'.

An assessment follows of the tangible economic value of the arts to the local economy (estimated three years later at £97 million and 3000 jobs), of community involvement, of the implications for the city's image and employment. A strategy is needed, it concludes, to provide a context for the Council's support for, and direct involvement in, this whole sector; to enable the Council to arbitrate between many competing claims; to guide the use of the City's own resources; to form a basis for discussion with the other Merseyside District Councils; and to assist efforts to attract additional funding (Liverpool lost £2.1 million [1983/84] when the Metropolitan County Council went). The 'key objective' of such a strategy should be: 'To maximise the contribution which the arts and cultural activities make to the economic and social well-being of the city'. There follow in detail proposed policies on the promotion of new arts activity and the means by which this should be brought about; on the possibility of a major annual arts festival; on employment and training for the cultural industries; on expanding the market for locally generated material; and on community involvement – together of course with sections on funding and organisational implications. Cardiff, Liverpool – two different approaches to arts planning. Each city will evolve its own appropriate strategy. What is evident is that *some* coherent framework is necessary for initiatives in this direction.

Much moving, at many different levels. The Arts Council report *An Urban Renaissance* listed eighty local initiatives of the kinds here touched on, but would in no way claim to be comprehensive. Indicative of the way things are going is the emergence, over recent years, of commissioning agencies who will advise on proposed programmes, assist in the commissioning process, undertake the administration and generally look after all the practicalities on behalf of – but of course in consultation with – the sponsor. However, euphoria can too easily set in. Funding remains an acute problem, and there is no way, as yet, that a per-cent-for-art policy can be *enforced.* Money, when it is available, will not of itself ensure talent and quality. To put the case for the arts on a purely economic basis is to diminish their essential nature, and the temptation to push the arts into purposes for which they are not fitted has to be resisted. There is no question but that they can provide a strong sub-structure for the renewal process, can generate energy and commitment locally to give coherence to the community. Baltimore, with a two thirds black population, is famous for the way it has pulled itself up over thirty years or so. There, Mayor Schaeffer's ambitious programme of concerts and other events in the Inner Harbor area before its redevelopment triumphantly brought life to what was virtually then a no-go area, brought blacks and whites together as never before, and demonstrated the potential of the area to developers who would otherwise never have considered it. Nonetheless, in the last analysis, it is in the release of the human spirit that the true role of art is to be found. We cannot live without dreams, myths, fables, the fulfilment that comes from creativity. 'There is potential in everybody,' says John Fox, of Welfare State International, 'but our educational system does not liberate creativity in people, does not enable people to realise their potential. People like solving problems as part of a team, not just earning to buy consumer goods. We are still working, in this country, with a silly Victorian "steam" mentality. The world is changing by the minute. We've *got* to

244

make these connections – spiritual, practical, artistic – or we're going to find ourselves in even deeper trouble.'

Art cannot solve the living conditions of Easterhouse, or Kirkby, or Newham. But, in conjunction with wider programmes, it can release the forces by which the civilised city is to be achieved.

THE PURSUIT OF QUALITY

For those personally involved in regeneration, or any kind of physical planning and development, it is hard not to become obsessed with the *process* – how to get around this snag or that: political, economic, technical. For those who come after, the users, process is irrelevant; the end *product* is all that matters. Does it work? Does it fulfil a need? Does it enrich and enhance the quality of community life? In the reshaping of our cities there are always pressing reasons for spending less, for speed and corner-cutting. Nothing could be more shortsighted, more wastefully profligate. The 1950s and 60s offer harsh testimony to idealisms hastily conceived and inadequately seen through. Down come the tower blocks, the elevated walkways and the rest, costly to erect, costly to demolish. Resources down the plughole. Who cares now that the urgency was so great, why resources were so stretched?

The *achievement* of quality, however, is not easy, and so often eludes us. Resources come into it – but flinging money at a problem, even if we are prepared to – of itself achieves nothing. The design process consists of a long chain of assessments and decisions, in the course of which any misjudgement is likely to invalidate subsequent assessments and decisions, to send the project down the wrong road, and thereby to compromise its final quality. The larger the scale of the undertaking the longer the chain, and the more disastrously wrong are the end consequences likely to be of mistakes made early in the process. The larger the scale of the project, moreover, the greater the number of interests at stake, the more voices there are claiming a right to have a say in the decision making. Our problem is how to formalise the collective representation of the legitimate interests of today's hydra-headed, corporate consortia, without destroying the creative leap of the imagination which alone can breathe life into a concept and ensure that it will continue to refresh the spirit for generations to come.

But what exactly *is* quality? It has been said that quality can always be appreciated, but never defined. For a start, urban quality has little to do with 'style', with a fashion-conscious view of façades as a form of theatre scenery. Buildings occupy space, but more importantly they create spaces. It is these spaces which, above all, make up the character of a town; which make this place different from that. In any built-up area, even one in decline, there are likely to be streets, one-time marketplaces, residential squares, parks – townscape assets on which to build a new urban form which nonetheless pays tribute to what was there before. If the area was so far gone that it has had to be cleared totally, if it is now no more than a featureless wasteland, what are the elements from which a new urban framework can be constructed? Water? The fall of the land? Earth moving and contouring? Sightlines to distant features – a church, a monument, a hilltop? There has to be a vision, embodied in a strategy, refined into smaller area plans or briefs, if the end result is to have coherence and dignity. In today's world, we may be certain, quality will not happen by chance.

Most of this kind of planning concerns 'the public realm', the public spaces of the development. Much is coupled with the provision of appropriate 'infrastructure': access by road and rail (but also properly planned traffic exclusion), the installation of essential services – water, power, telecommunications and much else. If these things are fudged at the outset, saving operations will have to be instituted, but they will be expensive, and forever unsatisfactory – a shutting of the stable door after the horse has bolted. Quality will have escaped once again. The Isle of Dogs – largely because of its status as an Enterprise Zone – is an example of failure to tackle planning and infrastructure at the outset; Salford Quays an example of the reverse, where vision and infrastructure were finalised before other serious development began, and will in fact outlast whatever may be slotted into and on to their armature.

What then of the buildings and structures that will flesh out this armature? In most areas there will be existing buildings – public and private, large and small, old and new, interesting and boring. How many are worth keeping? Some will be real or potential assets, not necessarily because they are old but because they embody character and quality. Refurbished and recycled, if necessary, they will enrich the new urban scene, lend continuity to its future and, for its citizens, ease the trauma of change.

But we need always to be clear as to exactly why we seek to retain this building or that. Its uniqueness? Its capacity, if converted, to meet new needs? Its value in townscape terms? Some building types, like warehouses, being solidly built but not of exceptional architectural interest, offer flexible space and lend

246

themselves readily to new uses. The greater the value of the building architecturally, the greater the sensitivity required in effecting any change to its nature. There can come a point when the exuberance of a conversion warrants the description 'having fun with the building' rather than 'conservation'. We have seen a wave of stripped brickwork and butcher's-block timber, of fibreglass columns and pediments, designed to make old buildings look new and new buildings look old. Steel and concrete structures are hooked on to period façades. 'Period' façades are cooked up to create instant 'villages' with 'the charm of a more gracious era'. Every falsification of this kind, which blurs the dividing line between the true and the spurious, demeans and diminishes the genuinely old and truly worthwhile.

Too much new construction is conceived lazily, designed to watered down, copycat formulae. Time was when local contractors built for local clients in local materials. This, and the nature of the terrain, helped to give every place its special identity. Today, developers and construction companies build for the same corporate clients in all parts of the country. Uniformity spreads across the land like a stain. Is this housing estate in Home Counties suburbia, or somewhere in Greater Manchester, on Tyneside, in Wales? Wherever they be the shopping centres boast the same atrium (prestige word of the eighties), the same greenery (some of it real), the same escalators and wall-creeping lifts, are 'anchored' by the same big stores offering the same merchandise. The marinas are decked out with the same quayside pubs, the same setts and bollards. The business parks sport the same glittering mirror-glass boxes, fronting the same lawns and satellite dishes . . .

Similar activities lead to similar building types, of course. But quality is not to be found in some across-the-counter kit of notions applied by rule of thumb. Every building, every structure, every space, must needs take account of its site, its neighbours, its bulk and form, its immediate surroundings, its effect upon more distant views. What may make sense in a confined space may constitute an eyesore when viewed across a dockland sheet of water or a big public square. A 'high-tech' design which looks dazzling in a science park is unlikely to make a good neighbour to the parish church or Town Hall. A high building which would look oppressive and ungainly in the middle of a small street might make an imposing focal point if it closed the end of the same street. A building can be excellent in itself but still fail to integrate itself in the surrounding urban fabric if it stands proud in a sea of tarmac parking spaces. And so on. Quality comes from the satisfying resolution of all these things, and many more.

The linked design decisions touch progressively smaller-scale matters: the ground surfaces and street furniture of the public realm, planting, things like overhead wires and outdoor advertising; perhaps fountains and water features, sculpture and exterior murals, floodlighting. They must needs be concerned with pollution, water quality, the cleanliness of streets and beaches and river banks, problems of vandalism and maintenance. Quality is not an all-time absolute. It has to be watched, maintained and enhanced right round the clock. Two examples. Studies by the University of Liverpool have suggested that half the trees planted in Britain to improve the environment are dead within five years. That represents wasted expenditure of millions of pounds. On the other hand we remain close-fisted in other ways. It has been pointed out that the four Central London Boroughs of Westminster, Kensington and Chelsea, Camden and Islington, having about 650,000 residents between them, spend £24.7 million a year on waste collection and street cleaning – or £38 per head. Central Paris, with more than three times that number of residents, spends around £70 per head. Allowing for all the difficulties inherent in such comparisons, there can still be no cause for surprise that Britain's reputation for street squalor stands almost unassailed in the western world. From the mediocre, the banal, the cheapjack, exceptions – for of course we are *capable* of quality – shine out like beacons. But if we can achieve quality, why do we so often fail to do so? Why does it all go so woefully wrong so much of the time? Having glanced, briefly, at one or two of the ingredients that go to make up urban quality, it is time to turn our attention to the means by which we seek to achieve it. How can we create places where people actually want to be?

Architects are fond of pointing out that the great cities of the past came into being without planning controls as we know them today. (In fact, Bologna's arcades stem from a fifteenth-century ordinance still in force; the controls exercised by ground landlords in Georgian London or Edinburgh New Town were rigid and detailed.) However, it is self-evident that glorious buildings result from good architects serving good clients. Unfortunately, not all architects are equally talented, and not all developers are minded to subordinate their profits to the public weal. The pirates of the fifties and sixties are by now an extinct species. Some of today's developers have shown a concern for quality which would have caused their forerunners of the previous generation to die laughing. Nonetheless, overall, corporations and developers lack the thirst for the prestige which quality brings, for example in North America. Recently the Chairman of the Royal Fine Art Commission, Lord St John of Fawley, put it succinctly in the Commission's twenty-sixth annual report. 'Too many schemes that we see,' he wrote, 'are not efforts to promote good architecture but are new ways of satisfying greed.'

It is not possible to legislate for masterpieces, but we have a right to demand mechanisms and procedures by which at least a minimum standard of architectural and townscape good manners can be ensured. This was one of the things our planning system was brought into being to do. All proposals to develop a site, or change its use, or alter a building which has been officially listed as of architectural or historic interest, must be submitted to the local planning authority for planning permission. The authority has powers, in the light of its local plans and policies, to grant or withhold consent – and thereby to control such things as the uses permitted for a particular site, the density of development, parking provision, the control of pollution and a multitude of allied matters. What has long been a matter of contention is the extent to which authorities have the power – and the right – to control purely aesthetic considerations. The dividing line between the functional and the aesthetic is anyway not always easy to define. Some authorities have pushed the legislation to extremes in their desire to ensure that development is appropriate in appearance. Some, seeking to be positive rather than negative, have offered advice to developers in the form of 'design guides', setting out the basic rules of the game as they see them. Some give the appearance of simply not caring at all. Some have given their blessing to schemes which should have been disallowed, in exchange for a donation from the company concerned of land, or some public facility, elsewhere – a process politely known as 'planning gain'.

It is a confused area, subject to regular skirmishing by the two main professions concerned – the architects (who would like total freedom from control) and the planners (who see the quality of the planning applications they actually receive – 80 per cent of which are not by architects at all). To make matters worse, it is an area which is mapped differently by different governments, and by successive Ministers in the same government. The general thrust of the Thatcherite eighties was towards a minimal use, if any, of aesthetic control. This was the message of two DoE Circulars in 1980 and 1985 (22/80 and 31/85), and of a Planning Policy

Guidance Note of 1989, which stated, with doubtless deliberate vagueness, that 'control over external appearance should only be exercised where there is a fully justified reason for doing so'. A number of planning authorities, notwithstanding, are embodying elements of design control in their draft Unitary Development Plans. For example Barnet's, in North London, is quoted as stating, 'All development proposals must be compatible with the established character and architectural identity of existing or adjoining proper-ties and the general locality in terms of scale, form and other design elements . . .'. New draft guidelines from the DoE in January 1990 implied that councils *could* indeed disallow housing schemes on aesthetic grounds alone. Unsurprisingly, the Royal Town Plan-ning Institute urged upon the government an extension of this approach to commercial building. In Parliament, the 'Sane Plan-ning Group' of nearly one hundred Conservative MPs, was likewise pressing for comprehensive controls. It was noised abroad that the Secretary of State was likely to take this line in the new planning bill he had in preparation. By March, however, it was made clear that no such thing was to be expected. It was the Royal Institute of British Architects' turn to be delighted.

This is not a twentieth-century equivalent to the mediaeval disputation about the number of angels on a pinhead. Lack of consensus, and therefore lack of clarity as to the position and responsibilities of the parties concerned, leads to muddle up and down the line. Never, until the second half of the eighties, had Secretaries of State for the Environment reversed so many of their Inspectors' recommendations and allowed so many appeals by developers against planning authorities' refusal of planning permis-sion. When nobody knows quite how they stand valuable time is wasted, issues are fudged, and the nation – usually – fails to get the quality it is quite capable of producing.

The public, aghast at much of the new development it sees around it, tends to blame it upon the wickedness or weakness of 'the planners'. In a democratic society it is not quite as simple as that. When public authorities themselves own land, their responsibility for the quality of development upon it – either as developer or as ground landlord in a position to call the tune – is clear-cut. All else falls to be dealt with by what the planning system allows – which, as we have seen, can appear contradictory. Consider, for example, the position of the Urban Development Corporations. The Cardiff Bay Corporation has been charged by successive Secretaries of State with creating 'a superlative environ-ment'. 'If Cardiff Bay makes a mess of it,' Peter Walker told a

Corporation seminar in 1989, 'that will have been the last chance for Cardiff for generations.' Looking back 'on all the opportunities lost in my lifetime', he said, he was determined that the CBDC should 'go for high quality and use their planning powers . . . to insist that high standards prevail. You may,' he said, 'be in for considerable battles with certain developers, government departments and the Treasury. These battles will have to be fought; I hope they won't have to be fought too hard.' Can this be squared with the official government line? John Pickup, Director of Planning, says unequivocally that there will be strong aesthetic control in the Development Corporation's area. The goals set by the government for the Corporation, he suggests, are taken by the Welsh Office as overriding the advice contained in the various circulars and notes referred to.

But how, in practice, are they to be achieved? Much of the land in Cardiff Bay is not owned by the Corporation. *Pace* Mr Walker, it has no direct planning-control powers. It can establish an overall strategy – and has done so; it can draw up area briefs, indicating in general terms the uses and types of development it would like to see – and has done so. It has published its *Policies for Urban Quality*, setting out generalised design guidelines. It can seek the views of its advisory Design Panel – and does so. In the last resort it can use its power of veto to block proposals it considers totally unsuitable or unworthy – but there is no way it can *ensure* one which is superlative. Political pressures moreover, here as elsewhere, to get things moving on the ground, and soon, are great. To public opinion, politicians, and certainly developers, quality may seem to take too long; insistence on standards to be no more than a stubborn and counter-productive perfectionism.

These problems have to be faced the length and breadth of the country. For smaller developments it is mostly a matter of persuasion, cajoling, suggesting. Unless the developer and his architect have come to discuss their project at the very outset, however, it is likely to be too late, when formal application is made, to do more than ameliorate some of its more glaring imperfections. For big, complex projects covering a considerable area, increasing use is being made – everywhere – of competitive bidding by architect-developer teams invited to submit package proposals to meet the requirements of broad area/site development briefs. In so far as the financial and qualitative elements of such packages are inextricably tangled, approaches of this kind are held by many to militate against quality. Certainly they offer fruitful opportunities for muddle and abortive waste of resources (a great deal of work is

251

involved in drawing up proposals for an area like, say, the Royal Docks in London). On their side, developers often feel that briefs are ambiguous and subject to alteration in mid process; they often feel, too, that they are given insufficient time properly to put together and solve the complex equations involved in big-scale work.

On the basis of his experience on the London Docklands Board, Sir Andrew Derbyshire, the distinguished architect, has suggested some ground rules for this type of operation. The criteria for judgement must be made crystal clear at the outset. Briefs, for example, must avoid the possibility of different land-use options, leading to differing land values confusing the selection process. They must specify design requirements with precision, so that the 'design bid' is as important as the 'money bid', not a chancy subsidiary element. Assessment teams should not be formed solely 'in house' but should include independent outside views with an understanding of design – perhaps in the form of advisory design panels (as now exist in Cardiff Bay and London Docklands). The selection process should be systematic. Teams should be invited to tender on the basis of their known track records. A first filtering process should reduce the number to a shortlist of perhaps six, three of these being selected on design grounds for final considera-tion. Terms should be such as to ensure that the architects employed on a submission are retained throughout the implementa-tion of the project (there have been cases where subsequent changes of architect have affected the nature and quality of the initial tender). Teams should be given adequate time for the preparation of their submissions, and it should be clearly under-stood that the sponsors will not deviate from the requirements set out in the brief.

Such a process approximates to that used by Swansea in the development of its Maritime Quarter, by LDDC outside the Isle of Dogs, and here and there elsewhere. Sometimes straight architectural competitions – limited by invitation, open, inter-national – may seem to open a door to otherwise unattainable heights. Unfortunately, history is littered with competition disasters (think only of the National Gallery extension in London). The Burrell Collection building in Glasgow gives proof that, if the brief and the assessing process can be got right, good can accrue from the architectural competition, but happy results are rather rare.

In the last analysis one is driven back to the lugubrious reflection that, as a nation, we do not rate quality as a very high priority. Market forces are powered by cost–profit ratios. Politicians long to be able to take credit for *action*, almost any action, but seldom see the results with their own eyes – and rarely *use* them. The professionals, hemmed in by these constraints, feel unable to hold to the big vision. The wider public accepts the second best which is foisted on to it because it has rarely been given the opportunity to experience anything else. (When presented with quality, it loves it, flocks to it, as like as not near kills it by sheer numbers.)

The second half of the eighties saw an unprecedented upsurge of interest in the nature of architectural style, triggered by Prince Charles and sustained by the media. From being the concern of specialists and pressure groups, the subject of urban design emerged centre stage. The debate has been often misconceived, sometimes mischievous, and nearly always disappointingly superficial – a rather uninformed 'battle of the styles'. Nonetheless, almost for the first time, the extent of public concern in these matters has become evident. Will it be pushed aside as other fashions and fads emerge – for we are conditioned to the delights of ceaseless novelty – or will the 1980s be seen by another generation as the moment when the nation began, dimly, to sense that, if it played its cards aright, quality might indeed be within its grasp? One piece of litmus by which to gauge the answer will be whether or not Calatrava's design is chosen for the East London River Crossing beyond the Royals in London's Docklands.

14

AN ATTITUDE OF MIND

WHY PRESERVE the inner city? Change is inevitable, change is desirable. Would it not be sensible explicitly to allow, even to encourage, the collapse of worn-out areas by making it known that no official rescue operations will be undertaken there? Land values would thereby plummet even further, to the point where commercial acquisition and redevelopment for new roles in the future would become economically feasible.

After all, 'no central machinery can ensure eternal life for all its cities at their historically highest level of prosperity'.[1] If, instinctively, we recoil from such brutal rationalities, is it perhaps connected with our sense of identity and our fear of change? Is it for reasons of social justice (for the community upheavals that would result from city-wide write-offs would make the clearance programmes of the sixties look like summer outings)? Or is it because, costly though salvage operations may be, their demands upon available resources will nonetheless prove less overwhelming? Incremental renewal is possible. *Total* clear-fell renewal – as Glasgow had to acknowledge after World War II – is beyond our means.

However, even 'the notion of salvaging inner cities presupposes a fairly precise idea of the alternative configuration which they are to have, and the scale of values and objectives to be attained'.[2] Do we, in fact, have any consensus vision of the future role of the city? Is there any real national strategy? How will all the effort, the achievements, of the past decade appear to our successors as the new century unfolds?

*

254

Let there be no argument about the achievements. The 1980s saw the most serious attempts to date to get to grips with the problems of urban decline. Things have been accomplished which would have seemed unbelievable a dozen years ago. Regeneration has been proved a practicable aim; renewal need no longer receive a shrug of the shoulders as a pipe dream. However, justifiable euphoria must not cloud the wider picture. Impressive battles have been won; the war has not. In many of the Boroughs of London, in the outer estates of Glasgow and Liverpool, in areas elsewhere which never make the news, desperation continues unabated. For millions of people nothing, but nothing, changed in the 1980s. Those headlines which crept into the Introduction to this book accurately reflect the two stories – of triumphant progress, of continuing despair. Both are true. It is the condition of the nation.

It matches the polarisation of political thought which so marked the eighties. It matches the ups and downs of the economy. It matches the underlying confusion and uncertainties attaching to policy options. Should the main emphasis of Exchequer aid be upon the alleviation of personal hardship, or should it be spent on measures designed to strengthen the economy? Should public money be directed to the blackest of the black spots, where decline has run its full course and hope is at its lowest ebb, or may it not prove more cost-effective if used to bolster the fire power of rather more buoyant areas where results can be more confidently expected? To what extent is the public realm to be seen as the responsibility of the private sector, and can an acceptable quality of development be achieved without objectives being spelled out, and up to a point regulated, by a public agency or authority? These are only some of the areas where differences of opinion exist, and policy falls between several stools.

Any appraisal of progress so far has to address: (a) the measures we have adopted to meet the known needs – are they the best possible? Are they adequate? Could they be improved? (b) the resources we make available – are they sufficient? Are they properly directed, geographically, and to the right purposes? (c) our long-term strategies – how certain are we as to our ultimate objectives? To what timescale are we working? Can we feel assured as to the continuity of essential programmes until their purpose has been achieved?

It is unnecessary here to reiterate the *needs* of those condemned to areas of decline and decay. The *extent* of those needs may be subject to disagreement but on their nature there is broad consensus. However, over the manner in which they are addressed two important matters of principle arise. First, to what extent is the meeting of immediate needs seen as a step towards an ultimate objective? Measures have to be devised and refined which will not only ease the hardships of social and demographic change, but will assist it. The shrinkage of cities which will never again boast the populations they supported in their heyday demands not merely a grudging acceptance but active encouragement, for it opens up the real possibility of greatly improved life-styles. To take but one obvious implication: encouragement of the greater mobility of labour calls for a much greater emphasis upon the provision of houses for rental, especially in areas of economic expansion. At the moment the whole thrust of government policy is towards home ownership; the provision of accommodation at affordable rents is given a very low priority. This creates a drag on the structural changes in society which are desirable, as well as creating hardship for those concerned.

Secondly, and colouring all else, is the need to give people a *real* say in what happens to them. Lip service is increasingly paid to the desirability of fuller public participation in community affairs, and brave attempts made to achieve it, but to what extent can genuine community involvement so far be said to form an integral thread of urban regeneration? Appropriate mechanisms for wider consultation, for better channels of communication, for shared decision-making, for the devolution of responsibility (which involves accountability) are beginning to evolve. They are not yet general. To make them work properly we need more trained '*animateurs*', enablers, project leaders, but above all greater corporate will to bring them about.

These two themes – the integration of short-term measures with long-term objectives and the meaningful participation by communities in decision-making which affects their own lives – *must* become central to the planning process. For urban regeneration, which is the subject of this book, must surely come to be seen as merely one aspect of an altogether bigger problem: the management of change – and innovation – in Britain.

This opens up the whole question of the changing role of local government and how it should function for the next half-century. During the 1980s, as we have seen, the functions, powers and resources of local authorities were markedly reduced. Functions have been passed to the private sector. Decision-making and financial control have been assumed increasingly by central government. At the same time, although their direct responsibilities have shrunk, the administrative burden upon Councils has grown no less – and in some respects (the switch from the rating system to the community charge provides but one example) has increased. Coupled with a continuing state of crisis management brought about by their financial difficulties, it is not surprising that many authorities – more especially those with proud records – feel bewildered and uncertain as to what is now expected of them. The fundamental changes of 1974/75, the coming and going of the Metro Counties, the creation of the UDCs, all created procedural upsets which have taken considerable time for the system to absorb. Now, it seems, with growing recognition that all is not as it should be after the last restructuring, and a feeling in some quarters that there is a level of administration too many, all is for the melting pot once again. The Labour Party and the Liberal Democrats are committed to the abolition of the County Councils. Over recent years conflicting nods and winks have come from the Conservatives, held back, one guesses, from openly putting the Counties on the chopping block by votes and tribal loyalties. The 1990 return of Michael Heseltine to the Department of the Environment, however, has brought the whole subject to the top of the agenda with a new urgency. His own views are well known. He has suggested that the bigger cities should be released from the two-tier system (in effect reverting to their previous County Borough status); that Councils should be led by full-time, directly elected mayors; that a Development Agency on the lines of the Scottish and Welsh model should be created for England. One of his first actions on resuming office was to announce a fundamental review of local government by his Department, with wide consultation. Not surprisingly, this provoked salvoes of special pleading from the local authority associations. The (Conservative-controlled) Association of District Councils redoubled its longstanding campaign for the abolition of the Counties; the (Conservative-controlled) Association of County Councils, usually reticent about taking part in public slanging matches, was stung into calling for the abolition of the Districts.

The time is clearly ripe for fundamental and wide-ranging consideration of the kind of local government we are likely to need in the coming century. What today are its proper responsibilities; what should fall to the private sector; what should be the *extent* of its obligations? How can its management structures be improved? What should be the basis for its finances (i.e. the split between Exchequer funding and local taxes in whatever form)? How best can fruitful partnerships be *ensured* with its own communities, the private sector, and other public authorities and agencies? Interim ministerial hints have suggested that some areas could end up with single-tier authorities, others with two tiers; that the single-tier authorities might in some cases be District Councils, in others Counties; that some areas might have elected mayors, others not. This would seem a design for total public confusion. Changes should not be made impetuously. It is imperative this time to get it right. The fullest possible consultation at all levels – not only within central and local government circles – is essential. If that should take the proposed new commission (to replace the Boundary Commission) longer than the two years suggested, so be it.

With all this goes a need to spell out afresh the objectives and purposes of planning. The 1947 Act embodied a vision of the world we sought to bring about, and a coherent and consistent system of machinery by which to achieve that vision. Since then it has been pulled about by all sorts of amendments and additions. Fashions have come and gone. Regional planning has found favour and fallen into disfavour. Two-tier planning has seemed imperatively desirable, but then imperatively undesirable. A system designed to control development in what was anticipated to be a steadily expanding economy has had to be put into reverse to *bolster* development in a period of decline. A whole new generation of politicians has grown up for whom the ethic and tenets of planning have lost their excitement – indeed are felt to be about as relevant to the final years of the century as the Reform Act of 1832. The basic system remains intact, and is administered conscientiously by the professionals within the constraints they face, but proper strategic frameworks are lacking. At times during the eighties planning appeals have been determined by Ministers in what has appeared to be a capricious fashion. A shared vision no longer exists. If we are not to blunder into the twenty-first century by-guess-and-by-God, that shared vision has to be re-established.

The future role of local government, the future role of planning – both turn about the same things: at the micro level, responsiveness to those they represent and serve; at the macro level, their strategic capabilities and resolve.

During the 1980s, partly as a result of government policies but perhaps even more because common sense and local circumstances have demanded it, authorities have become much more outward looking, much more entrepreneurial, much more ready and anxious to form working partnerships with other agencies – indeed themselves to set up new agencies for particular purposes. Of course earlier precedents exist – Norwich's imaginative 'Heritage-over-the-Wensum' programme of the early seventies for example.

But 'pragmatism' is a word now much in favour in city halls generally. We have seen something of these new partnerships in GEAR in Glasgow, in Birmingham's Heartlands programme, in Calderdale's association with the Civic Trust, and elsewhere; in the trusts and companies being set up by Councils to manage their housing estates and to promote investment and local enterprise.

Nonetheless, the gulf between Town Hall and *citizen* remains great. There is no wide understanding of the full nature of local government, its hierarchical structure, which departments should be approached for needed information, what help and support may be available. Councils have to become more accessible, more open and informative, more ready to take on board the views of those affected by proposed change, more ready to devolve responsibility in the day-to-day management of neighbourhood affairs. Many, perhaps most, will protest that they are already doing these things. They produce news-sheets, annual reports (not always, alas, as informative as Knowsley's), exhibitions, maybe videos; they conduct attitudes and needs surveys; they set up area outposts to which local residents can turn instead of trekking to the, possibly distant, Town or Shire Hall (Birmingham, as we have seen, is well on the way to completing a network of neighbourhood offices in all its thirty-nine wards, coupled to special Area Committees, and is committed to the eventual creation of Urban Parish Councils). Cardiff has a 'customer care' unit; John Scampion, the Chief Executive of Solihull, runs a personal 9 a.m. to 10 a.m. 'hotline' for complaints every day. And so on. All of it admirable. But all of it stemming, here and there, from particular Councils, particular individuals. These new approaches require to be codified and extended, to become part of local government practice generally – until they are taken for granted by the public no less than by those in authority. The concept of the Urban Parish Council, with powers and a commensurate budget, has been circulating now for some little time – and not merely in Birmingham. As part of an overall reassessment of local government, it should be taken into consideration. With a range of neighbourhood functions tacked on – area wardens, community workshops, resource centres, management committees and the like – its assumption of local responsibilities could serve to dispel some of the mistrust in which, in the past, the 'Corpies' have been held. Self-generating renewal could become part of the fabric of everyday life.

To look for new relationships at what I have termed the micro level in no way diminishes the need for more purposeful strategies at the macro level. This is inextricably bound up with the shortcomings of traditional local authority administration. Councils came into existence to undertake an increasing number of clearly defined tasks – in relation to housing, health, highways, education, policing, planning, among other things. Special departments and committees were created to handle each of these, their powers for the most part closely regulated by statute. As the complexities of their functions and responsibilities multiplied, departments have tended to become larger and consequently blinkered to other than their own work. It has become difficult to mount complex programmes cutting across departmental boundaries. In the 1970s the idea of 'corporate management' was introduced as a means to better coordination. Heads of departments met regularly round the table as do the executive directors of any private-sector business. Old habits, however, die hard. Departments still tend to be seen as separate fiefdoms, and messages agreed at the top do not always get sent down the line satisfactorily. When a question of priorities arises, one's own department tends to take precedence over others. This is not a problem peculiar to local government. All big organisations face it. In municipal affairs, however, it has been an inhibiting factor not only in day-to-day programmes but in relation to strategic planning.

Councils need urgently to restructure their affairs so that they can spend more time in thinking – not about the Parkinsonian bicycle shed but about the strategic issues which are going to shape their citizens' long-term destinies. Councillors have become prisoners to routines established long ago, designed to meet needs which have become outdated. Procedures have become a treadmill of committee meetings on the first and third Thursdays of the month, followed by a full Council meeting on the second Tuesday or whatever. Agendas are overlong and cover too many items which could be left for determination to their officers. The straitjacket of annual accounting encourages a preoccupation with day-to-day, or anyway half-year to half-year, mini-programmes rather than essential strategic infrastructure; or, conversely, frivolous expenditure at the end of the financial year because some budget head is underspent. Horizons have to be pushed further away, the corporate view of the terrain extended.

Several chief executives managed, during the eighties, to ease their Councils into two-, three-, four-year programmes – and in some cases even longer. In talking to them I had the feeling that they regarded this as almost the most important contribution they had been able to make to local affairs. One suggested that local consensus would be greatly strengthened if Councils not only gave more time to thinking but brought outside bodies more directly into their deliberations – the Unions, the business community, the voluntary associations. This is clearly one way in which the partnership ideal can be developed and strengthened. Holistic programmes call not only for wide community input and long-term budgeting; they call (as for example in Calderdale) for the creation of special teams or units which are free of departmental loyalties and can bring in specialist staff seconded from the private sector; they call for a much greater degree of collaboration than has existed in the past between neighbouring authorities. Here and there this is beginning to come about through European Community requirements for the submission of integrated schemes for Community funding. In the Metropolitan conurbations a degree of mutual cooperation was necessitated by the demise of the County Councils. Joint boards and consortia, technical liaison and coordinating committees, do exist in many areas – but for strictly practical purposes. In policy-making terms Councils generally remain wary of one another. Should, as seems possible, Borough and District Councils *all* become unitary authorities, wholly responsible for their own affairs, the need for agreed machinery by which regional and sub-regional strategies can be implemented is going to become ever more apparent and more urgent.

We are thus led to the much-debated need for more effective regional planning than is possible through the government's own regional offices; over the role of special government agencies such as the Urban Development Corporations; and the whole question of the now near-catastrophic relationship between Town Halls and Westminster/Whitehall. As we have seen, during the eighties, government has increasingly treated local Councils as ineffectual, profligate, and often untrustworthy – indeed, as more and more control has been drawn to the centre, almost irrelevant. As a result, over much of the country, Town Hall morale has slumped. Staffs have been slashed, departments closed down, services cut. Some hard-left Councils in inner-city areas, regarding themselves as under siege, have mounted the barricades with bands playing and flags flying. It is no way to deal with the nation's future. Of course there are authorities which are inefficient, overstaffed, feckless, reckless, self-indulgent, politically obstructive. They are in a minority in the 400-plus. Most, in differing degree, are at least reasonably efficient, pretty committed, understaffed and politically pragmatic. Of course there is need in the national interest to control national expenditure. But blanket mechanisms to this end tend to hit hardest the very areas most in need of regeneration.

Does not equity demand, for example, that the restrictions on Councils' spending of capital receipts from the sale of housing, which they themselves created, be lifted? It should not be beyond human ingenuity to devise means of loosening such restraints, if coupled with a strengthening of auditing procedures. Local authorities are, and must ever be, the most important single agencies in the renewal and wellbeing of our towns and cities. Within the enhanced frameworks suggested they must be allowed to set their own priorities; their planning capacity has to be recognised, their financial management strengthened rather than obstructed. It is not easy for Councils to act 'responsibly' unless they are treated as responsible.

None of which should be taken to diminish the need for specialist government agencies. In England, however, the UDC mechanism, as we have seen, has shown marked weaknesses, especially in its integration into local frameworks.* The better way in which to harness the clout of central government to local appreciation of local needs is surely, in England, through regional agencies modelled on the Scottish and Welsh Development Agencies. They would initiate programmes at the invitation of, and in collaboration with, the local authorities concerned. They would be able to tackle problems on a much wider geographical basis than the UDCs. They could exercise a powerful advisory/support function in relation to regional strategies which is lacking at the moment, and thereby assist local authorities in moving towards the new partnership roles suggested above. They will be doubly needed if, as the straws in the wind suggest, the whole tier of 'Shire' County administration should disappear in the future. The Counties have for long exerted a valuable balancing and mildly redistributive role, of an objective and relatively sophisticated kind, in relation to the District Councils within their boundaries. Transportation, investment policies, settlement, tourist planning, landscape management, cultural programmes – there are scores of matters which call to be dealt with across arbitrary boundaries. Strategic thinking will always be necessary on a wider basis than is provided by a single district, but closer to the ground than is possible for Whitehall. Regional Development Agencies – in conjunction of course with the other government quangos: the Housing Corporation, the Countryside Commission, English Heritage *et al.* – could be shaped to fill this gap. It now seems more than possible that such an agency, or agencies, will be one of the legacies left by Michael

---

* The Labour Party was at one time committed to killing off the UDCs, but later softened this to creating no new ones.

Heseltine's second term of office at the Department of Environment.

The ethic of the eighties was that all such matters can be left to market forces. At all levels government intervention must be minimised. However, to speak of a strategy need not at all imply all the rigidities of authoritarian centralised planning. A simple example: the green belt concept is strategic. The enabling legislation indicates a general objective; what, if anything, needs to be done in particular circumstances is left for local decision. Any public action, in whatever sphere, if it is to be meaningful must be policy-based. Policy, however, can only be formulated in relation to clear objectives. Unless national and regional objectives are spelled out, there is no rational framework for local decision-making, which must remain intuitive and possibly self-defeating.

Clear objectives have to be based on information. Today we have at our disposal more information than was available to any previous generation. Nonetheless, the overall picture, in many respects, remains far from clear. Complaints about the adequacy of the government's statistical information are raised fairly regularly. Consider, for example, the longstanding fudge represented by the lumping together of current spending/current receipts and capital spending/capital receipts as one single Public Sector Borrowing Requirement figure. This is mixing the balance sheet in with the profit and loss account. Some issues – notably, as we have seen, unemployment – have been clouded by the repeated use of differing bases for computation. Others are simply never brought together. For example, if we are to budget sensibly for essential maintenance, we need a comprehensive national survey of the state of Britain's infrastructure: roads and bridges, the railway system, the ports and airports, water supplies and sewerage, our publicly owned buildings – schools, hospitals, prisons, museums, libraries, government offices, civic buildings . . .

We nibble at all these things, each within its own context, its own budget, lashing out here, penny-pinching there. Privatisation, with its different economic criteria, has compounded the difficulties of getting such calculations on to a common basis. Yet how, without the hard information offered by a national survey and its associated costings, can national priorities and a national investment programme be established which will ensure at least a minimum basis for city life in the century to come? And this, after all, is but one of the many elements which call to be balanced and correlated before we can start to speak of a national strategy.

The government's 'Action for Cities' programme, by putting

together everything that a range of departments are doing in the inner cities, purports to present a coordinated drive upon the problem. It is no denigration of the many and admirable initiatives thus packaged to say that, to a very large extent, 'Action for Cities' has been a presentational device. The English UDCs touch their caps to the DoE. Until 1989 the Task Forces reported to the DTI. Problems relating to ethnic minorities are the responsibility of the Home Office; to roads and rail the DTp – and so on. Well – inevitable, it will be said; very right and proper. But to what extent can a real meeting of minds and community of purpose be said to exist between departments? Basically it is the story of the Town Hall again, writ large. When the fast rail Channel Tunnel links and feeders are under consideration, it is the inescapable route to London that causes nail-biting anguish; the immense potential for assisting the revival of the old industrial North, and Wales, is raised only by a few bolder characters from those areas. Far, far more is spent by government departments upon procurement every year than is paid out under the Urban Programme. From time to time a government department is decentralised to somewhere or other – but how often does it occur to those responsible that by placing their procurement requirements in the distressed areas they could more powerfully strengthen the latter's recovery? What steps are taken to correlate the provision of housing with availability of jobs? How often can investment decisions truly be said to be taken after full consideration of their secondary implications in other parts of the country? Down the line we have seen the fiscal kink which requires an authority to pay loan charges on money it has neither borrowed nor spent. Only connect ... The truth is that there is certainly abundant action to be observed, in many directions, but little policy. We have no housing policy. We have no transport policy. We have no policy for the maintenance of our infrastructure. We have no regional policy. We have no policy on poverty. Other than relinquishing it to market forces, we have no policy on the kind of world we are seeking to bring into being. And so it will continue until we can re-establish a vision which all can share.

Vision is an easy word. All those tower blocks and flyovers and upper-level walkways of the fifties and sixties were part of a vision, but a vision that turned sour. Is this how 'visions' must inevitably end, when the circumstances which gave them birth have passed into the night? A thousand cities around the world – or anyway substantial parts of them – cry otherwise. However, long before the balsawood models and the clever perspectives of another 'vision of the future' are unveiled, very fundamental questions need to have been asked and answered. And at the heart of those questions lie the *values* we consider important. 'The notion of salvaging inner cities presupposes a fairly precise idea of the alternative configuration which they are to have, and the scale of values and objectives to be obtained.' Any vision of the kind of cities at which we should be aiming presupposes a vision of the nation as a whole – of the interrelation between town and country, between North and South, between Britain and continental Europe. It certainly presupposes some idea of the *size* of towns in the next century. It presupposes some concept of their culture. The European Commission's 1988 report *Urban Problems and Regional Policy in the European Community* foresees the role of cities in the future 'not as dense concentrations of manufacturing and associated employment . . . but as something much closer to that of the major cities before the Industrial Revolution; as commercial and administrative centres in the broadest sense . . . and as the providers of high level urban services and of urban amenities'.[3]

How is such a change likely to come about? Left to its own devices in a free economy, business and industry will tend to continue to drift southwards – because of the gravitational pull of London, the Single Market and the Channel Tunnel, because of the weather and a less rugged life-style. As against this, a much weaker contrary movement can be discerned, resulting from inflated land values and property prices in the South, coupled with the frustrations of acute congestion – which makes, for instance, the life of the London commuter from South and East well-nigh intolerable. But there is a third strand, which is likely to bear increasingly upon the nature of the city everywhere: dispersal. The forces making for dispersal of labour, as, too, the shake-out of families wishing to live in, or nearer to, the country, can only grow. Electronics and the microchip, networked visual display units, fax machines and the rest, are already bringing about fundamental changes in the traditional distinction between home and workplace: they can now be one and the same. Shopping, banking, entertainment – and eventually, no doubt, much else – are likely to be done or enjoyed from home. Some of the functions always associated with the town in the past must inevitably become tenuous in the future.

None can see fully where these forces may take us, but the nature of their likely impact is clear enough. Are we taking sufficient account of it? There are considerable areas in the conurbations which are only kept going on public life-support systems (in the form of benefit and welfare payments), but which have in reality to be recognised as brain dead (in that they are incapable of useful life). There are no immutable tablets graven with the decree that land should not be returned to afforestation or countryside because it was once, for a hundred years, covered by heavy industry; that the existence of all the outer estates, hated by their inhabitants, has to be guaranteed in perpetuity. Let them not be renewed but phased out of existence. One is not suggesting draconian overnight measures – the clearance programmes of the fifties and sixties in reverse, from outer estate back into the city – but a gradual process worked out in conjunction with those involved. It is in this sense that some of our actions today seem unrelated to any long-term strategies. Might not some of the resources devoted to propping up such areas be more profitably devoted to the creation of alternatives?

At the other end of the process the pressures upon the South and upon the countryside have to be tackled imaginatively and creatively. It is an emotive subject – but no more so, for those directly concerned, than the 'deconstruction' of whole quarters of the big city. The same green-belt battles are fought with monotonous regularity, but each within fairly restricted terms of reference. Is it not time, as with the nation's infrastructure, to take a more comprehensive view of the countryside; to adopt policies which are not only restrictive – as they must continue to be – but positive as well? For a start, the boundaries – of what we call town and what we call country – are not immutable. If we wanted to, the amount of countryside could actually be increased. Considerable areas which at the moment contribute to neither town nor country – areas of industrial dereliction, the swathes of nothing at the urban fringe, soon to be swollen by the land released by the shrinking conurbations – these could all be given positive landscape value. New green wedges driving into the city would reduce the city dweller's desire to escape its confines. New villages, rather than spirit-crushing housing estates and overblown shopping complexes, could be embedded in the land thus released. Existing settlements could be consolidated by small-scale organic infill. Some towns have already marked themselves out as growth points. Instead of bemoaning the sadly commonplace commercial development this has mostly entailed, we should be concentrating on ensuring the infinitely higher qualitative levels of which we are perfectly capable. It will be possible to avoid a continuous, formless, self-defeating, Los Angeles-type sprawl between Bristol, London and Dover, but only by strategic thinking on a bigger scale than heretofore. Rule-of-thumb prohibitions and piecemeal planning permissions will not suffice. There are one or two welcome signs – of which the Countryside Commission's initiative for new urban forests is the most heartening. Overall, doubt remains as to the extent we are tailoring present programmes to any long-term vision of what might be.

If traditional patterns in both town and country are bound to change, then, the prospect should not alarm us. It offers an unprecedented opportunity to change the quality of urban life out of all recognition. A society's culture is built upon its centres of excellence – be they of learning, of the arts, or of any of its manifold activities from trade exhibitions to spectator sports. 'Towns,' it has been said, 'are incubators of new ideas and technology – essential for society's adaptation to the future.'[4] For the cross-fertilisation of ideas to take place, for the centre of excellence to 'work' – whether at national, regional or local level – a certain 'critical mass' of population, activity, energy, is necessary. Increasingly British towns and cities will be, are already, in competition, not only with one another, but with others in Europe, North America and even further afield. The biggest single factor in attracting that critical mass will be liveability and life-style. This is the opportunity that has to be grasped. Gradual dispersal from the swollen conurbations is unlikely to harm their essential functions – just the reverse; it could certainly bring new vitality to numerous smaller centres which have lapsed through the years into impoverished near-stagnation. Street life will be quieter and less frenetic. Reduced traffic congestion will return wide areas to the pedestrian. With less pressure on space the urban amenities will be closer to hand downtown, the countryside in the opposite direction.

> Forget six counties overhung with smoke,
> Forget the snorting steam and piston stroke,
> Forget the spreading of the hideous town;
> Think rather of the packhorse on the down,
> And dream of London, small and white and clean,
> The clear Thames bordered by its gardens green.[5]

Perhaps, a century later, give or take a packhorse or two, William Morris's dream does not seem so impossible after all.

Some questions were posed at the beginning of this chapter. I have resisted the temptation to set out a lengthy shopping list of

267

'helpful' practicalities by way of reply, partly because many, I think, should be self-evident from what has emerged in earlier pages; partly because there is no one formula – different mechanisms will suit different circumstances; but most of all because the very generalised principles, or aspirations, to which I have chosen to draw attention seem to me of far greater significance in the long run. To those struggling with the procedural and financial cat's cradles that entangle anything to do with environmental change these thoughts will seem simplistic, familiar, self-evident platitudes: naive and of no practical help whatsoever. They are indeed all of these things ... yet they remain fundamental. Unless they are kept firmly on the agenda for more intensive public debate, for fleshing out, refining, translating into agreed procedures – and legislation if necessary – we may well continue to meet limited challenges with success, but the real challenge, the big one, we shall have flunked. And history may not give us another chance.

Cities do not decline overnight and they cannot be nursed back to health overnight. Baltimore is everyone's favourite when it comes to regeneration, and not without reason – but Baltimore's revival has so far taken thirty-five years or so. Here, we set up UDCs for example (the third generation) for five to seven years. But it takes a third of that time to appoint the Board, find staff, find premises, undertake the first surveys and consultations, formulate initial proposals, cost them, draw up development briefs, start land acquisition, decide on a marketing strategy, begin to woo potential developers ... As we have seen in Calderdale and elsewhere, it is commonly only in the fifth year or so that real movement begins to take place, but it is never to be taken for granted. The lead times for anything to do with environmental change are very long. Taps simply cannot be turned on and off at whim. Long-term budgeting has to be assured. Commitment to a long-term strategy has to be assured. Without those any fundamental transformation must forever elude us.

Short-termism now colours all aspects of British life. In the private sector the profit and loss account has established supremacy over the balance sheet; asset stripping over investment in production. Companies now rent reach-me-down premises instead of building their own. Quick-buck opportunism leaves many of them mortally vulnerable to every shift in interest and exchange rates. Political horizons are dominated by the electoral cycle; the urge to demonstrate political dynamism emerges in demands for instant results; make-do-and-mend palliatives are too often preferred to investment in long-term solutions. This is regarded as 'prudent'.

The point has already been made, however, that society has yet to grasp the order of investment needed to keep our towns and cities in straightforwardly working order. Collapse is a real possibility. In the 1970s we saw New York reduced to bankruptcy; in the eighties Liège and other Belgian cities, in this country Liverpool. If worn-out cities, and not merely some quarters of some cities, are really to be kitted out afresh to fit them – and thereby the nation – for the unknown challenges which lie ahead, very large sums will require to be earmarked.

Every sector, of course, of our pluralist society is lobbying daily for increased funding – for health, for education, for research and development, and for everything else imaginable from the arts to prison reform and new football stadia. Calls for greater investment in our cities, however, are broad-based, from Royalty to the European Commission and OECD, from the Church to the CBI, from the local authority associations to the professional institutions and the voluntary organisations.

Let three considerations be tabled. First, on many aspects of the problem we really have no option. Sooner or later, on our own initiative or under pressure from the European Community, the urban infrastructure will have to be modernised, if things are not going to grind to a halt. As every householder knows, the longer essential maintenance is put off, the more cripplingly expensive it becomes. Secondly, there is no question of trying to do everything at once; even if the money were available it would be totally beyond our physical capacity. We have to be concerned with fifteen-, twenty-five-, thirty-five-year programmes. This probably means determining 'global' allocations – as is done with the UDCs – which can be drawn upon, with government approval, as and when required.

What is vital is the assurance of continuity: the elimination of uncertainty. 'Let us know the rules of the game,' cries the private sector. 'And please, *please*, stick to them. Don't keep moving the goal posts.' 'Don't encourage us to do so-and-so,' cry the local authorities, 'and then tell us there is no money for it.' With longer-term programming and budgeting, governing 'flywheels' can be built into the process to ensure greater stability and avoid the loss of opportunities through hiccups in the national or local economy – as has arisen, for example, with the Royals in London's Docklands. Within an assured programme things can click into place all the way down the line, to the individual tenant on the housing estate. When he or she sees improvement taking place over there, but not here – a common enough cause for bitterness – everyone can be told clearly, and believe it, exactly when their turn will come.

Thirdly, it has to be pointed out that difficulties in funding turn, not upon dwindling resources but upon how we cut the cake – upon the priorities we attach to competing claims. Today, Britain is richer by far than at any time in the past. Decade by decade, sometimes a little faster, sometimes a little slower, Britain grows wealthier. Some of that wealth we choose to spend on ephemeral frivolities: more satellite television channels, on Bingo or the pools or on fruit-machines. Some is simply wasted: on overheating and air-conditioning, for example, which better insulation would obviate; on delays in transport; on half-cock improvements which are all to do again in a few years' time; or, at another level, the £13 billion it has been estimated we spend annually on the unemployed,[6] when its use in a national drive to regenerate our cities would offer jobs instead. That, after all, is how Roosevelt lifted the United States out of the Great Depression. In allocating priorities the distinction between capital investment and current-account spending must always weigh heavily. It must never be said that we cannot afford to invest in the future; we cannot afford *not* to.

Let one figure put the subject in perspective. It was calculated by the Association of Metropolitan Authorities in 1986 that the money devoted to the Urban Programme in that year, as a proportion of total planned government spending, comprised *0.0002 per cent* of the total.[7] The figure would be marginally different today. It excludes, moreover, enormous sums spent on our cities under other heads. Nonetheless it provides an extraordinary comment upon our national priorities. It is upon the means by which these things are to be determined that we have to concentrate.

'We are on trial against the measure of our ambitions', as has been said in another connection. There would be no dispute about the objective: a decent life-style in decent surroundings in every part of the country, by the year 2015 or 2020; and that country vital, prosperous, civilised. But could we find it in ourselves to achieve consensus on the priority such an objective should be given in national affairs; on the strategies to be adopted; and on the funding necessary to make it a real proposition? Experience would label such a hope unrealistic, perhaps faintly ridiculous, certainly implausible in the extreme. But consider further for a moment before rubbishing the notion. A number of factors come together at the moment which possibly create a window of opportunity that will not recur.

The eighties were the Thatcher decade. The sense it gives of a discrete period, detached from the flow of recent political history, stems primarily, of course, from the intensely personal style of government which marked it, but seems to receive confirmation also from certain symmetries. It began with deep recession and ended in deep recession. Not without significance for the subject of this book, it began with Michael Heseltine presiding over the Department of the Environment and it ended with his return there. The decade profoundly changed attitudes in Britain. Nonetheless, even before the events of November 1990, there was a sense that the Thatcher 'revolution' had run its course. The urgent challenges of the 1990s are going to call for much lateral thinking, fresh and innovative responses. The Treaty of Rome is being redrafted. The watershed of 1992 is upon us. In a year or two the Channel Tunnel will have linked us irrevocably to the Continent in physical terms; whether it provides, for Britain, a refreshing stream of new prosperity or proves to be a drain through which our strengths ebb increasingly to the Continent will be determined by our own actions. The end of East–West confrontation opens up vast new commercial possibilities in Eastern Europe; the phased run-down of defence appropriations, if cautious to begin with, nonetheless offers a real opportunity to reorder the distribution of national resources. Over all there begins to hang that curious sense of anticipation which always, it seems, attends the turn of a century. Moulds, it is felt, can be broken, breakthroughs made in all directions, a fresh and better world opened up. All things seem possible.

It is a time of unparalleled opportunities, a time to look forward, a time to stop fighting the future. It is a time for Britain to forge for herself at last a sense of national purpose that goes beyond materialism and the 'politics of selfishness' (the phrase of Archbishop Runcie's); which can begin once more to unite the warring factions of our polarised society. The regeneration, not just of favoured enclaves, but of urban Britain as a whole; the elimination of decay and squalor everywhere; real improvement in the way people live – these, it seems to me, could provide such a cause. A cause beyond self, a cause to override party politics, a cause to catch the idealism of the young, bring new hope to the elderly and attract the support of men of goodwill everywhere. Who can doubt the existence of a widespread longing for an ethic

271

which goes beyond materialism to embody the deeper aspirations of mankind? There are many straws in the wind. Constitutional matters – note Charter 88, for example, and its backers – are to the fore as never before. A succession of opinion polls seem to agree that a majority would be prepared to pay higher taxes if that meant better funding for education, the health service, the relief of poverty. The fast-growing memberships of the environmental groups and the ballot-box rise of the 'Greens' – however unrealistic some of their policies – are indicative of a groundswell of popular opinion unknown to previous generations. The astonishing figures achieved by the new-style, media-sponsored, charitable appeals show the public's readiness to put its hand in its pocket for causes that touch its emotions. But if the aspirations are there, what is generally lacking are the mechanisms by which they can be realised. Exhortations, glossy brochures, demos – these accomplish little. How might real shape and purpose be given to the kind of crusade I have suggested? Call it 'programme' if you will, but that is hardly a word to catch the heart and mind.

In its scope such a national drive would be without parallel in peacetime, but precedents exist for elements within it. Many agencies, as we have seen in the foregoing pages, are already in place and need only to have their strategic and financial uncertainties removed. One possible pattern for enlarging the partnerships network, I would suggest, is offered by an example from the middle seventies. European Architectural Heritage Year was a pan-European campaign by the Council of Europe to alert its member nations to the dangers threatening their historic towns and cities, and to initiate action to save them while there was yet time. In the United Kingdom, under the administration of the Civic Trust, a national Council was set up representing over a hundred major organisations; the Duke of Edinburgh was its President, four Secretaries of State were its Patrons. National committees were set up in Scotland, Wales and Northern Ireland, their chairmen joining the English to form an Executive committee. Specialist panels were set up to initiate action in different areas of interest – education, film and television, tourism, business and industry, youth organisations and so on. This is not the place to spell out what was achieved during a three-year programme. Films were made, conferences held, publications issued, exhibitions mounted, competitions organised, and much else. Above all, thousands of practical projects were put in hand by government, local authorities, the private sector and the voluntary organisations. The committees met monthly, the Council twice a year, the panels probably every six weeks or so on average. The campaign culminated in a three-day conference in Amsterdam, when twenty-four nations adopted a declaration of intent which has largely governed their legislation and practice ever since. Several of the mechanisms then set up in Britain continue to flourish today. As an example of how the most diverse interests – political, public, private, academic, professional, voluntary – in all parts of the country can be brought into active partnership to a common end, European Architectural Heritage Year remains impressive.

Consider another such campaign. Five years earlier, the Council of Europe had initiated 'European Conservation Year', which, not to put too fine a point upon it, was an extension of an existing UK initiative by the Duke of Edinburgh: 'The Countryside in 1970'. What was of particular interest in this was that it was designed as a developing *process* over most of the sixties. Successive conferences were held every two or three years, to consider working papers produced by broad-based groups over the intervening periods. The research, the thinking, the policy proposals which were considered by the culminating conference in 1970, that is to say, had been thrashed out and refined in great detail over some seven years.

An example of a different kind. Memories have faded now, but the Festival of Britain was an extraordinary achievement, not just in the exhibitions and events it assembled on the South Bank site, but for the activities it contrived to mount in every part of the United Kingdom. It was a truly national manifestation, which succeeded in its aim of giving a genuine boost to national morale after ten years of austerity. As we approach the end of the century voices can be heard asking whether it is not the moment for another Festival of Britain. Not, of course, a direct repeat, for the world has changed. The 1951 Festival was essentially a celebration: of the British character, of what we are good at, of the things we made and did. But might not something of the same kind, on the same scale, carried through with the same *élan*, valuably focus national attention upon a new vision: a vision of challenges and opportunities, of the Britain we are trying to shape, of our place and role in Europe?

Precedents then – and more than these. Powerful agencies already in being and needing only to have their full potential released. Outside authoritarian countries the problem in putting such an operation together is always how to start. The status quo induces a general inertia which is not easily overcome. However, here is a notional scenario. A dozen others could be imagined.

It should not be difficult for the relevant quangos to agree the

273

wording of a joint commitment to certain long-term objectives. The Church, the CBI and the voluntary sector would find few problems, I believe, in doing likewise. Such statements might prove tenuous in their detail, but there is no reason why they should not be clear as to their objectives. From this base a joint committee representative of all these interests, chaired perhaps by a Law Lord, could commission consultants to examine the common ground established and draw up an outline strategy (in practice, a series of interlocking strategies) by which agreed objectives might be reached over such and such a period. If the broad lines of the consultants' report proved acceptable, working parties would then be set up to examine different aspects of the problem in greater detail – for example, administrative structures, possible changes in legislation, financial implications and programming, national and regional planning, the future role of the local authority, possibly a new Festival of Britain for the year 2000, and so on – and to develop proposals in greater detail. At this point the effort should be made to enlist all-party support for the great national campaign shaping up, the nature of which would be put to the wider public through a fully representative congress in London and a series of regional conferences throughout the country. Inevitably, formal provisos and reservations would have to be registered by government, but if sufficient momentum built up incrementally then and thereafter, one might expect to see a good many of the campaign's policies and recommendations creeping into government programmes. Eventually, one might hope, as the years went by and the results became evident, every decision-maker at every level, whatever his or her business, in whatever part of the country, would have so absorbed the purpose of the campaign that he or she would find themselves automatically measuring their every decision and action against the agreed national imperatives. A romantic fantasy? In the sense of a single, finely articulated machine, its every part meshing smoothly with every other, guaranteed to produce an earthly nirvana by 1 January 2015 (or whenever), of course. In the sense of an opportunist, pragmatic free-for-all which could nonetheless heave Britain into the next century more buoyantly than otherwise possible . . . surely at least worth trying.

We started with the ills of the inner city. It became clear, I hope, that the problems of multiple deprivation and urban decay spread much wider than that. In a highly urbanised society, it has been said, urban problems may be the problems of society itself. Here in Britain we have made a start in tackling some of those problems, but in relation to their totality our efforts to date have been woefully inadequate. Only by a national drive of unprecedented proportions, a new sense of national purpose, and participation by all of us, can we hope genuinely to solve those problems.

*

John Pickup is Director of Planning in the Cardiff Bay Development Corporation. On the wall of his office there is a small printed sheet. It reads:

A SAD, SAD STORY ABOUT NOBODY

This is a story about four people, named: Everybody, Somebody, Anybody and Nobody.

There was an important job to be done and Everybody was sure that Somebody would do it. Anybody could have done it, but Nobody did it.

Somebody got angry about that because it was Everybody's job. Everybody thought Anybody could do it, but Nobody realised that Everybody wouldn't do it.

It ended up that Everybody blamed Somebody when Nobody did what Anybody could have done.

APPENDICES

A: AGENCIES, MEASURES AND MECHANISMS

B: REFERENCES

C: SOME DATES, 1970–1990

APPENDIX A

Agencies, Measures and
Mechanisms

Listed here are some of the more important agencies and measures referred to in the foregoing pages. The entries are grouped alphabetically and make no claim to comprehensiveness.

BUSINESS IN THE COMMUNITY
Wider participation in community affairs by the private sector began to develop in the second half of the 1970s. By the end of the 1980s the number of organisations – many overlapping in objectives and membership – had become confusing to the casual observer. Enterprise Agencies, Business in the Community, Business in the Cities, the CBI Forum, the Phoenix Initiative, Education/Business Partnerships, Neighbourhood Development Partnerships – these are only some of the names likely to be encountered in relation to inner-city initiatives. Broadly, their objects and relationships are as follows.

The first *Enterprise Agency*, the Community of St Helens Trust, was brought into being by a retired managing director, Bill Humphrey, with the backing of Sir Alastair Pilkington of the glass firm, in 1978. In the same year Lord Byers, sometime Chairman of the Liberal Party, drew up a paper suggesting ways in which the private sector might involve itself more purposefully in community regeneration, through secondment and funding by a consortium of the bigger companies. This was circulated by Peter Shore, then at the DoE, to a number of leading chairmen in business and industry, who subsequently met for dinner at Lancaster House. From this meeting sprang the London Enterprise Agency, as a pilot project, on which in turn have been based the 320 or so Enterprise Agencies which now exist across the United Kingdom.

These differ in size, format and effectiveness, and their priorities depend upon a host of local circumstances. They offer encouragement and advice to those wishing to set up in business – on investment, production, training, recruitment, marketing, taxation and so on – though their negative advice in warning an aspiring starter off a project which is inevitably doomed may be no less helpful; they may seek to effect marriages between entrepreneurial skills which are not easily come by through other channels; they may provide managed workspace for small workshops and business units. Their combined annual budget is over £30 million, of which some 41 per cent comes from 6,000 sponsoring firms in business and industry, 35 per cent from central government and 24 per cent from local authorities. About two thirds of their directors are salaried, one third seconded from the private sector; their combined staffs number about 1,500. The network as a whole claims to have created, or saved, more than 100,000 jobs in 1988 alone.

Business in the Community was set up in 1981 as a national agency to coordinate and extend such work – in its own words 'to act as a focus and catalyst for the greater involvement of business in local economic development and regeneration ... [and] ... to promote corporate responsibility in British industry and commerce and the philosophy of private and public partnership'. Today its more than 330 corporate members include nearly two thirds of *The Times*' 'Top 100'; their Council representatives embrace practically every tycoon figure known to the general public. It is run by a Board of nineteen – which includes representatives of the Association of Metropolitan Authorities, the Department of Employment, the CBI and the TUC – under the Chairmanship of Sir Hector Laing. The Prince of Wales has been its indefatigable President since 1985 and has extended his association anyway until 1994. Activities are in the hands of ten programme directors.

During its first years BIC appeared somewhat uncertain as to how to position itself in relation to the public and private organisations already in the field. However, during the second half of the 1980s it consolidated and expanded its sphere of interest. Towards the end of 1987 it set up eight 'Target Teams' to be responsible for different aspects of the overall problem: Priority Hiring (aiming to target employers' recruitment and training opportunities on the unemployed young); Educational Partnerships (promoting school-based partnerships between employers and the education system with a view to improving school performance and job opportunities for school leavers); Finance for Enterprise (promoting loan funds for new enterprises); Enterprise Development (largely through Enterprise Agencies); Local Purchasing (aimed at helping small businesses through a national purchasing scheme); Urban Regeneration (in pilot areas); Voluntary Sector Initiatives (promoting business involvement in voluntary agencies); and Marketing Business Action (in effect a public relations campaign).

BIC now has nine regional offices in England, plus Scotland, Wales and Northern Ireland. It has set up area-based 'Business Action Teams' in Teesside, Tyneside, Wear and Northumberland, and the North West of England; others, in Nottingham, Sheffield and Stoke-on-Trent for example, are independent but have links with BIC. It has promoted a number of 'Neighbourhood Development Partnerships', in Finsbury Park and Spitalfields in London, Moss Side and Hulme in Manchester, in Walsall, Hartlepool and Wolverhampton. 'Education/Business Partnerships' are being set up in thirty inner-city areas under a new foundation. It has promoted the 'Per Cent Club', the nearly 150 members of which commit at least half of one per cent of pretax profits to the community or charity (British Telecom, to take but one example, donates more than £12 million a year to programmes in five main areas).

In 1987 the Confederation of British Industry established a 'task force' on regeneration. Its report *Initiatives Beyond Charity* recommended the formation of a Forum to bring together the organisations most active in promoting business participation in urban renewal programmes: BIC, the CBI and the Phoenix Initiative. The Forum adopted the title *Business in the Cities*, meeting for the first time at the end of 1988. Its stated objectives – to avoid duplication of effort (always an aspiration of every new organisation!), to pool knowledge and share experience – read a little wryly to those already in the field. Its first priorities included support for the Bristol Initiative, the Newcastle Initiative, the Wearside Opportunity, the Teesside Tomorrow Team, and teams in North-East London and the North West of England; with some involvement with the Birmingham Business Initiative, the Blackburn Partnership, the Calderdale Partnership, and groups in Bradford and Sheffield.

CITY ACTION TEAMS

City Action Teams (CATs) have as their function the coordination of government strategy under the 'Action for Cities' programme at local level. They are made up of senior officials from the regional offices of the Departments of Employment, the Environment, and Trade and Industry, plus representatives of other departments as and when necessary. CATs have small special budgets with which to assist local initiatives, and provide contact points for business and community organisations. At present CATs operate in Birmingham, Leeds/Bradford, Liverpool, London, Manchester/Salford, Nottingham/Derby/Leicester, and Tyne and Wear, with the Cleveland Coordinating Team exercising a similar function in that area.

CITY GRANT

Launched in May 1988, the government's City Grant replaced Urban Development Grant (dating from 1981 and directed to local authorities) and Urban Regeneration Grant (initiated only the previous year and available directly to private-sector companies). It also incorporates private-sector Derelict Land Grant (q.v.) in the areas of the fifty-seven authorities listed on page 292. It assists private-sector capital projects (normally in built-up areas) with a completed value of over £200,000. Grant is intended to bridge the gap between the estimated cost and the estimated value of a project (i.e. the amount by which the latter falls short of the former) where sufficient economic and social benefits – additional jobs, additional housing – are expected to accrue. Two types of project are eligible: property development and business development. Priority is given to applications within the fifty-seven areas listed. Some £55 million was available for England in City Grant for 1989/90 (with extra in the UDC areas). By July 1989, UDG/URG/City Grant Outlay of £229 million had brought about private investment of £931 million.

CIVIC TRUST

The Civic Trust is one of those organisations of which many in the wider public have heard but few could say exactly what it does – partly perhaps because of the very range of its activities; partly because, until recently, it has had no individual membership. The Trust's essential object is the improvement of the environment. It is a wholly independent charity, founded in 1957 by Lord (then Mr) Duncan Sandys and originally funded solely by business and industry. Its income now derives additionally from government, fees from local authorities and other earnings.

The Trust is the central reference point for over 1,000 local groups. Its annual awards scheme for good development is the oldest and largest of its kind anywhere. It publishes a bi-monthly magazine and has an active educational arm working with schools. It studies and reports on a wide range of environmental problems – for example, industrial dereliction, urban wasteland, the impact of heavy lorry and other traffic – and responds to government consultation papers on planning and related matters. It was closely associated with the drafting of the Civic Amenities Act 1967. It administered, in the UK, on behalf of the government, the Council of Europe's Architectural Heritage Year campaign in the mid seventies. It was instrumental in forming the Architectural Heritage Fund, a now £5.5 million revolving fund which offers low-interest loans to local historic buildings trusts.

Thirty years ago the Trust broke new ground by pioneering a cooperative approach locally to comprehensive environmental improvement, and this has remained one of its most important functions. In the early eighties its award-winning regeneration programme for the small town of Wirksworth in Derbyshire was widely praised. In 1987 the Trust formalised this work into a special Regeneration Unit, the purpose of which is to focus resources and professional expertise upon areas not covered by the main official campaigns and agencies – for example inner-city areas not touched by Urban Development Corporations; the 300-plus coastal resorts; 85 mining communities; 1,000 plus High Streets; 2,000 run-down council estates; rural areas in decline. Its projects fall into four broad categories: those in which a Civic Trust-appointed Project Leader is installed to stimulate and co-ordinate regeneration work locally; local authority-led partnerships (such as that in Calderdale); those under local grass-roots leadership (development trusts, community partnerships, etc); and business-led partnerships (such as Phoenix).

In 1989 the Regeneration Unit launched a national Regeneration Campaign, to foster a wider national thrust. At the end of 1990 it was handling six directly run projects; some 20 feasibility and project planning studies, with 12 more under consideration; in 12 other projects the Unit was acting as adviser. Around 80–100 projects were receiving information under the Regeneration Campaign, the whole programme ranging over all parts of England. The Unit consists currently of about 25 staff, of whom ten or so are in project offices outside London. Consultants are employed for particular purposes. Funding comes from private-sector sponsorship (with a big contribution from Grand Metropolitan): from government quango commissions, the DoE and the DTp; and from local authorities.

At the end of 1989 it launched a major initiative aimed at providing guidelines, legal advice, information and grants nationwide. This campaign was given additional thrust in 1991 by the launch of a manifesto – which received the blessing of Sir George Young, a DoE Minister – detailing the responsibilities of national and local government, business and industry, together with the Trust's own commitment to new forms of community partnerships.

Linked, though independent, Trusts operate in Scotland, Wales and (as we have seen) the North East of England. The earliest of these regional Trusts, that for the North-West of England, became a formal branch of the Trust in London in 1990.

COUNCIL OF EUROPE

The Council of Europe, born in London in 1949, is the oldest of the European agencies. Membership is open to all democratic nations subscribing to the European Convention on Human Rights (so that, for example, Spain under Franco and Greece under the colonels were not eligible for membership). Stretching as far as Turkey, the Council embraces some twenty member nations, and may be expected gradually to take under its wing at least some of the Eastern European countries. Organizationally, its two component elements are the Committee of Ministers (the inter-governmental body) and the Consultative Assembly (the parliamentary body).

As the Community institutions have developed, the Council of Europe has concentrated increasingly upon questions of human rights, social welfare, the role of regional and local government, and – strongly – the culture and spirit of Europe. In these fields it has provided a valuable clearing house for information and has acted as a kind of inter-governmental pressure group. In this capacity it has initiated a number of environmental campaigns of some significance. In 1970 it mounted a successful European Conservation Year (essentially dealing with ecology and the natural landscape); European Architectural Heritage Year in 1975 (the conservation of historic towns and architecture); and in 1980, Urban Renaissance Year (urban regeneration). It was thus within this general context that, for example, the Halifax conference, mentioned in earlier pages, was held.

DERELICT LAND GRANT

The official definition of derelict land is 'land so damaged by industrial or other development that it is incapable of beneficial use without treatment'. The 1982 Derelict Land Survey showed about 110,000 acres/ 45,000 ha to exist in England. Grant is available to local authorities and, outside the fifty-seven areas listed, to private-sector companies. Grant is paid as a percentage of the net cost to the owner of reclamation needed to bring land to 'green-field' standard – i.e. to ensure that subsequent development costs are no higher than for a comparable green-field site. The value of the cleared land is established by the District Valuer. To local authorities and public agencies (such as English Estates) in Assisted Areas and Derelict Land Clearance Areas the grant aid available is 100 per cent; in National Parks and Areas of Outstanding Natural Beauty 75 per cent; elsewhere 50 per cent. The 1980 Local Government Planning and Land Act provided for the first time for assistance to the private sector. In such cases the level of grant is up to 80 per cent in Assisted Areas and Derelict Land Clearance Areas; 50 per cent elsewhere. In 1988/89 £77 million was available in all for grant aid in England, of which £9 million was set aside for private-sector schemes. £25 million p.a. is currently available in Wales through the Welsh Development Agency; something of the order of £55 million is available in Scotland through the Scottish Development Agency.

DEVELOPMENT AGENCIES, SCOTTISH AND WELSH

The two Development Agencies for Scotland and Wales came into being in 1976, following the passage through Parliament of enabling legislation the previous year – possibly as a response by the then Labour government to the pressures of the day for political devolution. They are government funded. Their purposes were – and are – to further economic development and to provide, or safeguard, employment; to promote industrial efficiency and international competitiveness; and to improve the environment. To these ends they can compulsorily acquire land and bring it into use by clearance and reclamation, sale or lease; they can provide capital, loans, and a wide range of services. They do not, however, have plan-*making* powers, or exert powers of planning *control*, both of which remain in the hands of local planning authorities.

Each is controlled by a Board of a dozen or so members. Names tend to be well studded with CBEs; to be representative – informally – of local government, business and industry, academia and the Trade Unions; but to lack even a solitary 'statutory woman'. Boards are appointed by the respective Secretary of State, to whom, through their Chairman, they report. Salaries are broadly in line with comparable quangos. By way of comparison, the Chairmen of the Scottish Tourist Board and the Commission for New Towns receive more; the Chairmen of the English UDCs (with the partial exception of the LDDC) considerably less.

As their work has expanded, so have their staffs. The SDA currently employs nearly 700, the WDA a little over 500. (The SDA was the first government agency to reward staff on a performance-related basis.) Their gross incomes for 1988/89 were, respectively, £145 million (of which over £94 million was public money, by far the most of it government grant-in-aid) and nearly £115 million (of which £62 million represented government grant-in-aid). Government funding has increased steadily through the years – in Wales, for example, it has nearly doubled over five years – but so have receipts from sales (of land and property), rents, and investment income (from companies assisted). In 1988/89 such self-generated income produced £50 million for the SDA (over £18 million in rentals alone) and a comparable sum for the WDA. Both Agencies have benefited from European Community funds – notably from the European Coal and Steel Community and the European Social Fund.

The Agencies' undoubted strength derives largely from their ability to operate on both the demand and supply sides – bringing land and buildings into use, creating accommodation and facilities where they do not exist, while at the same time stimulating and assisting business and industry with analysis, training, loans and investment, and promotion worldwide (both have offices in Europe, America, Japan and elsewhere). This combination of powers, together with their steadily growing property portfolios and generally entrepreneurial approach, gives them considerable clout. Although in this book we have encountered them only in limited contexts, their remits and programmes of course run the full length and breadth of their countries. Both Agencies have a string of regional offices.

It is impossible in a short space to do more than hint at the range of their activities. Their complexity makes direct comparisons difficult. The Agencies sometimes act as the channels for government grant aid which in England would be dealt with directly between the applicant and the DoE. In some cases they have subsumed other organisations – as, for example, in Wales the Welsh Office Derelict Land Unit which had been in existence for ten years before the WDA. However, rather at random:

The SDA now administers factory space of around 17 million sq. ft./1.58 million sq. m. in which are employed some 44,000 people. (It announced in 1990 its intention to dispose of its industrial property holdings, valued at £100 million.) Loans made in 1987/88 amounted to £19 million; investments to nearly £10 million. In the same year 32 per cent of its expenditure – nearly £39 million – went on some 800 renewal projects, including the reclamation of 1,286 acres/520 ha. The SDA's Training and Employment Grants Scheme, which was started as part of the GEAR operation in Glasgow, is now operating in all the Agency's 'integrated area projects' and seven or so other areas as well (attracting 50 per cent of its costs from the European Social Fund). 'Integrated area projects' have been based upon Glasgow's East End, Clydebank, Dundee, Motherwell, Coatbridge, Inverclyde, Govan and Leith amongst other places.

In Wales the WDA's investment provision currently runs at over £7 million a year. The Agency's more than 19 million sq. ft./1.76 million sq. m. of factory space represents jobs for over 50,000 people. Expenditure on land reclamation was running, in 1989, at over £11 million; over 1,000 acres/over 400 ha were reclaimed in 1988/89; the Agency has a forward programme of work costed at £45 million, and has made such inroads into the problem that the end of the operation is actually within sight. So successful have the Principality's promotional efforts been that Wales consistently gains 20 per cent of all inward investment into the UK – about £1.12 billion, leading to some 14,000 new jobs – although having only about 5 per cent of the UK population.

Total gross expenditure by the WDA since its inception amounts to £990 million (1976/77 to 1989/90); that by the SDA rather higher. These figures indicate the scale of the Agencies' work, but neither its complexity (which renders impossible a simple total of the investment levered from the private sector) or, indeed, its variety. Activities range, for example, from an SDA seminar in Brazil for thirteen Scottish companies (which led to orders totalling £5.5 million), to a three-year research programme with the Clyde Port Authority on the use of dredged sediment as topsoil in reclamation schemes, to business advice for village shops. Some of their work in urban regeneration has been noted in previous pages. For a fuller picture the reader is referred to the Agencies' annual reports.

ENGLISH ESTATES
English Estates is an offshoot of the Development Commission (very long established and primarily concerned to strengthen the rural economy), which in turn comes under the umbrella of the Department of Trade and Industry. English Estates works with private-sector organisations to provide managed workspace for new and expanding small businesses.

ENTERPRISE AGENCIES
See Business in the Community.

ENTERPRISE ZONES
Enterprise zones seek to stimulate economic activity by easing financial and administrative burdens upon companies locating within defined areas designated by the DoE. The essential infrastructure having been created by the local authority or Development Agency, companies setting up within the Enterprise Zone receive exemption from rates/local taxes for ten years; 100 per cent allowances for corporation and income-tax purposes for capital expenditure on industrial and commercial development; and are subject to minimal planning restrictions. Twenty-six Enterprise Zones have been created since 1981, seventeen of them in England, four in Scotland, three in Wales and two in Northern Ireland. Sites vary widely in size, from under 110 acres/50 ha to over 970 acres/440 ha. Together, by 1987, they covered some 43,000 sq. ft/14,000 sq. m. and gave employment to nearly 72,000. Not all the jobs in the Zones are new jobs; a number of companies have simply relocated from outside the boundary to within the boundary in order to take advantage of the incentives offered. An evaluation carried out in 1986/87 by consultants for the government estimated that the cost of each new job in the Enterprise Zones and surrounding area affected by the Zones was in the range of £23,000 to £30,000. In one or two cases – the Canary Wharf development in London's Docklands, and perhaps the big MetroCentre shopping complex in Gateshead and its equivalents elsewhere – advantage has been taken of freedom from planning control to undertake development on a scale far beyond anything envisaged within the freedoms of the original Enterprise Zone concept, and which it is impossible to reconcile with the tenets of proper planning. At the end of 1987 the government decided to create new Zones only very exceptionally (for example one in Inverclyde in 1989); at the end of 1990 it announced that no more would be designated.

EUROPEAN COMMUNITY FUNDING
The regeneration policies of the European Community are evolving, a bit Topsy-like, as is the institutional system of the Community itself.

The European vision was originally embodied in a trinity of Communities: the European Coal and Steel Community (established in 1952); the European Economic Community (established in 1958); and the European Atomic Energy Community (formed in the same year). These are pushed, administered, directed, monitored, controlled by four institutions: the European Parliament; the Council (of member government Ministers, assisted by a Permanent Representatives Committee); the Commission (the administrative and policy-creating core of the system – its guardian and driving force); and the European Court of Justice (with which is linked the Court of Auditors).

At intervals moves have been made, on the one hand, to rationalise the administrative framework (initially, but no longer, the three Communities had separate Councils and Commissions); on the other hand to extend the European Community's fields of competence as delineated in the originating Treaties of Rome and of Paris. The enlargement of the Community from the original six member nations to the present twelve created additional pressures for change, coupled with the fresh political impetus which resulted in the Single European Act of 1986 – and now the changed situation in Eastern Europe.

The initiating Treaties were essentially concerned with economic 'harmonisation' between the member states; officially the Community had no competence, for example, in environmental matters (save in such things as the equitable control of industrial effluents). However, inevitably it has come, since the early seventies, to assume greater and greater responsibilities not only in the fields of industrial decline and development but in the social and environmental problems which attend them. It is now deeply concerned with the 'harmonisation' of living standards in whole regions.

These responsibilities are exercised, broadly, in two ways: through the controls embodied in the Commission's Directives (which have to be embodied in national legislation) and through the financial aid dispensed through Community funding. An example of the former is the 1987 Directive requiring an Environmental Impact Analysis to be undertaken before large developments of any kind are put in hand in sensitive areas; an example of the latter the £37 million grant towards the construction of the great Kielder Reservoir in Northumberland – the largest of its kind in Europe.

The Community's three 'structural' funds are the *Social Fund*, the *Regional Development Fund*, and the *Agricultural Guidance and Guarantee Fund*. The first of these makes grants for job creation, job training and resettlement schemes in areas of high unemployment. During 1985, for example, the UK received £91 million for its Youth Opportunities Programme. The European Regional Development Fund is aimed at reducing, if not eliminating, the disparities in development and wealth between different regions. Grants – as that for Kielder, already noted

288

– are for larger schemes; since 1985 resources have been disbursed on a percentage basis for each country, the UK's allocation having been between 14.50 per cent and 19.31 per cent. The third fund, the Agricultural Guidance and Guarantee Fund, need not concern us here. However, other sources of assistance are open to cities and areas in decline. Among these the *European Coal and Steel Community* can make grants and loans towards investment projects, and such things as low-cost housing and the resettlement or redeployment of workers in mining and steel-producing areas. For example, the National Coal Board received £130 million towards its twin-shaft mine at Selby and, in 1981, the UK received nearly £35.75 million to help pay for early-retirement schemes and retraining for 24,000 redundant steelworkers. As well as these, loans are available from the *European Investment Bank* for projects contributing to the 'balanced and steady' development of the Common Market – regional development schemes which reduce the level of Community oil imports, modernisation and the introduction of new technology, improved communications, and so on. Very roughly, the total volume of community assistance is split equally between grants and loans.

Clearly, considerable sums are at stake and the United Kingdom has benefited from Community funding to a greater extent than most of its partners. Between 1984 and 1987 the average level of the main receipts from the Social Fund was: Italy a little over 542 million ECU,* the UK nearly 535 million ECU, and Spain 404.6 million ECU; from the Regional Development Fund: Italy over 883 million ECU, Spain over 654 million ECU, the UK nearly 606 million ECU; from various other grants the UK was by far and away the biggest beneficiary. These mean figures disguise the upward trend of the annual figures (and the much smaller sums going elsewhere – Germany, for example, received something over 102 million ECU from the European Regional Development Fund, to compare with the UK's 606 million ECU shown above). However, the enlargement of the Community in 1986 to embrace its present twelve member nations will markedly affect its funding patterns: as resources are increasingly directed to the less developed countries, the proportion of grant aid to the UK must inevitably diminish.

Moreover, as already indicated, the Single European Act has affected these policies in a number of ways. Article 130(c) incorporates the Regional Development Fund into the EEC Treaty, where it now takes its place formally as a fundamental instrument of policy. Five objectives are set up for the Fund:

– helping to redress regional imbalances through development and

* The European Currency Unit, the basis of the Community's budgeting, is currently worth around £0.7.

adjustment, in those regions where development is lagging (that is to say, where per capita GDP is less than, or close to, 75 per cent of the Community average);

- assisting regions seriously affected by industrial decline (employment figures and diminishing industrial employment being the main criteria);
- combating long-term unemployment – for those over twenty-five and out of work for more than twelve months;
- facilitating the 'occupational integration' of (i.e. jobs for) young people *under* twenty-five;
- structural changes in agriculture and strengthening the economy of rural areas.

A number of reforms towards which the Community has been moving for some time are reinforced by the Act and were approved in 1989 – in particular, in the present connection, the shift from European Regional Development Fund support for individual projects to an integrated programme-based approach, probably covering several years. Operational programmes will predominate; greater coordination between funding channels will be effected, 'though leaving maximum scope for decentralised measures'; monitoring and assessment will be improved. The Community itself will initiate a number of programmes. Most significantly, the Community is doubling its appropriations to the three 'structural' funds between 1987 and 1993, from approximately 7 billion ECU (over £5 billion) to 14 billion ECU (over £10 billion). Areas covered by the first of the five objectives noted above stand to receive the greater part of these increases, the European Regional Development Fund devoting possibly up to 80 per cent of its budget to this end. The UK is likely to receive around 38 per cent of the funding going to the second objective – measures to combat industrial decline.

What does this mean at the receiving end? Some of these forms of assistance are available to private companies and agencies; most, however, are available primarily for local authorities, nationalised industries, statutory undertakers and similar public agencies. A good many authorities, and groups of authorities, now have their own representatives in Brussels to lobby their cause directly. However, formal applications normally have to be made through – and with the support of – the responsible government department of the country concerned. This is sensible enough if national and community programmes are to be properly coordinated, but does not guarantee automatic harmony. Some years ago a proposal from Birmingham found favour in Brussels (and the backing of M. Delors) but was blocked by our own government.

After the Commission has approved a project, grant aid is

transferred to the national government concerned. Here a measure of sleight of hand occurs. The rules of the game permit grants to be held back by the government as reimbursement of State aid made to the recipient. The latter, in other words, receives no *additional* funding over and above what his own government is making available to him anyway. The theory is that the government then uses the resources saved to assist additional projects, European funding thus making possible an increase in the number of projects assisted. On the local authority side, European funding reduces the loan charges that might otherwise have to be paid.

There is evidence that the government is beginning to apply the principle of 'additionality', as this process is called in Euro-Speak, more flexibly than at one time, and the small print of the Single Act calls for at least an equivalent increase to be made in national aid offered. Apart from the additional funding that will flow from the Community, its push towards integrated programmes is forcing local authorities into a degree of coordination and joint action which would probably not otherwise have come about. For example, as we have seen, the five District Councils on Merseyside have worked on a joint 'Integrated Development' submission; as have Manchester, Salford and Trafford – and many others in different parts of the country. In the long term, this may prove to have been one of the most important of the Community's contributions to urban regeneration in Britain.

FREEPORTS

As Simplified Planning Zones (q.v.) sprang from Enterprise Zones, so these in fact sprang from a seventies proposal by Professor Peter Hall for the creation in Britain of 'Freeports'. The concept has long been familiar in many parts of the world. Its essence is that the freeport is treated as though it were foreign territory. No tariffs or duties are levied on goods coming in; sorting, processing, remanufacture, finishing, are undertaken under reduced taxation and regulation levels; goods leaving the freeport are treated by the country of entry as though from any other foreign country. Experience elsewhere shows that, dynamically run, a freeport can create substantial employment. So far six have been created experimentally in Britain but it is not yet possible to assess their full impact.

GOVERNMENT GRANT AID

Total government input into the 'Action for Cities' programme is put, currently, at around £3 billion a year. Grant aid for regeneration programmes is channelled through a wide range of measures administered by a number of different departments – the DoE, the DTI, the Home Office, the Departments of Transport, Employment, Education and Science – as well as quasi-independent government

291

agencies such as the Scottish and Welsh Development Agencies (q.v.), the Housing Corporation (q.v.), English Estates (q.v.), English Heritage, the Tourist Boards and others. It is impossible in a short space to do more than touch upon the more important.

Before dealing with specific grants available, it is necessary to make some geographical distinctions. Left over from earlier regional policies, and aimed at the main areas of industrial and economic decline, are the 'Assisted Areas'. These cover much of the industrial Midlands, the North, Scotland and Wales. They comprise the *Development Areas* (where decline has been heaviest) and the *Intermediate Areas* (which have been hard hit, but less savagely).

Some grants arc available *only* in these areas; others are available at increased levels. In addition, the Assisted Areas are eligible for loans – for approved purposes – from the European Investment Bank and the European Coal and Steel Community (see under European Community Funding). Current government policy is now to make all such assistance discretionary rather than automatic.

An altogether separate 'priority areas' list is that of fifty-seven cities and towns in England, drawn up by the DoE in January 1987, to be the main recipients of assistance under the Urban Programme (see below). These include the thirty-two previously existing 'Partnership' and 'Programme' authorities, and twenty-five others which had had 'Other Designated District' or 'Traditional Urban Programme' status (the two latter categories were abolished from April 1987). The list of authorities now invited to bid for Urban Programme funding is as follows (these 'Programme Authority Areas' are also, perhaps confusingly, known as 'Inner City Target Areas'):

Barnsley	Halton	Leicester	Salford
Birmingham	Hammersmith and	Lewisham	Sandwell
Blackburn	Fulham	Liverpool	Sefton
Bolton	Haringey	Manchester	Sheffield
Bradford	Hartlepool	Middlesbrough	South Tyneside
Brent	Islington	Newcastle	Southwark
Bristol	Kensington and	Newham	Stockton-on-Tees
Burnley	Chelsea	North Tyneside	Sunderland
Coventry	Kingston-upon-	Nottingham	Tower Hamlets
Derby	Hull	Oldham	Walsall
Doncaster	Kirklees	Plymouth	Wandsworth
Dudley	Knowsley	Preston	Wigan
Gateshead	Lambeth	Rochdale	Wirral
Greenwich	Langbaurgh	Rotherham	Wolverhampton
Hackney	Leeds	St Helens	Wrekin

Comparable provisions apply in Scotland and Wales, although details of measures differ. (See also City Grant, Derelict Land Grant and Urban Programme.)

GROUNDWORK

The Groundwork Trusts are a network of charitable trusts working to improve environmental conditions, particularly in the urban fringes of industrial towns and cities. In 1978 the Countryside Commission decided to work towards a 'major urban-fringe experiment' to test the possibilities for improvements to, and better management of, damaged land round a big industrial city. It was seen as a large-scale public-sector initiative. By the following year agreement had been reached with the three local authorities concerned to launch the experiment in the St Helens/Knowsley area of Merseyside. However, after the change of government in that year, official policy no longer favoured a high-spending programme of this kind with substantial public-sector staffing. Michael Heseltine, the Environment Secretary, proposed instead the formation of a much smaller independent environmental trust. The local Councils agreed, subject to special funding from the government, and the first Groundwork Trust came into being at the end of 1981. Its staff of three, the then and still current Director has pointed out, was substantially less than the Countryside Commission had envisaged as necessary simply to *monitor* the experiment originally envisaged, let alone carry it out.

Today some twenty people are engaged in Operation Groundwork in Merseyside, and Sefton has joined the other two Districts in the programme. Five more Trusts were brought into being in 1983 in the North West – in Wigan, Salford, Macclesfield, Rossendale and Oldham. In 1985 the Groundwork Foundation was formed to take over the role of parent body from the Countryside Commission (in part to give legitimacy to more urban and inner-city work by the Trusts). And by 1989 eighteen Trusts were listed across the country – between them employing nearly 100 staff; their areas of concern cover an acreage twice that of Greater London. A further twenty-five Trusts are looked for over the next few years. The Foundation claims in its first five years to have completed more than 3,000 projects, to have reclaimed or refreshed 1,500 acres/600 ha of neglected land, and to have used the services of 6,000 volunteers.

Trusts were brought into being on government funding (originally £100,000 start-up money) on the understanding that they would become self-supporting after three years. That has not proved possible, though in 1987/88 Operation Groundwork raised about 70 per cent of its income by its own efforts. It having been judged impossible for the North-West Trusts to be totally self-sufficient, the DoE, in 1988/89, allocated £200,000 to be divided amongst them for 'core' funding.

293

A primary purpose of the Foundation is fund-raising at the national level to create a financial safety net for local Trusts faced by unavoidable deficits. Chairman is Sir Nigel Mobbs, in succession to Chris Chataway.

The problems and track records of the eighteen Trusts obviously vary widely. After an initially wary response, they have attracted good support from the private sector. Local authorities turn to them increasingly for all sorts of cleaning-up operations. They have placed stress on the monitoring and assessment of their operations. They have examined in detail the problems arising from the clash of urban and farming interests in fringe areas. They have sparked off the formation of other groups, from wildlife advisory groups in local authorities to canal-restoration associations in the voluntary sphere, ranger services to education groups in schools. They have a strong research base, have initiated a computer-based landscape management system, have undertaken research projects for the DoE and others, and in the second half of the eighties were commissioned by the European Community to examine the scope for the formation of like organisations in Lille, Nijmegen and Essen, with which three pairs of English Trusts have been paired.

THE HOUSING CORPORATION

The Housing Corporation exists 'to support social housing in England by working with housing associations and others to provide good homes for those in housing need'. The Corporation was established by Parliament in 1964, on the initiative of the then Minister for Housing and Local Government, Sir Keith Joseph. However, today's organisation, though its Board is still appointed by the Secretary of State for the Environment, bears little resemblance to that of a quarter of a century ago; apart from all else its functions in Scotland and Wales were transferred by the Housing Act of 1988 to two new bodies – Scottish Homes and Tai Cymru/Housing for Wales respectively.

For three years previous to 1964 the Ministry of Housing and Local Government and the National Federation of Housing Societies had administered a scheme by which the government contributed £38 million towards capital funding of voluntary housing societies building homes for letting at cost rents or for co-ownership. This had put around 5,600 new homes into the pipeline. A 1963 White Paper recognised the potential this represented, referring to the voluntary movement as 'the third arm in housing', and the purpose of the new Corporation, as set out in the Housing Act of the following year, was broadly to take over and expand the existing scheme. To this end £300 million was to be put at its disposal.

This is not the place to chronicle the convolutions of the Corporation's development since then. Initial assumptions proved shaky.

Management strengths and weaknesses, party politics, the mechanics of grant-delivery systems, but above all rising land values, construction costs and interest rates, have pulled its programmes this way and that. Stop-go swings in the national economy have led to stop-go crises for voluntary housing. There were moments when the Corporation's continued existence came into question. Nonetheless, by its own exertions, and the skilful machinations of two of its chairmen in particular – Lord Goodman and Sir Hugh Cubitt – it has contrived always to emerge from its tribulations increased in strength. In early 1965 the number of associations registered with the Corporation was thirty-one; today it is over 2,400, even after hiving off several hundred to Scottish Homes and Tai Cymru. It employs about 800, spread between its headquarters and eight regional offices in England. With the National Federation of Housing Associations, in 1987, it created the Housing Finance Corporation to generate additional private investment through the Stock Exchange and by other means. Its gross expenditure is set to rise from £818 million in 1990/91 to £1.22 billion in 1991/92 and no less than £1.736 billion in 1992/93, in which year it hopes to complete nearly 36,000 houses for rent and over 6,800 for sale – with a comparable number of new schemes agreed and put in hand. From the gap-filling initiative of the middle 1960s – characterised by Lord Goodman, only a touch unfairly, as 'a modest contribution to the housing needs largely of the indigent middle class' – the Corporation has emerged as the 'main engine of publicly subsidised housing', and therefore a major instrument of government housing policy.

Through the years its capabilities and responsibilities have been extended – for example in the direction of tighter supervision of associations' affairs (while releasing the Corporation itself from detailed DoE scrutiny of its every decision); and in enabling it to raise finance from the private sector in addition to its government funding. However, 1988/89 proved to be the real watershed year. The White Paper that preceded the Housing Act of 1988 set out four main aims:

- to reverse the decline in rented housing and to improve its quality;
- to give Council tenants the right to transfer to other landlords if they so wished (the 'Tenants' Choice' scheme);
- to target money more accurately on the most acute problems;
- to continue to encourage the growth of home ownership.

For the Housing Corporation the Act triggered several important developments. As has been noted, the Corporation's functions in Scotland and Wales passed to new agencies from April 1989. Its duties were extended to cover responsibility for the payment of capital and revenue grants to housing associations; assistance for tenants interested in 'Tenants' Choice'; and the approval and revocation of potential new landlords under that scheme. As its contribution to the £257 million package of extra help for the homeless, announced by the Secretary of State in November 1989, the Corporation has increased its own programme to that end by £80 million a year, resulting in 40 per cent of its 'approvals' in 1989/90 going to schemes aimed at the homeless. The Corporation works to a list of ninety-one designated 'stress areas', and a 'Housing Need Indicator' developed from the DoE's Generalised Needs Indicator; the Corporation's Housing Need Indicator has been adjusted to take greater account of homelessness. At the other end of the spectrum, its low-cost home-ownership programme is currently planned at about 20 per cent of the size of its rented programme.

At the end of the day what happens on the ground results from the policies and programmes of the 2,400 voluntary associations. Only to the extent that the Corporation can succeed in giving them a particular sense of direction at any particular moment, can encourage and cajole, and can control the flow of funds into their work, can it be held to shape this part of the national housing effort. Its commitment is obvious. Apart from whatever may be the policies of the government of the day, the Corporation – in day-to-day touch with local societies, co-operatives, ethnic minorities, tenants – has its own corporate ethos. It was clearly glad to record the results of a 1978 survey by the National Federation of Housing Associations, which showed that half those moving into housing association lettings had previously lived in substandard accommodation. A third had been homeless when rehoused. About 30 per cent were in retirement; 10 per cent were single-parent families. Only one in ten had an income which exceeded the average national wage. A decade later, in his 1988/89 annual report to the three Secretaries of State, Sir Hugh Cubitt, the Corporation's then Chairman, expressed the unease felt by associations that the 1988 legislation 'might be seen to be forcing the Movement "up market" to the detriment of those whom associations have always seen themselves as existing to help – those on low incomes and in housing need. It would be nice to be able to record that these anxieties no longer exist but I regret that this is not the case . . . For so long as these anxieties exist they will continue to constitute a de-motivating influence on Volunteer Committee Members and I cannot too strongly urge the Government . . . to do all that is in its power to allay them.' (See also Scottish Homes and Tai Cymru/Housing for Wales.)

LAND AUTHORITY FOR WALES
The Land Authority for Wales was set up under the Community Land Act of 1975, and re-established with modified powers and responsibili-

ties under the Local Government, Planning and Land Act 1980. Its essential purpose is to make land available for development where this is difficult or impossible for the private sector to do so unaided. By the end of March 1988 the Authority had invested some £44 million in acquiring and improving 4,310 acres/1,364 ha, of which 2,072 acres had subsequently been sold or was contracted to be sold. The land remaining in its ownership was valued at over £35 million. The Authority is run as a business and expected to pay its own way. Its income for the year 1987/88 amounted to about £62 million.

NATIONAL AUDIT OFFICE
The National Audit Office is a government-financed but independent body, set up in 1983 and headed by the Controller and Auditor General. Its purpose, through value-for-money audits (which frequently range beyond formal accountancy), is to provide independent information and advice to Parliament on the economy, efficiency and effectiveness with which government and public bodies use their resources.

PROGRAMME AUTHORITIES
See Government Grant Aid, City Grant, Derelict Land Grant and Urban Programme.

SCOTTISH HOMES
Scottish Homes was formed by the Housing (Scotland) Act, 1988, from two constituent bodies – the Scottish Special Housing Association and that part of the Housing Corporation which operated north of the Border. Both were government sponsored, the former having been set up in 1937 with very similar aims to those of the Housing Corporation. Amalgamation was therefore a rational move. The new body inherited a stock of 72,000 homes from the Scottish Special Housing Association, and 45,000 from the Housing Corporation's 210 Scottish associations. As an indication of the scale of the latter's operations in Scotland, its funding for its final year was £164 million; there were nearly 3,000 completions for rent, 355 for sale, with 3,850 approvals for new starts.

SIMPLIFIED PLANNING ZONES
Provisions were brought into operation in November 1987 by which local authorities may designate Simplified Planning Zones. Their essential purpose is the same as that of the Enterprise Zones. They enjoy the same relaxation of planning control as do Enterprise Zones and, like them, last for ten years. A number have been initiated but it is as yet too soon to gauge their effectiveness.

TAI CYMRU/HOUSING FOR WALES

Tai Cymru represents a straight transfer of Housing Corporation (q.v.) duties in the Principality to Welsh control. During the Corporation's last year before the restructuring its funding in Wales was, in all, nearly £73 million; nearly 1,600 new homes were completed or in hand; all but 2,500 new ones approved. One quarter of the Corporation's resources for Wales have in recent years been put into the South Wales Valleys.

TASK FORCES

Task Forces are small teams of about six to eight civil servants and others set up by the government in central 'shopfront offices' to coordinate and focus the main government programmes on small inner-city areas; to develop new approaches; to work with local authorities and voluntary groups and to encourage private-sector support and commitment. They have funding – about £750,000 – at their disposal with which to pump-prime local initiatives and strengthen existing projects.

Eight Task Forces were created in 1986; eight more a year later. They are not permanent, but are withdrawn after a few years, when it is considered appropriate, and replaced by others elsewhere. Thus those in Leicester, Preston and Wolverhampton ceased at the end of 1989. The following year saw Task Forces in East Birmingham, Bradford, Bristol, Coventry, Doncaster, Granby/Toxteth in Liverpool, Hartlepool, Leeds (Chapeltown and Harehills), Manchester (Moss Side and Hulme), Middlesbrough, Nottingham, Rochdale; and in the London area: Deptford, North Kensington, North Peckham and Spitalfields. Of these Doncaster and Rochdale were due to close at the end of 1990, to be replaced by new ones in Derby and Wirral.

The Task Forces (originally under the wing of the Department of Trade and Industry but now the DoE) have been active in training, business development and work with ethnic minorities. Over 450 companies work with them, and they claim to have supported over 1,000 projects, creating or safeguarding nearly 4,000 jobs and over 23,500 training places.

Two examples from London. The Spitalfields Task Force contributed nearly £119,000 towards the total cost of £403,000 required to set up a joinery trades centre in a disused pub. The North Kensington Task Force has assisted a pioneering scheme that has attracted attention: CHOICE – Children of the Inner City. CHOICE aims to motivate youngsters still at school by attaching them for a period to an undergraduate at a university, or staff in business and industry, thereby offering them new role models and the realisation that routes

298

to achievement are not automatically closed to them. First programmes are said to have had a high success rate.

TRAINING AGENCIES

Big changes took place during the late eighties in the government's provision for training for industry. Schools/Industry Compacts create links between schools and local employers, under which school leavers who meet agreed standards are guaranteed jobs, or training with the assurance of a job at the end. Some forty such partnerships are currently being developed.

City Technology Colleges are new secondary schools outside the local education authorities framework. Funded directly by the Department of Education and Science, in conjunction with industrial sponsorship, they offer free education with a special emphasis on science and technology.

From spring 1990 new industry- and business-led Training and Enterprise Councils began to take responsibility for the Training Agency's programmes. Each TEC has an annual budget of about £20 million. By mid 1991 there should be eighty such Councils covering the whole of England and Wales.

URBAN DEVELOPMENT CORPORATIONS

The Urban Development Corporations are set up by the government under the Local Government, Planning and Land Act of 1980. Their purpose is to bring about the regeneration of their designated areas – by bringing land and buildings into effective use; by encouraging the development of industry and commerce; by ensuring the availability of housing and social facilities so as to encourage people to live and work in the area. They are expected to maximise investment by the private sector, and to this end the rule-of-thumb 'gearing' they are meant to aim at is 1:4, public to private. Their thrust is largely, though not wholly, directed to removing the 'negative value' of land within their designated area and fitting it, by reclamation and the provision of essential infrastructure (roads, services and so on) for development by the private sector. To this end they can acquire, hold, manage, reclaim and dispose of land, and themselves carry out building operations. To a degree they are able to assist developers financially, on the basis of government funding within the Urban Programme generally. They are not plan-*making* authorities within the meaning of the Town and Country Planning legislation (though they can and do produce development strategies and briefs). They do, however, in England exercise planning *control* powers, enabling them to determine planning applications within their area (in the sole Welsh Corporation, that for Cardiff Bay, these powers remain with the local Planning authorities, though the Corporation can exercise a power of veto if, in its view, an application does not come up to the required standard). The Corporations are *not* housing, highway, health, education or police authorities, but their areas and functions do overlap those of the existing local authorities and this has in some cases provided ground for friction. A particular bone of contention has been the degree to which each side should take account of the other's planning strategies.

Eleven Development Corporations have been created. First, in 1981, were those for Merseyside and the London Docklands. They were followed, in 1987, after the abolition of the Metro County Councils, by four more – for the Black Country, Trafford Park, Teesside, and Tyne and Wear. A third generation, in 1988, added Cardiff Bay, Sheffield, Leeds, Central Manchester and, after a struggle by a reluctant City Council, Bristol. These are rather different, in that the earlier Corporations were faced with large tracts of industrial wasteland, whereas the third wave of English Corporations – with Sheffield possibly a bit of a 'rogue' among them – have been grafted on to areas where there is already substantial private-sector interest. Working to a shorter time span – of five to seven years – they are intended to ensure, by their additional push of concentrated attention, that such further possibilities as may exist in the area are in fact fully realised.

As might be expected, then, the areas covered by the Corporations (listed below) vary greatly, in their extent and in their nature.

	(acres)	(ha)
Teesside	11,260	4,560
Tyne and Wear	5,860	2,380
LDDC	5,100	2,070
Trafford Park	3,140	1,270
Cardiff Bay	2,700	1,100
Merseyside (now)	2,370	960
Black Country (now)	6,420	2,600
Sheffield	2,220	900
Leeds	1,330	540
Bristol	890	360
Central Manchester	460	187

(Merseyside and the Black Country have both had their areas extended since the initial designations. Figures approximate.)

The nature of their terrains varies no less. Some are compact, some are very dispersed; some lie outside, or on the fringes of, cities, while others are right in the middle. Some include large areas of water.

Tyne and Wear has to contend with long straggling strips on either side of two rivers, lengths of which have little directly in common. Cardiff Bay, on the other hand, is offered a relatively coherent area on which to realise, not just an intensification of what was there previously but a new potential never previously envisaged. Several Corporations – for example, Leeds and Merseyside – are responsible for unconnected areas. Conversely Greater Manchester sports two unconnected Corporations – though both together would make up less than one third of the territory covered by Teesside.

Policy is controlled by Boards appointed by the government Minister concerned, to whom their chairman reports. Board members, typically, are prominent in business and industry, local politics, perhaps academia and/or one of the land-based professions; women are very few and far between (though Cardiff Bay actually has *two*). The Corporations are seen as 'tight ships' administratively and a firm top limit is set by the government on their staffing. LDDC, perhaps unsurprisingly, is way above the others with, in 1990, around 150 'in-house'. Around fifty or sixty is the level for the middle range; the third generation may be half that (Leeds had twenty-one after eighteen months and was hoping to make it twenty-seven). These figures – a fraction of the number to be found in a District Planning Department – mean that the Corporations 'buy in' consultants from the private sector for almost everything, from planning to public relations.

Each Corporation is allotted, at the outset, a certain sum to cover its expected life span. This is then divided by the number of years, to be drawn upon as an annual grant-in-aid. It is sometimes possible to bring forward some of this money to cover the heavy expenditure required by essential infrastructure in the earlier years. The total sum can be increased by the government, if it sees fit, to cover additional work that could not have been foreseen at the outset (LDDC, for example, has had its grant boosted very considerably to enable it to meet its share of the costs of new transport provision). Over and above the Corporation's basic grant-in-aid, a tranche of Urban Programme money is allotted to it for use within its area (on the same terms as elsewhere). Total gross expenditure by the Corporations varied, in 1989–90, from £279 million by LDDC (of which £245.6 million was government grant-in-aid) to a few tens of millions by the more recent. These sums may be compared with, for example, the £168 million expenditure of the Scottish Special Housing Association (now Scottish Homes) in 1988–89; the nearly £133 million by the Scottish Development Agency and the £110 million by the Welsh Development Agency – even the £11 million by the Wales Tourist Board. The Corporations are not on a mad spending spree. Everything they do is 'shadowed' and monitored and approved – in England by the Regional Offices of the Departments of the Environment and Transport, and/or the Departments in London, and/or the Treasury. The absence of real delegated powers often prevents them, say some Corporations, from acting as entrepreneurially as they would wish. In relation to their terms of reference, the real test of the UDCs financially lies in the degree of private-sector investment they can bring about – and this, inevitably, is largely governed by the state of the economy. It is as yet early – even in the cases of London and Merseyside – to hazard a guess at the final reckoning; in the case of the second- and third-generation Corporations it is impossible.

URBAN AND ECONOMIC DEVELOPMENT GROUP (URBED)

A non-profit company founded in 1976 by Nicholas Falk with the aim of 'devising practical solutions to the problems of regenerating run-down areas and creating new work'. Since then it has steadily expanded its range of concerns. As consultant URBED works with government departments, public-service agencies and private-sector companies on feasibility studies and the development of imaginative strategies for regeneration. The Group undertakes research, for example, in the leisure and retail fields, the economics of reuse of redundant buildings (particularly industrial buildings) and similar matters. It handles project management, the formation of development trusts, public/private partnerships, and promotion. It also runs entrepreneurial training programmes (more than 2,500 went through its courses in 1987/88). URBED has been involved in important schemes in many parts of Britain (Sowerby Bridge in Calderdale and the Jewelry Quarter in Birmingham have both figured in the foregoing pages) and currently has bases in Leeds, Birmingham and Bristol in addition to its offices in London.

URBAN PROGRAMME

The first major government measure (Inner Urban Areas Act, 1978) targeted on the inner cities. It is intended to help tackle underlying economic, social and environmental problems, and provides support for a wide range of projects – from job creation to road improvements, from crime prevention to health care. Some 10,000 projects a year receive financial assistance in the form of grants or loans. Projects form part of the Inner Area Programmes prepared annually by the fifty-seven authorities listed above (page 292). Programmes are drawn up in consultation with the private and voluntary sectors, including ethnic-minority groups, and submitted to the DoE for funding. Ministerial guidelines were laid down in 1985, encouraging innovative and multi-objective projects. Increasingly, funding is used to support capital projects and increasingly authorities are encouraged to support appropriate private-sector schemes which contribute to their programmes. Approved Urban Programme projects receive 75 per

302

cent grant from the government, the local authority concerned paying the other 25 per cent. Urban Programme resources come from several different government departments – in 1987/88 67 per cent came from the DoE, 15 per cent from Education and Science, 15 per cent from Health and Social Security, 3 per cent from Transport. In 1988/89 a total of £279 million was available for Urban Programme use in England, of which about £25 million was earmarked for assistance to private companies at the discretion of the local authorities. In 1987/88 some 24 per cent, or £67 million, went to the voluntary sector; projects aimed specifically at ethnic-minority groups accounted for about 14 per cent, or £32 million (£37 million the previous year). Broadly, expenditure tends to be highest on social and economic measures, followed by environmental improvement, with housing at the bottom. Allocations at the start of the financial year remain provisional and may be adjusted (upwards or downwards) as the year progresses. From 1986 more rigorous monitoring of effectiveness was introduced. No projects are funded permanently.

APPENDIX B

REFERENCES AND SOURCES

A book of this nature does not call for the full academic panoply of references. Some of the more important or less obvious, however, are given below, and I am anxious moreover to acknowledge my debt to at least some of the many publications and documents consulted.

INTRODUCTION
1 *Poverty in Europe - Estimates 1975, 1980 & 1985*. Institute of Social Advisory Service, Rotterdam University, 1990.
2 *Sunday Times* photograph by Anita Corbin.
3 As reported by Geordie Greig in the *Sunday Times*, 18 June 1989.
4 *Daily Mirror*, 19 April 1989.

CHAPTER 2
1 Institute of Insurance Brokers' Ratings, August 1989.
2 D. Eversley and I. Begg, *Inner Cities Research Programme – National Studies*. For the Economic and Social Research Council. See also *People and Places: A Classification of Urban Areas and Residential Neighbourhoods*, Council for Environmental Studies.
3 Fact Sheet prepared for the Standing Conference of Outer Estates, London, November 1986.
4 Malcolm Wicks, Family Policy Studies Centre, writing in *The Times*, 12 May 1989.
5 *Low Income Statistics: Households below average income tables 1988*. HMSO, 1991.
6 *Broken Promises*, Southwark London Borough Council, 1989.
7 *Faith in the City*. Report of the Archbishop of Canterbury's Commission on Urban Priority Areas, Church House Publications, 1985.

8 *Inquiry into British Housing,* chaired by HRH The Duke of Edinburgh, National Federation of Housing Associations, 1985.

9 Chadwick's 1842 *Report to the Select Commission on Health of Towns.*

10 *Appraisal of Local Authority Housing for 1988,* DoE/HMSO, 1990.

11 *Wasting Money, Wasting Lives.* Report by SHELTER, the National Campaign for the Homeless, December 1990.

12 Paper No. 2, Merseyside Planning Conference, October 1987.

13 See *Paying for Britain's Housing,* Joseph Rowntree Foundation, 1990.

14 Dr Alice Coleman, *Utopia on Trial: Vision and Reality in Planned Housing,* Hilary Shipman, 1985.

15 Woolwich Building Society *Survey,* 1989.

16 Quoted by Peter Hennessy in *Whitehall,* Secker & Warburg, 1989.

Other

Peter Townsend, *Poverty in the United Kingdom,* Allen Lane/ Penguin Books Ltd, 1979.

Problems of Inner City Areas, Committee on the Challenges of Modern Society – Report No. 91, NATO, Brussels, 1978.

Lord Scarman, *The Brixton Disorders 10–12 April 1981,* HMSO.

Lord Gifford, *The Broadwater Farm Inquiry Report,* Karia Press, London, 1986.

Living Faith in the City. A progress report following up (7) above. The General Synod, 1990.

CHAPTER 3

1 *Liverpool Mercury,* 6 May 1833. Quoted by Asa Briggs in *Victorian Cities.*

2 Greater London Council brochure, 1977.

3 Michael Heseltine, *Where There's a Will,* Hutchinson, 1987. Also: speaking at a conference, 'Tomorrow's Cities', at Swansea, 17 June 1988.

4 J. Thompson, *Community Architecture: The Story of Lea View House, Hackney,* Conference paper (1984) reprinted by the Royal Institute of British Architects.

5 *Urban Regeneration and Economic Development: The Local Government Dimension,* National Audit Office, September 1989.

Other

HMSO has published a number of general brochures under the 'Action for Cities' tag, including

DoE Inner City Programmes, 1987/88

Action for Cities, 1988

Progress on Cities, 1989

People in Cities, 1990
Renewing the Cities, 1990.

These deal with England. Other publications cover Scotland and Wales, and some of those covering specific areas of interest – such as environmental improvement, Estate Action, Task Forces, etc. – are listed in the appropriate place below.

CHAPTER 4

1 Speaking at the conference cited above (3;3).
2 LDDC *Briefing* and *Fact Sheets*.
3 Speaking to the London Forum of civic and amenity societies, 21 May 1990.
4 Letter to the *Guardian*, 17 April 1989 and speaking at a Docklands Forum transport conference, 1989.
5 *Broken Promises*, London Borough of Southwark, 1989.

Other

LDDC *Annual Reports*.
Greenland Dock: A Framework for Development, LDDC, revised 1984.
Corporate Plan, LDDC, 1989.
Transport in Docklands, LDDC, November 1989.
Promotional and marketing brochures for Wapping and Poplar, Surrey Docks, Royal Docks, Isle of Dogs/Enterprise Zone. And other publications.

CHAPTER 5

1 *Architects' Journal*, July 1978.
2 Speaking at an international symposium, *Arts and the Changing City*, organised by the British American Arts Association, Glasgow, October 1988.
3 Levi Tafari, *Duboetry*, Windows Project, November 1987.
4 *New Brighton: Draft Area Strategy*, MDC, 1989.
5 Alan McDonald, *The Weller Way: The Story of the Weller Streets Housing Co-operative*, Faber and Faber, 1985.
6 A good general account of the movement is to be found in *Building Democracy: Housing Co-operatives on Merseyside*, Co-operative Development Services, Liverpool, revised 1987.
7 *Liverpool City Centre: Strategy Review*, City Council, November 1987.
8 *Op. cit.* (3;3 above).
9 Quoted in *Success Against the Odds*, Liverpool City Council, undated, 1986–87.

Other

Merseyside Development Corporation: The Liverpool Experience, City Council, July 1987.
An Economic Development Strategy for Liverpool, City Council,

October 1987.

A Tourism Strategy for Liverpool: A Framework, City Council, November 1987.

An Arts and Cultural Industries Strategy for Liverpool, City Council, November 1987.

Poverty in Liverpool, City Council, December 1988.

Locate in Liverpool, City Council, June 1989.

Population Trends and Prospects: Liverpool 2001, City Council, February 1989.

Annual Reports, Merseyside Development Corporation.

Liverpool Waterfront Development Plan, MDC, 1988.

Vauxhall Area Draft Strategy for Consultation, MDC.

Parliament Street Area: Draft Area Strategy, MDC, 1989.

Annual Reports and Accounts, Knowsley Borough Council.

Towards a Strategy for Knowsley District Council, Report prepared for the Council by the School of Advanced Urban Studies, Bristol, 1988.

CHAPTER 6

1 Figures from *Castlemilk Initiative . . . a Change for the Better*, Glasgow City Council, February 1989.
2 Quoted in the *Sunday Times*, 1988.
3 Figures from *The East End Experience*, East End Management Unit, August 1988.
4 Speaking at *Arts and the Changing City*, see above (5: 3).
5 *Miles Better, Miles to Go: The story of Glasgow's Housing Associations*, The Housetalk Group (of five associations), undated, perhaps 1985.

Other

GEAR: A Glasgow City Council Perspective, City Council, March 1987.

Glasgow Heritage: Caring for the City's listed buildings and conservation areas, City Council, September 1987.

Glasgow Planning Handbook, City Council, March 1988.

The Partick–Kelvin Project, City Council, December 1988.

Springburn into the 90s, City Council, 1988.

The Balmore/Saracen Corridor, City Council, undated, perhaps 1988.

J. B. Watson, *Let Glasgow Flourish! Glasgow's bold approach to urban renewal*, City Council, 1988.

Annual Reports, Strathclyde Region.

Glasgow Action: *Glasgow Means Business*, November 1988, and other brochures.

The Glasgow Canal Project, various publications, British Waterways Board.

CHAPTER 7

1 In a paper dated March 1989.
2 Speaking at a Council of Europe conference 'Planning for Enterprise' at Swansea, 16–18 September 1982.
3 Ian Kelsall, writing in *The Valleys in Focus*, Welsh Development Agency, 1989.
4 Paper, Valleys Conference, 23 June 1989.
5 *The Japanese Experience in Wales*, Arthur D. Little Ltd, Welsh Development Agency, undated, perhaps 1987.
6 Dafidd Elis Thomas, MP.

Other
Annual Reports, Swansea City Council.
Lower Swansea Valley – legacy and future, City Council, 1982.
Waterfront 89, Swansea City Council.
Annual Reports, Cardiff Bay Development Corporation.
Llewellyn-Davies Planning, *Cardiff Bay Regeneration Strategy*, CBDC, 1988. See also *The Regeneration Strategy – a commentary by the Corporation*.
Shepheard Epstein Hunter, *Public Realm Study*, CBDC, 1990.
Policies for Urban Quality, CBDC, 1990.
The Strategy for Public Art in Cardiff Bay, CBDC, 1990.
A Strategy for Training and Employment in South Glamorgan, CBDC and others, 1990.
Numerous development briefs and discussion documents relating to specific areas and problems.
Annual Reports, Welsh Development Agency.
Wales: Facts for Industry, WDA, 1989.
Numerous promotional brochures, marketing documents and papers on specific problems.
An Initiative for the Valleys, Welsh Office, February 1986.
The Valleys: A Programme for the People, Welsh Office, 1988.

CHAPTER 8
Annual Reports, Tyne and Wear Development Corporation.
Corporate Plan 1990–94, T & WDC.
Numerous promotional and marketing brochures for specific sites.
Annual Reports, Teesside Development Corporation.
Numerous promotional and marketing brochures for specific sites.

CHAPTER 9

1 Quoted in *Building Design*, 16 July 1989.

Other
Annual Reports, Leeds Development Corporation.

Leeds Waterways Strategy, LDC, undated.

Planning Frameworks for The Calls and Riverside, Clarence Dock, Hunslet Green, etc.

2 Quoted in the *Sunday Times*, 6 August 1989.

Other

Draft Local Plan for the Lower Don Valley, Sheffield City Council, 1987.

Annual Reports, Sheffield Development Corporation.

A Vision of the Lower Don Valley, SDC, October 1989.

3 John Punter in his impressive *Design Control in Bristol 1940– 1990*, Redcliffe, Bristol, 1990, to which I am indebted for much information in this chapter.

Other

Corporate Plan, Bristol Development Corporation, July 1989.

A Vision for Bristol, BDC, undated.

CHAPTER 10

1 The Highbury Initiative, *Proceedings of the Birmingham City Centre Challenge Symposium*, Birmingham City Action Team/City Council, March 1988.

Other

Annual Reports, Black Country Development Corporation.

Black Country Landscape Strategy, summary leaflet, undated.

Promotional and marketing brochures.

Developing the Jewelry Quarter's Unique Potential, URBED *et al.*, June 1987.

Jewelry Quarter Development Study, Report of City's Director of Development, June 1987.

Birmingham Heartlands: Development Strategy for East Birmingham, final report by Roger Tym and Partners for Birmingham Heartlands/City Council, January 1988.

Waterlinks Development Framework, Birmingham Heartlands/City Council, undated.

Bordesley Development Framework, Birmingham Heartlands, undated.

Nechells Development Framework, Birmingham Heartlands, September 1989.

Saltley Simplified Planning Zone, City Council/Birmingham Heartlands, 1989.

Birmingham Investment Programme, business support brochures, City Council.

Canal Improvement Programme, Birmingham Planning Committee paper, September 1989.

CHAPTER 11

Annual Reports, Trafford Park Development Corporation.

Promotional and marketing material for Wharfside, Northbank Industrial Park and other sites, TPDC.

Annual Reports and *Fact Sheets,* Central Manchester Development Corporation.

Opportunities, CMDC, July 1988.

Strategy for Consultation, CMDC, September 1989.

Salford Quays: the Development Plan for Salford Docks, prepared by Shepheard Epstein & Hunter for Salford City Council, April 1985.

Salford Quays: Development Strategy Review, City Council, August 1988.

Tony Struthers, City Technical Services Officer, *The Rebirth of a City and the Renewal of Derelict Docklands,* paper given in Paris, October 1989.

Annual Reviews and *Fact Sheets,* Salford Quays, City Council.

The Salford Centre, promotional brochure for an important cultural facility on Salford Quays, City Council, undated.

The Trinity Project, promotional brochure, City Council, undated.

Environmental Action, news-sheet on action to 'green' the city.

Lowry's Landscape Regenerated, Council's Landscape Group, *Landscape Design,* No. 185, November 1989.

CHAPTER 12

Little Germany: Bradford's Historic Merchant Quarter, City Council, undated, perhaps 1988.

Halifax in Calderdale: A Strategy for Prosperity, Civic Trust, June 1984.

Calderdale – The Challenge: A Strategy for Prosperity, Civic Trust, January 1986.

A New Heart for Sowerby Bridge, URBED/West Yorkshire Metropolitan Council, 1985.

Eric Webster, *Dean Clough and the Crossley Inheritance,* Dean Clough Publications, 1988.

Heritage and Successful Town Regeneration, report of the 1988 Halifax Colloquy, Council of Europe, Strasbourg, 1989.

Numerous reports on specific aspects of the programme – an interpretive strategy, on training, on the reuse of redundant rural buildings, etc.; newsletters and brochures, Calderdale Borough Council.

CHAPTER 13

1 I am beholden for these figures to Applied Property Research, whose report *UK 2000 – an overview of business parks* was published London, 1989.

2 *Survey of Derelict Land in England in 1982,* DoE/HMSO, 1984.

3 A. D. Bradshaw and A. Burt, *Transforming our Wasteland: The Way Forward*, DoE/HMSO, 1986.

4 M. Chisholm and P. Kivell, *Inner City Wasteland*, Institute of Economic Affairs, 1987.

5 Stephen Joseph, *Urban Wasteland Now*, Civic Trust, 1988.

6 Nick Michael and Professor Tony Bradshaw, 'A Hard Future for Derelict Land', *Landscape Design*, No. 117, February 1989.

7 B. D. Macgregor *et al.*, *Land Availability for Inner City Development*, University of Reading Department of Land Management, 1985.

8 *Mid Glamorgan County Structure Plan: Approved Plan incorporating Proposed Alterations No. 1*, County Council, September 1989.

9 Speaking to the Brick Development Association, 18 May 1988.

10 *The Green Quadratic*, Adam Smith Institute, 1988.

Other

Evaluation of Derelict Land Grand Schemes, HMSO, 1987.

Forests for the Community and other publications, Countryside Commission/Forestry Commission.

11 Quoted in *The Times*, 27 June 1989.

12 *An Investigation of Difficult-to-let Housing*, Occasional Papers 3/80, 4/80 and 5/80, DoE/HMSO.

13 See Anne Power, *The PEP Guide to Local Housing Management*, a model in three parts, Department of the Environment/Welsh Office, April 1987.

14 as for example in *The Castlemilk Initiative*. See 6: 1 above.

15 *Feasibility Study for the Redevelopment of Five Estates*, Hunt Thompson Associates for the London Borough of Waltham Forest, December 1987.

16 Quoted in the *Walthamstow Guardian*, week ending 9 December 1988.

Other

The Jubilee Album, National Federation of Housing Associations, Peter Jones, 1985.

The First Twenty-five Years, the Housing Corporation, 1985.

Development Programmes and *Programme for 1990–1993*, The Housing Corporation.

The National Federation of Housing Associations, *Annual Reports*, and its magazine *Voluntary Housing*.

Community Architecture: How People are Creating their own Environment. Nick Wates and Charles Knevitt. Penguin Books, 1987.

17 John Myerscough, *The Economic Importance of the Arts in Britain*, Policy Studies Institute, London, 1988.

18 See 5: 3 above.

19 *An Urban Renaissance: Sixteen Case Studies*, Arts Council, 1989.

20 Quoted in *The North-west Evening Mail*, 13 July 1987.

21 *The Guardian*, 11 July 1987.

22 See 7 above.

23 See 5 above.

Other

Two recent booklets on design, published by the Royal Fine Art Commission, are Tony Aldous, *Inner City Urban Regeneration and Good Design*, and Judy Hillman, *A New Look for London*, both HMSO, 1988.

CHAPTER 14

1 Dr Steve Savas, Department of Housing and Urban Development, USA, speaking at a Council of Europe Seminar, *Planning for Enterprise*, Swansea, September 1982.

2 *Problems of Inner City Areas*, CCMS Report No. 91, NATO, 1978.

3 Paul Cheshire, Dennis Hay, Gianni Carbonaro, Nick Bevan, of the Faculty of Urban and Regional Studies, University of Reading, *Urban Problems and Regional Policy in the European Community*, for the Commission of the European Communities, Brussels, 1988.

4 *Managing Urban Change: Policies and Finance*. OECD, Paris, 1983.

5 *The Wanderers*.

6 Estimated in *Working Brief*, The Unemployment Unit, August 1990.

7 Given in *Programme for Partnership. An urban policy statement*, Association of Metropolitan Authorities, London, 1986.

APPENDIX A

Business and the Inner Cities, Business in the Community, 1987.

Business in the Community Magazine.

Emile Noël, *Working Together: The Institutions of the European Community*, Luxembourg, 1988.

Groundwork: The Environmental Entrepreneurs, The Groundwork Foundation.

Breaking New Ground, Report of the Operation Groundwork Conference, July 1988.

APPENDIX C

Some Dates, 1970–1990

1970–75

1970 Conservative administration under Edward Heath. Creation of Department of the Environment; Peter Walker first Secretary of State.

1971 DoE and Greater London Council appoint consultants to report on London's docklands.

1972 Walker initiates six urban area studies.

1973 Geoffrey Rippon replaces Walker at DoE. Throws out GLC's grandiose redevelopment proposals for Covent Garden and proposals for a new civic centre in Liverpool.
Consultants' report on London's docklands; uproar from local groups; GLC sets up new committee with docklands councils.
Population projections for year 2000 dropped from 66.4 million to 52.2 million.
O P E C quadruples the price of oil.
Restructuring of local government in Scotland (1973–74).

1974 'Winter of discontent'.
Labour administration returned. Peter Shore at DoE. Restructuring of local government in England and Wales (1974–75). Creation of Metropolitan Counties and County Councils.
Swansea adopts plan to restore South Dock.

1975 Anthony Crosland at DoE. Heath replaced by Margaret Thatcher as Leader of the Opposition. European Architectural Heritage Year.

1976–80

1976 Cabinet Committee formed to consider problems of inner city.

Scottish and Welsh Development Agencies created. SDA initiates GEAR in Glasgow.

1977 Three Inner City reports published by government (Liverpool, Birmingham and London Borough of Lambeth). White Paper on inner urban areas follows.

Weller Streets Housing Co-operative set up in Liverpool.

1978 Peter Shore returns to DoE.

Rod Hackney wins battle with Macclesfield Council to retain threatened office in Black Street; launches 'community architecture' project there.

Inner Urban Areas Act. First 'Programme Authorities' designated.

1979 First Thatcher administration returned. Michael Heseltine at DoE. DoE budget cut by £440 million.

Department's Priority Estates Project started.

1980 Local Government Planning and Land Act (enabling Act for creation of Urban Development Corporations). Government announce proposals for London Docklands and Merseyside Corporations.

Parker Morris standards and the Housing Cost Yardstick abandoned, with loss of government control over public housing design standards.

GEAR Strategy for Glasgow East published after widespread consultation.

Covent Garden Market opened.

1981–85

1981 MDC and LDDC brought into being.

Toxteth riots. Michael Heseltine moved to Merseyside for three weeks.

Liverpool Task Force set up. First International Garden Festival announced for Liverpool.

'Business in the City' set up.

First Enterprise Zone designated (Lower Swansea Valley).

1982 Derelict Land Act. Urban Development Grant initiated.

LDDC designate Isle of Dogs Enterprise Zone. Plans for Docklands Light Railway announced. Non-cooperation policy adopted by Southwark Council.

MDC acquires Albert Dock.

Weller Streets Housing Co-operative's new homes opened, Liverpool.

Swansea Yacht Haven (first phase) opened in South Dock.

Bristol 'Watershed' development opened.

1983 Second Thatcher administration.

Heseltine succeeded at DoE by Tom King, in turn succeeded by Patrick Jenkin.

Surrey Docks vested in LDDC. Public Inquiry into STO airport. First speculative workspace completed.

National Museum of Photography, Film and Television opened in Bradford.

HM The Queen opens Burrell Collection, Glasgow. 'Glasgow's Miles Better' campaign.

Militant Tendency take control of Liverpool City Council.

Ernest Hall reopens the Dean Clough mill complex in Halifax for multiple use.

1984 Liverpool Garden Festival opened by HM The Queen.

First Civic Trust report to Calderdale Council.

Work starts on LDDC light railway.

1985 Kenneth Baker succeeds Jenkin at DoE.

Government grants LDDC outline permission for STO airport. 2,400 houses built in LDDC area; a further 4,600 under construction. First proposals for Canary Wharf announced.

Five City Action Teams set up. Urban Housing Renewal Unit formed within DoE.

Plan for redevelopment of 'Salford Quays'.

Faith in the City (report of the Archbishop of Canterbury's Commission on Urban Priority Areas) published.

Inquiry into British Housing (chaired by HRH The Duke of Edinburgh) published.

1986–90

1986 Nicholas Ridley succeeds Kenneth Baker at DoE.

Stoke-on–Trent Garden Festival.

Second Civic Trust report to Calderdale.

Study of South Cardiff commissioned by Welsh Office.

Greater London Council and Metropolitan County Councils abolished.

European Community passes the Single European Act.

1987 Third Thatcher administration; 'We must do something about these inner cities!'

UDCs established for Black Country, Teesside, and Tyne and Wear; announced for Bristol, Leeds, Central Manchester and Sheffield.

Peter Walker succeeds Nicholas Edwards at the Welsh Office.

'Estate Action' announced by the DoE.

Cardiff Bay Development Corporation announced by Welsh Office.

End of GEAR; replaced by Glasgow East End Executive.

MetroCentre, Gateshead, opened.

1988 Housing Act – 'Tenants' Choice'. Scottish Homes and Tai Cymru/Housing for Wales hived off.
Government announce 'Action for Cities'.
City Grant replaces Urban Development Grant and Urban Regeneration Grant.
Two more CATs set up (Nottingham, Leeds).
Welsh Office launches 'Valleys Initiative'.
Glasgow Garden Festival.
Albert Dock opened in Liverpool.
National Audit Office recommend Merseyside Development Corporation be wound up because of its failure to attract investment.
Black Country Development Corporation enlarged.
Merseyside Development Corporation's designated area nearly tripled.
Heartlands Development Strategy approved by Birmingham City Council.
CBI publishes 'Initiatives Beyond Charity'.
1989 St Enoch's Centre opened, Glasgow.
Government approval in principle for extension of Underground Jubilee Line to Isle of Dogs and Stratford.
Bristol City petitions against creation of an Urban Development Corporation; turned down by Parliamentary Select Committee.
Merry Hill Shopping Centre opens in the Black Country.
Christopher Patten succeeds Nicholas Ridley at Department of Environment.
1990 Gateshead Garden Festival.
Glasgow: European City of Culture. Concert hall opens.
Living Faith in the City published, the Church of England's follow-up to its 1985 report.
Peter Walker resigns from Cabinet and Welsh Office.
Main tower of Canary Wharf development, Isle of Dogs, 'topped out'.
John Major replaces Mrs Thatcher as Prime Minister. Michael Heseltine returns to Department of the Environment.
Fundamental review of local government announced.

INDEX

Figures underlined refer to illustration numbers.

317